POLLUTING TEXTILES

This book examines the critical issue of environmental pollutants produced by the textiles industry.

Comprised of contributions from environmental scientists and materials and textiles scientists, this edited volume addresses the environmental impact of microplastics, with a particular focus on microfibres released by textiles into marine and freshwater environments. The chapters in Part I offer environmental perspectives focusing on the measurement of microplastics in the environment, their ingestion by small plankton and larger filter feeders, the effects of consuming microplastics, and the role of microplastics as a vector for transferring toxic contaminants in food webs. Written by environmental and material scientists, the chapters in Part II present potential solutions to the problem of microplastics released from textiles, discussing parameters of influence, water treatment, degradation in aquatic environments, textile end-of-life management, textile manufacturing and laundry, and possible policy measures. This is a much needed volume which brings together in one place environmental research with technical solutions in order to provide a cohesive and practical approach to mitigating and preventing environmental pollution from the textiles industry going forward.

This book will be of great interest to students and scholars of environmental conservation and management, environmental pollution and environmental chemistry and toxicology, sustainability, as well as students and scholars of material and textiles science, textile engineering and sustainable manufacturing.

Judith S. Weis is Professor Emerita in the Department of Biological Sciences at Rutgers University, USA. She is the author/editor of over 250 scientific articles, multiple books, including *Marine Pollution: What Everyone Needs to Know* (2014) and *Biological Invasions and Animal Behaviour* (2016, with Daniel Sol).

Francesca De Falco is Post-Doctoral Research Fellow at the University of Plymouth, UK. She holds a PhD in Industrial Products and Process Engineering from the University of Naples, Italy, with a thesis on microplastic pollution from synthetic textiles. She is author of one patent, three book chapters and 15 scientific articles with over 400 citations.

Mariacristina Cocca is Permanent Researcher at Institute of Polymers, Composites and Biomaterials of the National Research Council of Italy. She is co-author of over 66 scientific papers, eight book chapters, four patents and was invited speaker in several national and international conferences.

Routledge Explorations in Environmental Studies

Environmental Defenders
Deadly Struggles for Land and Territory
Edited by Mary Menton and Philippe Le Billon

Globalization, Environmental Law and Sustainable Development in the Global South
Challenges for Implementation
Edited by Kirk W. Junker and Paolo Davide Farah

The Political Ecology of Austerity
Crisis, Social Movements, and the Environment
Edited by Rita Calvário, Maria Kaika and Giorgos Velegrakis

Sociology Saves the Planet
An Introduction to Socioecological Thinking and Practice
Thomas Macias

Polluting Textiles
The Problem with Microfibres
Edited by Judith S. Weis, Francesca De Falco and Mariacristina Cocca

Biocultural Rights, Indigenous Peoples and Local Communities
Protecting Culture and the Environment
Edited by Fabien Girard, Ingrid Hall and Christine Frison

For more information about this series, please visit: www.routledge.com/Routledge-Explorations-in-Environmental-Studies/book-series/REES

POLLUTING TEXTILES

The Problem with Microfibres

Edited by Judith S. Weis, Francesca De Falco and Mariacristina Cocca

Routledge
Taylor & Francis Group

LONDON AND NEW YORK

from Routledge

Cover image: Getty Images

First published 2022
by Routledge
4 Park Square, Milton Park, Abingdon, Oxon OX14 4RN

and by Routledge
605 Third Avenue, New York, NY 10158

Routledge is an imprint of the Taylor & Francis Group, an informa business

British Library Cataloguing-in-Publication Data
A catalogue record for this book is available from the British Library

Library of Congress Cataloging-in-Publication Data
A catalog record for this book has been requested

ISBN: 978-0-367-76078-6 (hbk)
ISBN: 978-0-367-76075-5 (pbk)
ISBN: 978-1-003-16538-5 (ebk)

DOI: 10.4324/9781003165385

Typeset in Bembo
by Apex CoVantage, LLC

CONTENTS

FIGURES

TABLES

PREFACE

The initial idea for this book was back in 2013 or 2014 when I (JSW) was at a workshop on microplastics, organized by the International Joint Commission (United States and Canada). At this workshop it became apparent that the majority of the microplastics in the Great Lakes and oceans were microfibers coming from textiles. When, later in the workshop, we were discussing ways to reduce the problem and I kept saying, "We need to get the textiles people into the discussion." It was clear that we environmental scientists could analyze the problems in great detail, but that we were not going to be able to ameliorate or solve them. I wrote a plea that was published in a textiles journal, and organized a meeting at the American Association for the Advancement of Science (AAAS) meeting, bringing together people from the environmental and textile fields. The idea of a book, with chapters on both the environmental problems and textile approaches to solve the problem, arose from that meeting. While it took a while to find the right co-editors to work with, we have come through the process with chapters contributed by outstanding scientists from both the environmental and textile side of the issue. FDF and MC were eager to collaborate on this book, providing more insights and contributions from the textile and material fields. A transdisciplinary approach among different research fields is of pivotal importance to correctly address and fight the problem of microfibre pollution.

ACKNOWLEDGEMENTS

JSW would like to thank Victor Serveis of the International Joint Committee (IJC) for inviting her to a workshop on microplastics, where she first realized the importance of microfibers from clothing to microplastics pollution problems, and which prompted her to connect with textile scientists. She also wishes to thank the American Association for the Advancement of Science (AAAS) for approving the workshop she coordinated for their Annual Meeting in 2019, at which environmental scientists and textile scientists discussed the problems and potential solutions.

We all are grateful to Hannah Ferguson and John Baddeley of Routledge/ Taylor & Francis for their encouragement and support of the book and for preparing the manuscript for publication and to Daniela Capuano research fellow at Institute for Polymers, Composites and Biomaterials – National Research Council of Italy for preparing the index.

1

INTRODUCTION TO TEXTILE POLLUTION

Judith S. Weis, Mariacristina Cocca and Francesca De Falco

Microplastics (MPs) are pieces of plastic ranging from 5 mm in size down to microscopic. They include different polymers, such as polyethylene, polystyrene, etc., and come in a variety of shapes, such as fragments, spheres, and fibres. There has been a virtual explosion of research on microplastics – where they are found, how organisms interact with them, and effects they may have on the organisms. Early studies focused on marine habitats where they were first found, but they have been found and studied in freshwater and terrestrial environments as well.

Environmental sampling

The number of MPs found in water samples depends on the collecting methods. Some studies use plankton nets to collect them, although it has been well documented that long thin fibers tend to go through the pores of nets and are greatly undercounted. Rocha-Santos and Duarte (2015) evaluated sampling methods and found that nets show microfibres (microplastic fibres, MFs, <5 mm) to be much less abundant than in whole water samples. Green et al. (2018) reported that plankton nets may underestimate concentrations of MFs by three to four orders of magnitude compared to grab (whole water) methods. A meta-analysis (Burns and Boxall 2018) found average sample proportions in the water column were 52% MFs, 29% fragments, with other shapes including beads/spherules, films, foams, and others making up only a small proportion. Constant et al. (2019) indicated that MFs were the most common shape in beached MPs as well. Personal care products, a source of spherical microbeads, received considerable attention years ago, but currently account for a very small percent of MPs in the ocean. MFs originate primarily from clothing via wastewater from washing machines (Browne et al. 2011). It is estimated that a single laundry wash releases approximately 121,465 acrylic, 82,672 polyester, and 22,992 poly-cotton microfibers

DOI: 10.4324/9781003165385-1

(www.vox.com/the-goods/2018/9/19/17800654/clothes-plastic-pollution-polyester-washingmachine). Chemical analysis methods such as GC-MS (Gas chromatography-mass spectrometry), Raman Spectroscopy, or Fourier Transform Infrared (FTIR) spectroscopy can determine the proportions of different plastic polymers.

Less attention has been paid to occurrence of MPs in the air, but in urban air they are predominantly MFs from synthetic textiles (Liu et al. 2019). A major source of airborne MFs is release from clothes dryers (Kapp and Miller 2020). Since MPs differ in chemical composition, size, shape, color, density, and effects on biota, they should be regarded as a suite of contaminants, somewhat comparable to metal pollutants, and samples should be characterized that way (Rochman et al. 2019). MFs from clothing, the most abundant type of MP in water (e.g. polyester and acrylic), tend to sink rather than float (Taylor et al. 2016); all MPs found in deep-sea organisms were MF.

Uptake

Ingestion has been reported in marine mammals, birds, fishes, macroinvertebrates and plankton. Most of the plastics found inside animals in the field are MFs, which may reflect their relative abundance in the environment, and/or potentially that they are not eliminated (egested) as readily as other shapes (Murray and Cowie 2011). Botterell et al. (2019) reviewed data on consumption of MPs by marine zooplankton and found 39 species that ingested them, most of which had been studied in the laboratory. They noted the importance of physical differences (size, shape, type, age) of MPs in determining ingestion and recommend that future research should use MP types representative of what is in the environment and in comparable concentrations. It is important to note that surface-dwelling organisms are more likely to encounter polystyrene, polypropylene, and polyethylene which are less dense than seawater and float, and that animals living deeper are more likely to encounter denser polyethylene terephalate and polyvinyl chloride (Cole et al. 2013). Most MPs found in animals' digestive systems are MFs and fragments (Mohsen et al. 2019). Spheres may be more likely to pass through easily and rapidly, while fragments with sharp edges are more likely to damage tissues, and fibres are more likely to form tangles and clog up the digestive system. Mussels and other filter-feeding bivalves reject undesirable particles during or right after capture by means of pseudofeces which are egested before being swallowed. In experimental studies, 71% of MFs in mussels were found in pseudofeces (Woods et al. 2018) and another 10% were found in feces after passing through the digestive system.

Transfer to other tissues and through the food web (trophic transfer)

It is important to study to what degree MPs can move out of the digestive system into other tissues rather than being egested. Anchovies, *Engraulis encrasicolus*, collected from the field had MPs, primarily polyethylene, in their livers (Collard et al.

2017). There are relatively few laboratory observations of MPs moving out from the digestive tract into tissues. Crabs exposed to 0.5 mm spheres showed translocation to the hemolymph, gills, and ovary (Farrell and Nelson 2013)

Most laboratory studies of trophic transfer used microspheres (MSs), despite the fact that they are scarce in the environment. In the laboratory, copepods (*Eurytemora affinis*) and polychaete larvae (*Marenzellaria* sp) ingested fluorescent polystyrene MSs and later passed them on to mysids which consumed them (Woods et al. 2018). Blue mussels, *Mytilus edulis*, took up green fluorescent polystyrene MSs before being fed to shore crabs (*Carcinus maenas*). Particles were subsequently detected in the hemolymph, stomach, hepatopancreas, ovary, and gills of the crabs (Farrell and Nelson 2013). Brown mussels (*Perna perna*) were fed polyvinylchloride (PVC) MSs and then fed to the fish *Spheroides greelyi*, and to crabs, *Callinectes ornatus* (Santana et al. 2017). The plastics were transferred to the predators. Thus, transfer up the food web has been demonstrated in the laboratory, but in some studies, prey organisms were fed only MPs and then were fed to predators prior to egestion; then MPs were measured in the predators prior to any egestion. This is an unrealistic experimental design.

Effects

The degree and type of effects that MPs produce depends on polymer type, size, shape, concentration, exposure time, and adsorbed chemicals. Because of aggregation and biofouling, MPs on the bottom may exceed the number in the water column and pose a greater risk to benthic fauna. However, most of the studies of effects have focused on pelagic organisms (Haegerbaeumer et al. 2019). Many studies find effects at concentrations far above environmental levels. In most studies, clean MSs are used, rather than fibers or weathered fragments. In amphipods, ingested MPs can block the digestive tract and reduce the amount of food they can eat (Au et al. 2015). MFs were more damaging than other shapes, possibly because they stay in the gut longer. Jovanovic (2017) found that MF ingestion by small fish can block the digestive system, interfere with feeding, and change behavior. While that study used MFs, many other studies use sizes, shapes, and/or concentration of MPs very different from those in the environment. In a study that used environmentally relevant levels of polyethylene MPs, Bour et al. (2018) found changes in energy reserves in the clam, *Ennucula tenuis*, exposed to the largest particles (125–500 μm). When MSs and MFs were compared for toxicity to Daphnids, MFs were more damaging (Ziajahromi et al. 2017).

Effects from plastic-associated chemicals

Two types of chemicals are of concern: (1) those in the plastic, including the polymer itself and additives like phthalates, pigments, or BPA (bisphenol A), and (2) environmental contaminants that adsorb onto the plastic, such as polychlorinated biphenyls (PCBs), metals, etc., which can be toxic, carcinogenic, or mutagenic.

Since MPs attract environmental chemicals, it is possible that they act as a vector to transfer pollutants to organisms. Leachate from raw resin pellets used for making plastic products affected behaviour of periwinkle snails (Seuront 2018), but the snails responded differently to virgin vs beached pellets. It is likely that the virgin plastic leached out additives, while the beached older plastic leached out adsorbed chemicals. In contrast, no toxicity was observed for extracts of virgin MPs on embryos of the medaka fish (*Oryzias latipes*) (Pannetier et al. 2019), while extracts of MPs coated with benzo [a] pyrene induced lethal effects with embryo mortality, low hatching rate, and DNA damage. Wardrop et al. (2016) indicated that ingested MSs can transfer adsorbed PBDEs (polybrominated diphenyl ethers) to the rainbow fish (*Melanotaenia fluviatilis*). Beckingham and Ghosh (2017) demonstrated uptake of PCBs from MPs in benthic worms, but uptake was much greater from sediments than from MPs, and the presence of MPs in the sediments reduced the transfer of the chemicals from MPs to the worms. In the laboratory, Batel et al. (2016) found that benzo [a] pyrene was transferred from MPs to *Artemia* nauplii, and from them to zebrafish, via trophic transfer. Most studies did not use MFs. Some chemicals may be more tightly bound to MPs of a certain shape and chemistry; how quickly they can be desorbed is a critical issue. Since some animals complete egestion relatively quickly, it is important to learn whether the plastic is in the gut long enough for significant desorption. Species with longer, more convoluted digestive tracts are likely to retain MPs longer and desorb more. The chemistry of the digestive tract could also be important. Bakir et al. (2014) found that acidic conditions promote desorption, but Bakir et al. (2016) modelled the transfer of adsorbed organic contaminants to an invertebrate, a fish, and a seabird, and determined that intake from food and water was the principal route of exposure to toxicants, with negligible input from MPs.

Quantification of MFs from textile

The washing process of textiles is identified as one of the major sources of MF pollution. In 2017, the International Union for Conservation of Nature (IUCN) estimated that the washing of synthetic textiles caused 35% of global emissions of primary MPs to the world oceans (Boucher and Friot 2017). Another recent report calculated that MPs generated from the washing of synthetic clothing are in the range of 18,430–46,175 tonnes per year, only in Europe (Eunomia 2018). Since 2016, several works have tried to evaluate the quantity of MFs that textiles may release during a washing cycle (Napper and Thompson 2016; Carney Almroth et al. 2018; De Falco et al. 2019). Each work applied a different methodology, ranging from tests in real washing machines (Hartline et al. 2016; Pirc et al. 2016; Belzagui et al. 2019) to laboratory simulations of washing processes (Hernandez et al. 2017; De Falco et al. 2018; Kelly et al. 2019). The type of textiles tested is varied: standard or ad hoc manufactured textiles (De Falco et al. 2018; Carney Almroth et al. 2018), new commercial garments (De Falco et al. 2019; Belzagui et al. 2019), or soiled consumer wash loads (Lant et al. 2020; Galvão et al. 2020). Moreover, the filtration and evaluation processes of the MFs in the washing water also differ among the studies in terms of volume of water filtered, filter pore size, quantification of the MFs released by number, or by weight. Some of these studies also investigated the influence on the release of factors like detergent (i.e. De Falco et al. 2018), washing program (i.e. Kelly et al. 2019), and textile characteristics (i.e. Carney Almroth et al. 2018). Due to the major differences in the methodologies applied across the different works, it is difficult to compare their results and draw general conclusions. Therefore, there is a strong need for development of a uniform methodology/protocol to assess MF release from the washing of textiles.

Wastewater treatment

Wastewater treatment plants (WWTPs) represent an important pathway for the release of MPs, especially MFs, in aquatic ecosystems. There is a double aspect of this problem since, via WWTPs, microplastics can reach both water via effluent and soil via sludge (Zhang and Chen 2020). The efficiency of WWTPs in retaining MPs depends on the treatment stage considered (primary, secondary, or tertiary), but also on the country regulations. The existing literature indicates that primary and secondary treatment stages can remove up to 88% of microplastics, and an additional 10% can be reached by applying a tertiary stage (Freeman et al. 2020). Ziajahromi et al. (2017) analysed wastewater from three WWTPs in Sydney (Australia), finding an average of 1.54, 0.48, and 0.28 MPs per litre of final effluent from primary, secondary, and tertiary treated effluent, respectively. By collecting wastewater samples from a secondary WWTP in Glasgow (UK), Murphy et al. (2016) estimated an efficiency of 98.41% in removing MPs but, despite this, they calculated that the WWTP could release 65 million MPs into receiving water every day, due to the great volumes of water discharged daily. Among the types of MPs found in wastewater samples, MFs represent the predominant fraction with around 50% (Sol et al. 2020), with two possible causes: the great quantity of MFs released during textile washing and the difficulties in their removal due to MF morphology that can facilitate their escaping from filtration systems. Another aspect to consider is that even if MPs are successfully retained by the WWTP, they can end up in the sludge, which is frequently used as fertilizer in agricultural soil, with MFs again as the most abundant shape (Corradini et al. 2019). For instance, after analysis of 79 sewage sludge samples collected from 28 WWTPs in 11 Chinese provinces, Li et al. (2018) reported an occurrence of MFs of 63%. Lares et al. (2018) analysed both water and sludge samples while monitoring WWTP in Mikkeli (Finland). They found that the 79.1% of the MPs collected were MFs, of which 96.3% and 3.1% were polyester and polyamide fibres, respectively. In light of such findings, the role of WWTPs as a route for MP release to the environment calls for mitigation measures to be applied at this level.

Degradation

Microplastics are generally divided into two categories: primary MPs when they are produced in micrometric size, secondary MPs when they result from fragmentation and degradation of larger plastic items (Arthur et al. 2009; GESAMP 2015). Degradation is a chemical change that decreases the molecular-weight of a polymer, compromising its mechanical integrity, that can be caused by UV radiation (photodegradation), reaction with water (hydrolysis), or oxidation at moderate temperatures (Andrady 2011). Another process to consider is biodegradation, microbial conversion of the organic constituents of plastics to CO_2 and mineral salts in aerobic conditions, and with the addition of methane in anaerobic conditions (SAPEA 2020). In a review, Gewert et al. (2015) analysed how the degradation process in marine environment depends on the polymer type, highlighting the risk of releasing additives that lead to the formation of other environmental pollutants. In the context of MF pollution, new studies examine the degradation of textile fibres under simulated conditions of marine environments (Zambrano et al. 2020; Sørensen et al. 2021). However, more studies are needed to better understand the degradation of textile fibres in the marine environment, particularly experiments that simulate realistic and reliable environmental conditions. In addition, these studies should examine not only synthetic fibres, but also natural ones. In fact, several works have reported the presence of cellulose-based MFs in aquatic ecosystems, raising questions on their actual persistence in the environment and possible impact as pollutants. An important aspect to consider is the possible influence of additives, finishes, and dyes on the biodegradation of natural fibres.

Textiles end-of-life

The current trends in textile production and consumption have led to millions of tonnes of fibers that are manufactured and disposed annually. In 2014, the world fiber production for textiles was 96 million tonnes (The Fiber Year 2015). At the same time, it has also been estimated that the textile industry generates more than 92 million tonnes of textile waste per year (Niinimäki et al. 2020). This is another important and concerning consequence of the textile and fashion industry, which is already recognized as one of the main industrial polluters due to its use of harmful chemicals, water and energy consumption, CO_2 emissions, etc. (Bruce et al. 2016). A relevant factor that aggravates waste generation is the rise and diffusion of the "fast fashion" production and consumption scheme. Consumers are incentivized to buy garments which are produced at very fast rates, resulting in low quality and durability. As a result of these current practices, great quantities of waste are produced, in terms of fibre, yarn, and fabric waste produced during manufacturing, unsold new garments, and garments discarded by consumers (Niinimäki et al. 2020). According to the Ellen MacArthur Foundation, 87% of fibres used in clothing manufacturing is landfilled or incinerated, and less than 1% is recycled (Ellen MacArthur Foundation 2017). Currently, there is no available information or data on the contribution of textile waste to the global emissions of MFs, but the massive amount of waste involved raises concerns and doubts on its impact on MF pollution. In order to get a complete assessment of MF sources and to identify mitigation strategies, the end-of-life of textiles is an aspect that needs to be taken into account.

Mitigation actions

The problem of MF pollution is of particular complexity, due to the different sources of MFs and the several parameters that influence MF release. Besides waste-water treatment and waste management, other intervention points for potential solutions include textile manufacturing and textile use. Up to now, commercially available solutions mostly involve the washing phase, like capturing devices to insert directly in the drum of the washing machine (Cora ball 2020; Guppyfriend 2020) or filtration systems to install in the washing machine (PlanetCare 2020; Xeros 2020). Other actions can be undertaken during the washing phase to mini-mize MF release, like choosing the right type of detergent (De Falco et al. 2018) or setting less stressing washing parameters (Lant et al. 2020). However, effective mitigation measures could be also applied in the production chain, by intervening at the textile design and manufacturing phase. Such measures could involve the research and development of new types of fibres (i.e. biosynthetic), the design of textiles with characteristics that reduce MF shedding, and implementation of pro-tective finishing treatments.

Policy

While many countries have banned the inclusion of microbeads in personal care products, attention is now being focused on reducing release of MFs into the environment. Policies are being discussed that focus on the manufacture of yarns, textiles, and clothing. Using a life-cycle approach, release can be evaluated at production of fibres, yarns, and fabric, manufacturing of the garment, distribu-tion, use, and end-of-life stage. Specifically, regarding the release of MFs from textiles, policies are just beginning. In California and Connecticut, bills were submitted to include a warning on clothing on the release of microplastic fibres in 2018, but none were scheduled for hearings or voting (California's Assembly Bill No. 2379; Connecticut General Assembly No. 341). In 2020, France became the first country in the world to adopt a law preventing microfibre pollution from textiles (LOI n° 2020–105, Art 79). As part of its circular economy law, new washing machines must be fitted with a filter for plastic microfibres as of January 2025.

In Part I of this book, we include chapters by experts covering the topics of environmental sampling, consumption, transfer out of the gut and through the food chain, effects, toxic effects of associated chemicals. Authors focus on MFs whenever possible, but in many fields, as mentioned earlier, there is an unfortunate deficiency of studies on MFs. While environmental scientists focus on understanding the environmental fate and effects of MPs, other disciplines are needed to learn how to reduce the problems. Since MFs from textiles are the most abundant MPs, Part II focuses on textiles and potential ways to reduce inputs into the environment. The chapters of this second part will cover the following different aspects: quantification of MF release from textiles; the role of WWTPs as a MF pathway but also as part of potential solutions; degradation of MPs, particularly MFs, in the marine environment; textile end-of life waste management; innovative mitigation measures to be applied at textile production and use levels and policy approaches.

References

Andrady A (2011) Microplastics in the marine environment. *Mar Pollut Bull* 62, 1596–1605. https://doi.org/10.1016/j.marpolbul.2011.05.030

Arthur C, Baker J, Bamford H (2009) *Proceedings of the International Research Workshop on the Occurrence, Effects and Fate of Microplastic Marine Debris*, 49. NOAA Technical Memorandum NOS-OR&R-30.

Au S, Bruce T, Bridges W (2015) Responses of *Hyalella azteca* to acute and chronic microplastic exposures. *Environ Toxicol Chem* 34(11), 2564–2572. https://doi.org/10.1002/etc.3093

Bakir A, O'Connor I, Rowland S, et al. (2016) Relative importance of microplastics as a pathway for the transfer of hydrophobic organic chemicals to marine life. *Environ Pollut* 219, 56–65. https://doi.org/10.1016/j.envpol.2016.09.046

Bakir A, Rowland S, Thompson R (2014) Enhanced desorption of persistent organic pollutants from microplastics under simulated physiological conditions. *Environ Pollut* 185, 16–23. https://doi.org/10.1016/j.envpol.2013.10.007

Batel A, Linti F, Scherer M, et al. (2016) Transfer of benzo [a] pyrene from microplastics to Artemia nauplii and further to zebrafish via a trophic food web experiment: CYP1A induction and visual tracking of persistent organic pollutants. *Environ Toxicol Chem* 35(7), 1656–1666. https://doi.org/10.1002/etc.3361

Beckingham, B, Ghosh, U (2017) Differential bioavailability of polychlorinated biphenyls associated with environmental particles: Microplastic in comparison to wood, coal, and biochar. *Environ Pollut* 220(A), 150–158.

Belzagui F, et al. (2019) Microplastics' emissions: Microfibers' detachment from textile garments. *Environ Pollut* 248, 1028–1035. https://doi.org/10.1016/j.envpol.2019.02.059

Botterell Z, Beaumont N, Dorrington T, et al. (2019) Bioavailability and effects of microplastics on marine zooplankton: A review. *Environ Pollut* 245, 98–110. https://doi.org/10.1016/j.envpol.2019.02.059

Boucher J, Friot D (2017) *Primary Microplastics in the Oceans: A Global Evaluation of Sources.* IUCN: Gland, Switzerland.

Bour A, Haarr A, Keiter S, et al. (2018) Environmentally relevant microplastic exposure affects sediment-dwelling bivalves. *Environ Pollut* 236, 652–660. https://doi.org/10.1016/j.envpol.2018.02.006

Browne MA, Crump P, Nivenet SJ, et al. (2011) Accumulation of microplastic on shorelines worldwide: Sources and sinks. *Environ Sci Technol* 45(21), 9175–9179. https://doi.org/10.1021/es201811s

Bruce N, Hartline N, Karba S, Ruff B, Sonar S (2016) *Microfiber Pollution and the Apparel Industry, Group Project Report, 2016.* Retrieved from http://brenmicroplastics.weebly.com/uploads/5/1/7/0/51702815/bren-patagonia_final_report_3-7-17.pdf

Burns E, Boxall A (2018) Microplastics in the aquatic environment: Evidence for or against adverse impacts and major knowledge gaps. *Environ Toxicol Chem* 37(11), 2776–2796. https://doi.org/10.1002/etc.4268

Carney Almroth B, Aström L, Roslund S, Petersson H, Johansson M, Persson, N (2018) Quantifying shedding of synthetic fibres from textiles; A source of microplastics released into the environment. *Environ Sci Pollut Res* 25(2), 1191–1199. https://doi.org/10.1007/s11356-017-0528-7

Cole M, Lindeque P, Fileman E, et al. (2013) Microplastic ingestion by zooplankton. *Environ Sci Technol* 47(12), 6646–6655. https://doi.org/10.1021/es400663f

Collard F, Gilbert B, Compere P, et al. (2017) Microplastics in the livers of European anchovies (*Engraulis encrasicolus* L.). *Environ Pollut* 229, 1000–1005. https://doi.org/10.1016/j.envpol.2017.07.089

Constant M, Kerherve P, Mino-Vercello-Verollet M, et al. (2019) Beached microplastics in the northwestern Mediterranean Sea. *Mar Pollut Bull* 142, 263–273. https://doi.org/10.1016/j.marpolbul.2019.03.032

Cora Ball (2020) *Cora Ball.* Retrieved from http://coraball.com/

Corradini F, et al. (2019) Evidence of microplastic accumulation in agricultural soils from sewage sludge disposal. *Sci Total Environ* 671, 411–420. https://doi.org/10.1016/j.scitotenv.2019.03.368

De Falco F, Di Pace E, Cocca M, Avella M (2019) The contribution of washing processes of synthetic clothes to microplastic pollution. *Sci Rep* 9, 6633. https://doi.org/10.1038/s41598-019-43023-x

De Falco F, et al. (2018) Evaluation of microplastic release caused by textile washing processes of synthetic fabrics. *Environ Pollut* 236, 916–925. https://doi.org/10.1016/j.envpol.2017.10.057

Ellen MacArthur Foundation (2017) *A New Textiles Economy: Redesigning Fashion's Future.* Retrieved from www.ellenmacarthurfoundation.org/publications

Eunomia (2018) Investigating options for reducing releases in the aquatic environment of microplastics emitted by (but not intentionally added in) products – final report. *Report for DG Environment of the European Commission*, p. 335. Retrieved from https://ec.europa.eu/environment/marine/good-environmental-status/descriptor-10/pdf/microplastics_final_report_v5_full.pdf

Farrell P, Nelson K (2013) Trophic level transfer of microplastic: *Mytilus edulis* (L.) to *Carcinus maenas* (L.). *Environ Pollut* 177, 1–3. https://doi.org/10.1016/j.envpol.2013.01.046

The Fiber Year (2015) *World Survey on Textiles and Nonwovens.* Editorial: Chemical Fibers.

Freeman S, et al. (2020) Between source and sea: The role of wastewater treatment in reducing marine microplastics. *J Environ Manag* 266, 110642. https://doi.org/10.1016/j.jenvman.2020.110642

Galvão A, Aleixo M, De Pablo H, et al. (2020) Microplastics in wastewater: microfiber emissions from common household laundry. *Environ Sci Pollut Res* 27(21), 26643–26649. https://doi.org/10.1007/s11356-020-08765-6

GESAMP (2015) Sources, fate and effects of microplastics in the marine environment: A global assessment. In: Kershaw, P.J. (Ed.), *IMO/FAO/UNESCO-IOC/ UNIDO/WMO/IAEA/UN/UNEP/UNDP Joint Group of Experts on the Scientific Aspects of Marine Environmental Protection.* Rep Stud GESAMP No. 90, 96 p.

Gewert B, Plassmann MM, Macleod M (2015) Pathways for degradation of plastic polymers floating in the marine environment. *Environ Sci: Processes Impacts* 17, 1513–1521 https://doi.org/ 10.1039/C5EM00207A

Green D, Kregting L, Boots B, et al. (2018) A comparison of sampling methods for seawater microplastics and a first report of the microplastic litter in coastal waters of

Ascension and Falkland Islands. *Mar Pollut Bull* 137, 695–701. https://doi.org/10.1016/j. marpolbul.2018.11.004

Guppyfriend (2020) *Guppyfriend Washing Bag*. Retrieved from http://guppyfriend.com/

Haegerbaeumer A, Mueller MT, Fueser H, et al. (2019) Impacts of micro-and nano-sized plastic particles on benthic invertebrates: A literature review and gap analysis. *Front Environ Sci* 7, 17. https://doi.org/10.3389/fenvs.2019.00017

Hartline NL, et al. (2016) Microfibre masses recovered from conventional machine washing of new or aged garments. *Environ Sci Technol* 50(21), 11532–11538. https://doi. org/10.1021/acs.est.6b03045

Hernandez E, Nowack B, Mitrano DM (2017) Polyester textiles as a source of microplastics from households: A mechanistic study to understand microfiber release during washing. *Environ Sci Technol* 51(12), 7036–7046. https://doi.org/10.1021/acs.est.7b01750

Jovanovic B (2017) Ingestion of microplastic by fish and its potential consequences from a physical perspective. *Integr Environ Assess Manage* 13(3), 510–515. https://doi. org/10.1002/ieam.1913

Kapp K, Miller R (2020) Electric clothes dryers: An underestimated source of microfiber pollution. *PLoS ONE*. https://doi.org/10.1371/journal.pone.0239165

Kelly M, et al. (2019) Importance of water-volume on the release of microplastic fibers from laundry. *Environ Sci Technol* 53(20), 11735–11744. https://doi.org/10.1021/acs. est.9b03022

Lant NJ, Hayward AS, Peththawadu MMD, Sheridan KJ, Dean JR (2020) Microfiber release from real soiled consumer laundry and the impact of fabric care products and washing conditions. *PLoS ONE* 15(6), e0233332. https://doi.org/10.1371/journal. pone.0233332

Lares M, Ncibi MC, Sillanpää M, Sillanpää M (2018) Occurrence, identification and removal of microplastic particles and fibers in conventional activated sludge process and advanced MBR technology. *Water Res* 133, 236–246. https://doi.org/10.1016/j. watres.2018.01.049

Li, et al. (2018) Microplastics in sewage sludge from the wastewater treatment plants in China. *Water Res* 142, 75–85. https://doi.org/10.1016/j.watres.2018.05.034

Liu D, Wang X, Fang T, et al. (2019) Source and potential risk assessment of suspended atmospheric microplastics in Shanghai. *Sci Total Environ* 675, 462–471 https://doi. org/10.1016/j.scitotenv.2019.04.110

Mohsen M, Wang Q, Zhang L, et al. (2019) Microplastic ingestion by the farmed sea cucumber *Apostichopus japonicus* in China. *Environ Pollut* 245, 1071–1078 https://doi. org/10.1016/j.envpol.2018.11.083

Murphy F, Ewins C, Carbonnier F, Quinn B (2016) Wastewater treatment works (WwTW) as a source of microplastics in the aquatic environment. *Environ Sci Technol* 50(11), 5800–5808. https://doi.org/10.1021/acs.est.5b05416

Murray F, Cowie P (2011) Plastic contamination in the decapod crustacean *Nephrops norvegicus* (Linnaeus 1758). *Mar Pollut Bull* 62(6), 1207–1217. https://doi.org/10.1016/j. marpolbul.2011.03.032

Napper IE, Thompson RC (2016) Release of synthetic microplastic plastic fibres from domestic washing machines: Effects of fabric type and washing conditions. *Mar Pollut Bull* 112(1–2), 39–45. https://doi.org/10.1016/j.marpolbul.2016.09.025

Niinimäki K, Peters G, Dahlbo H, Perry P (2020) The environmental price of fast fashion. *Nat Rev Earth Environ* 1(4), 189–200. https://doi.org/10.1038/s43017-020-0039-9

Pannetier P, Morin B, Clérandeau C, et al. (2019) Toxicity assessment of pollutants sorbed on environmental microplastics collected on beaches: Part II – adverse effects on Japanese medaka early life stages. *Environ Pollut* 248, 1098–1107. https://doi.org/10.1016/j.envpol.2018.10.129

Pirc U, Vidmar M, Mozer A, Kržan A (2016) Emissions of microplastic fibers from micro-fibre fleece during domestic washing. *Environ Sci Pollut Res* 23(21), 22206–222211. https://doi.org/10.1007/s11356-016-7703-0

PlanetCare (2020) *PlanetCare Household Filter.* Retrieved from www.planetcare.org/en/products/household-filter

Rocha-Santos T, Duarte A (2015) A critical overview of the analytical approaches to the occurrence, the fate and the behavior of microplastics in the environment. *Trends Anal Chem* 65, 47–53. https://doi.org/10.1016/j.trac.2014.10.011

Rochman C, Brookman C, Bikker J, et al. (2019) Rethinking microplastics as a diverse con-taminant suite. *Environ Toxicol Chem* 38(4), 703–711. https://doi.org/10.1002/etc.4371

Santana M, Moreira F, Turra A (2017) Trophic transference of microplastics under a low expo-sure scenario: Insights on the likelihood of particle cascading along marine food webs. *Mar Pollut Bull* 121(1–2), 154–159. https://doi.org/10.1016/j.marpolbul.2017.05.061

SAPEA, Science Advice for Policy by European Academies. (2020) *Biodegradability of Plastics in the Open Environment.* Berlin: SAPEA.

Seuront L (2018) Microplastic leachates impair behavioural vigilance and predator avoidance in a temperate intertidal gastropod. *Biol Lett* 14, 20180453. https://doi.org/10.1098/rsbl.2018.0453

Sol, D, Laca, A, Laca, A, Díaz, M (2020) Approaching the environmental problem of micro-plastics: Importance of WWTP treatments. *Sci Total Environ* 740, 140016. https://doi.org/10.1016/j.scitotenv.2020.140016

Sørensen L, et al. (2021) UV degradation of natural and synthetic microfibers causes frag-mentation and release of polymer degradation products and chemical additives. *Sci Total Environ* 755(2), 143170. https://doi.org/10.1016/j.scitotenv.2020.143170

Taylor ML, Gwinnett C, Robinson L, et al. (2016) Plastic microfibre ingestion by deep-sea organisms. *Sci Rep* 6, article 33997. https://doi.org/10.1038/srep33997

Wardrop P, Shimeta J, Nugegoda D, et al. (2016) Chemical pollutants sorbed to ingested microbeads from personal care products accumulate in fish. *Environ Sci Technol* 50(7), 4037–4044. https://doi.org/10.1021/acs.est.5b06280

Woods M, Stack M, Fields D, et al. (2018) Microplastic fiber uptake, ingestion, and eges-tion rates in blue mussel (*Mytilus edulis*). *Mar Pollut Bull* 137, 638–645. https://doi.org/10.1016/j.marpolbul.2018.10.061

Xeros (2020) *Xfiltra.* Retrieved from www.xerostech.com/technologies

Zambrano M, et al. (2020) Aerobic biodegradation in freshwater and marine environments of textile microfibers generated in clothes laundering: Effects of cellulose and poly-ester-based microfibers on the microbiome. *Mar Pollut Bull* 151, 110826. https://doi.org/10.1016/j.marpolbul.2019.110826

Zhang Z, Chen Y (2020) Effects of microplastics on wastewater and sewage sludge treatment and their removal: A review. *Chem Eng J* 382(3), 22955. https://doi.org/10.1016/j.cej.2019.122955

Ziajahromi S, Kumar A, Neale P, et al. (2017) Impact of microplastic beads and fibers on waterflea (*Ceriodaphnia dubia*) survival, growth, and reproduction: Implications of single and mixture exposures. *Environ Sci Technol* 51(22), 13397–13406. https://doi.org/10.1021/acs.est.7b03574

Ziajahromi S, Neale PA, Rintoul L, Leusch FDL (2017) Wastewater treatment plants as a pathway for microplastics: Development of a new approach to sample wastewater-based microplastics. *Water Res* 112, 93–99. https://doi.org/10.1016/j.watres.2017.01.042

PART 1
Environmental problems

2

MICROFIBRE METHODOLOGIES FOR THE FIELD AND LABORATORY

Abigail P.W. Barrows and Courtney A. Neumann

Introduction

While the scientific documentation of small pieces of plastic dates back to the 1960s (Buchanan, 1971; Carpenter & Smith, 1972; Colton et al., 1974; Thompson et al., 2004), the term *microplastic* was not coined until 2004 after researchers examining sediments around Plymouth, UK realized small plastics were often overlooked in field surveys and studies (Thompson et al., 2004). This study inspired a profound increase in microplastic research after highlighting the lack of quantification of these small particles (Rochman, 2018).

Early microplastic research focused primarily on documenting microplastic presence or absence, as well as geographical distribution. Microplastic is found worldwide. Field collection diversified from sampling solely the ocean surface to further include sampling in freshwater lakes, rivers, glaciers, the ocean's depths and terrestrial ecosystems. The more sampling conducted, the more apparent it became that microplastics were everywhere- even places as remote as Mt Everest (Napper et al., 2020) and the Mariana Trench (Jamieson et al., 2019).

As knowledge of microplastic distribution increased, more emphasis turned to identifying *types* of microplastic. The most prominent microplastic present in numerous field studies were microfibres (Salvador Cesa et al., 2017). Microfibres are small, fibrous threads, often synthetic in origin and generally accepted as having a diameter less than 20μm (Beverley et al., 2018) with a length between 1μm and 5mm and a width approximately 1.5 orders of magnitude shorter than their length (Barrows et al., 2017; Beverley et al., 2018). Microfibres are as pervasive as microplastic, and have similarly wide-reaching effects (Salvador Cesa et al., 2017). This realization prompted the scientific community to diversify field and laboratory research methods in order to better understand microfibre sources, sinks, exposures and potential effects.

DOI: 10.4324/9781003165385-3

Field sampling

Due to the ubiquitous nature of microfibres, field sampling techniques are both numerous and diverse, each method with advantages and disadvantages. In a perfect world, field methods would be standardized to allow geographical and temporal comparisons. While this ideal is acknowledged repeatedly by scientists, the diversity and range of microfibre environments and experiments require vastly different collection methods, some examples of which are detailed in Figure 2.1.

Sampling seawater

Thus far, most field-based microfibre studies focus sampling on surface seawater (Gago et al., 2018). In 2012, Hidalgo-Ruz, et al. wrote a review summarizing the quickly emerging, but not-yet standardized, microplastic field methodologies of the time. They identified three main categories of field sampling for microplastic: selective sampling, volume-reducing sampling and bulk sampling (Figure 2.1). Selective sampling involves identifying microplastic in the field and extracting them directly. This is the least common methodology employed, as it requires microplastic to be large enough to see with the naked eye. While some microfibres will be visible, many will not and field extraction will be impossible.

A much more popular method for microplastic sampling is volume-reducing sampling. This method boasts the advantage of sampling large volumes of water, thus providing a better overall representation of the composition of microplastic

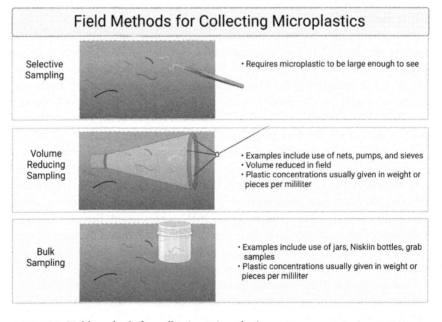

FIGURE 2.1 Field methods for collecting microplastics

in an area, and less variability due to chance. Volume-reducing sampling methods include nets, pumps and sieves (Prata et al., 2019).

Currently, the most common method for sampling surface water is trawling a neuston net from a boat. Neuston net mesh sizes most commonly measure 333mm or 335mm, but can range from 50 μm to 3mm (Hidalgo-Ruz et al., 2012). A disadvantage to neuston trawls is the undersampling of microplastic smaller than the net mesh size, as well as the incompatibility of cross-study comparison with different net mesh sizes. Smaller mesh sizes significantly increase the amount of microplastic collected (Lindeque et al., 2020; Zheng et al., 2021) and microplastic concentrations decrease as their size approaches the lower sampling limit (Filella, 2015). Furthermore, neuston nets can specifically complicate microfibre sampling. For one, microfibres become more easily trapped in nets than other plastic shapes and therefore may be sampled in higher quantities than other microplastic shapes. Secondly and conversely, since the average microfibre diameter is much smaller than the net mesh size, fibres may slip out of a neuston net. One study examined the average concentration of microfibres collected with two different mesh sizes, and found using an 80 μm net versus a 330 μm net increases the probability of capturing fibres in samples by 250 times (Dris et al., 2015).

Other popular net sampling methods include manta nets and plankton nets. The manta net has built-in wings for consistent floatation, keeping the net upright and fully open at all times, thus allowing for uniform water depth at collection. The manta net is designed to capture items at the water's surface, inspired by the two front extensions on the mouth of a manta ray, an animal that captures floating prey in a similar fashion (Brown & Cheng, 1981). The pore sizes of manta nets often correspond to neuston nets, and are similarly prone to underestimating microfibre presence (Tamminga et al., 2019). The plankton net was designed to sample plankton at the sea surface, but they are also useful for microplastic studies. Plankton nets have smaller pore size (generally 100 μm), which allows them to capture more microplastic, but also results in the nets becoming clogged much more quickly and easily by organic material (Prata et al., 2019).

Pumps and sieves also collect volume-reduced samples. Sieving can be done by hand, or in conjunction with a pump to mechanically increase the amount of water flowing through different-sized sieves. Sometimes water is passed through one filter (Covernton et al., 2019), while other times multiple filters are used with decreasing pore sizes: the largest pore size first to filter out debris, plankton and other suspended material, then increasingly finer pore sizes to isolate microplastic (Desforges et al., 2014). Other studies use their vessel's on-board seawater pump to sample very large volumes of water – as much as 150,000 litres (Lusher et al., 2015). Studies using vessel seawater intake must account for waves and turbulence affecting the depth of water sampled (will be a +/- range), the vessel's greywater overboard location and potential boat contamination from lines or sloughed paint. The designs of pump systems are continually being refined to reduce contamination and increase efficiency. Some up-and-coming designs include an enclosed pump system that can minimize environmental contamination while volume-reducing over 1000 L of water for samples in rivers, tributaries and wastewater treatment plants (Lenz & Labrenz, 2018). Both pumps and sieves allow for more accurate quantification of microplastic per volume than a towed net because the volume of water intake can be directly measured (Karlsson et al., 2019). Additionally, pump systems are generally enclosed, and thus provide more standardized means of reducing environmental contamination. The ability of pumps and sieves to capture microfibres is dependent on the filter pore size in the same manner as it is for all other methods: smaller pore size results in more microfibres captured.

Bulk sampling collects a whole volume of water without any reduction in the field. Bulk samples can range in volume, e.g. 100 ml in the Dubaish and Liebezeit (2013) study of the southern North Sea to 10 L in the Ng and Obbard's (2006) study of the beaches around Singapore. Bulk sampling is more prone to bias from high spatial variability than volume-reduced sampling because it samples a much smaller area, leaving samples vulnerable to irregular distributions. However, this method's strengths lie in quicker sample collection, as well as the ability to sample when neuston nets are not practical. Furthermore, potential for contamination is reduced because the sample is obtained more quickly, allowing less time for potential air or sampler-generated contamination. A study directly comparing the collection methods of one-litre bulk samples versus neuston net samples found more microplastic and a higher proportion of small microplastic in bulk samples. Interestingly, the amount and length of microfibres collected by both methods were not significantly different, but the neuston net collected wider microfibres (Barrows et al., 2017).

Sampling freshwater

While the methods mentioned earlier are most commonly used for surface seawaters, they are increasingly applied in freshwater systems as well. Lakes, rivers, streams and watersheds are all of concern as sinks and pathways of microfibre pollution. Sampling via boat with nets or pumps is possible in large freshwater bodies like the Great Lakes (e.g. Mason, 2019). Smaller freshwater bodies may require more creative field collection methods. When working from a boat is not feasible, for example, drifting plankton nets from bridges, or strategically positioning hand nets, could aid in collecting samples. Bulk water sampling works particularly well, especially in rivers and streams. Bulk samples have been used to sample microfibres in the Cumberland River in Tennessee (Said & Heard, 2020), and along the length of the Hudson River in New York (Miller et al., 2017b). In some cases, field collection may require persistence and ingenuity. In a 2018 study of the Gallatin watershed in southwest Montana and northwest Wyoming, field collection adapted to season and site as necessary, varying from wading to kayaking to sampling through holes in ice, to extending a pole with a collection jar from the shore (Barrows et al., 2018). Rivers are known to have high spatial and temporal variation in microplastic concentration (McCormick & Hoellein, 2016; Yonkos et al., 2014), therefore it is important to record and, if possible, sample over a variety of environmental factors such as rainfall, streamflow and season.

Sampling at depth

When field sampling, environmental factors must be considered, as they can easily affect the location of microfibres within the water column. Wind, waves, thermoclines, haloclines, upwelling, downwelling and currents can all change the distribution of microfibres within the water column. Furthermore, one study found microfibres to be distributed vertically throughout the water column regardless of density (Lenaker et al., 2019). Hence the need to sample at more than just the surface to understand pollution extent. Popular methods for sampling at depth include weighted plankton nets, bongo nets (plankton nets paired on a frame mounted next to each other), epibenthic sleds (a heavy steel frame with skids to ride along the sediment surface), Niskin bottles (a bottle open at both ends that is automatically closed when a weighted trigger is sent down a cable), a vessel's seawater intake, submersible pumps, or rosettes (a wheel of Niskin bottles usually paired with a conductivity-temperature-depth sampler). For deep water samples, landers are used (a metal platform sunk to depth, triggered to collect a water sample, and then floated to the surface for collection). A lander was used to collect sediment and water from the Mariana trench: the deepest sample collected was 10,903m deep (Peng et al., 2018). Remotely operated vehicles (ROVs) are also used to collect samples from deep in the water column.

Sampling wastewater

Wastewater treatment plants were first identified as a major source of microfibre pollution in 2011 (Browne et al., 2011) and since then, they have been further explored and documented by a number of studies (Hu et al., 2019). Samples are typically taken within or near the plant from the surrounding water, surrounding sediment, or directly at the wastewater outfall pipe. To localize findings even further, washing machines have been studied wherein samples are taken for analysis by collecting and filtering the washing water (Browne et al., 2011). A chapter later in this text is dedicated to further understanding the sampling of wastewater.

Sampling sediment

Sediment is a sink for microplastic (Thompson et al., 2004). Early on, microplastic was selectively sampled, often along beach shorelines. Microplastic was identified visually on the sediment surface and picked up with tweezers, spatulas, or by hand (Hidalgo-Ruz et al., 2012). This was very time-consuming and prone to underestimating the presence of microfibres, not only because sediment could easily cover fibres, but because of the challenge of seeing plastic < 5 mm in length. Similar to water samples, once researchers realized the ubiquity of microplastic in sediments, field sampling expanded to include many more environments besides just shorelines: freshwater sediments, sand, mud, estuaries, soil and benthos. Sediment samples are usually collected with cores to sample the top layer of sediment where microfibres settle. Cores can be collected on land, wading in shallow water, or even by scuba divers (Frias et al., 2016). To sample large quantities of sediment or sediment at depth while retaining sediment stratification, box-corers and multi-corers are popular. Multi-corers, due to their design, better preserve the sediment-water interface: they are lowered carefully to the seabed with the landing feet spread far from sample area, then a rack with tubes is lowered to collect the sediment.

Grab devices are also commonly used. Their jaws can be lowered to scoop up the top sediment layer before being lifted to the surface. Grab devices vary in size and do not keep the sediment stratified, nor can they preserve the sediment-water interface. Other methods include hand-trawls, whereby cotton sample bags are pulled along the sediment surface over a specified distance (Zobkov & Esiukova, 2017), long-term passive sediment traps consisting of a frame with collection cylinders set on a sea or lake floor to capture material falling through the water column (Dean et al., 2018), and the use of remote operated vehicles (ROV) to collect very deep sediment (Thompson et al., 2004).

Sampling air

Microplastic in the air is a concern for human and environmental health, as well as a potential source of contamination in microplastic studies. Early on, a few studies chose to completely eliminate microfibres from their results as it was contentious which microfibres were from the sample versus which were from airborne contamination (Torre et al., 2016). More recently, scientists have devised methodical and accurate ways to discern the source of microfibre contamination.

To document airborne microplastic abundance, scientists can measure passive deposition by leaving filters, adhesive pads, bottles, or petri dishes out for a specified amount of time to collect microplastics settling out of the air (Zhang et al., 2020). Rain samplers (funnel leading to a collection bottle) measure wet deposition of microplastics while simultaneously measuring rainfall. This is important as it has been suggested that rainfall can affect the amount of microplastics collected (Dris et al., 2015). Often, rain samplers (wet deposition) and passive deposition collectors (dry deposition) are used in conjunction to get a better overall idea of atmospheric microplastic concentrations. Another avenue for quantification is to collect deposited microplastics in settled dust. Dust can be collected from a defined area using pans and brushes, vacuum cleaners, or vacuum pumps with hoses (Zhang et al., 2020). Active collection of microplastics from the air can involve pumps equipped with filters that measure a specific volume of air per unit time (Mbachu et al., 2020). Other active methods of collection include particulate fallout collectors and ambient filter samplers both of which draw air in, capturing microplastic and other particulate through filters (reviewed in Enyoh et al., 2019). While none of these methods specifically sample microfibres, microfibres comprise the majority of microplastic collected from the air.

Sampling snow and ice

Snow, like rain, can be a means of wet deposition of microfibres (Zhang et al., 2020). Fresh fallen snow can be scooped up or cored, melted and examined for microfibres (Bergmann et al., 2019; Napper et al., 2020). Sea ice and glaciers can be cored with a drill, carefully stored and melted for examination (Bergmann et al., 2019; Napper et al., 2020). Ice cores allow for sampling temporally: the core can be sliced and analyzed based on specific criteria. This can contribute to an accurate historical perspective of microfibre presence over time (Cabrera et al., 2020).

Sampling items consumed by humans

There are many pathways for human ingestion of microfibres (Mishra et al., 2019). One estimate puts the microplastic consumption by an average American in the range of 39,000 to 52,000 microplastic particles annually (Cox et al., 2019). Another found eight human stool samples from around the world to have a median of 20 microplastics per 10 grams of stool (Schwabl et al., 2019). Microplastic is documented in bivalves, fish, salt, sugar, honey, tea bags, beer, milk and both tap and bottled water. When sampling these foods and beverages, scientists must consider what is ecologically and environmentally important in their research questions: where the food was obtained from, if it has been processed and does it accurately represent the item in a way that would be consumed? Once the samples accurately represent a research question, then the challenge becomes developing a method to process these items in the laboratory.

Sampling in animals

Ingestion of microfibres has been reported in a diversity of species from zooplankton (Desforges et al., 2015) to terrestrial snails (Song et al., 2019) to beluga whales (Moore et al., 2020). Animals can be collected in the field by trapping, trawling, hand-gathering, grab sampling, or collecting sediment samples along with its corresponding benthos (Lusher et al., 2017). For large and/or protected species, samples may be collected from animal excretions, or from stranded or hunted carcasses (Zantis et al., 2021). Again, once the samples accurately represent the intended research question, then the challenge becomes the laboratory processing.

Laboratory techniques

Most field samples will have to undergo a laboratory process to prepare for microfibre identification. The preparation technique is often determined by the matrices of the sample. Manipulation of the sample to remove non-plastic materials is often necessary to extract and/or measure microplastic. Most techniques have an impact on the plastic particles and the chosen methodology is usually a compromise based on available resources, time and research goals. Ultimately the methodology should be simple, affordable, precise, accurate and limit contamination at all steps (GESAMP, 2019).

Quality assurance and quality control

First and foremost, potential contamination needs to be considered when preparing a sample. Microfibres are the most common airborne contaminant in laboratories (Barrows et al., 2018; Miller et al., 2017b; Ryan et al., 2020). Incorporating strong quality assurance and quality control (QA/QC) measures are essential for microplastic studies. Control and/or blank samples should be conducted concurrently during the sample preparation process (Hung et al., 2020; Prata et al., 2020; Woodall et al., 2015). Laboratories should strive to be as plastic-free as possible: reduction of plastic equipment in contact with the sample, reduction of people and movement in the laboratory when processing samples and cotton laboratory coats should be worn at all times and noted in materials and methods. Another commonly implemented technique used to determine plastic recovery success is spiking a sample with a known quantity and shape or type of plastic, processing the sample following the study protocol and documenting plastic recuperation (Miller et al., 2017a; Quinn et al., 2017). A wide range of laboratory techniques are used to process environmental samples. Most focus broadly on capturing microplastic and don't specifically target microfibres. Microfibres pose distinct challenges for successful capture and quantification due to their unique thread-like shape, and too often longer microfibres are quantified more often than shorter ones (Lares et al., 2019). Their shape needs to be accounted for if specifically targeting microfibres in a sample. We will assess commonly used sample preparation techniques with consideration for microfibre isolation.

Density separation

Density separation of samples is commonly used for preparing sediment samples or samples with organic material. Most studies mix or shake a highly concentrated or saturated sodium, potassium formate or zinc solution in with the sample (Maes et al., 2017; Zhang et al., 2016). This method is based on extracting plastics with relatively low density, while certain polymers denser than the solution (PET and PVC, PE, PP) are not always captured with this technique (Qiu et al., 2016), which includes many of the polymers used to make microfibres.

Another relatively new technique for separating microplastic from aquatic, soil/sediment and biogenic samples is using oil (Crichton et al., 2017; Mani et al., 2019; Scopetani et al., 2020). The oleophilic and hydrophobic characteristics of most microplastic allows for a higher recovery rate than in density-separated samples (Crichton et al., 2017). This technique is efficient, non-toxic, low-cost and effective at extracting a range of polymer types, sizes (0.2 mm– 5 mm), shapes and high-density polymers (Crichton et al., 2017; Scopetani et al., 2020). Microfibres appear to have a high recovery rate using oil, with the exception of car tire rubber (styrene butadiene and butadiene rubber), which can sometimes be found in a fibre-like shape (Scopetani et al., 2020). Additionally, oil was not found to be suitable for extracting Polytetrafluoroethylene (PTFE) from solid samples (Scopetani et al., 2020). Oil type affects the affinity of microplastics – at this point, olive oil appears to have the best performance (Scopetani et al., 2020) – although further experimentation on oil type should continue to be explored for different sample matrices.

Filtration and sieving

Two laboratory techniques which may impact the quantity of microfibres captured more than other microplastic shapes are the filtration and sieving processes. Sometimes these processes are used in tandem to maximize the plastic captured (see Figure 2.2) (Hung et al., 2020; Wagner et al., 2017). Both of these techniques limit the diameter of the particle captured based on the pore (filtration) or mesh size (sieving). Commonly used filters have a pore size of $0.02\mu m$ to 10 μm (Oßmann et al., 2017), while sieves, often stacked to minimize plastic loss, range from 50 to 1000 μm mesh size (Conkle et al., 2017; Wagner et al., 2017). These often result in smaller diameter microfibre loss, as they are able to pass through the mesh lengthwise (Lares et al., 2019). Further consideration when processing sieved samples are if they are wet or dry sieved. Each have different separation efficiencies due to what remains in the sieve.

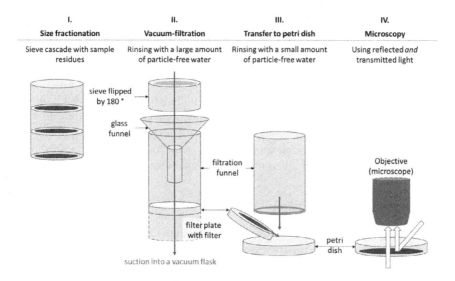

FIGURE 2.2 Method for sample transfer from sieve to microscope

Dye

Nile Red dye is frequently used to stain plastic particles in microplastic samples since it adheres to synthetics but not to most naturally occurring materials and fluoresces under specific light wavelengths (Erni-Cassola et al., 2017; Simmerman & Coleman Wasik, 2020). The technique is fast and efficient, especially for quantifying smaller plastic size fractions (<1 mm) (Erni-Cassola et al., 2017; Lavers et al., 2016). Nile Red needs to be dissolved with a solvent, commonly methanol (Erni-Cassola et al., 2017) or acetone (Maes et al., 2017; Mason et al., 2018; Shim et al., 2016), before being added to a sample. Different solvents can affect the efficacy or fluorescence of the filter material and therefore solvent choice will be determined by which filter material is used for processing (Erni-Cassola et al., 2017; Shim et al., 2016).

Digestion

Most microplastic samples undergo a digestion process to make microplastic quantification possible by reducing biogenic material (lignin, lipids, chitin) which may stain and create false positives if using dyes (Wagner et al., 2017). Samples are either treated with a chemical (e.g., KOH, H_2O_2, HCl, HNO_3) or undergo enzymatic digestion which can also be destructive or damaging to synthetic polymers (Stock et al., 2019; Wagner et al., 2017). Certain chemicals have been shown to completely dissolve (HNO_3) (Avio et al., 2015; Claessens et al., 2013), or degrade and cause color change (H_2O_2, NaOH) in common types of plastic (Dehaut et al., 2016; Hurley, et al., 2018; Karami et al., 2017). Microfibres may be particularly susceptible to degradation and loss due to their high surface area and thin thread shape. Depending on the type and quantity of organic matter in a sample, the current recommended chemical is either KOH (Dehaut et al., 2016), a low percentage solution of H_2O_2 (Frias et al., 2018) or H_2O_2 with an iron catalyst (Fenton's Reagent) (Dyachenko et al., 2017; Hurley et al., 2018) if color of the plastic is to be excluded from the study.

Enzymatic digestion successfully removes most types of biogenic matter in a sample, is non-hazardous and does not impact polymers (Cole et al., 2011; Stock et al., 2019). Unfortunately, this process is not frequently utilized due to the expense, especially for larger samples (Hurley et al., 2018), and it also requires a fair amount of time to process each sample (Lusher et al., 2017). For small samples this is considered an effective method for isolating microplastic.

Microplastic identification

Once samples have been collected and processed in the laboratory, the final step is to positively characterize the retrieved particles thought to be plastic (Figure 2.3). While the most simple and cost-effective characterization technique is visual identification, synthetic and natural microfibres of all sizes are very difficult to

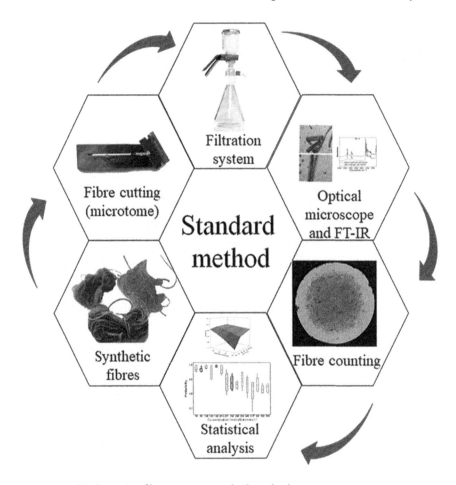

FIGURE 2.3 Testing microfibres using a standard method

differentiate if only relying on sight (Kavya et al., 2020; Shim et al., 2017; Song et al., 2015). Most microscope identification will miss many of the smaller sized microplastics and also do not allow for distinction between plastic microfibre and other natural material microfibre. Hence, the identification of material type within a sample is essential for results reporting, particularly when identifying smaller microplastics (<1 mm in size).

Most plastics contain additives and fillers or occur as copolymers, thus creating a complex and extensive chemical composition which, in turn, can create challenging identification (Crawford & Quinn, 2017). A range of analytical techniques are used to identify the polymer type in microplastic samples e.g. light microscopy, gas chromatography mass spectrometry (GC/MS), pyrolysis GC/MS (py-GC/MS), micro–Fourier-Transform Infrared spectroscopy (μ-FTIR) and μ-Raman (Frias et al., 2018).

Any method that reliably measures both the physical (size, shape, color) and chemical (polymer type) is valid for laboratory analysis. Mass spectrometry has often been utilized, but relies on thermal degradation and will destroy the sample upon analysis (Rios Mendoza & Balcer, 2019). Attenuated Total Reflectance (ATR) with μ-FTIR has been one of the most reliable techniques for microfibre material characterization for items removed from sample matrices, though it is expensive, time consuming and requires a trained technician (Rocha-Santos & Duarte, 2015). Additionally, samples do not need to undergo chemical treatment before analysis (Rios Mendoza & Balcer, 2019). ATR-μ-FTIR can only identify microplastics down to 10 μm (Löder & Gerdts, 2015), whereas μ-Raman spectroscopy can identify microplastics as small as 1 μm (Oßmann et al., 2017; Schymanski et al., 2018). μ-Raman spectroscopy has the noteworthy advantage in that it is rapid and the sample thickness or the presence of liquid or water/moisture will not negatively affect the measurement (Cabernard et al., 2018). If samples are processed through filtration, a compatible filter can be used.

When preparing any environmental sample for ATR-μ-FTIR or μ-Raman material characterization, a particular method is recommended. Once the sample has undergone initial laboratory processing (density separating, sieving, dying or digestion), particles smaller than 500 μm can be transferred directly via light rinsing through a glass funnel on to an aluminum oxide or gold polycarbonate other analytic filter for imaging (Prume et al., 2021). If the sample was processed using filtration, an analytical filter can be used, reducing the need for sample transfer. If the sample is too wet, it can be heated at no more than 65 °C until water is evaporated (Prume et al., 2021).

Consideration of environmental factors – lab

Ambient environmental conditions in laboratories also must be considered. Variables such as sampler clothing, foot traffic through the lab, tap water for rinsing equipment and air filtration are just some examples of factors that can potentially contribute to higher contamination levels in processed microfibre samples. Scientists must be aware of these variables to mitigate them if possible, or, to assess how they may impact their results.

Conclusion

Microfibre pollution will only become more prevalent in the coming decades. When initiating a study on microfibres, it is essential to consider the breadth of techniques available and select a methodology that will result in the most robust data possible, as well as suit the study site and researcher capacity. Recording comprehensive metadata is important for maximizing interstudy comparisons. Study results should be shared with local and global databases in order to further expand the knowledge on the presence of microfibres, and to inform effective next steps in research and/or local mitigation.

References

Avio, C. G., Gorbi, S., & Regoli, F. 2015. Experimental development of a new protocol for extraction and characterization of microplastics in fish tissues: First observations in commercial species from Adriatic Sea. *Mar. Environ. Res.*, *111*, 18–26. doi:10.1016/j. marenvres.2015.06.014

Barrows, A. P. W., Cathey, S. E., & Petersen, C. W. 2018. Marine environment microfiber contamination: Global patterns and the diversity of microparticle origins. *Environ. Pollut.*, *237*, 275–284. doi:10.1016/j.envpol.2018.02.062

Barrows, A. P. W., Christiansen, K. S., Bode, E. T., & Hoellein, T. J. 2018. A watershed-scale, citizen science approach to quantifying microplastic concentration in a mixed land-use river. *Water Res.*, *147*, 382–392. doi:10.1016/j.watres.2018.10.013

Barrows, A. P. W., Neumann, C. A., Berger, M. L., & Shaw, S. D. 2017. Grab vs. neuston tow net: A microplastic sampling performance comparison and possible advances in the field. *Anal. Methods*, *9*(9), 1446–1453. doi:10.1039/c6ay02387h

Bergmann, M., Mützel, S., Primpke, S., Tekman, M. B., Trachsel, J., & Gerdts, G. 2019. White and wonderful? Microplastics prevail in snow from the Alps to the Arctic. *Sci. Adv.*, *5*(8), eaax1157-eaax1157. doi:10.1126/sciadv.aax1157

Beverley, H., Kirsil, K., & Grimstad, I. 2018. *Microplastic pollution from textiles: A literature review*. Retrieved from https://fagarkivet.oslomet.no/handle/20.500.12199/5360

Brown, D. M., & Cheng, L. 1981. New net for sampling the ocean surface. *Mar. Ecol. Progr. Ser.*, *5*, 225–227. doi:10.3354/meps005225

Browne, M. A., Crump, P., Niven, S. J., Teuten, E., Tonkin, A., Galloway, T., & Thompson, R. 2011. Accumulation of microplastic on shorelines worldwide: Sources and sinks. *Environ. Sci. Technol.*, *45*, 9175. doi:10.1021/es201811s

Buchanan, J. B. 1971. Pollution by synthetic fibres. *Mar. Pollut. Bull.*, *2*(2), 23–23. doi:10.1016/0025-326x(71)90136-6

Cabernard, L., Roscher, L., Lorenz, C., Gerdts, G., & Primpke, S. 2018. Comparison of Raman and Fourier Transform Infrared Spectroscopy for the quantification of microplastics in the aquatic environment. *Environ. Sci. Technol.*, *52*(22), 13279–13288. doi:10.1021/acs.est.8b03438

Cabrera, M., Valencia, B. G., Lucas-Solis, O., Calero, J. L., Maisincho, L., Conicelli, B., . . . Capparelli, M. V. (2020). A new method for microplastic sampling and isolation in mountain glaciers: A case study of one antisana glacier, Ecuadorian Andes. *Case Stud. Chem. Environ. Eng.*, *2*, 100051. doi:10.1016/j.cscee.2020.100051

Carpenter, E. J., & Smith, K. L. 1972. Plastics on the Sargasso Sea Surface. *Science*, *175*(4027), 1240. doi: 10.1126/science.175.4027.1240

Claessens, M., Van Cauwenberghe, L., Vandegehuchte, M. B., & Janssen, C. R. 2013. New techniques for the detection of microplastics in sediments and field collected organisms. *Mar. Pollut. Bull.*, *70*(1–2), 227–233. doi:10.1016/j.marpolbul.2013.03.009

Cole, M., Lindeque, P., Halsband, C., & Galloway, T. S. 2011. Microplastics as contaminants in the marine environment: A review. *Mar. Pollut. Bull.*, *62*(12), 2588–2597. doi:10.1016/j.marpolbul.2011.09.025

Colton, J. B., Burns, B. R., & Knapp, F. D. 1974. Plastic particles in surface waters of the Northwestern Atlantic. *Science*, *185*(4150), 491–497. doi:10.1126/science.185.4150.491

Conkle, J. L., Báez Del Valle, C. D., & Turner, J. W. 2017. Are we underestimating microplastic contamination in aquatic environments? *Environ. Manag.*, *61*(1), 1–8. doi:10.1007/s00267-017-0947-8

Covernton, G. A., Pearce, C. M., Gurney-Smith, H. J., Chastain, S. G., Ross, P. S., Dower, J. F., & Dudas, S. E. 2019. Size and shape matter: A preliminary analysis of microplastic sampling technique in seawater studies with implications for ecological risk assessment. *Sci. Total Environ.*, *667*, 124–132. doi:10.1016/j.scitotenv.2019.02.346

Cox, K. D., Covernton, G. A., Davies, H. L., Dower, J. F., Juanes, F., & Dudas, S. E. 2019. Human consumption of microplastics. *Environ. Sci. Technol.*, *53*(12), 7068–7074. doi:10.1021/acs.est.9b01517

Crawford, C. B., & Quinn, B. 2017. Microplastic identification techniques. In C. B. Crawford & B. Quinn (Eds.), *Microplastic pollutants* (pp. 219–267). Amsterdam: Elsevier.

Crichton, E. M., Noël, M., Gies, E. A., & Ross, P. S. 2017. A novel, density-independent and FTIR-compatible approach for the rapid extraction of microplastics from aquatic sediments. *Anal. Methods*, *9*(9), 1419–1428. doi:10.1039/c6ay02733d

Dean, B. Y., Corcoran, P. L., & Helm, P. A. 2018. Factors influencing microplastic abundances in nearshore, tributary and beach sediments along the Ontario shoreline of Lake Erie. *J. Great Lakes Res.*, *44*(5), 1002–1009. doi:10.1016/j.jglr.2018.07.014

Dehaut, A., Cassone, A.-L., Frère, L., Hermabessiere, L., Himber, C., Rinnert, E., . . . Paul-Pont, I. (2016). Microplastics in seafood: Benchmark protocol for their extraction and characterization. *Environ. Pollut.*, *215*, 223–233. doi:10.1016/j.envpol.2016.05.018

Desforges, J.-P. W., Galbraith, M., Dangerfield, N., & Ross, P. S. 2014. Widespread distribution of microplastics in subsurface seawater in the NE Pacific Ocean. *Mar. Pollut. Bull.*, *79*(1–2), 94–99. doi:10.1016/j.marpolbul.2013.12.035

Desforges, J.-P. W., Galbraith, M., & Ross, P. S. 2015. Ingestion of microplastics by zooplankton in the Northeast Pacific Ocean. *Arch. Environ. Contam. Toxicol.*, *69*(3), 320–330. doi:10.1007/s00244-015-0172-5

Dris, R., Gasperi, J., Rocher, V., Saad, M., Renault, N., & Tassin, B. 2015. Microplastic contamination in an urban area: A case study in Greater Paris. *Environ. Chem.*, *12*(5), 592. doi:10.1071/en14167

Dubaish, F., & Liebezeit, G. 2013. Suspended microplastics and black carbon particles in the Jade System, Southern North Sea. *Water Air Soil Pollut.*, *224*(2), 1–8. doi:10.1007/s11270-012-1352-9

Dyachenko, A., Mitchell, J., & Arsem, N. 2017. Extraction and identification of microplastic particles from secondary wastewater treatment plant (WWTP) effluent. *Anal. Methods*, *9*(9), 1412–1418. doi:10.1039/C6AY02397E

Enyoh, C. E., Verla, A. W., Verla, E. N., Ibe, F. C., & Amaobi, C. E. 2019. Airborne microplastics: A review study on method for analysis, occurrence, movement and risks. *Environ. Monit. Assess.*, *191*(11), 1–17. doi:10.1007/s10661-019-7842-0

Erni-Cassola, G., Gibson, M. I., Thompson, R. C., & Christie-Oleza, J. A. 2017. Lost, but found with Nile Red: A novel method for detecting and quantifying small microplastics (1 mm to 20 µm) in environmental samples. *Environ. Sci. Technol.*, *51*(23), 13641–13648. doi:10.1021/acs.est.7b04512

Filella, M. 2015. Questions of size and numbers in environmental research on microplastics: Methodological and conceptual aspects. *Environ. Chem.*, *12*(5), 527. doi:10.1071/EN15012

Frias, J. P. G. L., Gago, J., Otero, V., & Sobral, P. 2016. Microplastics in coastal sediments from Southern Portuguese shelf waters. *Mar. Environ. Res.*, *114*, 24–30. doi:10.1016/j.marenvres.2015.12.006

Frias, J., Pagter, E., Nash, R., O'Connor, I., Carretero, O., Filgueiras, A., . . . Gerdts, G. 2018. *Standardised protocol for monitoring microplastics in sediments*. Retrieved from www.jpi-oceans.eu/baseman/main-page

Gago, J., Carretero, O., Filgueiras, A. V., & Viñas, L. 2018. Synthetic microfibers in the marine environment: A review on their occurrence in seawater and sediments. *Mar. Pollut. Bull.*, *127*, 365–376. doi:10.1016/j.marpolbul.2017.11.070

GESAMP. 2019. Guidelines or the monitoring and assessment of plastic litter and microplastics in the ocean. In P. J. Kershaw, A. Turra, & F. Galgani (Eds.), *IMO/FAO/UNESCO-IOC/UNIDO/WMO/IAEA/UN/UNEP/UNDP/ISA Joint Group of Experts on the Scientific Aspects of Marine Environmental Protection.* Rep. Stud. GESAMP No. 99, 130p.

Hidalgo-Ruz, V., Gutow, L., Thompson, R. C., & Thiel, M. 2012. Microplastics in the marine environment: A review of the methods used for identification and quantification. *Environ. Sci. Technol., 46*(6), 3060–3075. doi:10.1021/es2031505

Hu, Y., Gong, M., Wang, J., & Bassi, A. 2019. Current research trends on microplastic pollution from wastewater systems: A critical review. *Rev. Environ. Sci. Bio/Technol., 18*(2), 207–230. doi:10.1007/s11157-019-09498-w

Hung, C., Klasios, N., Zhu, X., Sedlak, M., Sutton, R., & Rochman, C. M. 2020. Methods matter: Methods for sampling microplastic and other anthropogenic particles and their implications for monitoring and ecological risk assessment. *Integ. Environ. Assess. Manag.,* doi:10.1002/ieam.4325

Hurley, R. R., Lusher, A. L., Olsen, M., & Nizzetto, L. 2018. Validation of a method for extracting microplastics from complex, organic-rich, environmental matrices. *Environ. Sci. Technol, 52*(13), 7409–7417. doi:10.1021/acs.est.8b01517

Jamieson, A. J., Brooks, L. S. R., Reid, W. D. K., Piertney, S. B., Narayanaswamy, B. E., & Linley, T. D. 2019. Microplastics and synthetic particles ingested by deep-sea amphipods in six of the deepest marine ecosystems on Earth. *R. Soc. Open Sci., 6*(2), 180667–180667. doi:10.1098/rsos.180667

Karami, A., Golieskardi, A., Choo, C. K., Romano, N., Ho, Y. B., & Salamatinia, B. 2017. A high-performance protocol for extraction of microplastics in fish. *Sci. Total Environ., 578*, 485–494. doi:10.1016/j.scitotenv.2016.10.213

Karlsson, T. M., Kärrman, A., Rotander, A., & Hassellöv, M. 2019. Comparison between manta trawl and in situ pump filtration methods, and guidance for visual identification of microplastics in surface waters. *Environ. Sci. Pollut. Res. Int., 27*(5), 5559–5571. doi:10.1007/s11356-019-07274-5

Kavya, A. N. V. L., Sundarrajan, S., & Ramakrishna, S. 2020. Identification and characterization of micro-plastics in the marine environment: A mini review. *Mar. Pollut. Bull., 160*, 111704. doi:10.1016/j.marpolbul.2020.111704

Lares, M., Ncibi, M. C., Sillanpää, M., & Sillanpää, M. 2019. Intercomparison study on commonly used methods to determine microplastics in wastewater and sludge samples. *Environ. Sci. Pollut. Res., 26*(12), 12109–12122. doi:10.1007/s11356-019-04584-6

Lavers, J. L., Oppel, S., & Bond, A. L. 2016. Factors influencing the detection of beach plastic debris. *Mar. Environ. Res., 119*, 245–251. doi:10.1016/j.marenvres.2016.06.009

Lenaker, P. L., Baldwin, A. K., Corsi, S. R., Mason, S. A., Reneau, P. C., & Scott, J. W. 2019. Vertical distribution of microplastics in the water column and surficial sediment from the Milwaukee River Basin to Lake Michigan. *Environ. Sci. Technol., 53*(21), 12227–12237. doi:10.1021/acs.est.9b03850

Lenz, R., & Labrenz, M. 2018. Small microplastic sampling in water: Development of an encapsulated filtration device. *Water (Basel), 10*(8), 1055. doi:10.3390/w10081055

Lindeque, P. K., Cole, M., Coppock, R. L., Lewis, C. N., Miller, R. Z., Watts, A. J. R., . . . Galloway, T. S. 2020. Are we underestimating microplastic abundance in the marine environment? A comparison of microplastic capture with nets of different mesh-size. *Environ. Pollut.* 114721. doi:10.1016/j.envpol.2020.114721

Löder, M. G. J., & Gerdts, G. 2015. Methodology used for the detection and identification of microplastics: A critical appraisal. In M. Bergmann, L. Gutow, & M. Klages (Eds.), *Marine anthropogenic litter* (pp. 201–227). Cham: Springer International Publishing.

Lusher, A. L., Tirelli, V., O'Connor, I., & Officer, R. 2015. Microplastics in Arctic polar waters: The first reported values of particles in surface and sub-surface samples. *Sci. Rep.*, *5*(1), 14947–14947. doi:10.1038/srep14947

Lusher, A. L., Welden, N. A., Sobral, P., & Cole, M. 2017. Sampling, isolating and identifying microplastics ingested by fish and invertebrates. *Anal. Methods*, *9*(9), 1346–1360. doi:10.1039/C6AY02415G

Maes, T., Jessop, R., Wellner, J., Haupt, K., & Mayes, A. G. 2017. A rapid-screening approach to detect and quantify microplastics based on fluorescent tagging with Nile Red. *Sci. Rep.*, *7*, 44501. doi:10.1038/srep44501

Mani, T., Frehland, S., Kalberer, A., & Burkhardt-Holm, P. 2019. Using castor oil to separate microplastics from four different environmental matrices. *Anal. Methods*, *11*(13), 1788–1794. doi:10.1039/C8AY02559B

Mason, S. A. 2019. Plastics, plastics everywhere. *Am. Scientist*, *107*(5), 284–287.

Mason, S. A., Welch, V. G., & Neratko, J. 2018. Synthetic polymer contamination in bottled water. *Front. Chem.*, *6*, 407. doi:10.3389/fchem.2018.00407

Mbachu, O., Jenkins, G., Pratt, C., & Kaparaju, P. 2020. A new contaminant superhighway? A review of sources, measurement techniques and fate of atmospheric microplastics. *Water Air Soil Pollut.*, *231*(2). doi:10.1007/s11270-020-4459-4

McCormick, A. R., & Hoellein, T. J. 2016. Anthropogenic litter is abundant, diverse, and mobile in urban rivers: Insights from cross-ecosystem analyses using ecosystem and community ecology tools. *Limnol. Ocean.*, *61*(5), 1718–1734. doi:10.1002/lno.10328

Miller, M. E., Kroon, F. J., & Motti, C. A. 2017a. Recovering microplastics from marine samples: A review of current practices. *Mar. Pollut. Bull.*, *123*(1), 6–18. doi: 10.1016/j.marpolbul.2017.08.058

Miller, R. Z., Watts, A. J. R., Winslow, B. O., Galloway, T. S., & Barrows, A. P. W. 2017b. Mountains to the sea: River study of plastic and non-plastic microfiber pollution in the northeast USA. *Mar. Pollut. Bull.*, *124*(1), 245–251. doi:10.1016/j.marpolbul.2017.07.028

Mishra, S., Rath, C. C., & Das, A. P. 2019. Marine microfiber pollution: A review on present status and future challenges. *Mar. Pollut. Bull.*, *140*, 188–197. doi:10.1016/j.marpolbul.2019.01.039

Moore, R. C., Loseto, L., Noel, M., Etemadifar, A., Brewster, J. D., MacPhee, S., . . . Ross, P. S. 2020. Microplastics in beluga whales (Delphinapterus leucas) from the Eastern Beaufort Sea. *Mar. Pollut. Bull.*, *150*, 110723. doi:10.1016/j.marpolbul.2019.110723

Napper, I., Davies, B., Clifford, H., Elvin, S., Koldewey, H. J., Mayewski, P. A., . . . Thompson, R. C. 2020. Reaching new heights in plastic pollution- preliminary findings of microplastics on Mount Everest. *One Earth*, *3*(5), 621–630. doi:10.1016/j.oneear.2020.10.020

Ng, K. L., & Obbard, J. P. 2006. Prevalence of microplastics in Singapore's coastal marine environment. *Mar. Pollut. Bull.*, *52*(7), 761–767. doi:10.1016/j.marpolbul.2005.11.017

Oßmann, B. E., Sarau, G., Schmitt, S. W., Holtmannspötter, H., Christiansen, S. H., & Dicke, W. 2017. Development of an optimal filter substrate for the identification of small microplastic particles in food by micro-Raman spectroscopy. *Anal. Bioanal. Chem.*, *409*(16), 4099–4109. doi:10.1007/s00216-017-0358-y

Peng, X., Chen, M., Chen, S., Dasgupta, S., Xu, H., Ta, K., . . . Bai, S. 2018. Microplastics contaminate the deepest part of the world's ocean. *Geochem. Persp. Lett.*, *9*, 1–5. doi:10.7185/geochemlet.1829

Prata, J. C., Castro, J. L., da Costa, J. P., Duarte, A. C., Rocha-Santos, T., & Cerqueira, M. 2020. The importance of contamination control in airborne fibers and microplastic sampling: Experiences from indoor and outdoor air sampling in Aveiro, Portugal. *Mar. Pollut. Bull.*, *159*, 111522. doi:10.1016/j.marpolbul.2020.111522

Prata, J. C., da Costa, J. P., Duarte, A. C., & Rocha-Santos, T. 2019. Methods for sampling and detection of microplastics in water and sediment: A critical review. *TrAC, Trends Anal. Chem. (Reg. ed.)*, *110*, 150–159. doi:10.1016/j.trac.2018.10.029

Prume, J. A., Gorka, F., & Löder, M. G. J. 2021. From sieve to microscope: An efficient technique for sample transfer in the process of microplastics' quantification. *MethodsX*, *8*, 101341. doi:10.1016/j.mex.2021.101341

Qiu, Q., Tan, Z., Wang, J., Peng, J., Li, M., & Zhang, Z. 2016. Extraction, enumeration and identification methods for monitoring microplastics in the environment. *Estuar. Coast. Shelf Sci.*, *176*, 102–109. doi:10.1016/j.ecss.2016.04.012

Quinn, B., Murphy, F., & Ewins, C. 2017. Validation of density separation for the rapid recovery of microplastics from sediment. *Anal. Methods*, *9*(9), 1491–1498. doi:10.1039/C6AY02542K

Rios Mendoza, L. M., & Balcer, M. 2019. Microplastics in freshwater environments: A review of quantification assessment. *TrAC Trends Anal. Chem.*, *113*, 402–408. doi:10.1016/j.trac.2018.10.020

Rocha-Santos, T., & Duarte, A. C. 2015. A critical overview of the analytical approaches to the occurrence, the fate and the behavior of microplastics in the environment. *TrAC Trends Anal. Chem.*, *65*, 47–53. doi:10.1016/j.trac.2014.10.011

Rochman, C. M. 2018. Microplastics research – from sink to source. *Science*, *360*(6384), 28–29. doi:10.1126/science.aar7734

Ryan, P. G., Suaria, G., Perold, V., Pierucci, A., Bornman, T. G., & Aliani, S. 2020. Sampling microfibres at the sea surface: The effects of mesh size, sample volume and water depth. *Environ. Pollut.*, *258*, 113413. doi:10.1016/j.envpol.2019.113413

Said, L., & Heard, M. J. 2020. Variation in the presence and abundance of anthropogenic microfibers in the Cumberland River in Nashville, TN, USA. *Environ. Sci. Pollut. Res.*, *27*(9), 10135–10139. doi:10.1007/s11356–020–08091-x

Salvador Cesa, F., Turra, A., & Baruque-Ramos, J. 2017. Synthetic fibers as microplastics in the marine environment: A review from textile perspective with a focus on domestic washings. *Sci. Tot. Environ.*, *598*, 1116–1129. doi:10.1016/j.scitotenv.2017.04.172

Schwabl, P., Köppel, S., Königshofer, P., Bucsics, T., Trauner, M., Reiberger, T., & Liebmann, B. 2019. Detection of various microplastics in human stool: A prospective case series. *Annals Inter. Med.*, *171*(7), 453–457. doi:10.7326/M19–0618

Schymanski, D., Goldbeck, C., Humpf, H.-U., & Fürst, P. (2018). Analysis of microplastics in water by micro-Raman spectroscopy: Release of plastic particles from different packaging into mineral water. *Water Res.*, *129*, 154–162. doi:10.1016/j.watres.2017.11.011

Scopetani, C., Chelazzi, D., Mikola, J., Leiniö, V., Heikkinen, R., Cincinelli, A., & Pellinen, J. 2020. Olive oil-based method for the extraction, quantification and identification of microplastics in soil and compost samples. *Sci. Tot. Environ.*, *733*, 139338. doi:10.1016/j.scitotenv.2020.139338

Shim, W. J., Hong, S. H., & Eo, S. E. 2017. Identification methods in microplastic analysis: A review. *Anal. Methods*, *9*(9), 1384–1391. doi:10.1039/C6AY02558G

Shim, W. J., Song, Y. K., Hong, S. H., & Jang, M. 2016. Identification and quantification of microplastics using Nile Red staining. *Mar. Pollut. Bull.*, *113*(1–2), 469–476. doi:10.1016/j.marpolbul.2016.10.049

Simmerman, C. B., & Coleman Wasik, J. K. 2020. The effect of urban point source contamination on microplastic levels in water and organisms in a cold-water stream. *Limnol. Ocean. Lett.*, *5*(1), 137–146. doi:10.1002/lol2.10138

Song, Y. K., Hong, S. H., Jang, M., Han, G. M., Rani, M., Lee, J., & Shim, W. J. 2015. A comparison of microplastic and spectroscopic identification methods for analysis of microplastics in environmental samples. *Mar. Pollut. Bull.*, *93*(1–2), 202–209. doi:10.1016/j.marpolbul.2015.01.015

Song, Y., Cao, C., Qiu, R., Hu, J., Liu, M., Lu, S., . . . He, D. 2019. Uptake and adverse effects of polyethylene terephthalate microplastics fibers on terrestrial snails (Achatina fulica) after soil exposure. *Environ. Pollut.*, *250*, 447–455. doi:10.1016/j.envpol.2019.04.066

Stock, F., Kochleus, C., Bänsch-Baltruschat, B., Brennholt, N., & Reifferscheid, G. 2019. Sampling techniques and preparation methods for microplastic analyses in the aquatic environment – A review. *TrAC Trends Anal. Chem.*, *113*, 84–92. doi:10.1016/j.trac.2019.01.014

Tamminga, M., Stoewer, S.-C., & Fischer, E. K. 2019. On the representativeness of pump water samples versus manta sampling in microplastic analysis. *Environ. Pollut.*, *254*, 112970. doi:10.1016/j.envpol.2019.112970

Thompson, R. C., Olsen, Y., Mitchell, R. P., Davis, A., Rowland, S. J., John, A. W. G., . . . Russell, A. E. 2004. Lost at sea: Where is all the plastic? *Science*, *304*(5672), 838. doi:10.1126/science.1094559

Torre, M , Digka, N., Anastasopoulou, A., Tsangaris, C., & Mytilineou, C. 2016. Anthropogenic microfibres pollution in marine biota. A new and simple methodology to minimize airborne contamination. *Mar. Pollut. Bull.*, *113*(1–2), 55–61. doi:10.1016/j.marpolbul.2016.07.050

Wagner, J., Wang, Z.-M., Ghosal, S., Rochman, C., Gassel, M., & Wall, S. 2017. Novel method for the extraction and identification of microplastics in ocean trawl and fish gut matrices. *Anal. Methods*, *9*(9), 1479–1490. doi:10.1039/c6ay02396g

Woodall, L. C., Gwinnett, C., Packer, M., Thompson, R. C., Robinson, L. F., & Paterson, G. L. J. (2015). Using a forensic science approach to minimize environmental contamination and to identify microfibres in marine sediments. *Mar. Pollut. Bull.*, *95*(1), 40.

Yonkos, L. T., Friedel, E. A., Perez-Reyes, A. C., Ghosal, S., & Arthur, C. D. 2014. Microplastics in four estuarine rivers in the Chesapeake Bay, U.S.A. *Environ. Sci. Technol.*, *48*(24), 14195–14202. doi:10.1021/es5036317

Zantis, L. J., Carroll, E. L., Nelms, S. E., & Bosker, T. 2021. Marine mammals and microplastics: A systematic review and call for standardisation. *Environ. Pollut.*, *269*, 116142. doi:10.1016/j.envpol.2020.116142

Zhang, K., Su, J., Xiong, X., Wu, X., Wu, C., & Liu, J. 2016. Microplastic pollution of lakeshore sediments from remote lakes in Tibet plateau, China. *Environ. Pollut.*, *219*, 450–455. doi:10.1016/j.envpol.2016.05.048

Zhang, Y., Kang, S., Allen, S., Allen, D., Gao, T., & Sillanpää, M. 2020. Atmospheric microplastics: A review on current status and perspectives. *Earth-Sci. Rev.*, *203*, 103118. doi:10.1016/j.earscirev.2020.103118

Zheng, Y., Li, J., Sun, C., Cao, W., Wang, M., Jiang, F., & Ju, P. 2021. Comparative study of three sampling methods for microplastics analysis in seawater. *Sci. Total. Environ.*, *765*, 144495. doi:10.1016/j.scitotenv.2020.144495

Zobkov, M., & Esiukova, E. 2017. Microplastics in Baltic bottom sediments: Quantification procedures and first results. *Mar. Pollut. Bull.*, *114*(2), 724–732. doi:10.1016/j.marpolbul.2016.10.060

3

ANIMALS AND MICROPLASTICS

Ingestion, transport, breakdown, and trophic transfer

Jennifer F. Provencher, Sarah Y. Au, Dorothy Horn,
Mark L. Mallory, Tony R. Walker, Joshua Kurek,
Lisa M. Erdle, Judith S. Weis, and Amy Lusher

Animals and microplastics, as habitat and food

Microplastics (MPs) in the environment can adhere to microbes, plants, and animals, thus they become vulnerable to being consumed, incorporated, enveloped, and altered by biota. The most common and studied type of exposure to MPs is by animals consuming them. It has been documented from field and laboratory studies that many pelagic (e.g., fish, plankton, invertebrates) and benthic animals (e.g., crabs, polychaete worms, mussels, sea cucumbers) eat MPs (Kühn et al., 2015; Walkinshaw et al., 2020). Furthermore, as MPs enter marine food webs, consumption by humans is likely via seafood (Devriese et al., 2015; Mohsen et al., 2019; Rochman et al., 2015b; Yang et al., 2015). Of course, consumption levels of MPs from seafood is going to be variable because the concentration of MPs varies by species and region, as do the MPs consumption rates of different species (Cox et al., 2019).

Organisms that inhabit marine surface waters are likely to encounter microplastics that are less dense than seawater, such as polystyrene (PS), polypropylene (PP), and polyethylene (PE), while benthic organisms are more likely to encounter denser polymers, including polyethylene terephthalate (PET) and polyvinyl chloride (PVC), so exposures are different depending on habitat (Cole et al., 2013). It is primarily the dense microfibres (MFs) that have been found in benthic invertebrates (Plee and Pomory, 2020), reflecting their prevalence in the environment (Figure 3.1). Deep-sea animals from three major taxa (Echinoderms, Cnidaria, and Arthropods) including sea pens, hermit crabs, and squat lobsters were found to have ingested exclusively MF of different chemical types (Taylor et al., 2016). Amphipods from the Marianas Trench, the deepest part of the ocean, and other abyssal trenches had predominantly MF in their digestive systems (Jamieson et al., 2021). However, organisms found in the water column also consume MFs, reflecting the

DOI: 10.4324/9781003165385-4

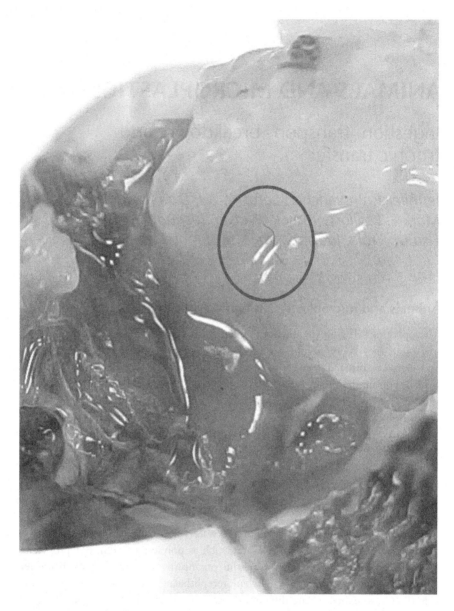

FIGURE 3.1 A sand crab stomach with microfiber (Identified as PE with FTIR)

widespread abundance of MPs within the pelagic environment (Amorim et al., 2020; McGregor and Strydom, 2020).

Why animals ingest plastics is debated among experts, and varies across taxa. Some animals are attracted by the appearance of plastics that resemble their natural food (Cadee, 2002; Ory et al., 2017). Ory et al. (2017) found that amberstripe scad (*Decapterus muroadsi*), a fish that normally eats blue copepods, consumes blue microparticles of similar size and colour. Cadee (2002) found that marks from bird beaks on cuttlefish bones and Styrofoam were similar, suggesting that the birds treat these two types of white floating objects similarly. In other animals, attraction is likely olfactory rather than visual. For example, corals appear to be attracted by the odor of virgin plastic and are less likely to consume MPs that have a biofilm (Allen et al., 2017), while other animals are attracted by the odor of the bacterial biofilm (Savoca et al., 2016). Savoca et al. (2016) found that microbes in the biofilm on marine MPs produced dimethyl sulfoxide (DMS), which may act as an attractant odor that increases ingestion of the plastic by zooplankton and also attracts seabirds.

Although it has been documented that animals eat MPs, few studies have investigated the rate of elimination. From a toxicological perspective, it is important to examine elimination (egestion, defecation) of MPs of different sizes, chemical make-up, and morphology to understand potential MP bioaccumulation and biomagnification. Experimental studies [usually using microspheres, which are uniform in shape, can be purchased commercially, but are rare in the environment due to regulatory restrictions (Xanthos and Walker, 2017)] have broadened our understanding of elimination of MPs by animals. To date, most laboratory studies show that microbeads may pass through the digestive system without causing detectable effects (Rochman et al., 2015a), although this work is ongoing in many laboratories globally and the literature on this topic is expected to greatly expand in the coming years.

It is probable that the morphology of the MPs that animals are exposed to in the environment may be important. It is likely that spheres could pass through more easily than sharp-edged fragments, which could injure walls of the gut, or fibres, which could become entangled and block the digestive system. Studies comparing MFs versus microspheres suggest that MFs caused more damage to the intestinal epithelial cells of zebrafish (*Danio rerio*) than microbeads (Qiao et al., 2019). This could be due partly to longer gut passage time, but also to the possibility that sharp-edged MFs could cause greater injury than smooth-spherical microbeads. A study of the amphipod *Hyalella azteca* reported slower egestion of MFs than microbeads, but eventually complete egestion occurred for both (Au et al., 2015). It has also been suggested that MFs had greater toxicity than microbeads because they were in the gut for a longer time. A study comparing plastic and cellulose MFs in the freshwater amphipod *Gammarus duebeni* exposed for 96 hours found more cellulose than polyester MFs in their digestive tracts (Mateos-Cárdenas et al., 2021). Animals exposed to polyester fibres along with food had the highest number of MFs in the gut. More MFs were found in the midgut or hindgut than in the foregut, suggesting that these fibres were being egested.

The gastric mill is a grinding apparatus in the gut of many crustaceans, consisting of several movable hard pieces. A study by Saborowski et al. (2019) found that the gastric mill of the Atlantic ditch shrimp (*Palaemon varians*) separates ingested microbeads from MFs. These two types of MPs are sent in different directions: the spheres continue along the gut to be defecated, while the fibres are sent back to where they came from, to be regurgitated from the mouth, demonstrating that animals may deal differently with different MP shapes. It is likely that this phenomenon exists in other crustaceans and in other invertebrates that have gastric mills (e.g., *Nephrops norvegicus*; Welden and Cowie, 2016).

If MPs merely pass through the gut, they are unlikely to do damage. If they get stuck and clog up the digestive tract, there is the possibility of malnutrition and starvation. However, if they can penetrate the gut lining and move elsewhere in the body, they are more likely to do greater damage. There are few studies that demonstrate MPs translocation out of the gut and into other tissues. One such study on the water flea (*Daphnia sp.*) found that after feeding with fluorescent microspheres, these MPs were later detected in various body tissues (Rosenkranz et al., 2009). However, a subsequent study found that it was the fluorescent dye itself, not the MPs, that had moved to the body tissues (Schür et al., 2019). A study of blue mussels (*Mytilus edulis*) provided further evidence of MP transfer to the digestive gland causing an inflammatory response (von Moos et al., 2012). Wang et al. (2021) showed accumulation and depuration (removal) of MPs in mussels after depurating from the gut, with a delay, suggesting MPs move from the gut to the mantle. Hurley et al. (2017) found greater accumulation of MFs than microbeads in the tissues of *Tubifex* worms, which was attributed to the greater likelihood of sharp-edged fibres to penetrate and embed in tissues.

There is a general tendency for smaller particles to have a greater impact than larger plastic particles (Chen et al., 2020). It also is reasonable that smaller particles are more likely to be able to move through the gut wall into tissues. The number of particles reaching other organs increases with decreasing particle size (Critchell and Hoogenboom, 2018; Jeong et al., 2016). However, in some cases, larger MPs can transfer from the intestinal tract. For example, more MPs were found in muscle than the gastrointestinal tract of a reef fish (Karami et al., 2017). Furthermore, considerable numbers of relatively large plastic particles (124–438 μm) were detected in the liver of three fish species (Collard et al., 2017). Consuming MPs instead of food could impact nutrition and energy reserves. Bour et al. (2018) studied impacts on two sediment-dwelling bivalves. *Ennucula tenuis* and *Abra nitida* were exposed to three size classes of MPs at 1, 10 and 25 mg/kg of sediment for four weeks. *E. tenuis* had a decrease in lipid content and total energy when exposed to the largest particles (125–500 μm). *A. nitida* did not have reduced total energy, but those exposed to the largest particles had reduced protein content.

Ingestion is not the only route of exposure to MPs. MFs can accumulate under the carapace of crustacean larvae (Woods et al., 2020). MPs have also been found in the gills of the green (shore) crab *Carcinus maenas* (Watts et al., 2016), suggesting that respiration is another route of intake that is poorly studied. It was noted by Hurt et al. (2020) that gizzard shad (*Dorosoma cepedianum*) had greater amounts of MPs in the gills than in the gut. Since MPs are ubiquitous in the air and soil, as well as aquatic environments, studies on respiratory intake in aquatic, land, and soil-dwelling animals are called for.

Animals and microplastics, transport and movement in the environment

While MPs have been referred to as inert contaminants, they can be subject to a variety of processes associated with biota. For example, many animals ingest MPs, therefore supporting the likelihood that MPs may undergo trophic transfer, passing from prey to predator, sometimes across ecosystem boundaries (Provencher et al., 2019). When migratory species ingest plastics, these species may move the plastic in their bodies hundreds of kilometres in the environment. Similarly, marine species with diurnal migration can facilitate the movement of plastics from surface waters to the deep-sea following ingestion and egestion. New research suggests that some biota may also be able to metabolize certain plastics on a small scale, and thus change the nature of microplastics in the environment. We explore these relationships here as biota are a main vector through which MPs and MFs are transported and biotransformed in the environment.

i)   Buoyancy: how it can change the movement of MPs in the water column

Conservative estimates of plastic inputs from land to global oceans was 5–13 million metric tonnes (Mt) in 2010, accounting for ~80% of plastic debris in the marine environment (Jambeck et al., 2015). Recently, Borrelle et al. (2020) estimated that twice that amount (19–23 Mt) entered global aquatic ecosystems in 2016. However, Eriksen et al. (2014) estimated that only 0.3 Mt of plastic was floating on the sea surface, representing a significant discrepancy between plastic inputs and floating plastics (van Sebille et al., 2015). Although plastics and MPs have been measured in many environments, such as along marine shorelines (e.g., Browne et al., 2010; Plee and Pomory, 2020), rivers (e.g., Eerkes-Medrano et al., 2015), floodplain soils (e.g., Scheurer and Bigalke, 2018), lakes (e.g., Corcoran et al., 2015; Eriksen et al., 2013), sea-ice (e.g., Obbard et al., 2014; Peeken et al., 2018), the atmosphere (e.g., Dris et al., 2018, Allen et al., 2019), aquatic sediments (e.g., Browne et al., 2010; Hamilton et al., 2021), and riparian or terrestrial soils (e.g., Crossman et al., 2020), changes in buoyancy by biota may represent a less recognized and underreported mechanism for the fate of plastic inputs to sink in aquatic ecosystems. Regardless of the absolute numbers, large amounts of MPs are buoyant and float near the surface of the water column.

In the aquatic environment, microbes can attach to and form a biofilm around MPs, suggesting that the surfaces of MPs can have a biome of their own (Wright et al., 2020, 2021). These biofilms can alter vertical transport as well as sorption and release of contaminants, which may have ecological consequences (Rummel et al., 2017). The composition of the microbial community of the biofilm is determined by MP physical characteristics (polymer, size, morphology) as well as spatial and seasonal factors (Oberbeckmann et al., 2015; Rummel et al., 2017). The community of microbes on MPs (the "plastisphere") is the subject of intense study by microbiologists (Zettler et al., 2013). Amaral-Zettler et al. (2020) reviewed information about the plastisphere and noted that while most studies have examined bacterial and archaeal diversity, eukaryotes (larger and more evolutionarily advanced single celled organisms) are also common members of the plastisphere. Among these are diatoms, at least on plastics that are exposed to sunlight. The dinoflagellate *Pfiesteria* is also abundant, as are ciliates. The presence of diatoms and dinoflagellates raises the intriguing possibility that eating microplastics might provide some nutritional value. *Vibrio* are amongst some of the bacteria found, so there is a possibility that MPs can also serve as vectors for pathogenic microorganisms (Oberbeckmann et al., 2015). Since the biofilm can concentrate pollutants (Richard et al., 2019) and toxin-producing microbes (e.g., *Pfiesteria piscicida*; Kettner et al., 2019), it may be a source of toxicity to consumers of MPs.

This process where algae and biofilms can accumulate on the surface of MPs and alter their buoyancy is called biofouling. Biofouling adds mass on plastic particles, which can alter density and increase sinking velocity (Fazey and Ryan, 2016; Kooi et al., 2016). For example, Tu et al. (2020) found that when PE film was exposed to coastal waters in the Yellow Sea, biofilms formed on the plastic surfaces that included mostly coccus-, rod-, disc-shaped bacteria and filaments. Furthermore, there may be organisms that selectively colonize plastic debris over other habitats in the marine environment. For example, niche partitioning was observed between the bacterial counts on plastic marine debris and other organic particle attachment (Dussud et al., 2018). Such "plastic specific bacteria" formed a distinct habitat of which the authors called for further consideration of the changing microbial diversity facilitated by anthropogenic debris.

Importantly, the thickness of biofilms on the PE increased with longer environmental exposure time, but decreased with the water depth at which the plastics were placed (Tu et al., 2020). Notably, biofouling of plastics varied between habitat type (Wright et al., 2020, 2021). For example, Kaiser et al. (2017) found that PE exposed to coastal water was colonized by the blue mussel, which caused an increase in density and settling velocity, although in estuarine water, PE did not sink during a 14-week incubation. The time required to sink a plastic particle depends on the particle morphology, size, surface texture and environmental conditions, but typically occurs within weeks or months (Fazey and Ryan, 2016). Sinking due to biofouling may occur most quickly when particles are small, due to their high surface area to volume ratio. Diverse taxa, including bacteria, microalgae, and invertebrates have been reported to colonize plastics and microplastics in marine (Amaral-Zettler et al., 2020; Lobelle and Cunliffe, 2011) and brackish (Wright et al., 2021) environments.

MP ingestion is another mechanism that can alter the movement of MPs in the water column. MP ingestion can impact transport of MPs via vertical migration and long-range geographical transport, and the buoyancy of particles can be altered through encapsulation in fecal pellets. MPs are ingested by zooplankton, fish, reptiles, birds, and mammals, and some of the ingested debris is egested contained in fecal pellets (e.g., Caron et al., 2018; Cole et al., 2016; Coppock et al., 2019;

Donohue et al., 2019; Katija et al., 2017; Setälä et al., 2014). Fecal pellets can alter the settling velocities of microplastics that are encapsulated (Cole et al., 2016; Coppock et al., 2019). Further, MPs may impact the structural integrity of fecal pellets and can change the fate of fecal pellets in the environment (Cole et al., 2016).

Marine snow is recognized as particles (> 0.5 mm) or aggregations of particles, both organic and inorganic, which can be observed sinking through the water column. When MPs are associated with sinking material, such as bacteria, phytoplankton, microzooplankton, or within fecal pellets and bio-deposits (Cole et al., 2016; Piarulli and Airoldi, 2020), feeding structures (larvacean houses; Katija et al., 2017) and detritus, this can facilitate the transport of microplastics in the global ocean. Laboratory experiments have shown that marine snows can transport MPs (of different morphologies and polymer types) through the water column from surface waters and enhance their bioavailability to benthic organisms (Porter et al., 2018).

Such buoyancy changes can alter movement of particles – and may be one of the processes accounting for fewer plastics on the sea surface (Cozar et al., 2014; Enders et al., 2015; Kukulka et al., 2016). This sinking of plastics due to a change in buoyancy associated with biofouling or encapsulation in fecal pellets is a likely mechanism to transport plastics and MPs to benthos and deep-sea habitats (e.g., Booth and Sørensen, 2020; Canals et al., 2020; Kvale et al., 2020; Woodall et al., 2014), and thus increase exposure for deep-sea organisms (Taylor et al., 2016; Zhu et al., 2019). Kvale et al. (2020) investigated the potential global sequestration of MPs in marine aggregated, including fecal pellets, and estimated that the MPs export to the seafloor could be between 7.3×10^3 and 4.2×10^5 Mt per year, or about 0.06–8.8% of annual ocean plastic pollution rates.

ii)   Trophic transfer: changes on small spatial scales and top predator exposure

MPs can move from prey to predator through trophic transfer, although this is not universal in all food webs. Essentially, this means that if prey has ingested or internalized MPs in their body, or adhered to their surfaces, and is consumed by a predator, the MPs themselves will be moved from one trophic level to another. In terms of the scientific literature, possibly the earliest description of plastics moving within the food web was shown for the scats of fur seals (*Arctocephalus* spp.) and Hooker's sea lions (*Phocarctos hookeri*) where the presence of plastics corresponded to otoliths of the prey species suggesting a trophic link (Eriksson and Burton, 2003; Goldsworthy et al., 1997; McMahon et al., 1999). The mesopelagic fish which are common prey for these species feed in the water column and have been shown to ingest MPs (Bellas et al., 2016; Burkhardt-Holm and N'Guyen, 2019; Choy et al., 2019; Lusher et al., 2016, 2015). To understand the consequences of MPs in prey species, Lusher et al. (2016) discussed how MPs, if retained within mesopelagic fish, could be transferred to larger marine organisms. With the understanding that: (1) mesopelagic fish account for 39–65% of the diet of striped dolphin in Irish waters (*Stenella coeruleoalba*); (2) ~ 0.18 tonnes of mesopelagic fish could be eaten annually by a single dolphin (Hernández-Milián, 2014); and (3) mesopelagic fish (average weight 5.6g) contained on average 1.2 MPs with an occurrence rate of 11% (Lusher et al., 2016). These figures can be used to estimate that a single dolphin may ingest ~4,300 MPs per year. The obvious limiting factor of these types of calculations is that they are estimates, and not empirical observations, and so further research is needed to understand the extent of annual ingestion rates for various species. Two recent analyses of MP ingestion in fish suggest consumption of MPs by fish may be increasing over time (Savoca et al., 2021), but that trophic transfer is not observable, and in fact, small planktivorous fish appear to ingest more MPs when compared with species at higher trophic levels (Covernton et al., 2021).

Ingestion of MPs is better quantified and understood in lower trophic level organisms (Bagheri et al., 2020; Rochman, 2019; Walkinshaw et al., 2020), whereas *in natura* studies have primarily demonstrated the consumption of larger plastic products by higher trophic level organisms from both terrestrial and aquatic ecosystems such as mammals (e.g., whales, deer, camels) and birds (e.g., Eriksen et al., 2021; Lavers and Bond, 2016; Lusher et al., 2015; Provencher et al., 2019). However, the exposure to MPs by organisms that preferentially consume prey larger than MPs (> 5 mm) is likely through both direct (i.e., filter feeders) and indirect consumption (i.e. trophic transfer) (Besseling et al., 2015; Moore et al., 2020), making it difficult to discern the exposure route in which MPs are ingested by higher trophic level organisms. Most of the available literature regarding MPs centres on their presence and toxicity to aquatic organisms (de Sà et al., 2018), and the same applies to the potential for bioaccumulation and trophic transfer in the environment. Feeding studies confirmed the earlier suggestions that MPs from prey pass through the digestive tracts of predators (e.g., De Sales-Ribeiro et al., 2020; Nelms et al., 2018). Another consideration that has resulted in variability between studies that evaluate the potential for MPs trophic transfer is geographically specific parameters that result in varying environmental concentrations of plastic debris and MPs.

The introduction of MPs into a food web does not necessarily need to originate from the consumption of organisms that have consumed prey exposed to MPs. Although there is considerably less research done on the role of primary producers on MP trophic transfers, field sampling of seagrasses and seaweed demonstrated the accumulation of MPs on aquatic vegetation surfaces (Goss et al., 2018; Gutow et al., 2016), resulting in the exposure to MPs of organisms that preferentially graze upon or consume aquatic vegetation. The common periwinkle (*Littorina littorea*) did not distinguish between seaweed blades with varying surface concentrations of MPs, suggesting that organisms may not avoid the direct consumption of MPs or other non-food matter when consuming biofilms or surface dwelling biota matrices containing MPs (Gutow et al., 2016). Many organisms preferentially graze upon or consume particulate and organic matter, suggesting that aquatic vegetation may serve as a source of MPs and introduce MPs into aquatic food webs (Goss et al., 2018; Gutow et al., 2016; Yokota et al., 2017). Most trophic transfer research regarding MP exposure has focused on carnivorous organisms; however, the consumption of vegetation and herbivorous species should also be considered when evaluating MP trophic transfers (Goss et al., 2018). Similarly, MPs may also adhere to the surfaces of organisms (Watts et al., 2014), demonstrating that organisms that may not ingest MPs can also introduce MPs into food webs (Au et al., 2017; Doucet et al., 2021).

The dietary preferences of humans could influence the extent to which MPs are consumed through trophic transfer. Discussions of MPs in the human diet have been focused on seafood, with greater concern voiced towards shellfish and species which are consumed whole (Cox et al., 2019; Yang et al., 2015). The number of MPs in seafood would depend on the original exposure concentrations in the environment. There has not currently been any similar discussion of terrestrial or farmed foods. In many instances, farmed animals are eaten as cuts of meat, so uptake by the digestive system becomes less relevant unless MPs have translocated into the edible tissues. Organs such as chicken gizzards and gastrointestinal tracts (tripe) may retain MPs, and so further research should be conducted.

iii)   *Species movements within foraging habitats: transport of MPs across small spatial scales*

Species that move across different habitats can also play a role as vectors and concentrators of MPs in the environment. In some cases, "biotransport" clearly plays a role in structuring (González-Bergonzoni et al., 2017; Hentati-Sundberg et al., 2020; Otero et al., 2018) or contaminating (e.g., Blais et al., 2005) local ecosystems. Several bird species have been studied to better understand how they facilitate movement of plastic pollution, including MPs, within biomes. For example, at the local scale, Ballejo et al. (2021) showed that vultures move plastics from areas where they acquire food (e.g., dumps and other anthropogenic sites) to roosting areas, creating new "hotspots" of plastic debris within terrestrial ecosystems, and effectively increasing the anthropogenic footprint of plastic waste.

Another example of the movement of MPs by birds has been shown by Hammer et al. (2016), who showed that great skuas (*Stercorarius skua*) were not only subject to the trophic transfer of MPs, but that through their regurgitation of MPs in their boluses, great skuas are transporting MPs from the marine environment back to the terrestrial environment. Similarly, a recent study focusing on fleshfooted shearwaters (*Ardenna carneipe*) that live on the isolated Lord Howe Island (Australia) have been estimated to bring over 688,000 pieces of plastic pollution to their breeding colony on the island each year (Grant et al., 2021). This biotransport of plastic pollution may lead to "hotspots" in the environment because migratory seabirds typically use the same sites year after year. It is important to consider that while both studies focused on mesoplastics, these plastics likely further mechanically breakdown in the environment leading to MPs.

MP transport has also been examined in seabirds using northern fulmars and thick-billed murres (*Uria lomvia*). Bourdages et al. (2021) showed that seabirds are

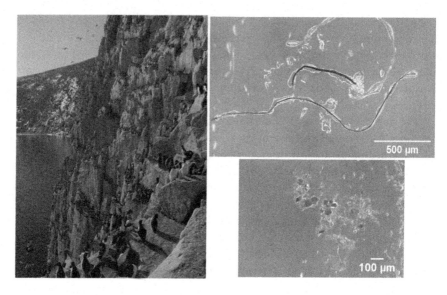

FIGURE 3.2 Left – A thick-billed murre (*Uria lomvia*) colony in Arctic Canada where they nest in dense colonies of tens of thousands. The cliffs are plant-free and covered in bird guano (photo courtesy of Jennifer Provencher). Right – Microplastics found in the guano of thick-billed murres collected by Inuit hunters

Source: (photo courtesy of Madelaine Bourdages).

bringing MPs from their diet in the ocean and depositing them back in the environment through their guano around their Arctic colony, with estimates of 3–45 million MPs per year (Figure 3.2). While a follow-up study found that the levels of MPs measured in the water, shoreline sediments, and atmospheric deposition do not show higher levels of MPs in the immediate vicinity of a fulmar colony as compared with more removed sites (Hamilton et al., 2021), there are many factors that may influence how birds act as concentrators of MPs in the environment. More research is needed to understand how colonial migratory seabirds may move significant quantities of MPs and mesoplastics around the environment.

iv) Migratory species: transport of MPs across large spatial scales

While we recognize that the transport of MPs in the environment is facilitated by atmospheric and oceanic currents, via wind and water movement, how biota may move plastics around at larger scales has also been studied. Overall, the role that migratory wildlife play in redistributing or concentrating chemicals or tiny materials (e.g., nutrients, contaminants, seeds, diseases) has received increasing attention (Martín-Vélez et al., 2020; Viana et al., 2016). Generally, plastics are designed to be resistant to degradation, and therefore are persistent in the environment; it is likely that the relocation of MPs to remote regions occurs due to the migratory behaviour of higher trophic level organisms. Depending on the nature of the material (i.e., chemical, particulate, biological), studies have demonstrated biotransport across habitat components by a variety of organisms, from invertebrates (Akamatsu and Toda, 2011) to fish (Walters et al., 2009), to birds (Blais et al., 2005), to mammals (Zantis et al., 2021).

Migration adds another twist to the challenges in understanding the fate of MPs in the environment, and their potential impacts on diverse habitats. Globally, thousands of species undertake annual migrations that may exceed 25,000 km one-way (e.g., Alerstam et al., 2019). MPs are small enough that they behave like other small, transported materials; that is, they can be ingested by migratory species, and then deposited at the terminus of the migration (colony or breeding area) in guano, regurgitations, or mortality of adults or young (note: the same process applies for local movements from a breeding or roosting area to foraging sites and back; Ballejo et al., 2021). Importantly, the distribution of MPs is clearly not uniform across environments; consequently, migratory organisms are exposed to differing concentrations of MPs during their annual cycle (Auta et al., 2017), and thus have the potential to ingest, move, and concentrate MPs in areas that do not necessarily have high concentrations from physical processes (Hale et al., 2020). As one example, Mallory (2008) showed that northern fulmars, a seabird found in the North Atlantic and Arctic, had more plastic debris earlier in the breeding season than later, and suggested that this represented mesoplastics consumed during the winter and migration, which may take months to break down (Ryan, 2015).

Two key features of MPs make them particularly amenable to movement and redistribution by migratory wildlife. First, MPs have been found across the range of organisms, from plankton (Setälä et al., 2014) to large mammals (Zantis et al., 2021), and are prevalent in migratory species like birds (e.g., Amélineau et al., 2016; Poon et al., 2017). While small organisms may directly ingest MPs as food items, thus allowing MPs to enter food webs (e.g. Doucet et al., 2021; Wang et al., 2018), larger organisms likely acquire many MPs through trophic transfer (Nelms et al., 2018; Provencher et al., 2019), rather than directly ingesting them, or they may create some MPs internally as breakdown products of consumed macroplastics (Lambert and Wagner, 2016; Weinstein et al., 2016). Moreover, it is unclear to what extent biomagnification of MPs may occur (Miller et al., 2020), although current evidence suggests that it does not in studied food webs (Gouin, 2020). However, if additional evidence suggests that MP biomagnification is analogous to the biomagnification process for chemical contaminants like persistent organic pollutants (e.g. Riget et al., 2010), this potentially puts higher trophic level species at even greater risk. In any case, MPs can bioaccumulate in many parts of food webs, thereby enhancing their exposure to migratory species. Indeed, Provencher et al. (2018) found MPs in faecal precursors of northern fulmars, seabirds that may forage 500 km away from its colony feeding on zooplankton, squid and fish (Mallory et al., 2019), and may bring plastic pollution acquired during winter feeding in the North Atlantic, 10,000 km away from its breeding area, break that down, and deposit it at Arctic colonies (Bourdages et al., 2021; Mallory, 2008).

Second, migratory wildlife often do not move randomly across their migratory routes, but if they stop during their travels, it is usually to refuel or rest in safe areas of high food supply (e.g. Silva et al., 2013). If these areas overlap with substantial MP occurrence, then the migratory organisms may experience high exposure, and move those acquired MPs on to destinations later in their route. For example, in the Bay of Biscay (France), migratory birds are thought to be at risk from exposure to concentrations of MPs in areas set aside to protect wildlife, and they can ingest those particles and move to other sites (Masiá et al., 2019).

Collectively, the prevalence of MPs in terrestrial and aquatic food webs, and the ability of MPs to accumulate in key foraging areas, means that uptake and biotransport by migratory wildlife are likely to occur in many regions. The scientific challenge now is to evaluate whether biotransport actually leads to the creation of local hotspots of MPs, particularly in areas remote from sources of these particles. In the Arctic, MPs have been found in water and ice (Bergmann et al., 2019; Peeken et al., 2018), and even in Arctic benthos (Fang et al., 2018). Thus, MPs may be so ubiquitous that effects of biotransport could be muted at many aggregation sites for migratory wildlife. For example, at a major, remote seabird colony in Arctic Canada, Hamilton et al. (2021) did not find higher concentrations of MPs closer to the colony, but MPs were present in all environmental media tested (air, water, soil, Wildlife).

v) *Sequestration and sedimentation: microplastics in aquatic environments by biota*

Sediments and soils can act as an important sink for MPs following weathering and transformation of plastics in the environment. In some cases, undisturbed sediments may even provide a useful temporal archive of plastic pollution (Bancone et al., 2020). Thus, how the process of sedimentation (or sequestration, including the role of biota in this process) occurs and varies under different conditions may be a critical mechanism to understand the integration of MPs into sedimentary deposits, including their re-suspension in shallow waters or high-energy aquatic environments (Cozar et al., 2014; Law et al., 2010). As discussed earlier, MPs such as PE and polypropylene (PP), have lower densities than water and so float (Moret-Ferguson et al., 2010), where they can be colonized by microbes (e.g., Wright et al., 2020, 2021). This biofouling reduces buoyancy and may be an important transport mechanism from the surface waters to sediments. But once MPs sink, they may not stay negatively buoyant. Particle aggregation and resulting taphonomic processes influencing MPs of varying morphology are also key to understanding MPs behaviour in aquatic environments, including integration into sediments (Alimi et al., 2018; de Haan et al., 2019).

Although there has been increasing research on MP ingestion by aquatic biota, especially benthic organisms, there is limited research on the pathways that MPs follow via integration into sediments or transport processes following post-burial, such as resuspension or bioturbation. Provencher et al. (2018) demonstrated that guano and the gastrointestinal tract of a seabird (northern fulmar, *Fulmarus glacialis*) contains appreciable amounts of MPs. Thus, seabird defecation may act as a unique marine-to-terrestrial pathway of plastic particles to lake sediments and soils adjacent to high-density colonies. Similarly, it has been shown that seabird boluses or regurgitation pellets can contain plastics (Hammer et al., 2016). Both studies suggested that migratory birds may play a role in introducing plastics back into sedimentation processes that occur in terrestrial ecosystems. This movement of plastic pollution by seabirds feeding at sea, then back to the land, via pellets regurgitated into the terrestrial environment leads to a facilitated movement from the marine to the terrestrial realm, which could lead to their inclusion to geological processes.

Another transport pathway for MPs to accumulate in sediments is via entrapment in coastal seagrass and dune communities, and subsequent ingestion by grazers of epibiont communities (Figure 3.3). For example, Goss et al. (2018) found that 75% of turtle grass (*Thalassia testudinum*) blades had encrusted MPs.

FIGURE 3.3 Microplastics trapped in the wrack line on the Oregon coast (USA); an adult foot for scale

Source: (photo credit Dorothy Horn)

Most (81%) were fibres, 16% were beads, and 3% were fragments. Research on the occurrence, abundance, and distribution of MPs in benthic invertebrates, surficial sediments, and also in deeper undisturbed sediment cores is a growing area of research (Doucet et al., 2021; Pohl et al., 2020; Vianello et al., 2013). Burial within sediments via biotic (ingestion, defecation, colonization by microbes, and bioturbation) or by abiotic (aggregation, resuspension, currents) processes, may play an important role in MP sequestration. Increased mechanistic understanding of sequestration may provide management solutions to effectively immobilize MPs from further breakdown, mobility, and trophic transfer (Uddin et al., 2021). This is important, because measurement of contaminants in well-dated, undisturbed sediment cores has been used to document historical trends in contamination inputs and estimate natural recovery or evaluate the effectiveness of strategic pollution controls (Smith et al., 2009; Walker et al., 2013). Given that MPs have differing physical characteristics than sediments, the movement of MPs once they are in sediments needs to be considered.

vi) Breakdown: how biota can breakdown microplastics

There has been relatively little research into the effect of biota on degradation of MPs. Recently several papers have shown that the larvae of the greater wax moth (*Galleria mellonella*) can consume and chemically degrade PE and polystyrene (PS) (Lou et al., 2020; Montazer et al., 2020). It is likely that bacteria found in the guts of waxworms are responsible for the metabolism of the plastics (Yang et al., 2014). Specifically, PE-degrading bacteria have also been isolated and cultured from dump sites in one study in Iran (Montazer et al., 2018). Other studies have found that bacteria from the genus *Pseudomonas* isolated from the environment have been observed to partially degrade PE, PP, PVC, PS, polyurethane (PUR), PET, polyethylene succinate, polyethylene glycol and polyvinyl alcohol (Wilkes and Aristilde, 2017). Most of these studies have taken place in laboratory settings, so it is unclear if plastic degradation occurs at similar rates in a natural environment. While this work has focused primarily on supplying the larvae or bacteria with films and fragments, it is likely that similar processes occur on fibres as well. Given that fibres are a dominant MP morphology in the environment, future studies on plastic metabolism by biota should focus on fibre morphology.

Biota can also have the ability to mechanically breakdown plastics in the environment via their digestive processes. For example, a freshwater amphipod (*Gammarus duebeni*) has been shown to be able to fragment PE, leading to the changes in the shape and sizes of the fragments, including nanoplastics (Mateos-Cárdenas et al., 2020). Additionally, a recent study on crickets (*Gryllodes sigillatus*) fed individuals 100 μm PE microbeads, but found that the crickets eliminated a variety of MP fragment sizes smaller than the original microbeads, suggesting that mechanical breakdown is occurring within the digestive tracts of the crickets (Provencher unpub. data, Figure 3.4). Additionally, an observation of a plastic film (possible bag) in the stomach of a Cuvier's beaked whale (*Ziphius cavirostris*)

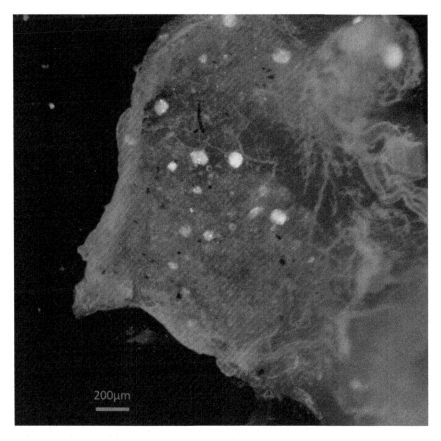

FIGURE 3.4 The gut of a cricket fed fluorescing 100 μm microbeads in a laboratory setting. Intact PE microbeads as well as smaller fragments can be seen in the
gut contents

Source: (photo courtesy of Marshall William Ritchie)

reported corresponding fragments, with matching Fourier Transform Infrared
(FTIR) spectroscopy polymer characteristics further along the digestive tract into
the intestines (Lusher, unpub. data). This observation suggests that fragmentation
of plastic materials can be facilitated within digestion processes. This breakdown
and subsequent release during egestion could lead to the release of smaller microplastics into the environment.

Considerations of biota-mediated fate of MPs for biomonitoring selection

As a result of all the ways biota can mediate the transport, movement, and fate of
MPs, the ingestion, elimination, transport, and alteration of MPs as described in
this chapter suggest consideration of biota as monitors and potential mitigation

tools for removal of MPs from the environment (Ogunola, et al., 2018; Rhodes, 2018). It is also important to consider that ingestion of MPs occurs in an array of sedentary and mobile organisms globally. In order to use this information, we must consider the biomechanical aspects related to capture of the different MPs morphologies (i.e., fragments, threads, fibres, etc.) from the environment by different organisms. The mechanics of ingestion ranging from stationary corals (Hall et al., 2015) and molluscs (Doucet et al., 2021; Piarulli and Airoldi, 2020; Su et al., 2018) to mobile organisms such as whales (Besseling et al., 2015; Fossi et al., 2016; Lusher et al., 2015) and birds (Baak et al., 2020b) that migrate annually and whose behaviours are vastly different. The consideration for biomechanical aspects of ingestion as well as environmental contamination can aid in the planning and implementation of monitoring plans. Current research into stationary organisms includes molluscs (Piarulli and Airoldi, 2020; Bråte et al., 2018), seagrasses (Agawin and Duarte, 2002) and mangroves (Nor and Obbard, 2014; Huang et al., 2020) in the marine environment, as well as freshwater molluscs (Doucet et al., 2021; Su et al., 2018) and terrestrial annelids (Baeza et al., 2020) that aid in the concept of a MP sink within different ecosystems.

Some have suggested that filter-feeding molluscs should be used as monitors for MPs in aquatic systems (Bonanno and Orlando-Bonaca, 2018; Bråte et al., 2018). Bivalves feed selectively, however, and in order to be used as a monitor, an animal should ingest most of the particles they encounter. Wang et al. (2021) measured the accumulation and depuration of particles in the gill, digestive tract, and mantle of mussels and found that ingestion of smaller particles was greater than larger particles, and large particles spent a longer time in the digestive tract. In the mantle, particles accumulated during the time when they were depurating from the gut, with a delay, suggesting they move from the gut to the mantle. Bivalves are known to be highly selective feeders (Ward et al., 2019). Doucet et al. (2021) observed that smaller freshwater mussels (*Margaritifera margaritifera*) contained more MFs than larger mussels from multiple rural watersheds in eastern Canada. Oysters (*Crassostrea virginica*) and blue mussels were offered different sized polystyrene microspheres and nylon MFs. Both species rejected up to 98% of the spheres, especially the larger sizes, and rejected most of the MFs. Particles to be rejected are first bound in mucus, transported to the mantle, and then expelled as pseudofeces. Of the small proportion of MPs that entered the digestive tract, differential defecation also occurred. Because of particle selection, concentrations of MPs in these shellfish are far lower than that in ambient water, and the relative proportions of different types of MPs are also very different from that in the surrounding environment. Thus, some have argued that bivalves may be poor biomonitors for MP pollution (Ward et al., 2019; Doucet et al., 2021). Others argue that because what mussels ingest can be consistent, they may be a useful biomonitoring tool across spatial and temporal scales within a planned program, as demonstrated by Bråte et al. (2018).

This example of sorting of MPs in bivalves demonstrates why it is necessary to select biomonitors with an understanding of how a species interacts with their immediate environment (air, water, and surrounding sediment), especially for sedentary species, or species with limited movements within a local area. Additionally, depending on the sampling location and media, MP properties can vary greatly (e.g., size, morphology, polymer composition), so species used as biomonitors may need to vary depending on the research question(s) and MPs of interest. Seasonal sampling of water, soil, and air along with a set of bioindicator species within the habitat can help to inform researchers and managers of potential spikes of pollution, as well as any population and community changes in these species.

When monitoring more mobile organisms such as benthic invertebrates, some fish species, mammals, and birds, knowing the seasonal and annual movements is key to understanding where the plastics are entering the environment (Baak et al., 2020a; Bonanno and Orlando-Bonaca, 2018). It is important that the spatial and temporal aspects of each sample organism's movements are included in the selection of biomonitor species, and in any resulting analysis of contaminants (Bonanno and Orlando-Bonaca, 2018; Kim et al., 2015; Pratte et al., 2020), especially migratory species that travel globally. Movements must include resting and staging areas where species may encounter plastic pollution, use it for nesting material, and ingest or egest plastics, causing a dispersal of plastics that needs to be accounted for (Ballejo et al., 2021; MacIvor and Moore, 2013; O'Hanlon et al., 2017). Even movement through the water column by large mammals, with egestion of plastics (Donohue et al., 2019; Harlacher, 2020; Moore et al., 2020), can change the immediate ecosystem density of plastics bioavailability. Therefore, use of mobile species as biomarkers is more indicative of the regional level of MPs as these species reflect a larger exposure to MPs than sedentary species exposed to local conditions only.

It may also be important to consider the commercial value of the species chosen for monitoring by using landing numbers from local fisheries (Bray et al., 2019). This can help rank the importance of the monitoring effort in relation to consumed species, as well as guide policy needs when the economic impact to highly rated fishery species is an argument for plastic pollution prevention. It can also help focus on species more readily available for MP analysis, which can help facilitate selection of biomonitoring approaches that can be more easily implemented with limited additional resources.

Importantly, MPs are found in both urban and remote regions around the world. However, the bioavailability of MPs may be significantly greater in urban areas where higher occurrences of anthropogenic activities likely contribute to the release of greater amounts of plastic debris. Freshwater and marine systems near urban areas generally have greater abundances of MPs than those in rural areas (Free et al., 2014; Pozo et al., 2019; Wang et al., 2017), and even in remote regions, MP concentrations have a negative relationship with proximity to populated areas (Free et al., 2014). Significantly greater concentrations of MPs are found in lakes that are associated with higher human populations than lakes in remote regions (Eriksen et al., 2013; Free et al., 2014); MP concentrations found in Lake Erie (Canada-United States) were 23 times higher than those found in Lake Hovsgol (Mongolia).

In Chile, MPs were found in all coastal fish sampled, and in greater quantities compared to the amounts found in oceanic fish, suggesting that habitat proximity to urban areas greatly influence MPs exposure and uptake (Pozo et al., 2019). MPs have also been found in greater quantities in surface water, sediment, and organisms sampled in rivers, and coastal areas receiving water from rivers (Campanale et al., 2020). Therefore, trophic transfer of MPs must be considered in context, and given that MPs likely do not accumulate in the same way as chemical contaminants, biomagnification or transfer in food webs is likely to be highly variable.

Choosing a bioindicator organism or organisms will be different in each ecosystem, but can be determined using a defined bioindicator index as discussed by Bray et al. (2019). By choosing specific organisms that are known to ingest plastics, identifying range and migratory patterns, as well documenting intestinal morphology and species distribution within the ecosystem in question, it is possible to complete a holistic measurement of the plastic pollution in the monitored area (Bray et al., 2019). Importantly, for some species other considerations may need to be included. For example, Bray et al. (2019) argue that "gut length" is crucial to calculate the digestion time when considering fish in order to understand residence time, but this may be of limited use in birds, for example, which have a very different gut morphology, and where residence time of plastics is of more concern (Ryan, 2015; van Franeker and Law, 2015). Therefore, bioindicators need to be considered within each taxa to ensure their applicability. In summary, given all the ways discussed in this chapter that biota can influence and mediate MPs in the environment, there is unlikely to be one "one size fits all" biomonitoring species. Thus, monitoring programs should consider a suite of biomonitoring species that target a variety of MPs of interest, and do so over the habitats of interest.

References

Agawin, N.S.R., Duarte C., 2002. Evidence of direct particle trapping by a tropical seagrass meadow. *Estuaries* 25, 1205–1209.

Akamatsu, F., Toda, H., 2011. Aquatic subsidies transport anthropogenic nitrogen to riparian spiders. *Environ. Pollut.* 159, 1390–1397. https://doi.org/10.1016/j.envpol.2011.01.005

Alerstam, T., Bäckman, J., Grönroos, J., Olofsson, P., Strandberg, R., 2019. Hypotheses and tracking results about the longest migration: The case of the arctic tern. *Ecol. Evol.* 9, 9511–9531. https://doi.org/10.1002/ece3.5459

Alimi, O.S., Farner Budarz, J., Hernandez, L.M., Tufenkji, N., 2018. Microplastics and nanoplastics in aquatic environments: Aggregation, deposition, and enhanced contaminant transport. *Environ. Sci. Technol.* 52, 1704–1724. https://doi.org/10.1021/acs.est.7b05559

Allen, A.S., Seymour, A.C., Rittschof, D., 2017. Chemoreception drives plastic consumption in a hard coral. *Mar. Pollut. Bull.* 124, 198–205. https://doi.org/10.1016/j.marpolbul.2017.07.030

Allen, S., Allen, D., Phoenix, V.R., Le Roux, G., Durántez Jiménez, P., Simonneau, A., Binet, S., Galop, D., 2019. Atmospheric transport and deposition of microplastics in a remote mountain catchment. *Nat. Geosci.* 12, 339–344. https://doi.org/10.1038/s41561-019-0335-5

Amaral-Zettler, L.A., Zettler, E.R., Mincer, T.J., 2020. Ecology of the plastisphere. *Nat. Rev. Microbiol.* 18 (139–151). https://doi.org/10.1038/s41579-019-0308-0

Amélineau, F., Bonnet, D., Heitz, O., Mortreux, V., Harding, A.M., Karnovsky, N., Walkusz, W., Fort, J., Grémillet, D., 2016. Microplastic pollution in the Greenland Sea: Background levels and selective contamination of planktivorous diving seabirds. *Environ. Pollut.* 219, 1131–1139. https://doi.org/10.1016/j.envpol.2016.09.017

Amorim, A.L.A. de, Ramos, J.A.A., Nogueira Júnior, M., 2020. Ingestion of microplastic by ontogenetic phases of *Stellifer brasiliensis* (Perciformes, Sciaenidae) from the surf zone of tropical beaches. *Mar. Pollut. Bull.* 158, 111214. https://doi.org/10.1016/j.marpolbul.2020.111214

Au, S.Y., Bruce, T.F., Bridges, W.C., Klaine, S.J., 2015. Responses of *Hyalella azteca* to acute and chronic microplastic exposures. *Environ. Toxicol. Chem.* 34, 2564–2572. https://doi.org/10.1002/etc.3093

Au, S.Y., Lee, C.M., Weinstein, J.E., van den Hurk, P., Klaine, S.J., 2017. Trophic transfer of microplastics in aquatic ecosystems: Identifying critical research needs. *Integr. Environ. Assess. Manag.* 13, 505–509. https://doi.org/10.1002/ieam.1907

Auta, H.S., Emenike, C., Fauziah, S., 2017. Distribution and importance of microplastics in the marine environment: A review of the sources, fate, effects, and potential solutions. *Environ. Int.* 102, 165–176. https://doi.org/10.1016/j.envint.2017.02.013

Baak, J.E., Linnebjerg, J.F., Barry, T., Gavrilo, M. V, Mallory, M.L., Price, C., Provencher, J.F., 2020a. Plastic ingestion by seabirds in the circumpolar Arctic: A review. *Environ. Rev.* 28, 506–516. https://doi.org/10.1139/er-2020–0029

Baak, J.E., Provencher, J.F., Mallory, M.L., 2020b. Plastic ingestion by four seabird species in the Canadian Arctic: Comparisons across species and time. *Mar. Pollut. Bull.* 158, 111386. https://doi.org/10.1016/j.marpolbul.2020.111386

Baeza, C., Cifuentes, C., González, P., Araneda, A., Barra, R., 2020. Experimental exposure of *Lumbricus terrestris* to microplastics. *Water Air Soil Pollut.* 231, 308. https://doi.org/10.1007/s11270-020-04673-0

Bagheri, T., Gholizadeh, M., Abarghouei, S., Zakeri, M., Hedayati, A., Rabaniha, M., Aghaeimoghadam, A., Hafezieh, M., 2020. Microplastics distribution, abundance and composition in sediment, fishes and benthic organisms of the Gorgan Bay, Caspian Sea. *Chemosphere* 257, 127201. https://doi.org/10.1016/j.chemosphere.2020.127201

Ballejo, F., Plaza, P., Speziale, K.L., Lambertucci, A.P., Lambertucci, S.A., 2021. Plastic ingestion and dispersion by vultures may produce plastic islands in natural areas. *Sci. Total Environ.* 755, 142421. https://doi.org/10.1016/j.scitotenv.2020.142421

Bancone, C.E.P., Turner, S.D., do Sul, J.A., Rose, N.L., 2020. The paleoecology of microplastic contamination. *Front. Environ. Sci.* 8, 154. https://doi.org/10.3389/fenvs.2020.574008

Bellas, J., Martínez-Armental, J., Martínez-Cámara, A., Besada, V., Martínez-Gómez, C., 2016. Ingestion of microplastics by demersal fish from the Spanish Atlantic and Mediterranean coasts. *Mar. Pollut. Bull.* 109, 55–60. https://doi.org/10.1016/j.marpolbul.2016.06.026

Bergmann, M., Mützel, S., Primpke, S., Tekman, M.B., Trachsel, J., Gerdts, G., 2019. White and wonderful? Microplastics prevail in snow from the Alps to the Arctic. *Sci. Adv.* 5. https://doi.org/10.1126/sciadv.aax1157

Besseling, E., Foekema, E.M., Van Franeker, J.A., Leopold, M.F., Kühn, S., Bravo Rebolledo, E.L., Heße, E., Mielke, L., Ijzer, J., Kamminga, P., Koelmans, A., 2015. Microplastic in a macro filter feeder: Humpback whale *Megaptera novaeangliae. Mar. Pollut. Bull.* 95, 248–252. https://doi.org/10.1016/j.marpolbul.2015.04.007

Blais, J.M., Kimpe, L.E., McMahon, D., Keatley, B.E., Mallory, M.L., Douglas, M.S. V, Smol, J.P., 2005. Arctic seabirds transport marine-derived contaminants. *Science* 309(445).

Bonanno, G., Orlando-Bonaca, M., 2018. Perspectives on using marine species as bioindicators of plastic pollution. *Mar. Pollut. Bull.* 137, 209–221. https://doi.org/10.1016/j.marpolbul.2018.10.018

Booth, A., Sørensen, L., 2020. Microplastic fate and impacts in the environment, in: *Handbook of Microplastics in the Environment*. Springer International Publishing, Cham, pp. 1–24.

Borrelle, S.B., Ringma, J., Lavender Law, K., Monnahan, C.C., Lebreton, L., McGivern, A., Murphy, E., Jambeck, J., Leonard, G.H., Hilleary, M.A., Eriksen, M., Possingham, H.P., De Frond, H., Gerber, L.R., Polidoro, B., Tahir, A., Bernard, M., Mallos, N., Barnes, M., Rochman, C.M., 2020. Predicted growth in plastic waste exceeds efforts to mitigate plastic pollution. *Science* 369, 1515–1518. https://doi.org/10.1126/SCIENCE.ABA3656

Bour, A., Avio, C.G., Gorbi, S., Regoli, F., Hylland, K., 2018. Presence of microplastics in benthic and epibenthic organisms: Influence of habitat, feeding mode and trophic level. *Environ. Pollut.* 243, 1217–1225. https://doi.org/10.1016/j.envpol.2018.09.115

Bourdages, M.P.T., Provencher, J.F., Baak, J.E., Mallory, M.L., Vermaire, J.C., 2021. Breeding seabirds as vectors of microplastics from sea to land: Evidence from colonies in Arctic Canada. *Sci. Total Environ.* 764, 142808. https://doi.org/10.1016/j.scitotenv.2020.142808

Bråte, I.L.N., Blázquez, M., Brooks, S.J., Thomas, K.V., 2018. Weathering impacts the uptake of polyethylene microparticles from toothpaste in Mediterranean mussels (*M. galloprovincialis*). *Sci. Total Environ.* 626, 1310–1318. https://doi.org/10.1016/J.SCITOTENV.2018.01.141

Bray, L., Digka, N., Tsangaris, C., Camedda, A., Gambaiani, D., de Lucia, G.A., Matiddi, M., Miaud, C., Palazzo, L., Pérez-del-Olmo, A., Raga, J.A., Silvestri, C., Kaberi, H., 2019. Determining suitable fish to monitor plastic ingestion trends in the Mediterranean Sea. *Environ. Pollut.* 247, 1071–1077. https://doi.org/10.1016/j.envpol.2019.01.100

Browne, M.A., Galloway, T.S., Thompson, R.C., 2010. Spatial patterns of plastic debris along estuarine shorelines. *Environ. Sci. Technol.* 44, 3404–3409. https://doi.org/10.1021/es903784e

Burkhardt-Holm, P., N'Guyen, A., 2019. Ingestion of microplastics by fish and other prey organisms of cetaceans, exemplified for two large baleen whale species. *Mar. Pollut. Bull.* 144, 224–234. https://doi.org/10.1016/j.marpolbul.2019.04.068

Cadee, G.C., 2002. Seabirds and floating plastic debris. *Mar. Pollut. Bull.* 44, 1294–1295. https://doi.org/10.1016/S0025-326X(02)00264-3

Campanale, C., Massarelli, C., Savino, I., Locaputo, V., Uricchio, V.F., 2020. A detailed review study on potential effects of microplastics and additives of concern on human health. *Int. J. Environ. Res. Public Health.* 17, 1212. https://doi.org/10.3390/ijerph17041212

Canals, M., Pham, C.K., Bergmann, M., Gutow, L., Hanke, G., van Sebille, E., Angiolillo, M., Buhl-Mortensen, L., Cau, A., Ioakeimidis, C., Kammann, U., Lundsten, L., Papatheodorou, G., Purser, A., Sanchez-Vidal, A., Schulz, M., Vinci, M., Chiba, S., Galgani, F., Langenkämper, D., Möller, T., Nattkemper, T.W., Ruiz, M., Suikkanen, S., Woodall, L., Fakiris, E., Jack, M.E.M., Giorgetti, A., 2020. The quest for seafloor macrolitter: A critical review of background knowledge, current methods and future prospects. *Environ. Res. Lett.* 16, 023001. https://doi.org/10.1088/1748-9326/abc6d4

Caron, A.G., Thomas, C.R., Berry, K.L., Motti, C.A., Ariel, E., Brodie, J.E., 2018. Ingestion of microplastic debris by green sea turtles (*Chelonia mydas*) in the Great Barrier

Reef: Validation of a sequential extraction protocol. *Mar. Pollut. Bull.* 127, 743–751. https://doi.org/10.1016/j.marpolbul.2017.12.062

Chen, Y., Ling, Y., Li, X., Hu, J., Cao, C., He, D., 2020. Size-dependent cellular internalization and effects of polystyrene microplastics in microalgae *P. helgolandica* var. *tsingtaoensis* and *S. quadricauda*. *J. Hazard. Mater.* 399, 123092. https://doi.org/10.1016/j.jhazmat.2020.123092

Choy, C.A., Robison, B.H., Gagne, T.O., Erwin, B., Firl, E., Halden, R.U., Hamilton, J.A., Katija, K., Lisin, S.E., Rolsky, C., S. Van Houtan, K., 2019. The vertical distribution and biological transport of marine microplastics across the epipelagic and mesopelagic water column. *Sci. Rep.* 9, 7843. https://doi.org/10.1038/s41598-019-44117-2

Cole, M., Lindeque, P.K., Fileman, E., Clark, J., Lewis, C., Halsband, C., Galloway, T.S., 2016. Microplastics alter the properties and sinking rates of zooplankton faecal pellets. *Environ. Sci. Technol.* 50, 3239–3246. https://doi.org/10.1021/acs.est.5b05905

Cole, M., Lindeque, P.K., Fileman, E., Halsband, C., Goodhead, R., Moger, J., Galloway, T.S., 2013. Microplastic ingestion by zooplankton. *Environ. Sci. Technol.* 47, 6646–6655. https://doi.org/10.1021/es400663f

Collard, F., Gilbert, B., Compère, P., Eppe, G., Das, K., Jauniaux, T., Parmentier, E., 2017. Microplastics in livers of European anchovies (*Engraulis encrasicolus*, L.). *Environ. Pollut.* 229, 1000–1005. https://doi.org/10.1016/J.ENVPOL.2017.07.089

Coppock, R.L., Galloway, T.S., Cole, M., Fileman, E.S., Queirós, A.M., Lindeque, P.K., 2019. Microplastics alter feeding selectivity and faecal density in the copepod, *Calanus helgolandicus*. *Sci. Total Environ.* 687, 780–789. https://doi.org/10.1016/j.scitotenv.2019.06.009

Corcoran, P.L., Moore, C., Jazvac, K., 2015. Benthic plastic debris in marine and freshwater environments. *Environ. Sci. Impacts* 17, 1363–1369. https://doi.org/10.1039/c5em00188a

Covernton, G.A., Davies, H.L., Cox, K.D., El-Sabaawi, R., Juanes, F., Dudas, S.E., Dower, J.F., 2021. A Bayesian analysis of the factors determining microplastics ingestion in fishes. *J. Hazard. Mater.* 413, 125405. https://doi.org/10.1016/j.jhazmat.2021.125405

Cox, K.D., Covernton, G.A., Davies, H.L., Dower, J.F., Juanes, F., Dudas, S.E., 2019. Human consumption of microplastics. *Environ. Sci. Technol.* 53, 7068–7074. https://doi.org/10.1021/acs.est.9b01517

Cozar, A., Echevarria, F., Gonzalez-Gordillo, J.I., Irigoien, X., Ubeda, B., Hernandez-Leon, S., Palma, A.T., Navarro, S., Garcia-de-Lomas, J., Ruiz, A., Fernandez-de-Puelles, M.L., Duarte, C.M., 2014. Plastic debris in the open ocean. *Proc. Natl. Acad. Sci.* 111, 10239–10244. https://doi.org/10.1073/pnas.1314705111

Critchell, K., Hoogenboom, M.O., 2018. Effects of microplastic exposure on the body condition and behaviour of planktivorous reef fish (*Acanthochromis polyacanthus*). *PLoS One* 13, e0193308. https://doi.org/10.1371/journal.pone.0193308

Crossman, J., Hurley, R.R., Futter, M., Nizzetto, L., 2020. Transfer and transport of microplastics from biosolids to agricultural soils and the wider environment. *Sci. Total Environ.* 724, 138334. https://doi.org/10.1016/j.scitotenv.2020.138334

de Haan, W.P., Sanchez-Vidal, A., Canals, M., 2019. Floating microplastics and aggregate formation in the Western Mediterranean Sea. *Mar. Pollut. Bull.* 140, 523–535. https://doi.org/10.1016/j.marpolbul.2019.01.053

de Sá, L.C., Oliveira, M., Ribeiro, F., Rocha, T.L., Futter, M.N., 2018. Studies of the effects of microplastics on aquatic organisms: What do we know and where should we focus our efforts in the future? *Sci. Total Environ.* https://doi.org/10.1016/j.scitotenv.2018.07.207

De Sales-Ribeiro, C., Brito-Casillas, Y., Fernandez, A., Caballero, M.J., 2020. An end to the controversy over the microscopic detection and effects of pristine microplastics in fish organs. *Sci. Rep.* 10, 12434. https://doi.org/10.1038/s41598-020-69062-3

Devriese, L.I., van der Meulen, M.D., Maes, T., Bekaert, K., Paul-Pont, I., Frère, L., Robbens, J., Vethaak, A.D., 2015. Microplastic contamination in brown shrimp (*Crangon, Linnaeus* 1758) from coastal waters of the Southern North Sea and Channel area. *Mar. Pollut. Bull.* 98, 179–187. https://doi.org/10.1016/j.marpolbul.2015.06.051

Donohue, M.J., Masura, J., Gelatt, T., Ream, R., Baker, J.D., Faulhaber, K., Lerner, D.T., 2019. Evaluating exposure of northern fur seals, *Callorhinus ursinus*, to microplastic pollution through fecal analysis. *Mar. Pollut. Bull.* 138, 213–221. https://doi.org/10.1016/j.marpolbul.2018.11.036

Doucet, C. V, Labaj, A.L., Kurek, J., 2021. Microfiber content in freshwater mussels from rural tributaries of the Saint John River, Canada. *Water Air Soil Pollut.* 232, 32. https://doi.org/10.1007/s11270-020-04958-4

Dris, R., Gasperi, J., Bruno, T., 2018. Sources and fate of microplastics in urban areas: A focus on Paris megacity, in: *Freshwater Microplastics: Emerging Environmental Contaminants?* Springer International Publishing, Cham, pp. 69–83.

Dussud, C., Meistertzheim, A.L., Conan, P., Pujo-Pay, M., George, M., Fabre, P., Coudane, J., Higgs, P., Elineau, A., Pedrotti, M.L., Gorsky, G., Ghiglione, J.F., 2018. Evidence of niche partitioning among bacteria living on plastics, organic particles and surrounding seawaters. *Environ. Pollut.* 236, 807–816. https://doi.org/10.1016/j.envpol.2017.12.027

Eerkes-Medrano, D., Thompson, R.C., Aldridge, D.C., 2015. Microplastics in freshwater systems: A review of the emerging threats, identification of knowledge gaps and prioritisation of research needs. *Water Res.* 75, 63–82. https://doi.org/10.1016/j.watres.2015.02.012

Enders, K., Lenz, R., Stdemon, C.A., Nielsen, T.G., 2015. Abundance, size and polymer composition of marine microplastics ≥ 10 μm in the Atlantic Ocean and their modelled vertical distribution. *Mar. Pollut. Bull.* 100, 70–81. https://doi.org/10.1016/j.marpolbul.2015.09.027

Eriksen, M., Lebreton, L.C.M., Carson, H.S., Thiel, M., Moore, C.J., Borerro, J.C., Galgani, F., Ryan, P.G., Reisser, J., 2014. Plastic pollution in the world's oceans: More than 5 trillion plastic pieces weighing over 250,000 tons afloat at sea. *PLoS One* 9, e111913. https://doi.org/10.1371/journal.pone.0111913

Eriksen, M., Lusher, A., Nixon, M., Wernery, U., 2021. The plight of camels eating plastic waste. *J. Arid Environ.* 185, 104374. https://doi.org/10.1016/j.jaridenv.2020.104374

Eriksen, M., Mason, S., Wilson, S., Box, C., Zellers, A., Edwards, W., Farley, H., Amato, S., 2013. Microplastic pollution in the surface waters of the Laurentian Great Lakes. *Mar. Pollut. Bull.* 77, 177–182. https://doi.org/10.1016/j.marpolbul.2013.10.007

Eriksson, C., Burton, H., 2003. Origins and biological accumulation of small plastic particles in fur seals from Macquarie Island. *AMBIO* 32, 380. https://doi.org/10.1639/0044-7447(2003)032[0380:OABAOS]2.0.CO;2

Fang, C., Zheng, R., Zhang, Y., Hong, F., Mu, J., Chen, M., Song, P., Lin, L., Lin, H., Le, F., Bo, J., 2018. Microplastic contamination in benthic organisms from the Arctic and sub-Arctic regions. *Chemosphere* 209, 298–306. https://doi.org/10.1016/j.chemosphere.2018.06.101

Fazey, F.M.C., Ryan, P.G., 2016. Biofouling on buoyant marine plastics: An experimental study into the effect of size on surface longevity. *Environ. Pollut.* 210, 354–360. https://doi.org/10.1016/j.envpol.2016.01.026

Fossi, M.C., Marsili, L., Baini, M., Giannetti, M., Coppola, D., Guerranti, C., Caliani, I., Minutoli, R., Lauriano, G., Finoia, M.G., Rubegni, F., Panigada, S., Bérubé, M., Urbán

Ramírez, J., Panti, C., 2016. Fin whales and microplastics: The Mediterranean Sea and the Sea of Cortez scenarios. *Environ. Pollut.* 209, 68–78. https://doi.org/10.1016/j. envpol.2015.11.022

Free, C.M., Jensen, O.P., Mason, S.A., Eriksen, M., Williamson, N.J., Boldgiv, B., 2014. High levels of microplastic pollution in a large, remote, mountain lake. *Mar. Pollut. Bull.* 85, 156–163. https://doi.org/10.1016/j.marpolbul.2014.06.001

Goldsworthy, S., Hindell, M.A., Crowley, H., 1997. Diet and diving behaviour of sympatric Fur seals *Arctocephalus gazella* and *A. tropicalis* at Macquarie Island, in: Hindell, M., Kemper, C. (Eds.), *Marine Mammal Research in the Southern Hemisphere. Status; Ecology and Medicine.* Beatty & Sons, New South Wales, Australia, pp. 151–163.

González-Bergonzoni, I., Johansen, K.L., Mosbech, A., Landkildehus, F., Jeppesen, E., Davidson, T.A., 2017. Small birds, big effects: The little auk (*Alle alle*) transforms high Arctic ecosystems. *Proc. R. Soc. B Biol. Sci.* 284, 20162572. https://doi.org/10.1098/rspb.2016.2572

Goss, H., Jaskiel, J., Rotjan, R., 2018. *Thalassia testudinum* as a potential vector for incorporating microplastics into benthic marine food webs. *Mar. Pollut. Bull.* 135, 1085–1089. https://doi.org/10.1016/j.marpolbul.2018.08.024

Gouin, T., 2020. Toward an improved understanding of the ingestion and trophic transfer of microplastic particles: Critical review and implications for future research. *Environ. Toxicol. Chem* 39, 1119–1137. https://doi.org/10.1002/etc.4718

Grant, M.L., Lavers, J.L., Hutton, I., Bond, A.L., 2021. Seabird breeding islands as sinks for marine plastic debris. *Environ. Pollut.* 276, 116734. https://doi.org/10.1016/j. envpol.2021.116734

Gutow, L., Eckerlebe, A., Giménez, L., Saborowski, R., 2016. Experimental evaluation of seaweeds as a vector for microplastics into marine food webs. *Environ. Sci. Technol.* 50, 915–923. https://doi.org/10.1021/acs.est.5b02431

Hale, R.C., Seeley, M.E., La Guardia, M.J., Mai, L., Zeng, E.Y., 2020. A global perspective on microplastics. *J. Geophys. Res. Ocean.* 125, e2018JC014719. https://doi.org/10.1029/2018JC014719

Hall, N.M., Berry, K.L.E., Rintoul, L., Hoogenboom, M.O., 2015. Microplastic ingestion by scleractinian corals. *Mar. Biol.* 162, 725–732. https://doi.org/10.1007/s00227-015-2619-7

Hamilton, B.M., Bourdages, M.P.T., Geoffroy, C., Vermaire, J.C., Mallory, M.L., Rochman, C.M., Provencher, J.F., 2021. Microplastics around an Arctic seabird colony: Particle community composition varies across environmental matrices. *Sci. Total Environ.* 773, 145536. https://doi.org/10.1016/j.scitotenv.2021.145536

Hammer, S., Nager, R.G., Johnson, P.C.D., Furness, R.W., Provencher, J.F., 2016. Plastic debris in great skua (*Stercorarius skua*) pellets corresponds to seabird prey species. *Mar. Pollut. Bull.* 103, 206–210. https://doi.org/10.1016/j.marpolbul.2015.12.018

Harlacher, J., 2020. *Whale, What Do We Have Here? Evidence of Microplastics in Top Predators: Analysis of Two Populations of Resident Killer Whale Fecal Samples.* PhD thesis, University of Washington. http://hdl.handle.net/1773/46085

Hentati-Sundberg, J., Raymond, C., Sköld, M., Svensson, O., Gustafsson, B., Bonaglia, S., 2020. Fueling of a marine-terrestrial ecosystem by a major seabird colony. *Sci. Rep.* 10, 15455. https://doi.org/10.1038/s41598-020-72238-6

Hernández-Milián, G., 2014. *Trophic Role of Small Cetaceans and Seals in Irish Waters.* University College Cork.

Huang, J.S., Koogolla, J.B., Li, H.I., Lin, L., Pan, Y.F., Liu, S., He, W.H., Maharana, D., Xu, X.R., 2020. Microplastic accumulation in fish from Zhanjiang mangrove wetland, South China. *Sci. Total Environ.* 708, 134839. https://doi.org/10.1016/j.scitotenv.2019.134839

Hurley, R.R., Woodward, J.C., Rothwell, J.J., 2017. Ingestion of microplastics by freshwater *Tubifex* worms. *Environ. Sci. Technol.* 51, 12844–12851. https://doi.org/10.1021/acs.est.7b03567

Hurt, R., O'Reilly, C.M., Perry, W.L., 2020. Microplastic prevalence in two fish species in two U.S. reservoirs. *Limnol. Oceanogr. Lett.* 5, 147–153. https://doi.org/10.1002/lol2.10140

Jambeck, J.R., Geyer, R., Wilcox, C., Siegler, T.R., Perryman, M., Andrady, A., Narayan, R., Law, K.L., 2015. Plastic waste inputs from land into the ocean. *Science* 347, 768–771. https://doi.org/10.1126/science.1260352

Jamieson, A.J., Brooks, L.S.R., Reid, W.D.K., Piertney, S.B., Narayanaswamy, B.E., Linley, T.D., 2021. Microplastics and synthetic particles ingested by deep-sea amphipods in six of the deepest marine ecosystems on Earth. *R. Soc. Open Sci.* 6, 180667. https://doi.org/10.1098/rsos.180667

Jeong, C.B., Won, E.J., Kang, H.M., Lee, M.C., Hwang, D.S., Hwang, U.K., Zhou, B., Souissi, S., Lee, S.J., Lee, J.S., 2016. Microplastic size-dependent toxicity, oxidative stress induction, and p-JNK and p-p38 activation in the monogonont rotifer (*Brachionus koreanus*). *Environ. Sci. Technol.* 50, 8849–8857. https://doi.org/10.1021/acs.est.6b01441

Kaiser, D., Kowalski, N., Waniek, J.J., 2017. Effects of biofouling on the sinking behavior of microplastics. *Environ. Res. Lett.* 12, 124003. https://doi.org/10.1088/1748-9326/aa8e8b

Karami, A., Golieskardi, A., Ho, Y. Bin, Larat, V., Salamatinia, B., 2017. Microplastics in eviscerated flesh and excised organs of dried fish. *Sci. Rep.* 7, 5473. https://doi.org/10.1038/s41598-017-05828-6

Katija, K., Choy, C.A., Sherlock, R.E., Sherman, A.D., Robison, B.H., 2017. From the surface to the seafloor: How giant larvaceans transport microplastics into the deep sea. *Sci. Adv.* 3, e1700715. https://doi.org/10.1126/sciadv.1700715

Kettner, M.T., Oberbeckmann, S., Labrenz, M., Grossart, H.-P., 2019. The eukaryotic life on microplastics in brackish ecosystems. *Front. Microbiol.* 10, 138. https://doi.org/10.3389/fmicb.2019.00538

Kim, I.S., Chae, D.H., Kim, S.K., Choi, S.B., Woo, S.B., 2015. Factors influencing the spatial variation of microplastics on high-tidal coastal beaches in Korea. *Arch. Environ. Contam. Toxicol.* 69, 299–309. https://doi.org/10.1007/s00244-015-0155-6

Kooi, M., Reisser, J., Slat, B., Ferrari, F.F., Schmid, M.S., Cunsolo, S., Brambini, R., Noble, K., Sirks, L.-A., Linders, T.E.W., Schoeneich-Argent, R.I., Koelmans, A.A., 2016. The effect of particle properties on the depth profile of buoyant plastics in the ocean. *Sci. Rep.* 6, 33882. https://doi.org/10.1038/srep33882

Kühn, S., Rebolledo, E.L.B., Van Franeker, J.A., 2015. Deleterious effects of litter on marine life, in: Bergmann, M., Gutow, L., Klages, M. (Eds.), *Marine Anthropogenic Litter.* Springer Open, Bremerhaven, Germany, pp. 75–116.

Kukulka, T., Law, K.L., Proskurowski, G., 2016. Evidence for the influence of surface heat fluxes on turbulent mixing of microplastic marine debris. *J. Phys. Oceanogr.* 46, 809–815. https://doi.org/10.1175/JPO-D-15-0242.1

Kvale, K., Prowe, A.E.F., Chien, C.-T., Landolfi, A., Oschlies, A., 2020. The global biological microplastic particle sink. *Sci. Rep.* 10, 16670. https://doi.org/10.1038/s41598-020-72898-4

Lambert, S., Wagner, M., 2016. Formation of microscopic particles during the degradation of different polymers. *Chemosphere* 161, 510–517. https://doi.org/10.1016/j.chemosphere.2016.07.042

Lavers, J.L., Bond, A.L., 2016. Ingested plastic as a route for trace metals in Laysan Albatross (*Phoebastria immutabilis*) and Bonin Petrel (*Pterodroma hypoleuca*) from Midway Atoll. *Mar. Pollut. Bull.* 110, 493–500. https://doi.org/10.1016/j.marpolbul.2016.06.001

Law, K.L., Moret-Ferguson, S., Maximenko, N.A., Proskurowski, G., Peacock, E.E., Hafner, J., Reddy, C.M., 2010. Plastic accumulation in the North Atlantic subtropical gyre. *Science* (80). 329, 1185–1188. https://doi.org/10.1126/science.1192321

Lobelle, D., Cunliffe, M., 2011. Early microbial biofilm formation on marine plastic debris. *Mar. Pollut. Bull.* 62, 197–200. https://doi.org/10.1016/j.marpolbul.2010.10.013

Lou, Y., Ekaterina, P., Yang, S.S., Lu, B., Liu, B., Ren, N., Corvini, P.F.X., Xing, D., 2020. Biodegradation of polyethylene and polystyrene by greater wax moth larvae (*Galleria mellonella* L.) and the effect of co-diet supplementation on the core gut microbiome. *Environ. Sci. Technol.* 54, 2821–2831. https://doi.org/10.1021/acs.est.9b07044

Lusher, A.L., Hernandez-Milian, G., O'Brien, J., Berrow, S., O'Connor, I., Officer, R., 2015. Microplastic and macroplastic ingestion by a deep diving, oceanic cetacean: The True's beaked whale *Mesoplodon mirus. Environ. Pollut.* 199, 185–191. https://doi.org/10.1016/j.envpol.2015.01.023

Lusher, A.L., O'Donnell, C., Officer, R., O'Connor, I., 2016. Microplastic interactions with North Atlantic mesopelagic fish. *ICES J. Mar. Sci.* 73, 1214–1225. https://doi.org/10.1093/icesjms/fsv241

MacIvor, J.S., Moore, A.E., 2013. Bees collect polyurethane and polyethylene plastics as novel nest materials. *Ecosphere* 4, art155. https://doi.org/10.1890/ES13-00308.1

Mallory, M.L., 2008. Marine plastic debris in northern fulmars from the Canadian high Arctic. *Mar. Pollut. Bull.* 56, 1501–1504. https://doi.org/10.1016/j.marpolbul.2008.04.017

Mallory, M.L., Gaston, A.J., Provencher, J.F., Wong, S.N.P., Anderson, C., Elliott, K.H., Gilchrist, H.G., Janssen, M., Lazarus, T., Patterson, A., Pirie-Dominix, L., Spencer, N.C., 2019. Identifying key marine habitat sites for seabirds and sea ducks in the Canadian Arctic. *Environ. Rev.* 27. https://doi.org/10.1139/er-2018-0067

Martín-Vélez, V., Mohring, B., van Leeuwen, C.H.A., Shamoun-Baranes, J., Thaxter, C.B., Baert, J.M., Camphuysen, C.J., Green, A.J., 2020. Functional connectivity network between terrestrial and aquatic habitats by a generalist waterbird, and implications for biovectoring. *Sci. Total Environ.* 705, 135886. https://doi.org/10.1016/j.scitotenv.2019.135886

Masiá, P., Ardura, A., Garcia-Vazquez, E., 2019. Microplastics in special protected areas for migratory birds in the Bay of Biscay. *Mar. Pollut. Bull.* 146, 993–1001. https://doi.org/10.1016/j.marpolbul.2019.07.065

Mateos-Cárdenas, A., O'Halloran, J., van Pelt, F.N.A.M., Jansen, M.A.K., 2021. Beyond plastic microbeads – Short-term feeding of cellulose and polyester microfibers to the freshwater amphipod *Gammarus duebeni. Sci. Total Environ.* 753, 141859. https://doi.org/10.1016/j.scitotenv.2020.141859

McGregor, S., Strydom, N.A., 2020. Feeding ecology and microplastic ingestion in *Chelon richardsonii* (Mugilidae) associated with surf diatom *Anaulus australis* accumulations in a warm temperate South African surf zone. *Mar. Pollut. Bull.* 158, 111430. https://doi.org/10.1016/j.marpolbul.2020.111430

McMahon, C.R., Holley, D., Robinson, S., 1999. The diet of itinerant male Hooker's sea lions, *Phocarctos hookeri*, at sub-Antarctic Macquarie Island. *Wildl. Res.* 26, 839–846. https://doi.org/10.1071/WR98079

Miller, M.E., Hamann, M., Kroon, F.J., 2020. Bioaccumulation and biomagnification of microplastics in marine organisms: A review and meta-analysis of current data. *PLoS One.* 15(10), e0240792. https://doi.org/10.1371/journal.pone.0240792

Mohsen, M., Wang, Q., Zhang, L., Sun, L., Lin, C., Yang, H., 2019. Microplastic ingestion by the farmed sea cucumber *Apostichopus japonicus* in China. *Environ. Pollut.* 245, 1071–1078. https://doi.org/10.1016/j.envpol.2018.11.083

Montazer, Z., Habibi Najafi, M.B., Levin, D.B., 2020. In vitro degradation of low-density polyethylene by new bacteria from larvae of the greater wax moth, *Galleria mellonella*. *Can. J. Microbiol.* 67, 249–258. https://doi.org/10.1139/cjm-2020-0208

Montazer, Z., Habibi-Najafi, M.B., Mohebbi, M., Oromiehei, A., 2018. Microbial degradation of UV-pretreated low-density polyethylene films by novel polyethylene degrading bacteria isolated from plastic dump soil. *J. Polym. Environ.* 26, 3613–3625. https://doi.org/10.1007/s10924-018-1245-0

Moore, R.C., Loseto, L., Noel, M., Etemadifar, A., Brewster, J.D., MacPhee, S., Bendell, L., Ross, P.S., 2020. Microplastics in beluga whales (*Delphinapterus leucas*) from the Eastern Beaufort Sea. *Mar. Pollut. Bull.* 150, 110723. https://doi.org/10.1016/j.marpolbul.2019.110723

Moret-Ferguson, S., Law, K.L., Proskurowski, G., Murphy, E.K., Peacock, E.E., Reddy, C.M., 2010. The size, mass, and composition of plastic debris in the western North Atlantic Ocean. *Mar. Pollut. Bull.* 60, 1873–1878. https://doi.org/10.1016/j.marpolbul.2010.07.020

Nelms, S.E., Galloway, T.S., Godley, B.J., Jarvis, D.S., Lindeque, P.K., 2018. Investigating microplastic trophic transfer in marine top predators. *Environ. Pollut.* 238, 999–1007. https://doi.org/10.1016/J.ENVPOL.2018.02.016

Nor, N.H., Obbard J.P., 2014. Microplastics in Singapore's coastal mangrove ecosystems. *Mar. Pollut. Bull.* 79, 278–283, 10.1016/j.marpolbul.2013.11.025.

O'Hanlon, N.J., James, N.A., Masden, E.A., Bond, A.L., 2017. Seabirds and marine plastic debris in the northeastern Atlantic: A synthesis and recommendations for monitoring and research. *Environ. Pollut.* 231, 1291–1301. https://doi.org/10.1016/j.envpol.2017.08.101

Obbard, R.W., Sadri, S., Wong, Q.Y., Khitun, A.A., Baker, I., Thompson, R.C., Wong, Y.Q., Khitun, A.A., Baker, I., Thompson, R.C., 2014. Global warming releases microplastic legacy frozen in Arctic sea ice. *Earth's Future*. 2. https://doi.org/10.1002/2014EF000240

Oberbeckmann, S., Löder, M.G.J., Labrenz, M., 2015. Marine microplastic-associated biofilms – a review. *Environ. Chem.* 12, 551–562. https://doi.org/10.1071/EN15069

Ogunola, O.S., Onada, O.A., Falaye A.E., 2018. Mitigation measures to avert the impacts of plastics and microplastics in the marine environment (a review). *Environ. Sci. Pollut. Res. Int.* 25 (10), 929 3–9310, doi: 10.1007/s11356–018–1499-z

Ory, N.C., Sobral, P., Ferreira, J.L., Thiel, M., 2017. Amberstripe scad *Decapterus muroadsi* (Carangidae) fish ingest blue microplastics resembling their copepod prey along the coast of Rapa Nui (Easter Island) in the South Pacific subtropical gyre. *Sci. Total Environ.* 586, 430–437. https://doi.org/10.1016/j.scitotenv.2017.01.175

Otero, X.L., De La Peña-Lastra, S., Pérez-Alberti, A., Ferreira, T.O., Huerta-Diaz, M.A., 2018. Seabird colonies as important global drivers in the nitrogen and phosphorus cycles. *Nat. Commun.* 9, 246. https://doi.org/10.1038/s41467-017-02446-8

Peeken, I., Primpke, S., Beyer, B., Gütermann, J., Katlein, C., Krumpen, T., Bergmann, M., Hehemann, L., Gerdts, G., 2018. Arctic sea ice is an important temporal sink and means of transport for microplastic. *Nat. Commun.* 9, 1505. https://doi.org/10.1038/s41467-018-03825-5

Piarulli, S., Airoldi, L., 2020. Mussels facilitate the sinking of microplastics to bottom sediments and their subsequent uptake by detritus-feeders. *Environ. Pollut.* 266, 115151. https://doi.org/10.1016/j.envpol.2020.115151

Plee, T.A., Pomory, C.M., 2020. Microplastics in sandy environments in the Florida Keys and the panhandle of Florida, and the ingestion by sea cucumbers (Echinodermata: Holothuroidea) and sand dollars (Echinodermata: Echinoidea). *Mar. Pollut. Bull.* 158, 111437. https://doi.org/10.1016/j.marpolbul.2020.111437

Pohl, F., Eggenhuisen, J.T., Kane, I.A., Clare, M.A., 2020. Transport and burial of microplastics in deep-marine sediments by turbidity currents. *Environ. Sci. Technol.* 54, 4180–4189. https://doi.org/10.1021/acs.est.9b07527

Poon, F., Provencher, J.F., Mallory, M.L., Braune, B.M., Smith, P.A., 2017. Plastic accumulation in four Arctic seabird species. *Mar. Pollut. Bull.* 116, 517–520. https://doi.org/10.1016/j.marpolbul.2016.11.051

Porter, A., Lyons, B.P., Galloway, T.S., Lewis, C., 2018. Role of marine snows in microplastic fate and bioavailability. *Environ. Sci. Technol.* 52, 7111–7119. https://doi.org/10.1021/acs.est.8b01000

Pozo, K., Gomez, V., Torres, M., Vera, L., Nuñez, D., Oyarzún, P., Mendoza, G., Clarke, B., Fossi, M.C., Baini, M., Přibylová, P., Klánová, J., 2019. Presence and characterization of microplastics in fish of commercial importance from the Biobío region in central Chile. *Mar. Pollut. Bull.* 140, 315–319. https://doi.org/10.1016/j.marpolbul.2019.01.025

Pratte, I., Noble, D.G., Mallory, M.L., Braune, B.M., Provencher, J.F., 2020. The influence of migration patterns on exposure to contaminants in Nearctic shorebirds: A historical study. *Environ. Monit. Assess.* 192, 256. https://doi.org/10.1007/s10661-020-8218-1

Provencher, J.F., Ammendolia, J., Rochman, C.M., Mallory, M.L., 2019. Assessing plastic debris in aquatic food webs: What we know and don't know about uptake and trophic transfer. *Environ. Rev.* 27(3), 304–317. https://doi.org/10.1139/er-2018-0079

Provencher, J.F., Vermaire, J.C., Avery-Gomm, S., Braune, B.M., Mallory, M.L., 2018. Garbage in guano: Microplastics found in fecal precursors of seabirds known to ingest plastics. *Sci. Total Environ.* 644, 1477–1488. https://doi.org/10.1016/j.scitotenv.2018.07.101

Qiao, T., Kim, S., Lee, W., Lee, H., 2019. Biodegradable and porous poly(lactic-co-glycolic acid) microbeads for in vitro evaluation of negatively charged fluorescent bacteria. *Macromol. Res.* 27, 321–326. https://doi.org/10.1007/s13233-019-7104-6

Rhodes, C.J., 2018. Plastic pollution and potential solutions. *Science Progress.* 101 (3), 207–260. https://doi.org/10.3184/003685018X15294876706211,

Richard, H., Carpenter, E.J., Komada, T., Palmer, P.T., Rochman, C.M., 2019. Biofilm facilitates metal accumulation onto microplastics in estuarine waters. *Sci. Total Environ.* 683, 600–608. https://doi.org/10.1016/j.scitotenv.2019.04.331

Riget, F., Bignert, A., Braune, B., Stow, J., Wilson, S., 2010. Temporal trends of legacy POPs in Arctic biota, an update. *Sci. Total Environ.* 408, 2874–2884. https://doi.org/10.1016/j.scitotenv.2009.07.036

Rochman, C.M., 2019. The role of plastic debris as another source of hazardous chemicals in lower-trophic level organisms, in: Takada, H., Karapanagioti, H.K. (Eds.). *Hazardous Chemicals Associated with Plastics in the Marine Environment.* Springer International Publishing, Cham, pp. 281–295. https://doi.org/10.1007/698_2016_17

Rochman, C.M., Brown, M., Underwood, A.J., van Franeker, J.A., Thompson, R.C., Amaral-Zettler, L.A., 2015a. The complex mixture, fate and toxicity of chemicals associated with plastic debris in the marine environment, in: Bergmann, M., Gutow, L., Klages, M. (Eds.), *Marine Anthropogenic Litter.* Springer International Publishing, Cham, pp. 117–140.

Rochman, Chelsea M., Tahir, A., Williams, S.L., Baxa, D.V., Lam, R., Miller, J.T., Teh, F.-C., Werorilangi, S., Teh, S.J., 2015b. Anthropogenic debris in seafood: Plastic debris and fibers from textiles in fish and bivalves sold for human consumption. *Sci. Rep.* 5, 14340. https://doi.org/10.1038/srep14340

Rosenkranz, P., Chaudhry, Q., Stone, V., Fernandes, T.F., 2009. A comparison of nanoparticle and fine particle uptake by *Daphnia magna*. *Environ. Toxicol. Chem.* 28, 2142–2149. https://doi.org/10.1897/08-559.1

Rummel, C.D., Jahnke, A., Gorokhova, E., Kühnel, D., Schmitt-Jansen, M., 2017. Impacts of biofilm formation on the fate and potential effects of microplastic in the aquatic environment. *Environ. Sci. Technol. Lett.* 4(7), 258 –267. https://doi.org/10.1021/acs.estlett.7b00164

Ryan, P., 2015. How quickly do albatrosses and petrels digest plastic particles? *Environ. Pollut.* 207, 438 –440. https://doi.org/10.1016/j.envpol.2015.08.005

Saborowski, R., Paulischkis, E., Gutow, L., 2019. How to get rid of ingested microplastic fibers? A straightforward approach of the Atlantic ditch shrimp *Palaemon varians*. *Environ. Pollut.* 254. https://doi.org/10.1016/j.envpol.2019.113068

Savoca, M.S., McInturf, A.G., Hazen, E.L., 2021. Plastic ingestion by marine fish is widespread and increasing. *Glob. Chang. Biol.* 27(10), 2188–2199. https://doi.org/10.1111/gcb.15533

Savoca, M.S., Wohlfeil, M.E., Ebeler, S.E., Nevitt, G.A., 2016. Marine plastic debris emits a keystone infochemical for olfactory foraging seabirds. *Sci. Adv.* 2, e1600395. https://doi.org/10.1126/sciadv.1600395

Scheurer, M., Bigalke, M., 2018. Microplastics in Swiss floodplain soils. *Environ. Sci. Technol.* 52, 3591–3598. https://doi.org/10.1021/acs.est.7b06003

Schür, C., Rist, S., Baun, A., Mayer, P., Hartmann, N.B., Wagner, M., 2019. When fluorescence is not a particle: The tissue translocation of microplastics in *Daphnia magna* seems an artifact. *Environ. Toxicol. Chem.* 38, 1495–1503. https://doi.org/10.1002/ctc.4436

Setälä, O., Fleming-Lehtinen, V., Lehtiniemi, M., 2014. Ingestion and transfer of microplastics in the planktonic food web. *Environ. Pollut.* 185, 7 7–83. https://doi.org/10.1016/j.envpol.2013.10.013

Silva, M.A., Prieto, R., Jonsen, I., Baumgartner, M.F., Santos, R.S., 2013. North Atlantic blue and fin whales suspend their spring migration to forage in middle latitudes: Building up energy reserves for the journey? *PLoS One* 8, e76507. https://doi.org/10.1371/journal.pone.0076507

Smith, J.N., Lee, K., Gobeil, C., Macdonald, R.W., 2009. Natural rates of sediment containment of PAH, PCB and metal inventories in Sydney Harbour, Nova Scotia. *Sci. Total Environ.* 407, 4858– 4869. https://doi.org/10.1016/j.scitotenv.2009.05.029

Su, L., Cai, H., Kolandhasamy, P., Wu, C., Rochman, C.M., Shi, H., 2018. Using the Asian clam as an indicator of microplastic pollution in freshwater ecosystems. *Environ. Pollut.* 234, 347–355. https://doi.org/10.1016/j.envpol.2017.11.075

Taylor, M.L., Gwinnett, C., Robinson, L.F., Woodall, L.C., 2016. Plastic microfibre ingestion by deep-sea organisms. *Sci. Rep.* 6, 33997. https://doi.org/10.1038/srep33997

Tu, C., Chen, T., Zhou, Q., Liu, Y., Wei, J., Waniek, J.J., Luo, Y., 2020. Biofilm formation and its influences on the properties of microplastics as affected by exposure time and depth in the seawater. *Sci. Total Environ.* 734. https://doi.org/10.1016/j.scitotenv.2020.139237

Uddin, S., Fowler, S.W., Uddin, M.F., Behbehani, M., Naji, A., 2021. A review of microplastic distribution in sediment profiles. *Mar. Pollut. Bull.* 163, 111973. https://doi.org/10.1016/j.marpolbul.2021.111973

van Franeker, J.A., Law, K.L., 2015. Seabirds, gyres and global trends in plastic pollution. *Environ. Pollut.* 203, 8 9–96. https://doi.org/10.1016/j.envpol.2015.02.034

van Sebille, E., Wilcox, C., Lebreton, L., Maximenko, N., Hardesty, B.D., van Franeker, J.A., Eriksen, M., Siegel, D., Galgani, F., Law, K.L., 2015. A global inventory of small floating plastic debris. *Environ. Res. Lett.* 10, 124006. https://doi.org/10.1088/1748-9326/10/12/124006

Viana, D.S., Gangoso, L., Bouten, W., Figuerola, J., 2016. Overseas seed dispersal by migratory birds. *Proc. R. Soc. B Biol. Sci.* 283, 20152406. https://doi.org/10.1098/rspb.2015.2406

Vianello, A., Boldrin, A., Guerriero, P., Moschino, V., Rella, R., Sturaro, A., Da Ros, L., 2013. Microplastic particles in sediments of Lagoon of Venice, Italy: First observations on occurrence, spatial patterns and identification. *Estuar. Coast. Shelf Sci.* 130, 54–61. https://doi.org/10.1016/j.ecss.2013.03.022

von Moos, N., Burkhardt-Holm, P., Köhler, A., 2012. Uptake and effects of microplastics on cells and tissue of the blue mussel *Mytilus edulis* l. after an experimental exposure. *Environ. Sci. Technol.* 46, 11327–11335. https://doi.org/10.1021/es302332w

Walker, T.R., MacAskill, D., Weaver, P., 2013. Environmental recovery in Sydney Harbour, Nova Scotia: Evidence of natural and anthropogenic sediment capping. *Mar. Pollut. Bull.* 74, 446–452. https://doi.org/10.1016/j.marpolbul.2013.06.013

Walkinshaw, C., Lindeque, P.K., Thompson, R., Tolhurst, T., Cole, M., 2020. Microplastics and seafood: Lower trophic organisms at highest risk of contamination. *Ecotoxicol. Environ. Saf.* 190, 110066. https://doi.org/10.1016/j.ecoenv.2019.110066

Walters, A., RT, B., Post, D., 2009. Anadromous alewives (*Alosa pseudoharengus*) contribute marine-derived nutrients to coastal stream food webs. *Can. J. Fish. Aquat. Sci.* 66, 439–448.

Wang, J., Zheng, L., Li, J., 2018. A critical review on the sources and instruments of marine microplastics and prospects on the relevant management in China. *Waste Manag. Res.* 36, 898–911. https://doi.org/10.1177/0734242X18793504

Wang, S., Hu, M., Zheng, J., Huang, W., Shang, Y., Kar Hei Fang, J., Shi, H., Wang, Y., 2021. Ingestion of nano/micro plastic particles by the mussel *Mytilus coruscus* is size dependent. *Chemosphere* 263, 127957. https://doi.org/10.1016/j.chemosphere.2020.127957

Wang, W., Ndungu, A.W., Li, Z., Wang, J., 2017. Microplastics pollution in inland freshwaters of China: A case study in urban surface waters of Wuhan, China. *Sci. Total Environ.* 575, 1369–1374. https://doi.org/10.1016/j.scitotenv.2016.09.213

Ward, J.E., Zhao, S., Holohan, B.A., Mladinich, K.M., Griffin, T.W., Wozniak, J., Shumway, S.E., 2019. Selective ingestion and egestion of plastic particles by the blue mussel (*Mytilus edulis*) and eastern oyster (*Crassostrea virginica*): Implications for using bivalves as bioindicators of microplastic pollution. *Environ. Sci. Technol.* 53, 8776–8784. https://doi.org/10.1021/acs.est.9b02073

Watts, A.J.R., Lewis, C., Goodhead, R.M., Beckett, S.J., Moger, J., Tyler, C.R., Galloway, T.S., 2014. Uptake and retention of microplastics by the shore crab *Carcinus maenas*. *Environ. Sci. Technol.* 48, 8823–8830. https://doi.org/10.1021/es501090e

Watts, A.J.R., Urbina, M.A., Goodhead, R., Moger, J., Lewis, C., Galloway, T.S., 2016. Effect of microplastic on the gills of the shore crab *Carcinus maenas*. *Environ. Sci. Technol.* 50, 5364–5369. https://doi.org/10.1021/acs.est.6b01187

Weinstein, J.E., Crocker, B.K., Gray, A.D., 2016. From macroplastic to microplastic: Degradation of high-density polyethylene, polypropylene, and polystyrene in a salt marsh habitat. *Environ. Toxicol. Chem.* 35, 1632–1640. https://doi.org/10.1002/etc.3432

Welden, N.A., Cowie, P.R., 2016. Environment and gut morphology influence microplastic retention in langoustine, *Nephrops norvegicus*. *Environ. Pollut.*, 214, 859–865.

Wilkes, R.A., Aristilde, L., 2017. Degradation and metabolism of synthetic plastics and associated products by *Pseudomonas* sp.: Capabilities and challenges. *J. Appl. Microbiol.* 123, 582–593. https://doi.org/10.1111/jam.13472

Woodall, L.C., Sanchez-Vidal, A., Canals, M., Paterson, G.L.J., Coppock, R., Sleight, V., Calafat, A., Rogers, A.D., Narayanaswamy, B.E., Thompson, R.C., 2014. The deep sea is a major sink for microplastic debris. *R. Soc. Open Sci.* 1, 140317–140317. https://doi.org/10.1098/rsos.140317

Woods, M.N., Hong, T.J., Baughman, D., Andrews, G., Fields, D.M., Matrai, P.A., 2020. Accumulation and effects of microplastic fibers in American lobster larvae (*Homarus americanus*). *Mar. Pollut. Bull.* 157, 111280.

Wright, R.J., Erni-Cassola, G., Zadjelovic, V., Latva, M., Christie-Oleza, J.A., 2020. Marine plastic debris: A new surface for microbial colonization. *Environ. Sci. Technol.* 54, 11657–1 1672. https://doi.org/10.1021/acs.est.0c02305

Wright, R.J., Langille, M.G., Walker, T.R., 2021. Food or just a free ride? A meta-analysis reveals the global diversity of the Plastisphere. *ISME J.* 15, 789–806. https://doi.org/10.1038/s41396-020-00814-9

Xanthos, D., Walker, T.R., 2017. International policies to reduce plastic marine pollution from single-use plastics (plastic bags and microbeads): A review. *Mar. Pollut. Bull.* 118, 17–26. https://doi.org/10.1016/j.marpolbul.2017.02.048

Yang, D., Shi, H., Li, L., Li, J., Jabeen, K., Kolandhasamy, P., Yang, D., Li, L., Jabeen, K., Shi, H., 2015. Microplastics in commercial bivalves from China. *Environ. Pollut.* 207, 13622–13627. https://doi.org/10.1016/j.envpol.2015.09.018

Yang, J., Yang, Y., Wu, W.M., Zhao, J., Jiang, L., 2014. Evidence of polyethylene biodegradation by bacterial strains from the guts of plastic-eating waxworms. *Environ. Sci. Technol.* 48, 13776–13784. https://doi.org/10.1021/es504038a

Yokota, K., Waterfield, H., Hastings, C., Davidson, E., Kwietniewski, E., Wells, B., 2017. Finding the missing piece of the aquatic plastic pollution puzzle: Interaction between primary producers and microplastics. *Limnol. Oceanogr. Lett.* 2, 91–104. https://doi.org/10.1002/lol2.10040

Zantis, L.J., Carroll, E.L., Nelms, S.E., Bosker, T., 2021. Marine mammals and micro plastics: A systematic review and call for standardisation. *Environ. Pollut.* 269, 11 6142. https://doi.org/10.1016/j.envpol.2020.116142

Zettler, E.R., Mincer, T.J., Amaral-Zettler, L.A., 2013. Life in the "Plastisphere": Microbial communities on plastic marine debris. *Environ. Sci. Technol.* 47, 7137–7146. https://doi.org/10.1021/es401288x

Zhu, L., Wang, H., Chen, B., Sun, X., Qu, K., Xia, B., 2019. Microplastic ingestion in deep-sea fish from the South China Sea. *Sci. Total Environ.* 677, 493–501. https://doi.org/10.1016/j.scitotenv.2019.04.380

4

CLOTHES ENCOUNTERS OF THE MICROFIBRE KIND

The effects of natural and synthetic textiles on organisms

Elise F. Granek, Summer D. Traylor, Alexandra G. Tissot, Paul T. Hurst, Rosemary S. Wood, and Susanne M. Brander

Introduction

When textiles – including apparel, towels, sheets, and rugs – are washed, they shed fibres into laundry water. These fibres are eventually released into wastewater and waterways, applied to agricultural fields in biosolids, and along with tire wear and other land-based emissions, are recognized as significant sources of microfibre input into the environment (Figure 4.1; Browne et al. 2011; Boucher & Friot 2017; Gavigan et al. 2020; Stone et al. 2020). Textile production and related processes may also generate fibres via shedding, though the contribution of this source to the environment is not well established (Carr 2017). As a result of fibre release and distribution through various pathways such as agricultural applications of sterilized wastewater sludge and effluent release, environmental microfibres are present in diverse terrestrial and aquatic ecosystems, including nearshore and deep sea marine ecosystems (Figure 4.1: Zubris & Richards 2005; Woodall et al. 2014; Taylor et al. 2016). Additionally, microfibres have been identified in hundreds of field-collected animal species ranging from zooplankton in the open ocean to riverine otters (Smiroldo et al. 2019), as well as human colon and placental tissue samples (Ibrahim et al. 2021; Ragusa et al. 2020).

The extent of fibre release from laundering is substantial, with acrylic, polyester, and polyester-cotton blended fabrics shedding hundreds of thousands of fibres per wash (728,789, 496,030, and 137,951 fibres/wash, respectively; Napper & Thompson 2016). Given that an average four-person household may release 18,000,000 synthetic microfibres in a 6 kg load of laundry (Galvão et al. 2020), laundering is considered a significant source of synthetic, textile-based microfibres found in the environment. New studies show that microfibre emissions to terrestrial environments may rival those of their aquatic counterparts, with annual emissions on land totaling 176.5 kilotons (kt) per year (Gavigan et al. 2020). Once

DOI: 10.4324/9781003165385-5

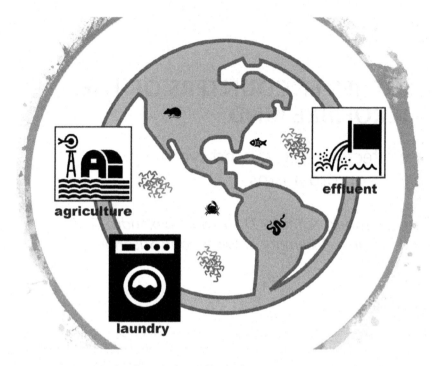

FIGURE 4.1 Framework of textile microfibres entering the environment and affecting organisms. Icons sourced from The Noun Project

Source: (www.thenounproject.com)

in the environment, microfibres can end up in organisms, sediments, the water column, and the atmosphere (e.g., Brahney et al. 2020; Büks et al. 2020; Ross et al. 2021).

The diversity of fibre types used in textile production (Figure 4.1) means that these fibres can have an array of effects on organisms and ecosystems (e.g., Napper & Thompson 2019; Shruti & Kutralam-Muniasamy 2019). Textile fibres range from fully synthetic, plastic-based materials including acetate (CA), acrylic, nylon (PA), general polyester, polypropylene (PP), polyvinyl chloride (PVC), rayon and spandex; to bioplastics such as poly-lactic acid (PLA), polyhydroxyalkanoates (PHAs), and thermoplastic starch (TPS); to natural fibres including bamboo, cotton, and wool. Not only do textile fibres possess numerous constituents, but the additives used to produce, process, or grow them can differ greatly (Carney Almroth et al. 2021). As a result, organism- and ecosystem-level effects of textile fibres and their associated additives are also highly variable. For example, polymer fibres (Figure 4.2) have additives ranging from anti-static agents and flame retardants to phthalates and nonylphenols that vary in their toxicological effects (Barker 1975; Hermabessiere et al. 2017). There is emerging evidence that fibres may be more toxic to organisms than other microplastic shapes, such as spheres and fragments (Stienbarger et al. 2021; Jacob et al. 2020).

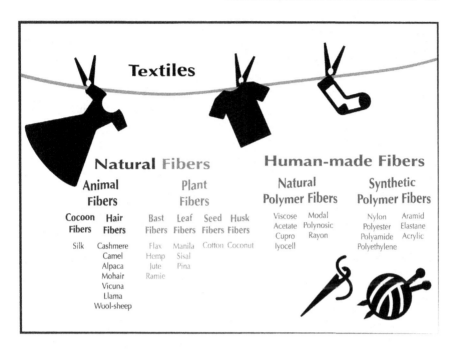

FIGURE 4.2 Textiles include a diverse array of fibre types from fully synthetic to natural
Source: Adapted from www.sewguide.com

Synthetic fibres (as defined by Kroon et al. 2018) are used to make clothing and other textiles, increasing their durability as well as to protect from staining, and to create specialty items, such as athletic wear, dry fit clothing, or wrinkle-free fabrics (McIntyre 2005). As the human population continues to grow, so does the use of highly durable synthetic clothing, linens, and even gardening cloth, both commercially and in home applications (Geyer 2020; Boucher & Friot 2017). Gavigan et al. (2020) estimated that 5.6 Mt of synthetic fibres were released from washing synthetic apparel from 1950 to 2016, with half of that released during the last decade. Synthetic fibres also contain a suite of chemicals from dyes and plasticizers added during production to chemicals adsorbed to their surface when in the environment (Meiyazhagan et al. 2020). Given their durability and widespread use that allow for multiple pathways of release into the environment, it is not surprising that synthetic, plastics-based fibres are the most abundant textile products found in the natural environment and that these fibres can negatively affect organisms (Kwon et al. 2021).

Bioplastics, on the other hand, have been developed and marketed as a green alternative to synthetic plastics, including fibres (Shruti & Kutralam-Muniasamy 2019; Schenker et al. 2020). However, increasing evidence indicates that they, too, are an emerging pollutant when introduced into the environment (Shruti & Kutralam-Muniasamy 2019). Bioplastics, simply defined, are any plastic material made of a biological component including (but not limited to) corn, algae, or hemp. These components are used to create materials such as poly-lactic acid (PLA), polyhydroxyalkanoates (PHAs), and thermoplastic starch (TPS); such compounds are mainly used in the food and agriculture industries, though they also are sometimes used in textiles (Shruti & Kutralam-Muniasamy 2019; Schenker et al. 2020). Bioplastics are used to make cups, plates, utensils, teabags, and storage solutions such as wraps, bags, and containers. In agriculture, these materials are made into films to suppress weeds and other unwanted plants in crop production or to facilitate harvestable crop or ornamental plant growth in domestic settings.

Bioplastics are designed to reduce waste, as they are capable of biodegradation under specific, mostly industrial, conditions specific to each bioplastic. Because they are biodegradable, bioplastics are marketed as a safe and responsible solution to plastic waste. However, these products are often disposed of in a way that will not allow them to biodegrade. Furthermore, more bioplastics are made than supported by the existing chain to return these materials to industry for biodegradation (Shruti & Kutralam-Muniasamy 2019; Napper & Thompson 2019; Schenker et al. 2020).

Improperly disposed bioplastics generally experience adequate conditions to begin biodegradation, such that these materials may break apart but do not biodegrade in soil (Shruti & Kutralam-Muniasamy 2019; Napper & Thompson 2019). Their degradation process is akin to that of microplastics in the environment – that is, breaking down into increasingly smaller fibres, beads, films, and fragments. These fibres can then affect organisms into whose habitats they disperse.

Both synthetic and bioplastic fibres can adhere to or be taken up and internalized by organisms, leading to biological effects from the cellular to the organismal levels, and potentially causing ecological effects on populations and communities (Figure 4.2, Table 1; Kolandhasamy et al. 2018). Though the effects of microfibre exposure vary by fibre type (Rochman et al. 2019), environmental degradation (Napper & Thompson 2019), and organism exposed, research indicates that most species uptake fibres and experience negative effects when exposed to both synthetic and bio-based plastics.

Though organisms may also uptake natural fibres, there is little research on how these fibres may affect organisms in the environment.

The lack of studies on the effects natural fibres may have on the environment is surprising, considering their widespread presence, particularly in aquatic environments (Remy et al. 2015; Zhao et al. 2016; Compa et al. 2018), reported findings in fish and birds (Zhao et al. 2016; Compa et al. 2018), frequently high use of chemicals in their production (Remy et al. 2015; Garcia et al. 2019), rapid degradability (Li et al. 2010; Zambrano et al. 2020), and resultant pathways through aquatic systems (Sillanpää & Sainio 2017; Belzagui et al. 2020; Galvão et al. 2020; Zambrano et al. 2019). Cotton textiles shed more fibres than synthetic materials when laundered (Zambrano et al. 2019; Galvão et al. 2020); once shed, these fibres are readily transported to aquatic systems via pathways such as stormwater runoff and wastewater treatment plant effluent (Rochman 2018; Ladewig et al. 2015; Belzagui et al. 2020; Galvão et al. 2020; Miller et al. 2020). As natural materials, it is frequently assumed that the physical properties of these fibres are unlikely to cause environmental damage. However, studies conducted on the physical structure and degradation of these materials stress that natural fibres not only sorb harmful chemicals such as surfactants (e.g., disinfectants, fungicides, fibre softeners; Grancaric et al. 2005) and already contain chemicals used in production and pre-treatment (Sillanpää & Sainio 2017; Garcia et al. 2019), but, due to their rapid biodegradability (Li et al. 2010; Ladewig et al. 2015; Zambrano et al. 2020), may be transported and released much more quickly into the environment.

In this chapter, we explore the effects of various microfibre types (ranging in size from 100μm to 6mm, based on laboratory research) on biota – from the subcellular to population levels, as reported in peer-reviewed laboratory studies. We broadly categorize these materials as synthetic and semi-synthetic, bioplastics, and natural fibres, primarily because the latter two are marketed as potentially having a lesser environmental effect based on their makeup. For the purpose of this analysis, we have defined each category of microfibre following the classification established by Kroon et al. (2018; Figure 4.2).

Synthetic and semi-synthetic fibres

Synthetic plastics are heavily used in textile production for their durability and versatility in specialty clothing items (McIntyre 2005); such plastics include acetate (CA), acrylic, nylon (PA), general polyester, polypropylene (PP), polyvinyl chloride (PVC), rayon, and spandex (Sait et al. 2021). Research on the impacts of synthetic fibres on aquatic and terrestrial organisms document effects ranging from subcellular to population levels (Figure 4.3, Table 4.1). Laboratory studies on the effects of synthetic microfibre ingestion focus on several marine taxa, but fish make up the majority of such studies on aquatic organisms. effects have been documented in many aquatic taxa including fish (20), crustacea (23), mollusca (8), echinodermata (9), and rotifera (2) (De Sá et al. 2018). Studies on the effects of synthetic fibres on terrestrial organisms are not as numerous as those on aquatic organisms. There are documented effects in a small number of terrestrial organisms, including insects (2), worms (1), and nematodes (1) (Büks et al. 2020; El-Gendy et al. 2020; Liu et al. 2021).

In addition to animals in the environment, recent studies have documented microplastic fibres in both the human intestinal tract and placental tissue, though major data gaps remain regarding exposure effects on humans (Ibrahim et al. 2021; Ragusa et al. 2020). We ingest microplastics through food items and drinking water (Hernandez et al. 2019; Kosuth et al. 2018; Rochman et al. 2015; Liebezeit & Liebezeit 2015) and inhale microplastics both indoors and outdoors (Dris et al. 2017). Occupational exposure to microplastics in industries like textile production or plastic manufacturing (Zarus et al. 2021; Pimentel et al. 1975; Stratton-Powell et al. 2019; Urban et al. 2000; Hicks et al. 1996) is documented to cause inflammation of the lungs in occupational workers; surgical exposure can decrease the immune response in patients with plastic implants and the translocation of microplastics from implants to the lymph nodes has been observed (Zarus et al. 2021). General public exposure to and effects of microplastics remains a priority area for future research (Zarus et al. 2021).

TABLE 4.1 Ecological and biological effects of fibers on organisms by species and material type

Level	Type of Effect	Organism Clade	Genus species	Plastic Material Type	Fiber Size	MP Concentration	In Text Citation
Sub/Cellular	**Adverse Immune Response**	Bivalves	*Mytilus spp.*	polyamide nylon	10 × 30 µm	~186 fibers/mL	(Cole et al. 2020)
		Coral	*Acropora sp.*	n/a	0.1–1 cm	0.1 mg/L	(Mendrik et al. 2021)
		Coral	*Seriatopora hystrix*	n/a	0.1–1 cm	0.1 mg/L	(Mendrik et al. 2021)
	Cellular Response	Annelid Worms	*Lumbricus terrestris*	polyester	Avg length (361.6 ± 387.0 um); diameter (40.7 ± 3.8 um)	0, 0.1% (0.3g MF), 1.0% (3.0g MF)	(Prendergast-Miller et al. 2019)
		Bivalves	*Mytilus galloprovincialis*	composite household lint	Length: 35.1 um mean (22.0–743 um); Width (<30 um)	56–180 mg/L	(Alnajar et al. 2021)
		Coral	*Acropora sp.*	n/a	0.1–1 cm	0.1 mg/L	(Mendrik et al. 2021)
		Coral	*Seriatopora hystrix*	n/a	0.1–1 cm	0.1 mg/L	(Mendrik et al. 2021)
		Crustaceans	*Nephrops norvegicus*	polypropylene	length (3–5mm); diameter (0.2 mm)	5 fibers/feeding; total exposure (360 fibers)	(Welden & Cowie 2016)
		Humans	*Homo sapiens*	nylon, polyester	nylon (11x30 µm); Polyester (15x53 µm)	n/a	(Dijk et al. 2020)
		Nematodes	*Caenorhabditis elegans*	polyethylene terephthalate	length (250 µm); diameter (17.4 µm)	0, 36, 36x5, 36x10 pieces of MF/0.5 mL	(Liu et al. 2021)
		Nematodes	*Caenorhabditis elegans*	polyethylene terephthalate	length (250 µm); diameter (17.4 µm)	0, 36, 36x5, 36x10 pieces of MF/0.5 mL	(Liu et al. 2021)

Nematodes	*Caenorhabditis elegans*	polyethylene terephthalate	length (250 µm); diameter (17.4 µm)	0, 36, 36x5, 36x10 pieces of MF/0.5 mL	(Liu et al. 2021)
Rodents	*Mus musculus*	nylon, polyester	nylon (11x30 µm); Polyester (15x53 µm)	n/a	(Dijk et al. 2020)
Oxidative Stress					
Annelid Worms	*Lumbricus terrestris*	polyester	Avg length (361.6 ± 387.0 um); diameter (40.7 ± 3.8 um)	0, 0.1% (0.3g MF), 1.0% (3.0g MF)	(Prendergast-Miller et al. 2019)
Bivalves	*Mytilus spp.*	polyamide nylon	10 × 30 µm	~186 fibers/mL	(Cole et al. 2020)
Bivalves	*Mytilus spp.*	polyamide nylon	10 × 30 µm	~186 fibers/mL	(Cole et al. 2020)
Coral	*Acropora sp.*	n/a	0.1–1 cm	0.1 mg/L	(Mendrik et al. 2021)
Coral	*Seriatopora hystrix*	n/a	0.1–1 cm	0.1 mg/L	(Mendrik et al. 2021)
Echinoderms	*Apostichopus japonicus*	n/a	n/a	MFs/g food+sediment mix (0.6 MFs/g; 1.2 MFs/g; 10 MFs/g)	(Mohsen et al. 2021)
Fish	*Dicentrachus labrax*	polyethylene (80%); polyester (19%); rayon (1%)	GIT = 501–1500um (>36%); Gills = 151–500um (>50%); Dorsal Muscle = 501–1500um (58%)	GIT (1.3 ± 2.5 MP items/individual); Gills (0.8 ± 1.4 MP items/individual); Dorsal Muscle (0.4 ± 0.7 MP items/g)	(Barboza et al. 2020)

(Continued)

TABLE 4.1 (Continued)

Level	Type of Effect	Organism Clade	Genus species	Plastic Material Type	Fiber Size	MP Concentration	In Text Citation
		Fish	Trachurus	polyethylene (80%); polyester (19%); rayon (1%)	GIT = 501–1500um (>36%); Gills = 151–500um (>50%); Dorsal Muscle = 151–500um (39%)	GIT (1.0 ± 1.9 MP items/individual); Gills (0.7 ± 1.9 MP items/individual); Dorsal Muscle (0.2 ± 1.3 MP items/g)	(Barboza et al. 2020)
		Fish	Scomber colias	polyethylene (80%); polyester (19%); rayon (1%)	GIT = 501–1500um (>36%); Gills = 151–500um (>50%); Dorsal Muscle = 501–1500um (58%)	GIT (1.2 ± 1.6 MP items/individual); Gills (0.7 ± 1.0 MP items/individual); Dorsal Muscle (0.6 ± 0.8 MP items/g)	(Barboza et al. 2020)
		Fish	Danio rerio	polypropylene	25 mm	10 ug/L (~680 fibers/L)	(Qiao et al. 2019)
		Nematodes	Caenorhabditis elegans	polyethylene terephthalate	length (250 μm); diameter (17.4 μm)	0, 36, 36x5, 36x10 pieces of MF/0.5 mL	(Liu et al. 2021)
		Terrestrial Snails	Achatina fulica	polyethylene terephthalate	length (1257.8 um); diameter (76.3 um)	0.14–0.71 g/kg	(Song et al. 2019)

Organ		Species	Polymer	Size	Concentration	Reference
Growth Development	Bivalves	*Mytilus galloprovincialis*	composite household lint	Length: 85.1 um mean (22.0–743 um); Width (<30 um)	56–180 mg/L	(Alnajar et al. 2021)
	Crustaceans	*Emerita analoga*	polypropylene	0.03–6 mm long	3 fibers/L	(Horn et al. 2020)
	Crustaceans	*Artemia franciscana*	polypropylene, polyethylene terephthalate	1mm long	75, 125, 250, 500, 1000 mg/L	(Kim et al. 2021)
	Fish	*Carassius auratus*	ethylene vinyl acetate (EVA)	length (0.7–5.0 mm)	0.03g fibers/15 food pellets; 55–76 fibers/pellet (fed 3x/wk for 6 wks, 3 pellets/fish)	(Jabeen et al. 2018)
Inflammation	Fish	*Carassius auratus*	ethylene vinyl acetate (EVA)	length (0.7–5.0 mm)	0.03g fibers/15 food pellets; 55–76 fibers/pellet (fed 3x/wk for 6 wks, 3 pellets/fish)	(Jabeen et al. 2018)
	Fish	*Danio rerio*	polypropylene	25 mm	10 ug/L (~680 fibers/L)	(Qiao et al. 2019)
	Rodents	*Cavia porcellus*	polyester	n/a	2g airborne dust 3x/day for 325 days	(Pimentel et al. 1975)
	Zooplankton	*Artemia franciscana*	polyethylene terephthalate	length (0.02–200 mm); mean diameter (22.8 ± 6.11 um)	100 mg/L concentration (50667.03 fibers/mg)	(Kokalj et al. 2018)

(Continued)

TABLE 4.1 (Continued)

Level	Type of Effect	Organism Clade	Genus species	Plastic Material Type	Fiber Size	MP Concentration	In Text Citation
	Oxidative Stress	Crustaceans	*Homarus americanus*	polyethylene terephthalate	<0.5mm	0, 1, 10, 25 fibers/mL	(Woods et al. 2020)
		Fish	*Danio rerio*	polypropylene	25 mm	10 ug/L (~680 fibers/L)	(Qiao et al. 2019)
	Physical Organ Damage	Bivalves	*Mytilus galloprovincialis*	composite household lint	Length: 85.1 um mean (22.0–743 um); Width (<30 um)	56–180 mg/L	(Alnajar et al. 2021)
		Crustaceans	*Artemia franciscana*	polypropylene, polyethylene terephthalate	1mm long	75, 125, 250, 500, 1000 mg/L	(Kim et al. 2021)
		Crustaceans	*Nephrops norvegicus*	polypropylene	length (3–5mm); diameter (0.2 mm)	5 fibers/feeding; total exposure (360 fibers)	(Welden & Cowie 2016)
		Fish	*Dicentrarchus labrax*	polyethylene (80%); polyester (19%); rayon (1%)	GIT = 501–1500um (>36%); Gills = 151–500um (>50%); Dorsal Muscle = 501–1500um (58%)	GIT (1.3 ± 2.5 MP items/individual); Gills (0.8 ± 1.4 MP items/individual); Dorsal Muscle (0.4 ± 0.7 MP items/g)	(Barboza et al. 2020)

Fish	*Trachurus*	polyethylene (80%); polyester (19%); rayon (1%)	GIT = 501–1500um (>36%); Gills = 151–500um (>50%); Dorsal Muscle = 151–500um (39%)	GIT (1.0 ± 1.9 MP items/individual); Gills (0.7 ± 1.9 MP items/individual); Dorsal Muscle (0.2 ± 1.3 MP items/g)	(Barboza et al. 2020)
Fish	*Scomber colias*	polyethylene (80%); polyester (19%); rayon (1%)	GIT = 501–1500um (>36%); Gills = 151–500um (>50%); Dorsal Muscle = 501–1500um (58%)	GIT (1.2 ± 1.6 MP items/individual); Gills (0.7 ± 1.0 MP items/individual); Dorsal Muscle (0.6 ± 0.8 MP items/g)	(Barboza et al. 2020)
Fish	*Carassius auratus*	ethylene vinyl acetate (EVA)	length (0.7–5.0 mm)	0.03g fibers/15 food pellets; 55–76 fibers/pellet (fed 3x/wk for 6 wks, 3 pellets/fish)	[Jabeen et al. 2018]
Fish	*Danio rerio*	polypropylene	25 mm	10 ug/L (~680 fibers/L)	(Qiao et al. 2019)

(Continued)

TABLE 4.1 (Continued)

Level	Type of Effect	Organism Clade	Genus species	Plastic Material Type	Fiber Size	MP Concentration	In Text Citation
		Humans	Homo sapiens	polycarbonate, polyamide, polypropylene	length (range: 0.8–1.6 mm) (average = 1.1–0.3 mm)	fibers (96.1% of total MP found); total MP avg (331 particles/individual specimen); total MP avg (28.1 +/- 15.4 particles/g tissue)	(Ibrahim et al. 2021)
		Humans	Homo sapiens	polyester	n/a	n/a	(Pimentel et al. 1975)
		Rodents	Cavia porcellus	polyester	n/a	2g airborne dust 3x/day for 325 days	(Pimentel et al. 1975)
		Terrestrial Snails	Achatina fulica	polyethylene terephthalate	length (1257.8 um); diameter (76.3 um)	0.14–0.71 g/kg	(Song et al. 2019)
		Zooplankton	Artemia franciscana	polyethylene terephthalate	length (0.02–200 mm); mean diameter (22.8 ± 6.11 um)	100 mg/L concentration (50667.03 fibers/mg)	(Kokalj et al. 2018)
Organism	**Adverse Reproductive Response**	Crustaceans	Emerita analoga	polypropylene	0.03–6 mm long	3 fibers/L	(Horn et al. 2020)
		Nematodes	Caenorhabditis elegans	polyethylene terephthalate	length (250 μm); diameter (17.4 μm)	0, 36, 36x5, 36x10 pieces of MF/0.5 mL	(Liu et al. 2021)
		Nematodes	Caenorhabditis elegans	polyethylene terephthalate	length (250 μm); diameter (17.4 μm)	0, 36, 36x5, 36x10 pieces of MF/0.5 mL	(Liu et al. 2021)

	Species	Material	Description	Concentration	Reference
Terrestrial Veg	Lolium perenne	high-density polyethylene (HDPE); polylactic acid (PLA)	HDPE avg length (102.6 μm; range = 0.48–316 μm; PLA avg length (65.6 μm; range = 0.6–363 μm)	0.1% dry soil w/w	(Boots et al. 2019)
Worm	Aporrectodea rosea	high-density polyethylene (HDPE); polylactic acid (PLA)	HDPE avg length (102.6 μm; range = 0.48–316 μm; PLA avg length (65.6 μm; range = 0.6–363 μm)	0.1% dry soil w/w	(Boots et al. 2019)
Zooplankton	Ceriodaphnia dubia	polyethylene terephthalate	avg length 280 ± 50 μm (25.7 ±10μm – 1150 ±160μm)	48 hrs (31.25, 62.5, 125, 250, 500, 1000 ug/L); 8 days (429 ug/L (345–539 ug/L))	(Ziajahromi et al. 2017)
Behavioral Change					
Annelid Worms	Lumbricus terrestris	polyester	Avg length (361.6 ± 387.0 um); diameter (40.7 ± 3.8 um)	0, 0.1% (0.3g MF), 1.0% (3.0g MF)	(Prendergast-Miller et al. 2019)
Bivalves	Mytilus galloprovincialis	composite household lint	Length: 85.1 um mean (22.0–743 um); Width (<30 um)	56–180 mg/L	(Alnajar et al. 2021)
Bivalves	Mytilus edulis	nylon	length (30 um)	24,000 fibers/L	(Christoforou et al. 2020)
Bivalves	Macomona liliana	polyethylene terephthalate	1.8 μm fibers	0–0.5 g/kg sediment	(Hope et al. 2020)

(Continued)

TABLE 4.1 (Continued)

Level	Type of Effect	Organism Clade	Genus species	Plastic Material Type	Fiber Size	MP Concentration	In Text Citation
		Cnidarians	*Aiptasia pallida*	nylon, polyester, polypropylene	50 μm – 1000μm	10mg MF/L	(Romanó de Orte et al. 2019)
		Crustaceans	*Hyalella azteca*	polypropylene	Length (20–75 um); diameter (20 um)	Acute 10 day LC50% exposure (71.43 fibers/mL)	(Au et al. 2015)
		Crustaceans	*Nephrops norvegicus*	polypropylene	length (3–5mm); diameter (0.2 mm)	5 fibers/feeding; total exposure (360 fibers)	(Welden & Cowie 2016)
		Nematodes	*Caenorhabditis elegans*	polyethylene terephthalate	length (250 μm); diameter (17.4 μm)	0, 36, 36x5, 36x10 pieces of MF/ 0.5 mL	(Liu et al. 2021)
		Terrestrial Snails	*Achatina fulica*	polyethylene terephthalate	length (1257.8 um); diameter (76.3 um)	0.14–0.71 g/kg	(Song et al. 2019)
		Zooplankton	*Daphnia magna*	nylon, polyethylene terephthalate	n/a	Exposure concentration – (50%, 5%, and 0.5% concentration (non/dialyzed leachate); Preparation –100% leachate from A+B (3.55 teabags/mL water) C+D (2.95 teabags/mL water)	(Hernandez et al. 2019)

	Species	Polymer	Size	Exposure	Reference
Zooplankton	*Tigriopus japonicus*	polyester	0.86 μm	MF/copepod ratios: 96hr exposure (0.1, 1.0, 2.5, 5.0, 25.0, 50.0); 168hr exposure (1.6, 166.6)	(Kang et al. 2020)
Growth Development					
Bivalves	*Macomona liliana*	polyethylene terephthalate	1.8 μm fibers	0–0.5 g/kg sediment	(Hope et al. 2020)
Crustaceans	*Hyalella azteca*	polypropylene	Length (20–75 um); diameter (20 um)	Acute 10 day LC50% exposure (71.43 fibers/mL)	(Au et al. 2015)
Crustaceans	*Emerita analoga*	polypropylene	0.03–6 mm long	3 fibers/L	(Horn et al. 2020)
Crustaceans	*Carcinus maenas*	polypropylene	500 μm	% fibers / 2 mg feed: 0% (0mg); 0.3% (0.6mg); 0.6% (1.2 mg); 1% (2.0 mg)	(Watts et al. 2015)
Crustaceans	*Nephrops norvegicus*	polypropylene	length (3–5mm); diameter (0.2 mm)	5 fibers/feeding; total exposure (360 fibers)	(Welden & Cowie 2016)
Crustaceans	*Homarus americanus*	polyethylene terephthalate	<0.5mm	0, 1, 10, 25 fibers/ mL	(Woods et al. 2020)
Microphytobenthos	Cyanobacteria	polyethylene terephthalate	1.8 μm fibers	0–0.5 g/kg sediment	(Hope et al. 2020)
Nematodes	*Caenorhabditis elegans*	polyethylene terephthalate	length (250 μm); diameter (17.4 μm)	0, 36, 36x5, 36x10 pieces of MF/ 0.5 mL	(Liu et al. 2021)

(Continued)

TABLE 4.1 (Continued)

Level	Type of Effect	Organism Clade	Genus species	Plastic Material Type	Fiber Size	MP Concentration	In Text Citation
		Nematodes	*Caenorhabditis elegans*	polyethylene terephthalate	length (250 μm); diameter (17.4 μm)	0, 36, 36x5, 36x10 pieces of MF/ 0.5 mL	(Liu et al. 2021)
		Terrestrial Veg	*Lolium perenne*	high-density polyethylene (HDPE); polylactic acid (PLA)	HDPE avg length (102.6 μm; range = 0.48–316 μm); PLA avg length (65.6 μm; range = 0.6–363 μm)	0.1% dry soil w/w	(Boots et al. 2019)
		Worm	*Aporrectodea rosea*	high-density polyethylene (HDPE); polylactic acid (PLA)	HDPE avg length (102.6 μm; range = 0.48–316 μm); PLA avg length (65.6 μm; range = 0.6–363 μm)	0.1% dry soil w/w	(Boots et al. 2019)
		Zooplankton	*Daphnia magna*	nylon, polyethylene terephthalate	n/a	Exposure concentration – (50%, 5%, and 0.5%) concentration (non/ dialyzed leachate); Preparation – 100% leachate from A+B (3.55 teabags/mL water) C+D (2.95 teabags/mL water)	(Hernandez et al. 2019)

Zooplankton	*Artemia franciscana*	polyethylene terephthalate	length (0.02–200 mm); mean diameter (22.8 ± 6.11 um)	100 mg/L; concentration (50667.03 fibers/mg)	(Kokalj et al. 2018)
Zooplankton	*Ceriodaphnia dubia*	polyethylene terephthalate	avg length 280 ± 50 μm (25.7 ±10μm – 1150 ±160μm)	48 hrs (31.25, 62.5, 125, 250, 500, 1000 ug/L); 8 days (429 ug/L (345–539 ug/L))	(Ziajahromi et al., 2017)
Neurological Fish	*Dicentrachus labrax*	polyethylene (80%); polyester (19%); rayon (1%)	GIT = 501–1500um (>36%); Gills = 151–500um (>50%); Dorsal Muscle = 501–1500um (58%)	GIT (1.3 ± 2.5 MP items/individual); Gills (0.8 ± 1.4 MP items/individual); Dorsal Muscle (0.4 ± 0.7 MP items/g)	(Barboza et al., 2020)
Fish	*Trachurus trachurus*	polyethylene (80%); polyester (19%); rayon (1%)	GIT = 501–1500um (>36%); Gills = 151–500um (>50%); Dorsal Muscle = 151–500um (39%)	GIT (1.0 ± 1.9 MP items/individual); Gills (0.7 ± 1.9 MP items/individual); Dorsal Muscle (0.2 ± 1.3 MP items/g)	(Barboza et al., 2020)

(Continued)

TABLE 4.1 (Continued)

Level	Type of Effect	Organism Clade	Genus species	Plastic Material Type	Fiber Size	MP Concentration	In Text Citation
	Fish		Scomber colias	polyethylene (80%); polyester (19%); rayon (1%)	GIT = 501–1500um (>36%); Gills = 151–500um (>50%); Dorsal Muscle = 501–1500um (58%)	GIT (1.2 ± 1.6 MP items/individual); Gills (0.7 ± 1.0 MP items/individual); Dorsal Muscle (0.6 ± 0.8 MP items/g)	(Barboza et al., 2020)
Survivorship or Mortality	Crustaceans		Hyalella azteca	polypropylene	Length (20–75 um); diameter (20 um)	Acute 10 day LC50% exposure (71.43 fibers/mL)	(Au et al., 2015)
		Crustaceans	Emerita analoga	polypropylene	0.03–6 mm long	3 fibers/L	(Horn et al. 2020)
		Crustaceans	Emerita analoga	polypropylene	0.03–6 mm long	3 fibers/L	(Horn et al. 2020)
		Crustaceans	Artemia franciscana	polypropylene, polyethylene terephthalate	1mm long	75, 125, 250, 500, 1000 mg/L	(Kim et al. 2021)
		Crustaceans	Nephrops norvegicus	polypropylene	length (3–5mm); diameter (0.2 mm)	5 fibers/feeding; total exposure (360 fibers)	(Welden & Cowie 2016)
		Crustaceans	Homarus americanus	polyethylene terephthalate	<0.5mm	0, 1, 10, 25 fibers/mL	(Woods et al. 2020)

Population					
Zooplankton	*Daphnia magna*	polyethylene terephthalate	length (62–1400 mm); width (31–528 mm); diameter (1–21.5 mm)	0 mg/L; 12.5 mg/L; 25 mg/L; 50 mg/L; 100 mg/L	(Jemec et al. 2016)
Zooplankton	*Ceriodaphnia dubia*	polyethylene terephthalate	avg length 280 ± 50 μm (25.7 ±10μm – 1150 ±160μm)	48 hrs (31.25, 62.5, 125, 250, 500, 1000 ug/L); 8 days (429 ug/L (345–539 ug/L))	(Ziajahromi et al. 2017)
Adverse Reproductive Response					
Crustaceans	*Emerita analoga*	polypropylene	0.03–6 mm long	3 fibers/L	(Horn et al. 2020)
Nematodes	*Caenorhabditis elegans*	polyethylene terephthalate	length (250 μm); diameter (17.4 μm)	0, 36, 36x5, 36x10 pieces of MF/ 0.5 mL	(Liu et al. 2021)

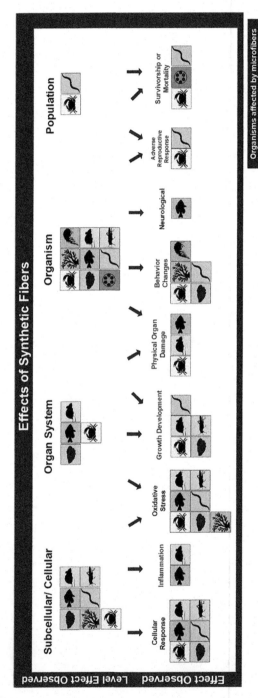

FIGURE 4.3 The effects of synthetic fibres on organism health have been documented across biological levels in a diverse array of species. Slanted arrows show an effect on more than one level

Cellular and subcellular

Cellular and subcellular level effects of synthetic fibres include changes in gene expression and enzyme activity, DNA damage, and retention of zinc (El-Gendy et al. 2020). In mussels, measured microplastic effects include changes in DNA repair, cellular stress response, and immunity, indicating effects on the gills and digestive glands (Alnajar et al. 2021). In the marine mussel *Mytilus galloprovincialis*, exposure to concentrations of synthetic microfibres ranging from 56–180 mg/L caused an increased retention of trace elements like zinc as well as damage to DNA structure (Alnajar et al. 2021). The abundance of zinc in synthetic fibres and the retention of this zinc by *M. galloprovincialis* demonstrates the potential for the uptake of other harmful chemicals into cells of marine bivalves (Alnajar et al. 2021). Additionally, tail DNA damage increased by more than 10% and 20% when *M. galloprovincialis* was exposed to 100 and 180 mg/L of microfibres, respectively (Alnajar et al. 2021). In *M. galloprovincialis* individuals exposed to microfibres, gill and digestive gland abnormalities increased from 15% in control groups to 87% in exposed groups (Alnajar et al. 2021). These abnormalities appeared as atrophy, loss of cell definition, and necrosis. While some of the fibre concentrations tested are not regularly encountered in the environment, these findings indicate future risks for organisms as plastic concentrations in the environment increase.

The sea cucumber *Apostichopus japonicus* experiences changes in acid phosphatase and alkaline phosphatase activity levels, which are key biomarkers of immune system health after exposure to environmentally relevant concentrations of synthetic microfibres (Mohsen et al. 2021). These environmentally relevant concentrations of 0.6 MF/g, 1.2 MF/g, and 10 MF/g also caused oxidative stress in both juvenile and adult *A. japonicus* (Mohsen et al. 2021).

The **earthworm** *Lumbricus terrestris* experiences changes in gene expression after exposure to 361.6 μm polyester microfibres at concentrations of 0.3 g/ 300 g of soil (Prendergast-Miller et al. 2019). This exposure resulted in the reduction of heat shock protein (hsp70) expression, an important chaperone protein that facilitates proper protein folding and protects the cell from stress (Prendergast-Miller et al. 2019). An increase in metallothionein (mt-2) expression, another stress biomarker, was also observed. Responses of specific genes among earthworms like *L. terrestris* varies depending on material, contaminant concentration, and exposure time, suggesting further study is needed across a wide range of fibre types to fully understand *L. terrestris* transcriptional response to fibres (Prendergast-Miller et al. 2019). It is also important to note microfibre exposure lowered cast production (excrement) in *L. terrestris*, an important ecosystem service offered by earthworms (Prendergast-Miller et al. 2019).

Tissue and organ systems

It is hypothesized that cells may uptake thin fibres, or that fibres may enter the body through lesions in the skin. Once in the bloodstream, they may circulate to other organs (Barboza et al. 2020). Organ systems of many species experience negative effects when exposed to synthetic fibres (Bucci et al. 2020; Jacob et al. 2020; Mishra et al. 2019). Physical organ damage – including inflammation and tissue damage – has been observed in several fish species (n = 4), crustaceans (n = 2), rodents, and humans (in vitro) (Qiao et al. 2019; Barboza et al. 2020; Kim et al. 2021; Welden & Cowie 2016; Dijk et al. 2020). Microfibres of polyester, PET, and cellulose of sizes ranging from 150 to 1500 μm can be internalized by fish and enter non-digestive tissues such as the dorsal muscle, though pathways are poorly understood (Barboza et al. 2020; Abbasi et al. 2018). This may be possible due to their small diameter but further studies are needed to determine what size microfibres can pass into the body of fish through this method and what impact those fibres have on organism health. Size and shape are important factors when examining the effects of microfibres on organ systems and a number of effects (6) have been observed with plastics of sizes ≤ 20 μm (Jacob et al. 2020).

Through accumulation in the gills, synthetic fibres (PET, 459 ± SE 2.25 μm) decrease or increase respiration rates in crustaceans, such as the American lobster (*Homarus americanus*), as well as bivalves and fish (Stienbarger et al., 2021; Woods et al. 2020; Cole at el. 2020; Barboza et al. 2020); such changes in respiration can lead to permanent neurological damage and effects on survivorship. In brine shrimp (*Artemia franciscana*), three types of synthetic fibres commonly used for clothing caused a decrease in gut width and increased permeability of the intestinal layer (Kim et al. 2021). This damage to the gut led to the eventual mortality of *A. franciscana*, especially when exposed to polyethylene terephthalate fibres (Kim et al. 2021). Nylon microfibres (10–100 μm) have been shown to accumulate in the gut of *Mytilus edulis* and affect long-term clearance rate of phytoplankton biomass from the water column (Christoforou et al. 2020). Mussels exhibited an average decrease of 21.3% in phytoplankton removal ability after exposure to microfibres (Christoforou et al. 2020). Continued exposure to microfibres could affect *M. edulis*'s ability to mitigate eutrophication and harmful algal blooms, both of which are important ecosystem services (Christoforou et al. 2020).

Research involving human subjects is limited by ethical concerns. However, researchers have developed a method using organoid-in-vitro tissue cells used to model the effects on specific organs (Rossi et al. 2018). Using this method, Dijk et al. (2020) found that rodent and human organoid growth is reduced in the lungs after exposure to nylon microfibres [size: 11x30 μm; density: 39 μg/ml] or polyester [size: 15x53 μm; density: 122 μg/ml], resulting in fewer and smaller organoids. Airway organoid development is significantly affected by the presence of synthetic fibres (Djik et al. 2020).

Studies evaluating effects in rodents and humans are currently at the in vitro stage and signal a high probability that in vivo studies would result in similar organ-level effects (Dijk et al. 2020).

Organism

At the organismal level, synthetic fibres can cause physical and neurological damage across an array of not only aquatic taxa like fish and crustaceans, but also terrestrial taxa ranging from hexapods (insects) to rodents (McCormick et al. 2020; Büks et al.

2020; da Costa Araújo & Malafaia 2021). Entanglement negatively impacted the movement of the copepod *Tigriopus japonicus* after exposure to polyester microfibres of size 0.86 μm (Kang et al. 2020). Microfibres became entangled around antennae, setae, bristles of appendages, and caudal rami of *T. japonicus*, affecting their mobility through water (Kang et al. 2020). Although this entanglement did not occur at environmentally relevant concentrations, increased encounters with microfibres lead to increased entanglement, and as concentrations of microfibres in the environment increase, copepod encounters with microfibres and other microplastics is likely to increase (Borrelle et al. 2020; Kang et al. 2020). As copepods are found in diverse fresh- and saltwater habitats and play an important role in many food webs, the potential for copepods and other similarly sized aquatic arthropods to be affected by synthetic fibre pollution is high.

Synthetic fibre exposure can impede growth and development in fish and crustaceans (Jabeen et al. 2018; Yin et al. 2018; Kokalj et al. 2018). By filling the gut with microplastics, an organism can become falsely satiated, leading to depletion in energy, protein, and lipid reserves and ultimately inhibiting growth potential (Welden & Cowie 2016); and this phenomenon, termed, 'food dilution', is now being used to model species sensitivity to microplastic pollution (Kooi & Koelmans 2019). In general, survivorship decreases and mortality increases when crustaceans, marine bivalves, copepods, and fish are exposed to increasing amounts of microfibres (Kim et al. 2021; Cole et al. 2013). The Pacific mole crab (*Emerita analoga*) is a widely distributed species along the North and South American coasts. Exposure to polypropylene fibres at environmentally relevant concentrations of 3 fibres/L every four days produced several adverse effects on these crabs (Horn et al. 2020). Crab lifespan decreased by approximately 5 days with every fibre ingested and exposure to microfibres at any life stage resulted in reduced incubation time of viable eggs (Horn et al. 2020). As Pacific mole crabs occupy an important niche in the food web, microfibre pollution poses a serious threat to individuals, the population (through reproductive effects), and other species such as fishes and seabirds who depend on them as a food source.

In fish, exposure to synthetic fibres and microspheres of length 1–5μm at concentrations of 0.26 and 0.69 mg/L can slow swim speed and alter behaviour (Barboza et al. 2018; Yin et al. 2018; Chisada et al. 2019), making fish more likely to exhibit erratic behaviour and end up farther from the shelter of reefs (Barboza et al. 2018). This could increase predation of fish exposed to synthetic fibres, which may contribute to further decline of fisheries stocks. Fibres were also observed in the gills and gastrointestinal tracts of the fish *Carassius auratus* (Jabeen et al. 2018). Exposed *C. auratus* experienced lowered condition index, inflammation in the liver, and slight changes to the jaw bone after ingestion of 0.7–5.0 μm ethylene vinyl acetate (EVA) fibres in food (Jabeen et al. 2018).

Exposure to environmentally relevant concentrations (0.1 mg/L) of 500–10,000 μm polystyrene microfibres resulted in reduced photosynthetic ability by the photosynthetic algae living in Acroporid corals, triggering stress responses by the corals and indicating a new ecological stressor on a taxon already stressed by the effects of climate change (Mendrik et al. 2021; Worm et al. 2006). Decreased PSII (a protein complex that results in the production of oxygen) capacity was also observed after exposure to microfibres, a sign of heightened oxidative stress (Mendrik et al. 2021).

When exposed to 10 mg nylon and polyester microfibres/L, 80% of anemones ingested 50–1000μm microfibres (Romanó de Orte et al. 2019). Bleached anemones also ingested more nylon and polyester fibres than symbiotic, or unbleached anemones (Romanó de Orte et al. 2019). Bleached anemones retained fibres longer than symbiotic anemones which, after chronic exposure, could be energetically costly on these organisms with compromised health (Romanó de Orte et al. 2019).

Even microalgae are affected at this biological level, with chronic exposures to synthetic fibres causing growth inhibition and trophic transfer to its predator, *Artemia franciscana* (Bergami et al. 2017). Exposure to synthetic fibres can also cause an extracellular stress mechanism in the green algae, *Dunaliella tertiolecta*, releasing polysaccharides (Bergami et al. 2017). Photosynthesis may also be negatively affected in *D. tertiolecta*, but more comprehensive studies are needed to confirm this.

Population

Research on population level effects of microfibres on organisms is extremely limited. However, population level effects are predicted by much of the research presented earlier. For example, with the high microfibre concentrations found in terrestrial, aquatic, and marine sand/sediment/soil (Gavigan et al. 2020; Auta et al. 2017), chronic exposure could decrease fitness and survival in sediment dwelling organisms (Hope et al. 2020). Additionally, a soil-dwelling, rapidly reproducing nematode species, *C. elegans*, has been used as a model organism for scientific research since the 1960s, and generational effects have been documented after multigenerational exposure to PET microfibres (Liu et al. 2021). After sampling eight generations of *C. elegans*, decreased reproductive rates (70%) were triggered by microfibre concentrations of 36 x 100 MF/0.5 mL after the second generation (Liu et al. 2021). Reproductive rates recovered in the fourth and fifth generations, signaling a possible adaptation to microfibre exposure. However, a significant decrease in reproductive success in the experimental group relative to the control group demonstrates that continuous exposure to microfibres can reduce overall reproductive success (Liu et al. 2021). The documented effects on reproduction across species (e.g. Liu et al. 2021; Horn et al. 2020) signal the need for further study of population-level effects and possible changes to ecosystem dynamics, particularly given that decreased reproduction resulting from exposure to other classes of contaminants is predicted to affect population size (e.g. White et al. 2017), and such models have been preliminarily extended to studies on the effects of microplastic exposure (Marn et al. 2020).

Across taxa for which synthetic fibre exposure effects have been studied, fish – ranging from nearshore rockfish to pelagic tuna, invertebrates, and even algae – experience negative effects across biological levels. It is important to note that with the exception of Mohsen et al. 2021 and Horn et al. 2020, most studies, including those discussed here, utilize microfibre concentrations considered higher than those in the environment. While these concentrations do not reflect current levels of microfibres in the environments, some of these concentrations may become environmentally relevant in the future (e.g., Everaert et al. 2018). Terrestrial species, though not widely studied, are exposed to microplastics through water, soil, and air (Büks et al. 2020). It is expected that synthetic fibres negatively affect terrestrial organisms, either through fibre inhalation or consumption of contaminated algae, plants, and animals.

However, reversing the effects of synthetic fibres in the environment is not as simple as switching to more natural alternatives. Evidence suggests marketed alternatives such as bioplastics produce effects similar to synthetic plastics when degrading in the environment (Zimmermann et al. 2020; Straub et al. 2017).

Bioplastics

Bioplastics are marketed as a greener alternative to synthetic plastics, in part because they are frequently developed to biodegrade under certain conditions, and are therefore portrayed as a product type designed to reduce the anthropogenic waste stream and dependence on fossil fuels (Napper & Thompson 2019). Certainly, reducing our waste stream is a first step in curbing the effects of plastic pollution. Unfortunately, the limited research on bioplastics as a pollutant in ecosystems points to their potential as a contaminant with similar effects as synthetics on organisms.

Existing research on bioplastics indicates a wide range of effects, from no adverse effect to effects on organism growth, reproduction, and membrane damage (Shruti & Kutralam-Muniasamy 2019; Palsikowski et al. 2018; Zuo et al. 2019), however, the majority of these studies utilize high concentrations that generally far exceed environmental relevance. No adverse effect reported is most common, though some studies do report adverse effects to organisms.

These include studies on *Allium sepia*, *Daphnia magna*, and *Chlamydomonas reinhardtii*, with *A. sepia* experiencing potential cytotoxic and genotoxic effects upon exposure to PLA at treatments of either 50g or 300g per litre of filtered water for 76 days, and *D. magna* and *C. reinhardtii* exposed to PHB nanoplastics exhibit reduced growth and severe membrane damage after a 2-day exposure (Shruti & Kutralam-Muniasamy 2019; Napper & Thompson 2019; Palsikowski et al. 2018). Plants experience a change in soil chemistry, causing them to distance further from one another, therefore decreasing density (Shruti & Kutralam-Muniasamy 2019; Napper & Thompson 2019). The various results seen throughout the small body of literature signal an important yet understudied topic in need of attention.

The lack of research on bioplastic effects on organisms may be due to its marketing as a green alternative to conventional plastics (Shruti & Kutralam-Muniasamy 2019; Schenker et al. 2020). For example, though cellulosic packaging has been used in the food industry longer than conventional plastics (Shruti & Kutralam-Muniasamy 2019; Napper & Thompson 2019; Straub et al. 2017), new cellulosic types, such as PLA, have only been used since the 1980s, and their ability to biodegrade in the environment has only been questioned since the 1990s (Napper & Thompson 2019; Schenker et al. 2020). The lack of research into organismal effects of bioplastics could prevent implementation of appropriate management and policy for this set of potential emerging contaminants in our ecosystems. Being composed primarily of natural compounds, effects of these heavily processed materials have been largely overlooked, much like those of natural fibres in textiles.

Natural fibres

Studies of the environmental effects of natural microfibres, in comparison to synthetics and bioplastics, are almost completely absent from the literature. In terms of microfibre pollution research, the most studied natural fibres are cotton and wool, with research on other material types largely absent. The absorption capacity and environmental persistence of synthetic fibres has made them prime candidates for toxicity research, however the physical properties of natural fibres should not be ignored. Grancaric et al. (2005) compared the electrokinetic properties of textiles, finding that the point of zero charge (PZC, essentially the sorption capacity of fibres with cationic surfactants) is much higher in natural fibres than in synthetics. Differently stated, natural fibres are more likely to sorb surfactants (i.e., disinfectants, detergents, and emulsifiers), which have been found to cause neurological damage in the gastrointestinal tract of rodents, with similar effects predicted for humans when ingested on their own (Gelberg 2018). Residues from chemical treatments applied during the manufacturing of cotton and wool textiles, such as the addition of the dye Direct Red 28, pesticides, and anti-shrink chemicals, could potentially increase the toxicity of natural fibres, should these substances desorb off of the fibres once ingested (Remy et al. 2015; Sillanpää & Sainio 2017; Stone et al. 2020). When considering the environmental impact of natural fibres, their relatively rapid degradation time has been hailed as environmentally friendly as they do not persist in the environment as long as plastics may. However, given the sorption capacity of these fibres, their quick degradability could instead mean they are even more toxic in the short term than synthetic fibres (Ladewig et al. 2015; Remy et al. 2015; Zhao et al. 2016; Compa et al. 2018; Stone et al. 2020).

Once in the environment, the biodegradability of fibres differs by material: cotton and wool are much more quickly biodegraded than polyester, both in the laboratory as well as in industrial compost settings (Figure 4.4; Li et al. 2010; Stone et al. 2020; Zambrano et al. 2020). Cotton fibres likely break down faster in the marine environment due to the presence of microbes that metabolize and consume cellulose (Ladewig et al. 2015).

Additionally, cotton and wool fibres are compostable by both aerobic degradation and enzymatic breakdown in soils (Li et al. 2010; Arshad et al. 2014). Though biodegradability is viewed positively when considering persistence of microfibres in aquatic environments, this breakdown process may increase the rate of delivery of toxicants into the environment and to organisms, relative to more slowly degrading synthetic fibres (Ladewig et al. 2015; Remy et al. 2015; Compa et al. 2018; Stone et al. 2020).

Due to differences in physical structure and rapid degradability, natural fibres are likely to transport various toxicants to the environment and release them at a quicker rate than synthetic fibres, potentially causing previously unknown effects (Ladewig et al. 2015; Remy et al. 2015; Compa et al. 2018; Stone et al. 2020).

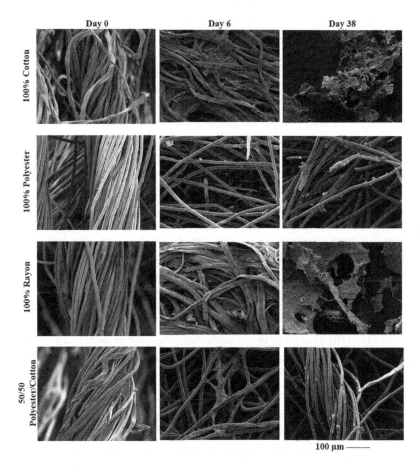

FIGURE 4.4 SEM images of spun yarns throughout the biodegradation process

Source: Reprinted with permission from Zambrano et al. (2020)

While no studies currently report the effects of natural fibres on the environment, their presence and capacity to deliver toxicants to the environment upon degradation create a strong argument for further research. Given the heavy pesticide use in cotton and wool production and chemical treatments before textile manufacturing (Remy et al. 2015; Sillanpää & Sainio 2017; Garcia et al. 2019; Stone et al. 2020), along with the capacity to sorb surfactants in waterways (Grancaric et al. 2005; Ivanković & Hrenović 2010), natural fibres released into the environment may pose a risk to organisms in natural systems, necessitating further study.

Conclusions

Environmental exposure to microfibres is affecting a diverse array of organisms across taxonomic groups, trophic levels, and ecosystem types (freshwater, marine, terrestrial).

The effects range from subcellular and cellular to organ, organismal, and multi-species, with the potential for population level impacts in light of effects on fitness-relevant endpoints such as growth, reproduction, and behaviour. Additionally, there is growing evidence that exposure to bioplastics as well as fully or semi-synthetic plastic fibres is detrimental to animals, and likely plants, though less information is available for primary producer species. More data on terrestrial impacts, particularly on primary producers grown in agricultural lands to which biosolids are applied and consumed as food crops, are anticipated over the coming years (Zubris & Richards 2005; Gavigan et al. 2020). Based on chemical adsorption to and rapid degradation of natural fibres, there may be negative effects of exposure (Ladewig et al. 2015; Stone et al. 2020), particularly since many natural fibre-based textiles use fibres that are grown and/or produced with extensive chemical use. Therefore, the data currently available suggest that bioplastics may not be a sustainable solution to plastics-based fibres, and that use of natural fibres as a substitute will need to consider the production processes in order to yield a more sustainable, less ecologically disruptive fibre. Despite the growing body of literature documenting the wide range of effects caused by such an array of fibre types across a diversity of organisms, many data gaps remain (Figure 4.5).

There is a critical need to better understand the ratio of synthetic to bioplastic to natural fibres in organisms, water, and sediments and the effects of fibre contamination on both wild and domesticated terrestrial organisms, as well as

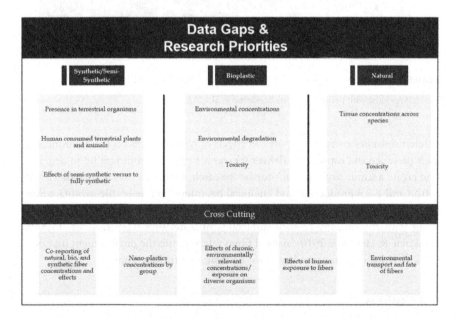

FIGURE 4.5 Data gaps and research priorities for understanding environmental and health effects of environmental microfibres

on humans. Additionally, further research to determine bioplastic and natural fibre toxicity and whether some bioplastics and/or natural fibres are safer than others when ingested by organisms would fill major data gaps. Standardization of studies on the occurrence and effects of microfibres, including strict quality control to account for background contamination, is critical as well (e.g., Cowger et al. 2020; Brander et al. 2020; Provencher et al. 2020). This will ensure the generation of comparable datasets, so that accurate risk assessments can be performed on this ubiquitous and potentially more hazardous microplastic type.

Across all textile types, better regulations as well as improved production and design will require a better understanding of the migration of different fibre types and sizes throughout an organism, how chronic effects vary by material type, and the effects of nano-sized fibres on organisms and humans (Figure 4.5). Emerging solutions to address microfibre uptake by organisms include: a) mandating catchment systems in household and commercial washing machines and dryers to prevent or reduce release into the environment (Erdle et al. 2020); b) re-examining application of wastewater sludge to agricultural fields (Zubris and Richards 2005); and c) developing synthetic and possibly natural fibres more resistant to shedding. In fact, as of early 2021 the State of California is considering two pieces of legislation that require filtration devices to be installed on all new washing and machines by 2024 and overall reduction of microfibre pollution (AB 802, AB 622). Additionally, the phasing out of top loading washers and transition to front loading washers and use of cold water cycles can reduce microfibre release from laundering of textiles (e.g., Hartline et al. 2016; de Falco et al. 2018; Kelly et al. 2019). Other practices that may reduce microfibre releases into the environment include the installation of filtration devices on dryer exhaust outlets, as well as washing clothes less frequently.

However, before discarding your synthetic textiles to purchase natural materials, it is important to recognize that the shedding rate of some synthetic fibres decreases with fibre age (Lant et al. 2020) and that, in combination with the increased bioavailability of natural fibres to animal systems, the choice of fibre type is far from clear-cut. Given that clothing and other fabric-based consumer goods are necessities, solutions on the horizon targeted at source reduction, such as better filtration during laundering, reconsideration of widespread biosolids application and increased research on more sustainable textiles (Choudhury 2017; Muthu & Gardetti 2020), are recommended paths forward to ensure that inputs to sensitive ecosystems and human food sources are reduced in the future.

Acknowledgements

We thank Britta Baechler for assistance with paper collection and editing; Corinne Heath and Katalin Plummer for input on the chapter draft; and Kimberly Brown for the idea behind the chapter title. We are grateful to the reviewer and editor for suggestions that improved the chapter.

References

AB 622, 2021. CALIFORNIA LEGISLATURE, 2021–2022 REGULAR SESSION, Part 15 of Division 104 Health and Safety Code (2021). https://leginfo.legislature.ca.gov/faces/billTextClient.xhtml?bill_id=202120220AB622

Abbasi, S., Soltani, N., Keshavarzi, B., Moore, F., Turner, A., & Hassanaghaei, M., 2018. Microplastics in different tissues of fish and prawn from the Musa Estuary, Persian Gulf. *Chemosphere*, 205, 80–87. https://doi.org/10.1016/j.chemosphere.2018.04.076

Alnajar, N., Jha, A. N., & Turner, A., 2021. Impacts of microplastic fibres on the marine mussel, Mytilus galloprovinciallis. *Chemosphere*, 262, 128290. https://doi.org/10.1016/j.chemosphere.2020.128290

Arshad, K., Skrifvars, M., Vivod, V., Volmajer Valh, J., & Vončina, B., 2014. Biodegradation of natural text mater soil. *Tekstilec*, 57(2), 118–132. https://doi.org/10.14502/Tekstilec2014.57.118–132Au, S. Y., Bruce, T. F., Bridges, W. C., & Klaine, S. J., 2015. Responses of Hyalella azteca to acute and chronic microplastic exposures: Effects of Microplastic Exposure on Hyalella azteca. *Environ Toxicol Chem*, 34(11), 2564–2572. https://doi.org/10.1002/etc.3093

Auta, H. S., Emenike, C. U., & Fauziah, S. H., 2017. Distribution and importance of microplastics in the marine environment: A review of the sources, fate, effects, and potential solutions. *Environ Int*, 102, 165–176. https://doi.org/10.1016/j.envint.2017.02.013

Barboza, L. G. A., Lopes, C., Oliveira, P., Bessa, F., Otero, V., Henriques, B., Raimundo, J., Caetano, M., Vale, C., & Guilhermino, L., 2020. Microplastics in wild fish from North East Atlantic Ocean and its potential for causing neurotoxic effects, lipid oxidative damage, and human health risks associated with ingestion exposure. *Sci Total Environ*, 717, 134625. https://doi.org/10.1016/j.scitotenv.2019.134625

Barboza, L. G. A., Vieira, L. R., & Guilhermino, L., 2018. Single and combined effects of microplastics and mercury on juveniles of the European seabass (Dicentrarchus labrax): Changes in behavioural responses and reduction of swimming velocity and resistance time. *Environ Pollut*, 236, 1014–1019. https://doi.org/10.1016/j.envpol.2017.12.082

Barker, R. H., 1975. Additives in fibres and fabrics. *Environ Health Persp*, 11, 41–45. https://doi-org.proxy.lib.pdx.edu/10.1289/ehp.751141

Belzagui, F., Gutiérrez-Bouzán, C., Álvarez-Sánchez, A., & Vilaseca, M., 2020. Textile microfibres reaching aquatic environments: A new estimation approach. *Environ Pollut*, 265, 114889. https://doi.org/10.1016/j.envpol.2020.114889

Bergami, E., Pugnalini, S., Vannuccini, M. L., Manfra, L., Faleri, C., Savorelli, F., Dawson, K. A., & Corsi, I., 2017. Long-term toxicity of surface-charged polystyrene nanoplastics to marine planktonic species Dunaliella tertiolecta and Artemia franciscana. *Aquat Toxicol*, 189, 159–169. https://doi.org/10.1016/j.aquatox.2017.06.008

Boots, B., Russell, C. W., & Green, D. S., 2019. Effects of Microplastics in Soil Ecosystems: Above and Below Ground. *Environ Sci Technol*, 53(19), 11496–11506. https://doi.org/10.1021/acs.est.9b03304

Borrelle, S. B., Ringma, J., Law, K. L., Monnahan, C. C., Lebreton, L., McGivern, A., Murphy, E., Jambeck, J., Leonard, G. H., Hilleary, M. A., Eriksen, M., Possingham, H. P., De Frond, H., Gerber, L. R., Polidoro, B., Tahir, A., Bernard, M., Mallos, N., Barnes, M., & Rochman, C. M., 2020. Predicted growth in plastic waste exceeds efforts to mitigate plastic pollution. *Science*, 369(6510), 1515–1518. https://doi.org/10.1126/science.aba3656

Boucher, J., & Friot, D., 2017. Primary microplastics in the oceans: A global evaluation of sources. *IUCN International Union for Conservation of Nature*. https://doi.org/10.2305/IUCN.CH.2017.01.en

Brahney, J., Hallerud, M., Heim, E., Hahnenberger, M., & Sukumaran, S., 2020. Plastic rain in protected areas of the United States. *Science*, 368(6496), 1257–1260. https://doi.org/10.1126/science.aaz5819

Brander, S. M., Renick, V. C., Foley, M. M., Steele, C., Woo, M., Lusher, A., Carr, S., Helm, P., Box, C., Cherniak, S., & Rochman, C., 2020. Sampling and Quality Assurance and Quality Control: A Guide for Scientists Investigating the Occurrence of Microplastics Across Matrices. *Appl Spectrosc*, 74, 1099–1125.

Browne, M. A., Crump, P., Niven, S. J., Teuten, E., Tonkin, A., Galloway, T., & Thompson, R., 2011. Accumulation of Microplastic on Shorelines Worldwide: Sources and Sinks. *Environ Sci Technol*, 45(21), 9175–9179. https://doi.org/10.1021/es201811s

Bucci, K., Tulio, M., & Rochman, C. M., 2020. What is known and unknown about the effects of plastic pollution: A meta-analysis and systematic review. *Ecol Appl*, 30(2). https://doi.org/10.1002/eap.2044

Büks, F., Loes van Schaik, N., & Kaupenjohann, M., 2020. What do we know about how the terrestrial multicellular soil fauna reacts to microplastic? *SOIL*, 6(2), 245–267. https://doi.org/10.5194/soil-6-245-2020

Carney Almroth, B., Cartine, J., Jönander, C., Karlsson, M., Langlois, J., Lindström, M., Lundin, J., Melander, N., Pesqueda, A., Rahmqvist, I., Renaux, J., Roos, J., Spilsbury, F., Svalin, J., Vestlund, H., Zhao, L., Asker, N., Ašmonaitė, G., Birgersson, L., Boloori, T., Book, F., Lammel, T., & Sturve, J., 2021. Assessing the effects of textile leachates in fish using multiple testing methods: From gene expression to behavior. *Ecotox Environ Safe*, 207, 111523. https://doi.org/10.1016/j.ecoenv.2020.111523

Carr, S. A., 2017. Sources and dispersive modes of micro-fibres in the environment: Environmental Microfibre Sources. *Integr Environ Asses*, 13(3), 466–469. https://doi.org/10.1002/ieam.1916

Chisada, S., Yoshida, M., & Karita, K., 2019. Ingestion of polyethylene microbeads affects the growth and reproduction of medaka, Oryzias latipes. *Environ Pollut*, 254, 113094. https://doi.org/10.1016/j.envpol.2019.113094

Choudhury, A. K. R., 2017. Sustainable chemical technologies for textile production. In *Sustainable Fibres and Textiles* (pp. 267–322). Elsevier. https://doi.org/10.1016/B978-0-08-102041-8.00010-X

Christoforou, E., Dominoni, D. M., Lindström, J., Stilo, G., & Spatharis, S., 2020. Effects of long-term exposure to microfibres on ecosystem services provided by coastal mussels. *Environ Pollut*, 266, 115184. https://doi.org/10.1016/j.envpol.2020.115184

Cole, M., Liddle, C., Consolandi, G., Drago, C., Hird, C., Lindeque, P. K., & Galloway, T. S., 2020. Microplastics, microfibres and nanoplastics cause variable sub-lethal responses in mussels (Mytilus spp.). *Mar Pollut Bull*, 160, 111552. https://doi.org/10.1016/j.marpolbul.2020.111552

Cole, M., Lindeque, P., Fileman, E., Halsband, C., Goodhead, R., Moger, J., & Galloway, T. S., 2013. Microplastic ingestion by zooplankton. *Environ Sci Technol*, 47(12), 6646–6655. https://doi.org/10.1021/es400663f

Compa, M., Ventero, A., Iglesias, M., & Deudero, S., 2018. Ingestion of microplastics and natural fibres in Sardina pilchardus (Walbaum, 1792) and Engraulis encrasicolus (Linnaeus, 1758) along the Spanish Mediterranean coast. *Mar Pollut Bull*, 128, 89–96. https://doi.org/10.1016/j.marpolbul.2018.01.009

Cowger, W., Booth, A. M., Hamilton, B. M., Thaysen, C., Primpke, S., Munno, K., Lusher, A. L., Dehaut, A., Vaz, V. P., Liboiron, M., Devriese, L. I., Hermabessiere, L., Rochman, C., Athey, S. N., Lynch, J. M., De Frond, H., Gray, A., Jones, O. A. H., Brander, S., Steele, C., Moore, S., Sanchez, A., & Nel, H., 2020. Reporting guidelines to increase the reproducibility and comparability of research on microplastics. *Appl Spectrosc*, 0003702820930292.

da Costa Araújo, A. P., & Malafaia, G., 2021. Microplastic ingestion induces behavioral disorders in mice: A preliminary study on the trophic transfer effects via tadpoles and fish. *J Hazard Mater*, 401, 123263. https://doi.org/10.1016/j.jhazmat.2020.123263

De Falco, F., Gullo, M. P., Gentile, G., Di Pace, E., Cocca, M., Gelabert, L., Brouta-Agnésa, M., Rovira, A., Escudero, R., Villalba, R., Mossotti, R., Montarsolo, A., Gavignano, S., Tonin, C., & Avella, M., 2018. Evaluation of microplastic release caused by textile washing processes of synthetic fabrics. *Environ Pollut*, 236, 916–925. https://doi.org/10.1016/j.envpol.2017.10.057

de Sá, L. C., Oliveira, M., Ribeiro, F., Rocha, T. L., & Futter, M. N., 2018. Studies of the effects of microplastics on aquatic organisms: What do we know and where should we focus our efforts in the future? *Sci Total Environ*, 645, 1029–1039. https://doi.org/10.1016/j.scitotenv.2018.07.207

Dijk, F. van, Eck, G. V., Cole, M., Salvati, A., Bos, S., Gosens, R., & Melgert, B., 2020. Exposure to textile microplastic fibres impairs epithelial growth. *Eur Respir J*, 56(suppl 64). https://doi.org/10.1183/13993003.congress-2020.1972

Dris, R., Gasperi, J., Mirande, C., Mandin, C., Guerrouache, M., Langlois, V., & Tassin, B., 2017. A first overview of textile fibres, including microplastics, in indoor and outdoor environments. *Environ Pollut*, 221, 453–458. https://doi.org/10.1016/j.envpol.2016.12.013

El-Gendy, A. H., Augustyniak, M., Toto, N. A., Al Farraj, S., & El-Samad, L. M., 2020. Oxidative stress parameters, DNA damage and expression of HSP70 and MT in midgut of Trachyderma hispida (Forskål, 1775) (Coleoptera: Tenebrionidae) from a textile industry area. *Environ Pollut*, 267, 115661. https://doi.org/10.1016/j.envpol.2020.115661

Erdle, L. M., 2020. Microplastics Impacts [Environmental charity dedicated to scientific research and public education on Georgian Bay's aquatic ecosystem]. *Georgian Bay Forever*. Retrieved from https://georgianbayforever.org/microplastics-impacts/

Everaert, G., Van Cauwenberghe, L., De Rijcke, M., Koelmans, A. A., Mees, J., Vandegehuchte, M., & Janssen, C. R., 2018. Risk assessment of microplastics in the ocean: Modelling approach and first conclusions. *Environ Pollut*, 242, 1930–1938.

Galvão, A., Aleixo, M., De Pablo, H., Lopes, C., & Raimundo, J., 2020. Microplastics in wastewater: Microfibre emissions from common household laundry. *Environ Sci Pollut R*, 27(21), 26643–26649. https://doi.org/10.1007/s11356-020-08765-6

Garcia, S., Cordeiro, A., Nääs, I. de A., & Costa Neto, P. L. de O., 2019. The sustainability awareness of Brazilian consumers of cotton clothing. *J Clean Prod*, 215, 1490–1502. https://doi.org/10.1016/j.jclepro.2019.01.069

Gavigan, J., Kefela, T., Macadam-Somer, I., Suh, S., & Geyer, R., 2020. Synthetic microfibre emissions to land rival those to waterbodies and are growing. *PLoS ONE*, 13.

Gelberg, H., 2018. Pathophysiological mechanisms of gastrointestinal toxicity. In *Comprehensive Toxicology* (pp. 139–178). Elsevier. https://doi.org/10.1016/B978-0-12-801238-3.10923-7

Geyer, R., 2020. Chapter 2 – Production, use, and fate of synthetic polymers. In T. M. Letcher (Ed.), *Plastic Waste and Recycling* (pp. 13–32). Academic Press. https://doi.org/10.1016/B978-0-12-817880-5.00002-5

Grancaric, A. M., Tarbuk, A., & Pusic, T., 2005. Electrokinetic properties of textile fabrics. *Color Technol*, 121(4), 221–227. https://doi.org/10.1111/j.1478-4408.2005.tb00277.x

Hartline, N. L., Bruce, N. J., Karba, S. N., Ruff, E. O., Sonar, S. U., & Holden, P. A., 2016. Microfibre masses recovered from conventional machine washing of new or aged garments. *Environ Sci Technol*, 50(21), 11532–11538. https://doi.org/10.1021/acs.est.6b03045

Hermabessiere, L., Dehaut, A., Paul-Pont, I., Lacroix, C., Jezequel, R., Soudant, P., & Duflos, G., 2017. Occurrence and effects of plastic additives on marine environments and organisms: a review. *Chemosphere*, 182, 781–793.

Hernandez, L. M., Xu, E. G., Larsson, H. C. E., Tahara, R., Maisuria, V. B., & Tufenkji, N., 2019. Plastic teabags release billions of microparticles and nanoparticles into tea. *Environ Sci Technol*, 53(21), 12300–12310. https://doi.org/10.1021/acs.est.9b02540

Hicks, D. G., Judkins, A. R., Sickel, J. Z., Rosier, R. N., Puzas, J. E., & O'keefe, R. J., 1996. Granular histiocytosis of pelvic lymph nodes following total hip arthroplasty. The presence of wear debris, cytokine production, and immunologically activated macrophages*. *J Bone Joint Surg*, 78(4), 482–496. https://doi.org/10.2106/00004623-199604000-00002

Hope, J. A., Coco, G., & Thrush, S. F., 2020. Effects of polyester microfibres on microphytobenthos and sediment-dwelling infauna. *Environ Sci Technol*, 54(13), 7970–7982. https://doi.org/10.1021/acs.est.0c00514

Horn, D. A., Granek, E. F., & Steele, C. L., 2020. Effects of environmentally relevant concentrations of microplastic fibres on Pacific mole crab (Emerita analoga) mortality and reproduction. *Limnol Oceanogr Lett*, 5(1), 74–83. https://doi.org/10.1002/lol2.10137

Ibrahim, Y. S., Tuan Anuar, S., Azmi, A. A., Wan Mohd Khalik, W. M. A., Lehata, S., Hamzah, S. R., Ismail, D., Ma, Z. F., Dzulkarnaen, A., Zakaria, Z., Mustaffa, N., Tuan Sharif, S. E., & Lee, Y., 2021. Detection of microplastics in human colectomy specimens. *JGH Open*, 5(1), 116–121. https://doi.org/10.1002/jgh3.12457

Ivanković, T., & Hrenović, J., 2010. Surfactants in the Environment. *Arch Ind Hyg Tox*, 61(1), 95–110. https://doi.org/10.2478/10004-1254 61-2010-1943

Jabeen, K., Li, B., Chen, Q., Su, L., Wu, C., Hollert, H., & Shi, H., 2018. Effects of virgin microplastics on goldfish (Carassius auratus). *Chemosphere*, 213, 323–332. https://doi.org/10.1016/j.chemosphere.2018.09.031

Jacob, H., Besson, M., Swarzenski, P. W., Lecchini, D., & Metian, M., 2020. Effects of virgin micro- and nanoplastics on fish: Trends, meta-analysis, and perspectives. *Environ Sci Technol*, 54(8), 4733–4745. https://doi.org/10.1021/acs.est.9b05995

Jemec, A., Horvat, P., Kunej, U., Bele, M., & Kržan, A., 2016. Uptake and effects of microplastic textile fibres on freshwater crustacean Daphnia magna. *Environ Pollut*, 219, 201–209. https://doi.org/10.1016/j.envpol.2016.10.037

Kang, J.-H., Kwon, O.-Y., Hong, S. H., & Shim, W. J., 2020. Can zooplankton be entangled by microfibres in the marine environment?: Laboratory studies. *Water*, 12(12), 3302. https://doi.org/10.3390/w12123302

Kelly, M. R., Lant, N. J., Kurr, M., & Burgess, J. G., 2019. Importance of water-volume on the release of microplastic fibres from laundry. *Environ Sci Technol*, 53(20), 11735–11744. https://doi.org/10.1021/acs.est.9b03022

Kim, L., Kim, S. A., Kim, T. H., Kim, J., & An, Y.-J., 2021. Synthetic and natural microfibres induce gut damage in the brine shrimp Artemia franciscana. *Aquat Toxicol*, 232, 105748. https://doi.org/10.1016/j.aquatox.2021.105748

Kokalj, A. J., Kunej, U., & Skalar, T., 2018. Screening study of four environmentally relevant microplastic pollutants: Uptake and effects on Daphnia magna and Artemia franciscana. *Chemosphere*, 208, 522–529. https://doi.org/10.1016/j.chemosphere.2018.05.172

Kolandhasamy, P., Su, L., Li, J., Qu, X., Jabeen, K., & Shi, H., 2018. Adherence of microplastics to soft tissue of mussels: A novel way to uptake microplastics beyond ingestion. *Sci Tot Environ*, 610–611, 635–640. https://doi.org/10.1016/j.scitotenv.2017.08.053

Kooi, M., & Koelmans, A. A., 2019. Simplifying microplastic via continuous probability distributions for size, shape, and density. *Environ Sci Tech Let*, 6(9), 551–557. https://doi.org/10.1021/acs.estlett.9b00379

Kosuth, M., Mason, S. A., & Wattenberg, E. V., 2018. Anthropogenic contamination of tap water, beer, and sea salt. *PLoS ONE*, 13(4), e0194970. https://doi.org/10.1371/journal.pone.0194970

Kroon, F. J., Motti, C. E., Jensen, L. H., & Berry, K. L. E., 2018. Classification of marine microdebris: A review and case study on fish from the Great Barrier Reef, Australia. *Sci Rep*, 8(1), 16422. https://doi.org/10.1038/s41598-018-34590-6

Kwon, D., Yi, S., Jung, S., & Kwon, E. E., 2021. Valorization of synthetic textile waste using $CO2$ as a raw material in the catalytic pyrolysis process. *Environ Pollut*, 268, 115916. https://doi.org/10.1016/j.envpol.2020.115916

Ladewig, S. M., Bao, S., & Chow, A. T., 2015. Natural fibres: A missing link to chemical pollution dispersion in aquatic environments. *Environ Sci Technol*, 49(21), 12609–12610. https://doi.org/10.1021/acs.est.5b04754

Lant, N. J., Hayward, A. S., Peththawadu, M. M. D., Sheridan, K. J., & Dean, J. R., 2020. Microfibre release from real soiled consumer laundry and the impact of fabric care products and washing conditions. *PLoS ONE*, 15(6), e0233332. https://doi.org/10.1371/journal.pone.0233332

Li, L., Frey, M., & Browning, K. J., 2010. Biodegradability study on cotton and polyester fabrics. *J Eng Fiber and Fabr*, 5(4), 155892501000500. https://doi.org/10.1177/155892501000500406

Liebezeit, G., & Liebezeit, E., 2015. Origin of synthetic particles in honeys. *Pol J Food Nutr Sci*, 65(2), 143–147. https://doi.org/10.1515/pjfns-2015-0025

Liu, H., Kwak, J. I., Wang, D., & An, Y.-J., 2021. Multigenerational effects of polyethylene terephthalate microfibres in Caenorhabditis elegans. *Environ Res*, 193, 110569. https://doi.org/10.1016/j.envres.2020.110569

Marn, N., Jusup, M., Kooijman, S. A. L. M., & Klanjscek, T., 2020. Quantifying impacts of plastic debris on marine wildlife identifies ecological breakpoints. *Ecol Lett*, 23(10), 1479–1487. https://doi.org/10.1111/ele.13574

McCormick, M. I., Chivers, D. P., Ferrari, M. C. O., Blandford, M. I., Nanninga, G. B., Richardson, C., Fakan, E. P., Vamvounis, G., Gulizia, A. M., & Allan, B. J. M., 2020. Microplastic exposure interacts with habitat degradation to affect behaviour and survival of juvenile fish in the field. *P Roy Soc B: Biol Sci*, 287(1937), 20201947. https://doi.org/10.1098/rspb.2020.1947

McIntyre, J. E. (Ed.), 2005. *Synthetic Fibres: Nylon, Polyester, Acrylic, Polyolefin.* Taylor & Francis US.

Meiyazhagan, S., Yugeswaran, S., Ananthapadmanabhan, P. V., & Suresh, K., 2020. Process and kinetics of dye degradation using microplasma and its feasibility in textile effluent detoxification. *J Water Proc Eng*, 37, 101519. https://doi.org/10.1016/j.jwpe.2020.101519

Mendrik, F. M., Henry, T. B., Burdett, H., Hackney, C. R., Waller, C., Parsons, D. R., & Hennige, S. J., 2021. Species-specific impact of microplastics on coral physiology. *Environ Pollut*, 269, 116238. https://doi.org/10.1016/j.envpol.2020.116238

Miller, E., Sedlak, M., Lin, D., Box, C., Holleman, C., Rochman, C. M., & Sutton, R., 2021. Recommended best practices for collecting, analyzing, and reporting microplastics in environmental media: Lessons learned from comprehensive monitoring of San Francisco Bay. *J Hazard Mater*, 409, 124770. https://doi.org/10.1016/j.jhazmat.2020.124770

Mishra, S., Rath, C. charan, & Das, A. P., 2019. Marine microfibre pollution: A review on present status and future challenges. *Mar Pollut Bull*, 140, 188–197. https://doi.org/10.1016/j.marpolbul.2019.01.039

Mohsen, M., Zhang, L., Sun, L., Lin, C., Wang, Q., Liu, S., Sun, J., & Yang, H., 2021. Effect of chronic exposure to microplastic fibre ingestion in the sea cucumber Apostichopus japonicus. *Ecotox Environ Saf*, 209, 111794. https://doi.org/10.1016/j.ecoenv.2020.111794

Muthu, S. S., & Gardetti, M. A. (Eds.), 2020. *Sustainability in the Textile and Apparel Industries* (1st ed.). Springer. https://doi-org.proxy.lib.pdx.edu/10.1007/978-3-030-37929-2

Napper, I. E., & Thompson, R. C., 2016. Release of synthetic microplastic plastic fibres from domestic washing machines: Effects of fabric type and washing conditions. *Mar Pollut Bull*, 112(1–2), 39–45. https://doi.org/10.1016/j.marpolbul.2016.09.025

Napper, I. E., & Thompson, R. C., 2019. Environmental deterioration of biodegradable, oxo- biodegradable, compostable, and conventional plastic carrier bags in the sea, soil, and open- air over a 3-year period. *Envir Sci Technol*, 53(9), 4775–4783. https://doi.org/10.1021/acs.est.8b06984

Palsikowski, P. A., Roberto, M. M., Sommaggio, L. R. D., Souza, P. M. S., Morales, A. R., & Marin-Morales, M. A., 2018. Ecotoxicity evaluation of the biodegradable polymers PLA, PBAT and its blends using Allium cepa as test organism. *J Polym Environ*, 26(3), 938–945. https://doi.org/10.1007/s10924-017-0990-9

Pimentel, J. C., Avila, R., & Lourenco, A. G., 1975. Respiratory disease caused by synthetic fibres: A new occupational disease. *Thorax*, 30(2), 204–219. https://doi.org/10.1136/thx.30.2.204

Prendergast-Miller, M. T., Katsiamides, A., Abbass, M., Sturzenbaum, S. R., Thorpe, K. L., & Hodson, M. E., 2019. Polyester-derived microfibre impacts on the soil-dwelling earthworm Lumbricus terrestris. *Environ Pollut*, 251, 453–459. https://doi.org/10.1016/j.envpol.2019.05.037

Provencher, J. F., Covernton, G. A., Moore, R C., Horn, D. A., Conkle, J. L., & Lusher, A. L., 2020. Proceed with caution: The need to raise the publication bar for microplastics research. *Sci Total Environ*, 748, 141426. https://doi.org/10.1016/j.scitotenv.2020.141426

Qiao, R., Deng, Y., Zhang, S., Wolosker, M. B., Zhu, Q., Ren, H., & Zhang, Y., 2019. Accumulation of different shapes of microplastics initiates intestinal injury and gut microbiota dysbiosis in the gut of zebrafish. *Chemosphere*, 236, 124334. https://doi.org/10.1016/j.chemosphere.2019.07.065

Ragusa, A., Svelato, A., Santacroce, C., Catalano, P., Notarstefano, V., Carnevali, O., Papa, F., Rongioletti, M. C. A., Baiocco, F., Draghi, S., D'Amore, E., Rinaldo, D., Matta, M., & Giorgini, E., 2020. Plasticenta: First evidence of microplastics in human placenta. *Environ Int*, 146, 106274. https://doi.org/10.1016/j.envint.2020.106274

Remy, F., Collard, F., Gilbert, B., Compère, P., Eppe, G., & Lepoint, G., 2015. When microplastic is not plastic: The ingestion of artificial cellulose fibres by macrofauna living in seagrass macrophytodetritus. *Envir Sci Technol*, 49(18), 11158–11166. https://doi.org/10.1021/acs.est.5b02005

Rochman, C. M., 2018. Microplastics research – From sink to source. *Science*, 360(6384), 28–29. https://doi.org/10.1126/science.aar7734

Rochman, C. M., Brookson, C., Bikker, J., Djuric, N., Earn, A., Bucci, K., Athey, S., Huntington, A., McIlwraith, H., Munno, K., De Frond, H., Kolomijeca, A., Erdle, L., Grbic, J., Bayoumi, M., Borrelle, S. B., Wu, T., Santoro, S., Werbowski, L. M., Zhu, X., Giles, R. K., Hamilton, B. M., Thaysen, C., Kaura, A., Klasios, N., Ead, L., Kim, J., Sherlock, C., Ho, A., & Hung, C., 2019. Rethinking microplastics as a diverse contaminant suite. *Environ Toxicol Chem*, 38(4), 703–711. https://doi.org/10.1002/etc.4371

Rochman, C. M., Tahir, A., Williams, S. L., Baxa, D. V., Lam, R., Miller, J. T., Teh, F.-C., Werorilangi, S., & Teh, S. J., 2015. Anthropogenic debris in seafood: Plastic debris and fibres from textiles in fish and bivalves sold for human consumption. *Sci Rep*, 5(1), 14340. https://doi.org/10.1038/srep14340

Romanó de Orte, M., Clowez, S., & Caldeira, K., 2019. Response of bleached and symbiotic sea anemones to plastic microfibre exposure. *Environ Pollut*, 249, 512–517. https://doi.org/10.1016/j.envpol.2019.02.100

Ross, P. S., Chastain, S., Vassilenko, E., Etemadifar, A., Zimmermann, S., Quesnel, S.-A., Eert, J., Solomon, E., Patankar, S., Posacka, A. M., & Williams, B., 2021. Pervasive distribution of polyester fibres in the Arctic Ocean is driven by Atlantic inputs. *Nature Commun*, 12(1), 106. https://doi.org/10.1038/s41467-020-20347-1

Rossi, G., Manfrin, A., & Lutolf, M. P., 2018. Progress and potential in organoid research. *Nature Rev Genet*, 19(11), 671–687. https://doi.org/10.1038/s41576-018-0051-9

Sait, S. T. L., Sørensen, L., Kubowicz, S., Vike-Jonas, K., Gonzalez, S. V., Asimakopoulos, A. G., & Booth, A. M., 2021. Microplastic fibres from synthetic textiles: Environmental degradation and additive chemical content. *Environ Pollut*, 268, 115745. https://doi.org/10.1016/j.envpol.2020.115745

Schenker, U., Chardot, J., Missoum, K., Vishtal, A., & Bras, J., 2020. Short communication on the role of cellulosic fibre-based packaging in reduction of climate change impacts. *Carbohyd Polym*, 254, 117248. https://doi.org/10.1016/j.carbpol.2020.117248

sewguide.com., n.d. Fibres-types.png (700×400). *sewguide.com* [Digital]. Retrieved March 2, 2021, from https://sewguide.com/wp-content/uploads/2019/03/fibres-types.png

Shruti, V. C., & Kutralam-Muniasamy, G., 2019. Bioplastics: Missing link in the era of Microplastics. *Sci Total Environ*, 697, 134139. https://doi.org/10.1016/j.scitotenv.2019.134139

Sillanpää, M., & Sainio, P., 2017. Release of polyester and cotton fibres from textiles in machine washings. *Environ Sci Pollut R*, 24(23), 19313–19321. https://doi.org/10.1007/s11356-017-9621-1

Smiroldo, G., Balestrieri, A., Pini, E., & Tremolada, P., 2019. Anthropogenically altered trophic webs: Alien catfish and microplastics in the diet of Eurasian otters. *Mammal Res*, 64(2), 165–174. https://doi.org/10.1007/s13364-018-00412-3

Song, Y., Cao, C., Qiu, R., Hu, J., Liu, M., Lu, S., Shi, H., Raley-Susman, K. M., & He, D., 2019. Uptake and adverse effects of polyethylene terephthalate microplastics fibres on terrestrial snails (Achatina fulica) after soil exposure. *Environ Pollut*, 250, 447–455. https://doi.org/10.1016/j.envpol.2019.04.066

Stienbarger, C.D., Joseph, J., Athey, S.N., Monteleone, B., Watanabe, W., Andrady, A.L., Seaton, P., Taylor, A.R., Brander, S.M., 2021. Direct ingestion, trophic transfer, and physiological effects of microplastics in the early life stages of Centropristis striata, a commercially and recreationally valuable fishery species. *Environ Pollut* (in revision)

Stone, C., Windsor, F. M., Munday, M., & Durance, I., 2020. Natural or synthetic – How global trends in textile usage threaten freshwater environments. *Sci Total Environ*, 718, 134689. https://doi.org/10.1016/j.scitotenv.2019.134689

Stratton-Powell, A. A., Pasko, K. M., Lal, S., Brockett, C. L., & Tipper, J. L., 2019. Biologic Responses to Polyetheretherketone (PEEK) wear particles. In *Peek Biomaterials Handbook* (2nd ed., pp. 367–384). Portland State University. https://doi.org/10.1016/B978-0-12-812524-3.00022-3

Straub, S., Hirsch, P. E., & Burkhardt-Holm, P., 2017. Biodegradable and petroleum-based microplastics do not differ in their ingestion and excretion but in their biological effects in a freshwater invertebrate Gammarus fossarum. *Int J Env Res Pub He*, 14(7), 774. https://doi.org/10.3390/ijerph14070774

Taylor, M. L., Gwinnett, C., Robinson, L. F., & Woodall, L. C., 2016. Plastic microfibre ingestion by deep-sea organisms. *Sci Rep*, 6(1), 33997. https://doi.org/10.1038/srep33997

Urban, R. M., Jacobs, J. J., Tomlinson, M. J., Gavrilovic, J., Black, J., & Peoc'h, M., 2000. Dissemination of wear particles to the liver, spleen, and abdominal lymph nodes of patients with hip or knee replacement*. *JBJS*, 82(4), 457.

Watts, A. J. R., Urbina, M. A., Corr, S., Lewis, C., & Galloway, T. S., 2015. Ingestion of plastic microfibres by the crab carcinus maenas and its effect on food consumption and energy balance. *Envir Sci Technol*, 49(24), 14597–14604. https://doi.org/10.1021/acs.est.5b04026

Welden, N. A. C., & Cowie, P. R., 2016. Long-term microplastic retention causes reduced body condition in the langoustine, Nephrops norvegicus. *Environ Pollut*, 218, 895–900. https://doi.org/10.1016/j.envpol.2016.08.020

White, J. W., Cole, B. J., Cherr, G. N., Connon, R. E., & Brander, S. M., 2017. Scaling up endocrine disruption effects from individuals to populations: Outcomes depend on how many males a population needs. *Envir Sci Technol*, 51(3), 1802–1810. https://doi.org/10.1021/acs.est.6b05276

Woodall, L. C., Sanchez-Vidal, A., Canals, M., Paterson, G. L. J., Coppock, R., Sleight, V., Calafat, A., Rogers, A. D., Narayanaswamy, B. E., & Thompson, R. C., 2014. The deep sea is a major sink for microplastic debris. *Roy Soc Open Sci*, 1(4), 140317. https://doi.org/10.1098/rsos.140317

Woods, M. N., Hong, T. J., Baughman, D., Andrews, G., Fields, D. M., & Matrai, P. A., 2020. Accumulation and effects of microplastic fibres in American lobster larvae (Homarus americanus). *Mar Pollut Bull*, 157, 111280. https://doi.org/10.1016/j.marpolbul.2020.111280

Worm, B., Barbier, E. B., Beaumont, N., Duffy, J. E., Folke, C., Halpern, B. S., Jackson, J. B. C., Lotze, H. K., Micheli, F., Palumbi, S. R., Sala, E., Selkoe, K. A., Stachowicz, J. J., & Watson, R., 2006. Impacts of biodiversity loss on ocean ecosystem services. *Science*, 314(5800), 787–790. https://doi.org/10.1126/science.1132294

Yin, L., Chen, B., Xia, B., Shi, X., & Qu, K., 2018. Polystyrene microplastics alter the behavior, energy reserve and nutritional composition of marine jacopever (Sebastes schlegelii). *J Hazard Mater*, 360, 97–105. https://doi.org/10.1016/j.jhazmat.2018.07.110

Zambrano, M. C., Pawlak, J. J., Daystar, J., Ankeny, M., Cheng, J. J., & Venditti, R. A., 2019. Microfibres generated from the laundering of cotton, rayon and polyester based fabrics and their aquatic biodegradation. *Mar Pollut Bull*, 142, 394–407. https://doi.org/10.1016/j.marpolbul.2019.02.062

Zambrano, M. C., Pawlak, J. J., Daystar, J., Ankeny, M., Goller, C. C., & Venditti, R. A., 2020. Aerobic biodegradation in freshwater and marine environments of textile microfibres generated in clothes laundering: Effects of cellulose and polyester-based microfibres on the microbiome. *Mar Pollut Bull*, 151, 110826. https://doi.org/10.1016/j.marpolbul.2019.110826

Zarus, G. M., Muianga, C., Hunter, C. M., & Pappas, R. S., 2021. A review of data for quantifying human exposures to micro and nanoplastics and potential health risks. *Sci Total Environ*, 756, 144010. https://doi.org/10.1016/j.scitotenv.2020.144010

Zhao, S., Zhu, L., & Li, D., 2016. Microscopic anthropogenic litter in terrestrial birds from Shanghai, China: Not only plastics but also natural fibres. *Sci Total Environ*, 550, 1110–1115. https://doi.org/10.1016/j.scitotenv.2016.01.112

Ziajahromi, S., Kumar, A., Neale, P. A., & Leusch, F. D. L., 2017. Impact of microplastic beads and fibres on Waterflea (Ceriodaphnia dubia) survival, growth, and reproduction: implications of single and mixture exposures. *Envir Sci Technol*, 51(22), 13397–13406. https://doi.org/10.1021/acs.est.7b03574

Zimmermann, L., Dombrowski, A., Völker, C., & Wagner, M., 2020. Are bioplastics and plant-based materials safer than conventional plastics? In vitro toxicity and chemical composition. *Environ Int*, 145. https://doi.org/10.1016/j.envint.2020.106066

Zubris, K. A. V., & Richards, B. K., 2005. Synthetic fibres as an indicator of land application of sludge. *Environ Pollut*, 138(2), 201–211. https://doi.org/10.1016/j.envpol.2005.04.013

Zuo, L.-Z., Li, H.-X., Lin, L., Sun, Y.-X., Diao, Z.-H., Liu, S., Zhang, Z.-Y., & Xu, X.-R., 2019. Sorption and desorption of phenanthrene on biodegradable poly(butylene adipate co-terephtalate) microplastics. *Chemosphere*, 215, 25–32. https://doi.org/10.1016/j.chemosphere.2018.09.173

5

TOXIC CHEMICALS IN TEXTILES AND THE ROLE OF MICROPLASTIC FIBRES AS A SOURCE AND VECTOR FOR CHEMICALS TO THE ENVIRONMENT

Bethanie Carney Almroth and Samantha Athey

1 Introduction

A recent estimation of national and regional chemical inventories across the globe indicated that over 350,000 chemicals (including individual compounds and chemical mixtures) have been registered for production and use (Wang, Walker et al. 2020); many of these are unknown and understudied, and many are used in the production of textiles (Commission 2003; Lacasse and Baumann 2004; ECHA 2021). The European REACH database of registered substances currently include 2,233 registration dossiers within the Sector of Use 'SU 5: manufacture of textiles, leather and fur' (as per April 2021). Three-quarters of these registered substances are textile dyes and finishing products (ECIA 2021).

The textile industry is regarded as one of the most chemical intensive industries on the planet. In fact, over 8,000 different chemical compounds are used across the entire production chain from agricultural production of natural materials and synthesis of manufactured materials from fossil fuels, to fibre production, garment production, shipment, storage, sales and consumer use (Lacasse and Baumann 2004; KemI 2013). Globally, nearly 43 million tonnes of chemicals and 93 billion cubic meters of water are used in textile production annually, rendering the textile industry one of the largest consumers of both chemicals and water (Kant 2012; Verma, Dash et al. 2012). More than 3,600 individual dyes are used in the production of textiles, and these are often discharged in a textile mill's industrial wastewater effluent, which on average produce 1.6 million liters of effluent per day at a site producing 8,000 kg of fabric (Kant 2012). In addition to chemicals, synthetic or microplastic fibres (the basic unit of textiles) can also become dislodged and released into the environment via contaminated wastewater from textile production (Zhou, Zhou et al. 2020; Chan, Park et al. 2021). For these reasons, the textile industry, including mass-produced and inexpensive 'fast fashion', has accordingly

DOI: 10.4324/9781003165385-6

been identified as having a high environmental price (Niinimäki, Peters et al. 2020; Liu, Liang et al. 2021).

Textile fibre production has increased from a global average of 7.6 kg fibres per person in 1995 to approximately 14 kg per person in 2018 (Peters, Li et al. 2021), with current average European consumption at 19 kg per EU citizen annually (JRC 2014). Similarly, the production of chemicals used in textile manufacturing has seen a steady linear increase since the 1930s (Alpizar, Backhaus et al. 2019). The current state of textile production and consumption is in direct conflict with the goals of a circular economy, which calls for decreases in linear models of production (from resource extraction to production to consumer use to waste management), and for a decrease in the numbers and amounts of chemicals intentionally added into consumer products, which can inhibit safe material recycling.

Production and consumption of textiles continues to increase, as does the proportion of fibres used that are synthetic in origin (Stone, Windsor et al. 2020). Currently, the market is dominated by a small number of synthetic polymers, namely polyester (polyethylene terephthalate; PET), nylon (PA), acrylic (polyacrylonitrile; PAN), and elastane, also called spandex (polyurethane; PU) (Ellen MacArthur Foundation 2017). Most synthetic polymers are produced using fossil fuels as raw materials (Law 2019). Textile fibres may also be produced from natural and regenerated materials, including both animal-based and plant-based fibres (Wilding 1995). Examples of animal-based or proteinaceous fibres include wool, angora, mohair, cashmere and silk. Common cellulosic or plant-based fibres include cotton, linen and hemp. Regenerated natural materials can also be used to create semi-synthetic, also called regenerated, fibres, such as lyocell and rayon or viscose (described further in chapter by Granek et al.).

Numerous chemicals are used in the production of fibres made from both natural materials (e.g., pesticides used in cotton farming) and synthetic raw materials (petrochemicals and additives used in production of polymers). Further, finishing treatments are often applied to final garments, including pigments and dyes, wrinkle-resistance finishing, antimicrobial agents, water- and stain-resistant coatings (KemI 2015). Although they are derived from natural sources, semi-synthetic and natural fibres also undergo heavy chemical processing, requiring the use of numerous chemicals, to achieve desired market qualities and therefore cannot be considered chemical-free or 'eco-friendly' (Islam 2020).

The textile production sites, where most chemical usage associated with textile occurs, are often located in low-wage countries, where workers, the local communities and environment are directly impacted by chemical pollution introduced to waterways via industrial wastewater. Exposure to chemicals is not limited to contaminated waterways as chemical exposure during use of finished textiles on the consumer market can also occur via dermal absorption (Morrison, Weschler et al. 2016; Licina, Morrison et al. 2019). Further, consumer laundering of textiles may lead to the unintentional release of textile chemicals to the environment (discussed further in Section 4.2) (Schreder and La Guardia 2014, Saini, Rauert et al. 2016). Chemical release from textiles is not limited to production and consumer use phases, as the management of textile waste can lead to further environmental contamination as discarded materials are either landfilled, escape to the environment as litter or are incinerated (Mitrano, Limpiteeprakan et al. 2016; Stubbings, Kajiwara et al. 2016; Harrad, Drage et al. 2020). The Swedish Chemical Agency estimates that the degradation of textiles in landfills accounts for the release of over 2,000 tonnes of hazardous colorants in the EU each year (KemI 2013). Humans may thus be exposed to chemical additives and residues in textiles both directly (during the textile use phase) and indirectly through releases to the environment throughout the product's life cycle. These chemicals include azo-dyes (organic compounds that often contain functional groups that are aromatic rings), pigments (can include metals), flame-retardants, fluorinated compounds used in surface treatments, phthalates, among others. Further, many of these compounds have known adverse human and environmental health impacts, often acting as endocrine disruptors, allergens and/or carcinogens (Kemi 2016; Wang, Zhang et al. 2019; Carney Almroth, Cartine et al. 2021).

While the release of additive chemicals from textiles is of concern, the degradation or shedding of textiles during production and consumer use (including laundering) also results in the release of large amounts of synthetic microfibres to the environment (Zhou, Zhou et al. 2020; Ramasamy and Subramanian 2021). Textile microfibres have now been documented in nearly every environmental compartment on Earth, including surface and deep-sea waters, limnetic systems, soil, snow and throughout the atmosphere; from urbanized areas close to land-based sources to remote regions (e.g., deep-sea, polar regions, remote mountain catchments) (Jamieson, Brooks et al. 2019; Athey and Erdle 2021; Ross, Chastain et al. 2021). When the fabric is made of synthetic materials (i.e., plastic), the fibres generated are defined as microplastics (Napper and Thompson 2016).

Microfibres, as defined in the microplastics literature, are contaminant particles that are flexible, have relatively equal thickness throughout their length, have a length-to-width aspect ratio of at least 3 to 1, and originate from textiles, upholstery, carpeting, among other fibrous sources (Liu, Yang et al. 2019; Rochman, Brookson et al. 2019). Typically, a specific size classification is also incorporated into this definition of microfibres, as with microplastics as a whole. The size classifications of microfibres vary in the literature, but it is most commonly reported as fibres 1–5000 μm in length (Browne, Crump et al. 2011; Liu, Yang et al. 2019). Recently, there has been an effort to broaden the environmental science definition of microfibres to include anthropogenic fibres created from natural and regenerated feedstocks (Athey and Erdle 2021). The definition of the term 'microfibres' used widely in the microplastics field varies from the textile industry, which defines a 'microfibre' specifically as an ultra-fine manufactured fibre that is less than 1 denier in width (MicrofiberConsortium 2020). For this reason, the textile industry uses the term 'fibre fragment' to describe the fibres that are released from the main textile construction (MicrofiberConsortium 2020). Keeping consistent with the large body of environmental science literature on the topic, in this chapter, the term 'microfibre' will be used generally and interchangeably with the term 'fibre' to refer to the basic elements of textile, including those released into the environment (see Table 5.1 for terminology and definitions used in this chapter).

Shedding of microfibres, including synthetic fibres, during textile production, laundering and wear is well-documented (see chapter by Thompson and Napper and (Hernandez, Nowack et al. 2017)). Several textile industrial processes such as

TABLE 5.1 List of reference terms and definitions

Term	Abbreviation	Definition
Microfibre or fibre		As defined in an environmental science context and throughout the present chapter, a microfibre is a contaminant particle that is flexible, has relatively equal thickness throughout their length, has a length-to-width aspect ratio of at least 3 to 1, and originates from textiles, upholstery, carpeting, among other fibrous sources (Rochman et al. 2019).
Fibre fragment		The textile industry term for 'microfibre'. Describes short piece of textile fibre, broken from the main textile construction (MicrofibreConsortium 2020).
Microplastic	MP	Particle between 1 and 5000 μm in size derived from plastic materials (Browne et al. 2011).
Fast fashion		A global phenomenon to produce inexpensive clothing on a massive scale in response to changing fashion trends that has led to increased generation of textile waste (Liu et al. 2021).
Synthetic fibre		Fibres generated from synthetic or plastic materials, such as polyester, polypropylene and polyurethane.
Semi-synthetic or regenerated fibre		Fibers derived from regenerated natural materials that have been chemically processed and extruded in a similar fashion to those of synthetic origin. These include rayon or viscose fibres.
Natural fibre		Fibres derived directly from natural materials. Despite being called 'natural', the natural fibres used in textile production involve the use of numerous chemicals applied during production.
Chemical additive		Chemicals that are intentionally added into consumer products to enhance their inherent properties. Because these chemicals are not inherently bonded to the material in which they are incorporated, fibres may act as a source of chemical additives to the environment.

(Continued)

TABLE 5.1 (Continued)

Term	Abbreviation	Definition
Chemical contaminant		Chemicals, which are not directly used in the production of textiles, that may sorb to fibres from the environment. Fibres may act as vectors for these chemicals to move throughout the environment, including into biota.
Non-intentionally added substances	NIAS	These include chemicals that are not intentionally added during textile production, but may be incorporated into the material unintentionally. These include reaction byproducts, degradation products and contamination from the raw materials (Groh et al. 2019).
Endocrine disrupting compounds	EDC	Chemical compounds that disrupt normal endocrine function (KemI 2015).
Forever chemicals		This term refers to PFAS, which are the most persistent synthetic chemicals produced to date. They hardly degrade in the natural environment and have been found in the blood and breastmilk of people and wildlife all round the world. These chemicals are EDCs, immunotoxic, reprotoxic and possible carcinogens.
Per- and polyfluorinated alkyl substances	PFAS	A large chemical family of over 4,700 highly persistent synthetic chemicals, used on a wide range of consumer products due to their ability to repel both fats and water. Examples of uses include paper food packaging, textiles, cosmetics and electronics. They are also found in fire-fighting foam. PFAS are designated as persistent, bioaccumulative and toxic (PBT).

brushing and padding of fabrics release fibres into air and dust (Mellin, Jönsson et al. 2016). The fibre-laden dust itself can cause health problems for textile workers (Zarus, Muianga et al. 2021). Further, these microfibres may act as a vehicle for chemical exposure via accidental ingestion and inhalation of contaminated dust and air (Prata 2018). Fibres can also be shed during normal consumer use, such as wear and laundering, in non-occupational settings, where they can contaminate indoor air and dust (Dris, Gasperi et al. 2017; Carney Almroth, Åström et al. 2018; Tunahan Kaya, Yurtsever et al. 2018; Zhang, Zhao et al. 2020). The deposition of fibres onto surfaces, including cookware and food surfaces, as well as the incorporation into indoor dust and air is of concern as they may cause health complications upon inhalation and/or accidental ingestion. These pathways are of particular concern for infants and toddlers, who are at elevated risk for contaminant exposure via dust ingestion (Vethaak and Leslie 2016; Liu, Li et al. 2019). Finally, when released into the environment, textile fibres and their associated chemical mixtures may cause harm to biota (see chapter by Granek et al.). Here, we will discuss the presence of additive chemicals, which are intentionally added to textile fibres; the propensity of the fibres to act as vectors for chemical contaminants that unintentionally accumulate on fibres in the environment, including to biota; and the possible health consequences of such exposures.

2   Which chemicals are found in synthetic textiles?

Chemicals are used in all stages of the life cycle of textiles. This begins at the first stages including extraction of raw materials, commonly fossil fuel resources, through the production of synthetic polymers and extrusion of fibres. Chemicals are also used in dyeing and finishing of textiles, as well as preparation for shipping and storage (Lacasse and Baumann 2004; KemI 2013). Releases occur at all of these life stages (Li, Luo et al. 2020; Niinimäki, Peters et al. 2020) as shown in Figure 5.1.

2.1   Chemicals used in production of synthetic fibres

Production of synthetic polymer fibres begins with extraction of raw materials, including fossil fuels and monomers. These monomers are then used in polymerization reactions. Acrylic fibres are formed via addition polymerization, which joins monomers end to end. Condensation polymerization also joins monomers end to end, thereby liberating a by-product (e.g. water), and is used in the production of nylon. Polycondensation is used in production of polyethylene

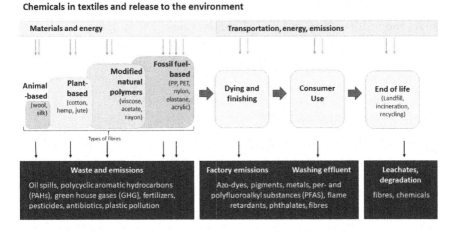

FIGURE 5.1 Chemicals in textiles and release into the environment

terephthalate (PET), whose constituent molecules contain ester functional groups. Many of these reactions will require the addition of catalysts, often oxygen or peroxides, while some reactions will require Ziegler-Natta catalysts such as titanium (III) chloride or titanium (IV) chloride (these catalysts contain inorganic transition metals and polymerize terminal alkenes containing a carbon-carbon double bond). Antimony (Sb) is a metalloid element commonly used in production of PET fibres, in the form of antimony oxides or antimony acetate, used to regulate polymerization, increasing the reaction rate and decreasing activation energy (Duh 2002; Dodd, Cordella et al. 2013). Caprolactam, a colorless organic compound and known irritant and mild toxicant, is commonly used in the polymerization of nylon and polyurethane synthetic leather (Dodd, Cordella et al. 2013). The polymer products used to create textile fibres will contain polymer chains, but may also contain unreacted monomers, intentionally added substances (IASes, such as TiCL3), including those driving polymerization reactions, antioxidants and UV-stabilizers. Synthetic polymers also contain non-intentionally added substances (NIASes) including reaction byproducts, degradation products and contamination from the raw materials. The types and amounts of NIASes present in synthetic materials are, by their nature, not well known (Groh, Backhaus et al. 2019).

While natural fibres are not the focus of this chapter, it is important to note that production of natural fibres also entails the use of large amounts of chemicals. Many garments or products will contain blends of synthetic and natural fibres. Therefore, garments may include substances used in production of plant-based fibres; pesticides, including herbicides, insecticides and rodenticides are applied during cultivation (Dolez and Benaddi 2018). The use of many chemicals applied in production of natural raw materials has been flagged as an important source of these compounds to the environment, and they pose great threats to environmental health (biodiversity loss, changes in microbial community function, such as N-fixation). However, greater amounts of chemicals are used in the production of synthetic textiles, and many of these remain in the marketed products (Luongo 2015). Biocides, for example, are also commonly applied to synthetic fibres and textiles during storage and transportation. This includes antimicrobial and antifungal agents like formaldehyde, arsenic and, in more modern materials, silver nanoparticles (Nayak and Padhye 2014).

2.2 Chemicals that are intentionally added to textiles and garments

Following production of raw materials and fibres, additive chemicals are used in the manufacturing of textiles and garments. Several reports document the chemicals found in consumer textiles (KemI 2013; KemI 2015). These are used to give the finished products specific qualities including stain or water resistance, anti-microbial properties, wrinkle resistance and dimensional stability, and flame resistance (Möller, Ahrens et al. 2010). Numerous studies have indicated that several important groups of synthetic chemicals used in textile production and finishing are toxic as discussed further in Section 3 (Rovira and Domingo 2019; Li, Luo et al. 2020). Polybrominated diphenyl ethers (PBDEs) are a group of brominated flame retardant chemicals used in textiles, and whose physical-chemical properties are similar to other environmental pollutants such as polychlorinated biphenyls (PCBs) and DDT. Many of these chemicals are persistent, bioaccumulative, toxic and have been identified as potential endocrine disrupting compounds (EDCs) (KemI 2015). Flame retardants, including PBDEs, are broadly used in textiles as well as other synthetic products, including the casing of electronic products, furniture foam and construction material (Wang, Peng et al. 2016). Perfluorinated chemicals (PFCs) are a group of chemicals that include per- and poly-fluorinated alkylated substances (PFAS). PFCs are applied to textiles as well as many other consumer products (e.g., food packaging, cookware and electronics) during production, as well as during consumer use. Perfluorohexanoic acid (PFHxA also referred to as 'C6') is a short-chained PFAS that is used to manufacture textiles with oil- and water-repellent properties. The German Environmental Agency (UBA) has proposed an EU restriction on PFHxA due to the risk they pose to the environment and human health (ECHA and Germany 2019). As with PBDEs, they are often persistent, bioaccumulative and toxic (Hill, Taylor et al. 2017). Phthalates comprise yet another problematic group of chemicals used as softening agents in plastic manufacturing. In textiles, phthalates are often used in polyvinyl chloride (PVC) prints and coatings used in decorative images on clothing items (Weil, Levchik et al. 2006). Numerous studies highlight phthalates as harmful to human reproduction and they are classified as EDCs (Meeker, Sathyanarayana et al. 2009).

Other chemicals commonly used in textile manufacturing include pigments and dyes. Traditional colorants, including pigments and dyes, can also have hazardous effects, such as an increased risk of cancer and developmental defects, and increased risk of allergy (Kemi 2016). Among the most toxic types of colorants are azo dyes, which produce carcinogenic degradation compounds when in contact with skin (Nguyen and Saleh 2016). This occurs when the dye molecules undergo oxidative-reduction reactions in microbiota, thereby releasing the mutagenic moieties (e.g. benzidine or p-phenylenediamine) present in the dyes (Chung 2016). Azo dyes currently constitute 60–70% of the global dye market (Singh, Chatterji et al. 2015). Textile industrial wastewater has been shown to carry high amounts of heavy metals, unfixed pigments and dyes, salts, persistent organic pollutants, as well as microfibres to the environment (Zhou, Zhou et al. 2020; Chan, Park et al. 2021; Kishor, Purchase et al. 2021). Of the 70,000 tonnes of dyes used in textile production annually, approximately 50% were discharged to textile industrial wastewater during manufacturing (Slokar and Majcen Le Marechal 1998), and while there have been advances in water usage, dye techniques and wastewater remediation, there is still evidence of environmental impacts and risks to aquatic organisms (Alves de Lima, Bazo et al. 2007; Tkaczyk, 2020 #3673).

There has been a push to for greener, more sustainable practices in the textile industry (Ellen MacArthur Foundation 2017; Palm, Cornell et al. 2021). The amounts of chemicals used in the production of textile garments has been the subject of much discussion. Generally, the weight of chemicals that are used during the production of textiles, including those that remain on the final products, exceeds the weight of the final material itself (Olsson, Posner et al. 2010; Lacasse and Baumann 2012). For example, 1 kg of cotton garments uses up to 3 kg of chemicals and final cotton garments can contain up to 30% chemical by weight, with many of these chemicals being hazardous to human and environmental health (discussed further in section 1.3) (Lacasse and Baumann 2012; Saxena, Raja et al. 2017). While the amount of chemicals used in the production of different textiles varies, synthetic textiles generally require 0.59 kg of chemicals for each kg of textile produced, not including the petrochemicals from which the plastic feedstocks are originally derived (Stone, Windsor et al. 2020; Palacios-Mateo, van der Meer et al. 2021). Initiatives to reduce the chemical footprint of synthetic textiles and fibres are many and can be applied at all stages of the life cycle of the products (Figure 5.1).

Chemical manufacturers can commit to avoiding the use of restricted chemicals, including a number of dyes and finishing treatments (e.g., to increase water resistance or anti-wrinkle and anti-static treatments). Safer alternatives are available in some cases, including oil- and formaldehyde-free dyes (Welch 1992; Ibrahim, Eid et al. 2019). In addition to substituting hazardous dyes with safer and more sustainable compounds, there are technological advancements, such as waterless dyeing processes, that reduce not only water usage but also contamination of industrial wastewater (Hussain and Wahab 2018). Another important group of chemicals that have been targeted for substitution in textile usage are PFCs (Ellen MacArthur Foundation 2017; Cousins, Richter et al. 2019; Cousins, Goldenman et al. 2019). Currently there are efforts within the textile industry to phase out the use of long-chained PFAS, the persistence and negative effects of which have been best demonstrated. However, these compounds are being replaced with alternative chemicals, such as fluorocarbon-based polymers, the direct effects of which remain unknown, but have been shown to release PFCs when washed and degraded (Ellen MacArthur Foundation 2017; Schellenberger, Jönsson et al. 2019; Sheriff, Debela et al. 2020; van der Veen, Hanning et al. 2020).

2.3   Chemicals that unintentionally accumulate on textiles

Because many chemicals used in the production of products within the home and office are not inherently bonded to the material and may migrate into the surrounding environment, it is possible for textiles to accumulate chemicals from the environment that were not introduced during production (Morrison, Li et al. 2015; Saini, Okeme et al. 2017; Morrison, Andersen et al. 2018). Sorption-desorption is a process by which a chemical interacts with another material as dictated by the physical-chemical properties of both the sorbate and sorbent. Sorption can involve absorption, wherein the sorbate penetrates into the sorbent; whereas in adsorption, the sorbate interacts with the surface of the sorbent (Schwarzenbach, Gschwend et al. 2016). Saini, Rauert et al. (2016) have demonstrated gas and particle phase accumulation of halogenated flame retardants and plasticizers (including PBDEs, phthalates and OPEs) from air to clothing. The sorption and desorption of chemicals from textiles is not limited to production and can continue throughout consumer use.

Clothing has a well-documented and large sorption capacity for volatile organic compounds (VOCs) (Mukhtar Abdul-Bari, McQueen et al. 2020) and semi-volatile organic compounds (SVOCs) (Morrison, Li et al. 2015; Saini, Okeme et al. 2017; Morrison, Andersen et al. 2018). In fact, the typical volume of clothing worn by an adult (2 m^2) can sequester the equivalent of 100 m^3 of air per day (Saini, Rauert et al. 2016). Clothing, carpeting, upholstery, among other textiles found in indoor environments can act as a sink and tertiary source for chemicals (Morrison, Li et al. 2015; Saini, Rauert et al. 2016; Morrison, Andersen et al. 2018). Further, synthetic microfibres emitted from textiles that enter the environment can sorb chemicals from surrounding environmental media, including PAHs, PCBs and other persistent organic pollutants (Wang, Chen et al. 2018; Lionetto and Esposito Corcione 2021; Jin, Yu et al. 2020).

3 Toxicity of textile chemicals and fibres

As described earlier, textile products and garments are constructed of fibres and treated with numerous chemicals. Within the field of microplastic research, including microfibres, attention has been placed on discerning the drivers of toxicity resulting from exposure (Prokić, Radovanović et al. 2018; Bucci, Tulio et al. 2020). Numerous factors should be considered when differentiating between impacts caused by exposure to physical particles versus chemical leachates. Firstly, the bulk of microplastic toxicity testing does not measure the effects of fibres, yet Bucci et al. (2020) suggest that the effects of fibre ingestion may differ from other particle shapes (e.g., microbeads or fragments). Further, the gut retention time of fibres can be longer than other particles (Qiao, Deng et al. 2019; Bour, Hossain et al. 2020). Secondly, the chemical composition of microfibres should be considered in toxicity testing. The chemical composition of microfibres can be complex, including the type of polymer (i.e., synthetic or natural) and associated cocktail of chemical additives and sorbed chemicals. Currently, only two studies have compared the effects of different polymer types on microfibre toxicity (Kim, Kim et al. 2021; Mateos-Cárdenas, O'Halloran et al. 2021). These studies suggest that microfibre toxicity of fibres created from natural polymers (e.g., cotton) are equivalent or only slightly reduced compared to synthetic fibres. However, more testing involving a variety of natural, semi-synthetic and synthetic polymers is needed to better understand the role of polymer composition in toxicity. Some of the chemicals intentionally added to textiles and those that are unintentionally sorbed from the environment are known toxicants that can have varying effects on exposed organisms (KemI 2015). The chemical mixture associated with fibres is of concern for biota as microfibres may act as vectors for chemical contaminants that unintentionally accumulate on fibres, as well as sources for chemicals intentionally applied to textile fibres during manufacturing.

3.1 Effects of exposure to fibres

As advances are made in the identification of microplastics in the environment, and techniques allow for analyses of smaller and smaller particles, researchers have been able to describe the presence of synthetic fibres in increasing numbers in numerous environmental matrices (Bergmann, Mützel et al. 2019; Allen, Allen et al. 2020; Athey, Adams et al. 2020). A recent study conducted by Athey and Erdle (2021) reviewed over 450 studies documenting microfibres in 17 environmental compartments, including soil, biota, surface and sub-surface waters, air, and dust. They reported that 58% of studies reported the presence of natural and semi-synthetic fibres (e.g., cotton, rayon), nearly half of which found non-synthetic fibres to be more abundant than synthetic fibres (Athey and Erdle 2021). These studies include those in marine and freshwater biota (Markic, Niemand et al. 2018; Athey, Adams et al. 2020; Le Guen, Suaria et al. 2020).

The number of studies addressing the effects of exposure to synthetic fibres in aquatic organisms have presented a knowledge gap, but recent studies have given us a better understanding of potential impacts. This is discussed in more detail in the chapter by Granek et al., describing impacts of fibre exposure on different levels of biological organization, from sub-cellular to population, and a wide range of organisms from different trophic levels and habitats. Here, we would like to emphasize the potentially different effects driven by either the fibres themselves, which could induce physical impacts via interactions with a particle, and/or the chemicals inherent to these materials. This differentiation can be determined experimentally if proper controls are employed, where organisms are exposed to 'control fibres', i.e., particles that are not contaminated with chemicals, or chemical exposures without fibres.

In vivo microfibre toxicity testing has been investigated using marine invertebrates (N. norvegicus, C. maenas, A. franciscana, M. liliana, and C. finmarchicus) (Watts, Urbina et al. 2015; Welden and Cowie 2016; Cole, Coppock et al. 2019; Hope, Coco et al. 2020; Kim, Kim et al. 2021), freshwater aquatic plants (L. minor) (Mateos-Cárdenas, O'Halloran et al. 2021), invertebrates (G. duebeni, C. riparius, D. magnus, H. azteca and C. elegans) (Au, Bruce et al. 2015; Jemec, Horvat et al. 2016; Belzagui, Buscio et al. 2021; Mateos-Cárdenas, O'Halloran et al. 2021; Setyorini, Michler-Kozma et al. 2021), fish (D. rerio) (Stienbarger, Joseph et al. 2021; Zhao, Qiao et al. 2021) and terrestrial invertebrates (E. crypticus, F. candida, P. scaber, A. fulica and O. nitens) (Song, Cao et al. 2019; Selonen, Dolar et al. 2020) as model organisms. The majority of these studies have addressed the impacts of microfibre ingestion on the gut, the main organ or exposure. For example, authors have shown that ingestion of fibres can induce histopathological damage to intestinal tissues, and subsequent changes in food intake and metabolism. In zebrafish, the extent of damage was positively correlated to fibre length, possible due to increased retention time of the longer fibres (Zhao, Qiao et al. 2021), and changes in metabolism of glycerophospholipids metabolism and fatty acyls was observed.

Important to note here is the fact that these studies do not attempt to delineate the relative importance of the particulate nature of the fibres versus the chemical contaminants (Bour, Hamann Sandgaard et al. 2021). Microplastics (and fibres) will always be a complex mix of numerous factors that can drive physiological responses and toxicity, including the material composition of the particle, the size, shape, density and surface properties of the particle, as well as the chemical profile of the particle (Hartmann, Hüffer et al. 2019). Chemical exposure routes can be many (e.g. direct uptake from the environment, uptake via food chain), and the role of ingested fibres as a vector remains to be determined.

3.2 Toxicity of virgin microplastic versus microplastic vectors

The microplastic research field has developed rapidly over the past 10 years, as have the collective knowledge base and research questions. A number of studies have compared the toxicity of fresh (virgin) plastics with that of 'weathered' plastics that have been in the environment and have had time to adsorb contaminants from the surrounding ocean or freshwater. However, few studies have applied this framework to fibres, as opposed to particles, so these is little information on the effects of virgin microfibres. Virgin MPs have been, in some cases, assumed to have no sorbed toxicants, while weathered ones would be expected to have accumulated toxicants from the environment (Jahnke, Arp et al. 2017). This type of exposure study can be instrumental in differentiating between the effects of an interaction with a particle and the chemicals sorbed to the particle, and might inform similar processes for microfibres, though sorption-desorption might differ between spheres and fibres, given differences in polymer type, crystallinity, surface area, etc. (Velez, Shashoua et al. 2018).

Seuront (2018) exposed intertidal snails (*Littorina littorea*) to leachates from both virgin and beached pellets. While virgin pellets slightly impaired vigilance and anti-predator behavior, beached pellets severely inhibited these behaviors. These results indicate that the biological effects from MP leachates may have major implications for organisms that rely on chemosensory cues to escape predation. In a study of medaka early life stages, Le Bihanic et al. (2020) exposed marine medaka *Oryzias melastigma* embryos and larvae to suspended microplastics spiked with benzo(a) pyrene (MP-BaP), perfluorooctanesulfonic acid (MP-PFOS) or benzophenone-3 (MP-BP3) for 12 days. The microplastics agglomerated on the surface of the egg chorion (outer membrane) but did not penetrate it. While embryos exposed to virgin MPs showed no toxic effects, those exposed to microplastics with PFOS had decreased embryonic survival and did not hatch. Larvae exposed to microplastics with BaP or with BP3 had reduced growth, developmental anomalies, and abnormal behavior. These investigators found that, compared to equivalent concentrations in the water, BaP and PFOS spiked on microplastics appeared to be more embryotoxic. These results suggest pollutant transfer by direct contact of microplastics on fish embryos. Rios-Fuster et al. (2021) performed a 21-day exposure of *Sparus aurata* juveniles to virgin and weathered microplastics. Fish were subsequently analyzed for a suite of enzyme biomarkers and behavioral changes, specifically social interactions and feeding behavior. While results indicated an increase in cellular stress from virgin microplastics, a significantly larger stress response, measured as oxidative stress, resulted from weathered microplastics. Behavioral effects of microplastic exposure indicated that fish exposed to either virgin or weathered microplastics were significantly bolder during social interactions than controls. It is important to note here that other studies have shown the opposite, where aging microplastics in the environment can reduce toxicity (Schür, Weil et al. 2021). Microplastics that have been weathered in the marine environment can thus produce a greater physiological response than virgin microplastics, but the opposite may also be true, owing to complex process of biofouling and chemical leaching.

3.3 Toxicity of chemicals associated with textiles

Many chemicals used in production of textiles have been shown to cause toxic effects in numerous organisms. Following Figure 5.1, the first step of production is in fact the extraction of raw materials. Production of natural fibres often requires the use of pesticides. These are, by design, toxic to specific groups of organisms (microbes, pests) but can also exhibit toxicity in non-target organisms (DeLorenzo, Scott et al. 2001; Lawrence, Neu et al. 2016; Nagy, Duca et al. 2020; Singh and Leppanen 2020). Residues of pesticides, or their degradation products, have been identified in cotton fibres, raising concerns about waste from fibre production, and exposure to the chemicals via the fibres themselves (Ma, Dong et al. 2019).

Synthetic fibres, however, are usually produced from fossil fuels, for example PET, and the environmental pollution association with extraction practices, and the release of numerous chemical compound at this stage, is well described (Law 2019). Once the raw materials have been obtained, numerous compounds are used in production of plastic polymers from the monomer extracted from oil and gas. Caprolactam, which is commonly used in polymerization reactions, can affect the growth and physiology of environmental bacteria, though at relatively high concentrations (10 g/L) (Baxi 2013). The compound is also moderately toxic to rats, with a LD50 of 1.1 g/kg (Unger, Salerno et al. 1981).

Numerous chemicals applied during dyeing, finishing and shipping/storage are known toxicants. For example, azo dyes can induce genotoxicity in aquatic organisms (Al-Sabti 2000), and dyes used in blue jeans (e.g. Blue HFRL, benzopurpurine 4B, Everzol Navy Blue FBN, direct red 89 BNL) have agonistic and antagonistic estrogen activity (Bazin, Ibn Hadj Hassine et al. 2012). In addition, chemicals that are intentionally added to textiles during wet-dying phases of production, such as dimethyl siloxane and 2-methyl-4-isothiazolin-3-one, are major contributors to the toxic chemical footprint of the textile industry (Li, Luo et al. 2020).

Throughout the consumer-use stage of the textile life-cycle, chemicals may be released sorbed to fibres that are shed during use or laundering; partition into air or surrounding surfaces (including skin); or solubilized into wash water during washing (Schreder and La Guardia 2014; Saini, Rauert et al. 2016). In a recent study addressing leachates from several different consumer garments, including jeans, sportswear and towels, authors found induced toxicity on several different model systems for aquatic organisms, including both *in vivo* and *in vitro* studies with freshwater fish (Carney Almroth et al. 2021). Leachates were shown to be cytotoxic in rainbow trout gill cell lines, measured as decreased cell viability. The leachates produced from synthetic sportswear resulted in increased mortality in zebrafish embryos and decreased locomotion in surviving larvae. The authors also observed oxidative stress and cytochrome P450 induction in exposed trout, indicating that the leachates contained AhR receptor agonists (like PAHs) and redox cycling compounds.

4 The importance of textiles fibres as a source of additives and an exposure vector for chemicals

4.1 Mechanisms that drive chemical and microplastic interactions

When discussing the role of microplastic fibres as vectors for chemicals in the environment, there are two main categories of chemicals to be considered: (1) chemicals intentionally added to products during production and consumer use (detailed in Section 2.2) and (2) chemicals that are unintentionally accumulated from the environment (detailed in Section 2.3 and shown in Figure 5.2). Most studies focusing on sorption and desorption of chemicals to microplastic fibres have focused on the latter category of chemicals, including heavy metals, pharmaceuticals and organic contaminants (e.g., PAHs, PCBs) ((Brennecke, Duarte et al. 2016; Li, Zhang et al. 2018; Wang, Chen et al. 2018; Torres, Dioses-Salinas et al. 2021; Torres et al. 2021).

Several important factors affect the sorption and desorption of chemicals to microplastic, including microplastic textile fibres. These include physical properties of

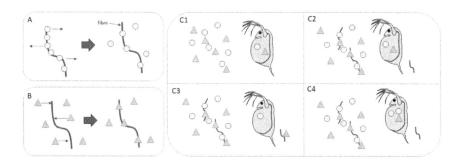

FIGURE 5.2 Chemicals from textiles can leach into the environment (A, O) and environmental chemicals can sorb onto particles including microfibres (B, Δ.). Further, there are three possible scenarios pertaining to the role of fibres as vectors in the bioaccumulation of chemicals in biota: (1) fibres may not affect bioaccumulation (C1-C2); (2) fibres may act as a sink of chemicals via a 'cleaning out' effect (C3); or (3) fibres may act as a vector, introducing chemicals to biota, thereby increasing bioaccumulation (C4)

Source: (Redrawn from Tourinho, Koči et al. 2019)

microplastics, such as particle size, crystallinity, degree of weathering and biofouling, and surface area, as well as the chemical properties of the particle, including polymer type, surface charge and hydrophobicity. Further, the properties of the environmental media in which the particle and chemical interacts dictates sorption-desorption processes (Fred-Ahmadu, Bhagwat et al. 2020; Jin, Yu et al. 2020). Understanding the sorption-desorption behaviors of environmental contaminants to microplastic fibres is critical for establishing their role as vectors for chemical exposure.

While most research on sorption behaviors of environmental contaminants to microplastics has focused on microplastic fragments or spheres (Rochman, Hoh et al. 2013; Velez, Shashoua et al. 2018; Bour, Sturve et al. 2020), a few studies have investigated sorption to synthetic microfibres released from textiles, including those composed of polyamide (or nylon), polyethylene and polyethylene terephthalate (or polyester). (Wang, Zhang et al. 2019; Jin, Yu et al. 2020; Lionetto and Esposito Corcione 2021). While textiles have been shown to accumulate chemicals that are not intentionally incorporated during production (discussed in Section 2.3), relatively few studies have investigated the sorptive capacity of the fibres released from textiles. Wang et al. demonstrated sorption of phenanthrene, a PAH, to nylon and polyethylene fibres (White, Clark et al. 2018).

While research has shown a high variation in sorption-desorption among chemicals and microplastic types (e.g., fibres versus spheres), chemical sorption may play an important role in determining bioavailability (Koelmans, Besseling et al. 2013). Fibres may not affect bioaccumulation at all; fibres may act as a sink of chemicals, decreasing bioaccumulation via a 'cleaning out' effect; or fibres may introduce chemicals to biota, increasing bioaccumulation (Tourinho, Koči et al. 2019).

4.2 Release of chemicals from textiles – synthetic fibres as vectors

It is well known that synthetic microfibres are released from textiles during laundering (De Falco et al. 2020; Napper and Thompson 2016; Zambrano et al. 2019). Zambrano et al. (2020) recently demonstrated that durable-press treatments (for wrinkle resistance) alter the mechanical properties of textile fibres and significantly increase microfibre release during washing. And conversely, not only can surface treatment with chemicals enhance microfibre emissions, these treatments may influence fibre degradation (Li, Frey et al. 2010; Zambrano, Pawlak et al. 2020) and the chemical sorption-desorption properties of fibres, although the latter has not been investigated.

Additionally, several studies have demonstrated that in addition to fibres, chemicals associated with textiles can be released from textiles during washing and drying. These include chemicals that are intentionally applied to textiles (e.g., PFCs, UV filters, bisphenol A, heavy metals) and those that are unintentionally accumulated from the environment (e.g., PBDEs, organophosphate esters or OPEs) (Schreder and La Guardia 2014; Saini, Rauert et al. 2016; Lindmark 2019; Schellenberger,

Jönsson et al. 2019; Wang, Zhang et al. 2019). However, recent work from Kvasnicka et al. (2021) suggests that laundering is not a significant pathway for chemicals to move from indoors to the outdoor environment when compared to other pathways, such as ventilation. While microfibres themselves have been shown to contain chemicals (Sait, Sørensen et al. 2021), their role as vectors in chemical release during laundering has not been directly investigated and remains unknown.

Not only can chemicals be released throughout production and consumer use (i.e., laundering), chemical additives can be released from textiles following disposal into landfill leachate (Mitrano, Limpiteeprakan et al. 2016; Stubbings, Kajiwara et al. 2016; Harrad, Drage et al. 2020). Microfibres are also documented in landfill leachate, most of which are likely released from textile waste in landfills (Su, Zhang et al. 2019; Sun, Zhu et al. 2021). However, the role of microfibres in chemical release from landfilled textile waste is currently unknown.

As far as we know, there is currently no empirical, experimental evidence demonstrating release of chemicals from textile fibres in the environment, confirming their potential importance as vectors and/or sources of chemicals. Sait et al. (2021) measured additives in microfibres, but samples were purchased from a supplier and not found in environmental samples. A number of studies have reported both categories of chemicals in dryer lint, which contains released fibres as well as dust, hair and soil (Stapleton, Dodder et al. 2005; Schecter, Shah et al. 2009). Collectively, these studies suggest that microfibres act as vectors for chemical release, but experimental evidence is still lacking. However, we hypothesize that releases from fibres are minimal compared to other emissions (e.g., ventilation, dust removal/disposal), likely due in part to the low total mass of microfibres discharged during laundering and the fact that evidence indicates that chemicals are removed from fibres and solubilized into wash water (Saini, Rauert et al. 2016; Kvasnicka, Cohen Huba et al. 2021).

4.3   Synthetic fibres in the environment, aging, weathering and chemical vectors

As with other synthetic polymer-particles, fibres from synthetic textiles will undergo degradation in the environment. All fibres, including synthetic, natural and semisynthetic or modified-natural fibres are susceptible to degradation via UV light. Sait et al. (2021) showed that both PET and nylon were significantly degraded after 10 months of UV exposure, with fragmentation and changes in surface morphology, while acrylic fibres were more persistent. In that study, the authors also used non-target chemical profiling to identify chemical leachates from both synthetic and wool fibres, finding, among others, monomers, degradation products and UV stabilizers in both pristine synthetic and wool fibres, as well as after 5- and 10-months of UV exposure.

There is a growing body of evidence to suggest that synthetic microfibres act as vectors for chemical release and transport in the environment; however, there are currently no studies that have directly investigated this. However, the significance of microplastics, including synthetic fibres, as vectors for chemicals to enter environmental compartments is debated. A number of authors have suggested that while microplastics may act as vectors for chemicals into the environment, their contribution to total chemical contamination is likely low compared to other sources of chemicals. This is likely true for biota, especially when compared to the flux of these compounds that is bioaccumulated from natural prey at levels that overwhelm exposure via microplastic fibres (Koelmans, Bakir et al. 2016). A few of studies have shown that, under laboratory conditions, ingested microplastic polyethylene spheres act as vectors for sorbed contaminants, which then cause adverse effects compared to pristine or uncontaminated particles (as discussed in Section 3.2; (Browne, Niven et al. 2013; Batel, Linti et al. 2016; Athey, Adams et al. 2020). However, these studies do not consider or compare other exposure pathways. When other pathways are considered, microplastics contribute little to the bioaccumulation of chemicals in environmental food webs (Bakir, O'Connor et al. 2016; Koelmans, Bakir et al. 2016; Besseling, Foekema et al. 2017).

4.4 Potential exposure to 'forever chemicals' via fibres in the aquatic environment

In order to exemplify the potential vector capacity of textile fibres, we discuss potential exposure to a specific group of chemicals of concern, namely PFAS (per- and polyfluoroalkyl substances), which comprises a group of 4,700 diverse substances used in numerous applications (Cousins, DeWitt et al. 2020). PFAS are commonly used in the impregnation of textiles in order to make garments and other textile products, such as furniture and carpets, water and dirt resistant (Wang, Goldenman et al. 2020) and are referred to as 'forever chemicals' due to their extremely persistent nature. PFAS are known to be hazardous to human and environmental health. They have intrinsic properties that include a range of bioaccumulation potentials, toxicity, mobility and molecular size (Cousins, DeWitt et al. 2020). There are indications that textiles are an important source of PFAS to humans, via direct contact, and to the environment (PFAS), though other uses account for the vast majority of sources of PFAS to the environment, including fire-fighting foam, the electronic industry, and lubricants and greases (Mumtaz, Bao et al. 2019; Glüge, Scheringer et al. 2020). PFAS can be released from textiles via several possible mechanisms, including loss of volatile substances to the air, washing out with rain, of loss during laundering and drying (Holmquist, Schellenberger et al. 2016). Fluorine mass measurements in textiles (used as a proxy of PFAS mass) indicate that PFAS can both be leached out of the products and retained in the materials, depending on the individual compounds (which may be volatile or ionic in nature), production methodologies and age of products (Robel, Marshall et al. 2017). In addition, the presence of PFAS chemicals in textile fibres can in fact decrease biodegradability of the fibres (Zambrano, Pawlak et al. 2021).

PFAS have been reported in tissues of wildlife, including in remote regions (Kelly, Ikonomou et al. 2009; Ali, Langberg et al. 2021). Given the chemical qualities of PFAS chemicals (including persistence and hydrophobicity (Cousins, Ng et al. 2019), their extensive use, the large volume of textile fibre production, and the ubiquitous nature of microfibre contamination in the environment, there is a risk that aquatic organisms could be exposed to PFAS via fibres. We have calculated potential exposure to PFAS via microplastic particles. Details can be found in Box 5.1.

BOX 5.1 A CASE STUDY CALCULATING POTENTIAL EXPOSURE TO FOREVER CHEMICALS IN MICROFIBRES IN THE AQUATIC ENVIRONMENT

Box 1. A case study calculating potential exposure to forever chemicals in microfibres in the aquatic environment

Here, we calculate the amount of PFAS to which an organism may be exposed, in order to assess whether microfibres are an important exposure route. We used available data on measurements of PFAS in textiles and calculate exposure in blue mussels (*Mytilus edulis*), which are one of the most well-studied aquatic organisms in the microfibre literature. Several pieces of information are need in order to perform such a calculation (data can be found in the table below):

1. Data on concentrations of PFAS substances textiles.
2. PFAS concentration in microfibres (calculated from the PFAS mass in textiles and the mass of PET fibres (based on density and cylindrical shape of fibres)).
3. Reported number of microfibres in blue mussels.

$$PFAS_{bivalve} = PFASgPETg * m_{average}MP * n_{ingested}$$

Given that information, we can calculate the worst-case scenario for exposure to PFAS via fibres, based on high concentrations used in textiles, and high levels of fibre ingestion, as well as a complete release of PFAS from the fibres into the biota upon ingestion, see scenario C4 from Figure 2. (Note, this assumption is not going to hold true in the environment, as many factors will affect desorption of PFAS from fibres, as discussed in the text). We can use reported weights of mussels to convert PFAS concentration per individual to nanograms of PFAS per g mussel.

	Parameter	Literature data	Converted units
Table 1. Calculations of potential mass of PFAS in blue mussels, based on number of ingested fibres and PFAS content in textiles and average mussel weights. a. Danish EPA (2015), b. Zhu and Kannan (2020), c. Kaynak and Babaarslan (2012), d. Napper and Thompson (2016), e. IFA (2018), f. Mathalon and Hill (2014), g. Scott, Porter et al. 2019. h. Mathalon and Hill (2014).	[PFAS] g/m² (high conc)	163,000 μg/m² [a]	0.163 g/m²
	[PFAS] g/m² (low conc)	0.521 μg/m² [b]	$5.21*10^{-7}$ g/m²
	PET g/m²	100 g/m² [c]	100 g/m²
	Diameter fibre	11.91 μm [d]	$11.91*10^{-6}$ m
	Radius fibre	diameter/2	$5.96*10^{-6}$ m
	Length fibre	7.79 mm [d]	$7.79*10^{-3}$ m
	Density PET	1.38 g/cm³ [e]	$1.38*10^{6}$ g/m³
	volume$_{average}$MP fibre (cylindrical shaped)	$\pi r^2 l$	$8.67*10^{-13}$ m³
	$m_{average}$ MP	Volume*density	$1.20*10^{-6}$ g
	$n_{ingested}$ MP (high number)	178 MP/individual [f]	178 MP/individual
	$n_{ingested}$ MP (low number)	1 MP/individual [g]	1 MP/individual
	Concentration of PFAS in mussels	**Calculated data**	**Converted units** **Based on avg mussel wt 34.6 g** [h]
	[PFAS] ng/ mussel (high)	348 ng/ individual	$1.81*10^{-8}$ ng/ g mussel
	[PFAS] ng/mussel (low)	$0.625*10^{-6}$ ng/ individual	10.0 ng/ g mussel

Result: PFAS concentrations may range from $0.625*10^{-6}$ to 348 ng PFAS per mussel, or $1.81*10^{-8}$ to 10.0 ng PFAS per g wet weight.

Conclusion: Given that reported concentrations of PFAS in farmed mussels range from 0.5 to 14.9 ng/ g wet weight Zafeiraki et al (2019), we conclude that in areas of high fibre contamination, this exposure route could be important.

First, we addressed concentration data of PFAS substances textile products. Regarding concentrations in textiles, the Danish EPA reported that PFOS are commonly used at concentrations of 2% wt/wt (Danish EPA 2015a, b). They also reported measured concentrations of an average of 72,700 $\mu g/m^2$ in children's clothing, with levels of up to 163,000 $\mu g/m^2$ in foul weather gear. Mumtaz et al. (2019) studied the levels of short-chain PFAS in clothing in China, one of the biggest manufacturers of clothing, and found an average of 0.29 mg/L, which exceeds the limits stated in the European Chemical Agency guidelines (0.025 mg/L) by more than 10-fold. In another study, researchers measured 13 different compounds and found the highest levels in fire-retardant textiles (13.3 $\mu g/m2$; 59.4 ng/g), followed by water repellent textiles (2.88 $\mu g/m2$; 12.9 ng/g) and infant clothes (0.521 $\mu g/m2$; 2.33 ng/g) (Zhu and Kannan 2020).

The levels of PFAS that might be present in microfibres in the aquatic environment will be governed by a number of factors, including the amount of chemicals present in the garments prior to release in the environment, as well as hydrophobic interactions driving the partitioning of organic compounds between the aqueous phase and the polymeric particles (Lionetto and Esposito Corcione 2021), and the presence of organic matter. In a recent study, Scott et al. (2021) conducted experiments quantifying the adsorption of PFAS onto MPs. They measured the abundance of PFAS on different polymer types of MPs after 1- and 3-months incubation in a lake, and results were compared to a controlled experiment that was conducted to assess adsorption in the absence of associated inorganic and organic matter. The adsorption of PFAS was much greater on field-deployed pristine MPs than in the laboratory (24 to 259 times versus one-seventh to one-fourth times background levels), indicating that the presence of inorganic and/or organic matter greatly influenced sorption. These authors measured concentrations of 67 ng/kg up to 730 ng/kg in MPs (compared to 2.8 ng/L and 3.3 ng/L in water samples). Note that these MPs used there were relatively large nurdles (2–4 mm in size) and not fibres which have a much larger surface area:volume ratio and could therefore potentially adsorb more PFAS per weight.

We then used published studies to find data on the number of microfibres in bivalves, specifically blue mussels (*Mytilus edulis*), which are one of the most well-studied aquatic organisms in the microfibre literature (Athey and Erdle 2021). We use bivalves to exemplify maximum possible PFAS uptake since both natural predators and humans consume the entire bodies of these animals. While there is evidence that oysters and blue mussels will reject fibres in pseudofeces, though to a lesser extent than microspheres, and that retention time of fibres is on the order of hours to days (Ward, Zhao et al. 2019), microfibres are commonly found in filter feeders in the environment. Numbers of fibres identified in mussels in the field range from ~1 particle per individual in wild mussels (Digka, Tsangaris et al. 2018; Qu, Su et al. 2018; Scott, Porter et al. 2019) to ~178 per individual in farmed mussels (Mathalon and Hill 2014). Note that not all of the fibres found were confirmed to be synthetic polymers, and many were confirmed to be natural fibres like cellulose, or anthropogenically modified cellulose. These fibres likely originate from production, use and laundering of textile garments, such as denim blue jeans (Athey, Adams et al. 2020). The chemical profile might differ between these fibres and products.

While several studies have investigated adsorption of PFAS microplastics (Llorca, Schirinzi et al. 2018; Scott, Gunderson et al. 2021), there is little data on concentrations of PFAS measured on environmental microfibres (i.e., those collected in the aquatic environment through sampling campaigns). Therefore, when calculating exposure potential to PFAS via textile fibres, we used a worst-case scenario based on high concentrations used in textiles, and high levels of fibre ingestion, as well as a complete release of PFAS from the fibres into the biota upon ingestion; see scenario C4 from Figure 5.2. (Note, this assumption is not going to hold true in the environment, as many factors will affect desorption of PFAS from fibres, as discussed earlier).

We estimate that uptake of PFAS from microfibres could result in concentrations that may range from 0.625×10^{-6} to 348 ng PFAS per individual, or using average bivalve mass reported by Mathalon and Hill (2014) of 34.6 g wet weight, from fibres ranging from 1.81×10^{-8} to 10.0 ng PFAS per g wet weight. We can then compare these calculated PFAS exposure values to measured levels of PFAS in bivalves. Zafeiraki et al. (2019) reported PFAS concentrations ranging from 0.5 to 14.9 ng g^{-1} wet weight for farmed and wild marine mussels. While these reported PFAS concentrations are orders of magnitude higher than our low exposure estimate, our high PFAS exposure scenario falls into the reported range. This finding could suggest that fibres may be vectors for PFAS to marine bivalves under high exposure scenarios. However, it is likely that ingested fibres exhibit bidirectional transfer of PFAS, as with other contaminants (Thaysen, Sorais et al. 2020), and do not offload their total PFAS concentration before excretion. While it is possible that fibres may become embedded in the gut epithelium, studies addressing gut retention of ingested textile fibres show relatively short retention times and little evidence of incorporation into tissues in both invertebrates and fish (Bour, Hossain et al. 2020). However, the potential for increased gut retention could affect desorption.

While our theoretical calculations here might suggest that, under high exposure scenarios, ingested fibres may act as vectors for PFAS to aquatic organisms, more research is needed to experimentally assess the capacity for fibres as vectors. Nevertheless, exposure routes to chemicals are many (for example, PFAS can be taken up into aquatic organisms via food (Miranda, Benskin et al. 2021)) and the widespread use of many of these substances, together with their ubiquitous presence in the environment, strengthen a call for banning their use in textiles.

5 Implications for future textile design, increased sustainability and transitions towards a circular economy

The role of synthetic microfibres as vectors for chemical contaminants in the environment and into biota remains to be determined, even if the textile industry is a clear contributor to the global burden of toxic chemicals (KemI 2015; Niinimäki,

Peters et al. 2020). Future research could help us understand the mechanisms driving the physiological and toxic responses to exposure to textile fibres, and identification of especially problematic materials or compounds could be informative for more sustainable choices in textile production.

The complex and often unknown chemical mixtures often associated with synthetic textiles make it difficult to recycle materials safely. Recycling of textiles is generally regarded as beneficial from an environmental perspective, compared to landfilling or incineration, though reuse is better than recycling (Sandin and Peters 2018). Recycling of textiles can be categorized into four different strategies: material recycling, mechanical recycling (e.g. pulping of cotton and linen), chemical recycling (e.g. hydrolysis and pyrolysis), or waste-to-energy conversion (incineration, discussed in greater detail in the chapter by Cocca and De Falco) and chemicals could play a role in each of these steps. There are several different policy instruments that can be applied to reduce the presence of chemicals on the textile market, including bans of specific compounds, or taxes, which can be used to encourage phasing out of certain problematic substances via economic pressures (one example is the proposed tax on harmful chemicals in clothing and shoes in Sweden (Bergman, Berntsson et al. 2020)).

In addition to chemicals, the fibres themselves are important to consider when addressing sustainability in the textile industry. Textiles release fibres to the environment during their life cycle, from production, use, to end-of-life disposal. As nearly 60% of textiles are synthetic, petroleum-based fibres, and these are now ubiquitous in the environment, it is prudent to consider microfibres in ecological risk assessment. Henry et al. (2019) have explored the potential to include a metric for microplastic pollution in quantifying the environmental performance of apparel and home textiles, concluding that the simple metric of mass or number of microfibres released, combined with data on their persistence in the environment, could provide a useful indicator in sustainability assessment tools.

6 Acknowledgements

We are grateful for Nanna B. Hartman's input in conceptualizing this chapter. We are also grateful for the work of Maria Eriksson Andin, a Master's student who worked with BCA at the University of Gothenburg, and her co-advisor, Sandra Roos, whose work was the inspiration for the PFAS calculations here (Andin 2018). BCA would like to acknowledge financial support from the Swedish Research Council for Sustainable Development FORMAS (2016–00895). This research was supported by the Swedish Research Council for Sustainable Development FORMAS (2016–00895).

References

Ali, A. M., H. A. Langberg, S. E. Hale, R. Kallenborn, W. F. Hartz, Å.-K. Mortensen, T. M. Ciesielski, C. A. McDonough, B. M. Jenssen and G. D. Breedveld, 2021. The fate of poly-and perfluoroalkyl substances in a marine food web influenced by land-based sources in the Norwegian Arctic. *Environ. Sci. Proc. Imp.*, 23(4), 588–604. doi:10.1039/ D0EM00510J

Allen, S., D. Allen, K. Moss, G. Le Roux, V. R. Phoenix and J. E. Sonke, 2020. Examination of the ocean as a source for atmospheric microplastics. *PLoS ONE* 15(5), e0232746. doi:10.1371/journal.pone.0232746

Alpizar, F., T. Backhaus, N. Decker, I. Eilks, N. Escobar-Pemberthy, P. Fantke, K. Geiser, M. Ivanova, O. Jolliet, H.-s. Kim, K. Khisa, H. Gundimeda, D. Slunge, S. Stec, J. Tickner, D. Tyrer, N. Urho, R. Visser, M. Yarto and V. G. Zuin, 2019. *Global chemicals outlook II. From legacies to innovative solutions*. Nairobi, Kenya, UN Environment.

Al-Sabti, K., 2000. Chlorotriazine reactive Azo Red 120 textile dye induces micronuclei in fish. *Ecotox. Environ. Saf.*, 47(2), 149–155. doi:10.1006/eesa.2000.1931

Alves de Lima, R. O., A. P. Bazo, D. M. F. Salvadori, C. M. Rech, D. de Palma Oliveira and G. de Aragão Umbuzeiro, 2007. Mutagenic and carcinogenic potential of a textile azo dye processing plant effluent that impacts a drinking water source. *Mutat. Res./Genet. Toxicol. Environ. Mutagen*, 626(1), 53–60. doi:10.1016/j.mrgentox.2006.08.002

Andin, M. E. (2018). *Microplastic polyester fiber as a source and vector of toxic substances: Risk assessment and evaluation of toxicity*. Master's of Science, University of Gotheburg.

Athey, S. N., J. K. Adams, L. M. Erdle, L. M. Jantunen, P. A. Helm, S. A. Finkelstein and M. L. Diamond, 2020. The widespread environmental footprint of indigo denim microfibers from blue jeans. *Environ. Sci. Technol. Lett.*, 7(11), 840–847. doi:10.1021/ acs.estlett.0c00498

Athey, S. N. and L. M. Erdle, 2021. Are we underestimating anthropogenic microfiber pollution? A critical review of occurrence, methods and reporting. *Environ. Toxicol. Chem.*, doi:10.1002/etc.5173

Au, S. Y., T. F. Bruce, W. C. Bridges and S. J. Klaine, 2015. Responses of Hyalella azteca to acute and chronic microplastic exposures. *Environ. Toxicol. Chem.*, 34(11), 2564–2572. doi:10.1002/etc.3093

Bakir, A., I. A. O'Connor, S. J. Rowland, A. J. Hendriks and R. C. Thompson, 2016. Relative importance of microplastics as a pathway for the transfer of hydrophobic organic chemicals to marine life. *Environ. Pollut.*, 219, 56–65. doi:10.1016/j. envpol.2016.09.046

Batel, A., F. Linti, M. Scherer, L. Erdinger and T. Braunbeck, 2016. The transfer of benzo[a] pyrene from microplastics to Artemia nauplii and further to zebrafish via a trophic food web experiment – CYP1A induction and visual tracking of persistent organic pollutants. *Environ. Toxicol. Chem.*, 34(7). doi:10.1002/etc.3361

Baxi, N. N., 2013. Influence of ε-caprolactam on growth and physiology of environmental bacteria. *Ann. Microbiol.*, 63(4), 1471–1476. doi:10.1007/s13213-013-0610-4

Bazin, I., A. Ibn Hadj Hassine, Y. Haj Hamouda, W. Mnif, A. Bartegi, M. Lopez-Ferber, M. De Waard and C. Gonzalez, 2012. Estrogenic and anti-estrogenic activity of 23 commercial textile dyes. *Ecotox. Environ. Saf.*, 85, 131–136. doi:10.1016/j.ecoenv.2012.08.003

Belzagui, F., V. Buscio, C. Gutiérrez-Bouzán and M. Vilaseca, 2021. Cigarette butts as a microfiber source with a microplastic level of concern. *Sci. Total Environ.*, 762, 144165. doi:10.1016/j.scitotenv.2020.144165

Bergman, Å., V. Berntsson, H. Bertell, F. Gisselman, T. Gärdström, M.-O. Hansson, R. Lönn, M. Nikkarinen, D. Slunge, A. Stewart, M. Wallin and L. Westman (2020). *Skatt på modet – för att få bort skadliga kemikalier S. O. U. SOU*. SOU 2020:20.

Bergmann, M., S. Mützel, S. Primpke, M. B. Tekman, J. Trachsel and G. Gerdts, 2019. White and wonderful? Microplastics prevail in snow from the Alps to the Arctic. *Sci. Adv.*, 5(8), eaax1157. doi:10.1126/sciadv.aax1157

Besseling, E., E. M. Foekema, M. J. van den Heuvel-Greve and A. A. Koelmans, 2017. The effect of microplastic on the uptake of chemicals by the Lugworm Arenicola marina (L.) under environmentally relevant exposure conditions. *Environ. Sci. Technol.*, 51(15), 8795–8804. doi:10.1021/acs.est.7b02286

Bour, A., M. Hamann Sandgaard, K. Syberg, A. Palmqvist and B. Carney Almroth, 2021. Comprehending the complexity of microplastic organismal exposures and effects, to improve testing frameworks. *J. Hazard. Mater.*, 415, 125652. doi:10.1016/j.jhazmat.2021.125652

Bour, A., S. Hossain, M. Taylor, M. Sumner and B. Carney Almroth, 2020. Synthetic microfiber and microbead exposure and retention time in model aquatic species under different exposure scenarios. *Front. Environ. Sci.*, 8 (83). doi:10.3389/fenvs.2020.00083

Bour, A., J. Sturve, J. Höjesjö and B. Carney Almroth, 2020. Microplastic vector effects: Are fish at risk when exposed via the trophic chain? *Front. Environ. Sci.*, 8(90). doi:10.3389/fenvs.2020.00090

Brennecke, D., B. Duarte, F. Paiva, I. Caçador and J. Canning-Clode, 2016. Microplastics as vector for heavy metal contamination from the marine environment. *Estuarine, Coast Shelf Sci.*, 178, 189–195. doi:10.1016/j.ecss.2015.12.003

Browne, M. A., P. Crump, S. J. Niven, E. Teuten, A. Tonkin, T. Galloway and R. Thompson, 2011. Accumulation of microplastic on shorelines woldwide: Sources and sinks. *Environ. Sci. Technol.*, 45(21), 9175–9179. doi: 10.1021/es201811s

Browne, M. A., S. J. Niven, T. S. Galloway, S. J. Rowland and R. C. Thompson, 2013. Microplastic moves pollutants and additives to worms, reducing functions linked to health and biodiversity. *Current Biol.*, 23(23), 2388–2392. doi:10.1016/j.cub.2013.10.012

Bucci, K., M. Tulio and C. M. Rochman, 2020. What is known and unknown about the effects of plastic pollution: A meta-analysis and systematic review. *Ecol. Appl.*, 30(2), e02044. doi:10.1002/eap.2044

Carney Almroth, B. M., L. Åström, S. Roslund, H. Petersson, M. Johansson and N.-K. Persson, 2018. Quantifying shedding of synthetic fibers from textiles; A source of microplastics released into the environment. *Environ. Sci. Pollut. Res.*, 25(2), 1191–1199. doi:10.1007/s11356-017-0528-7

Carney Almroth, B., J. Cartine, C. Jönander, M. Karlsson, J. Langlois, M. Lindström, J. Lundin, N. Melander, A. Pesqueda, I. Rahmqvist, J. Renaux, J. Roos, F. Spilsbury, J. Svalin, H. Vestlund, L. Zhao, N. Asker, G. Ašmonaitė, L. Birgersson, T. Boloori, F. Book, T. Lammel and J. Sturve, 2021. Assessing the effects of textile leachates in fish using multiple testing methods: From gene expression to behavior. *Ecotox. Environ. Saf.*, 207, 111523. doi:10.1016/j.ecoenv.2020.111523

Chan, C. K. M., C. Park, K. M. Chan, D. C. W. Mak, J. K. H. Fang and D. M. Mitrano, 2021. Microplastic fibre releases from industrial wastewater effluent: A textile wet-processing mill in China. *Environ. Chem.*, 18(3), 93–100. doi:10.1071/EN20143

Chung, K.-T., 2016. Azo dyes and human health: A review. *J. Environ. Sci. Health, Part C* 34(4), 233–261. doi:10.1080/10590501.2016.1236602

Cole, M., R. Coppock, P. K. Lindeque, D. Altin, S. Reed, D. W. Pond, L. Sørensen, T. S. Galloway and A. M. Booth, 2019. Effects of nylon microplastic on feeding, lipid accumulation, and moulting in a coldwater copepod. *Environ. Sci. Technol.*, 53(12), 7075–7082. doi:10.1021/acs.est.9b01853

Cousins, E. M., L. Richter, A. Cordner, P. Brown and S. Diallo, 2019. Risky business? Manufacturer and retailer action to remove per- and polyfluorinated chemicals from consumer products. *NEW SOLUTIONS: J. Environ. Occup. Health Pol.*, 29(2), 242–265. doi:10.1177/1048291119852674

Cousins, I. T., J. C. DeWitt, J. Glüge, G. Goldenman, D. Herzke, R. Lohmann, M. Miller, C. A. Ng, M. Scheringer and L. Vierke, 2020. Strategies for grouping per-and polyfluoroalkyl substances (PFAS) to protect human and environmental health. *Environ. Sci.: Process. Imp.*, 22(7), 1444–1460. doi:10.1039/D0EM00147C

Cousins, I. T., G. Goldenman, D. Herzke, R. Lohmann, M. Miller, C. A. Ng, S. Patton, M. Scheringer, X. Trier and L. Vierke, 2019. The concept of essential use for determining when uses of PFASs can be phased out. *Environ. Sci.: Process. Imp.*, 21(11), 1803–1815. doi:10.1039/c9em00163h

Cousins, I. T., C. A. Ng, Z. Wang and M. Scheringer, 2019. Why is high persistence alone a major cause of concern? *Environ. Sci.: Process. Imp.*, 21(5), 781–792. doi:10.1039/C8EM00515J

Danish EPA, 2015a. *Polyfluoroalkyl substances (PFASs) in textiles for children Survey of chemical substances in consumer products.* Ministry of Environment. Food No. 136.

Danish EPA, 2015b. *Short-chain Polyfluoroalkyl Substances (PFAS); A literature review of information on human health effects and environmental fate and effect aspects of short-chain PFAS.* Environmental Project No. 1707.

De Falco, F., M. Cocca, M. Avella and R. C. Thompson, 2020. Microfibre release to water, via laundering, and to air, via everyday use: A comparison between polyester clothing with differing textile parameters. *Environ. Sci. Technol.* doi:10.1021/acs.est.9b06892

DeLorenzo, M. E., G. I. Scott and P. E. Ross, 2001. Toxicity of pesticides to aquatic microorganisms: A review. *Environ. Toxicol. Chem.*, 20(1), 84–98. doi:10.1002/etc.5620200108

Digka, N., C. Tsangaris, M. Torre, A. Anastasopoulou and C. Zeri, 2018. Microplastics in mussels and fish from the Northern Ionian Sea. *Mar. Poll. Bull.*, 135, 30–40. doi:10.1016/j.marpolbul.2018.06.063

Dodd, N., M. Cordella, O. Wolf, J. Waidløw, M. Stibolt and E. Hansen, 2013. *Revision of the European Ecolabel and Green Public Procurement (GPP) criteria for textile products.* Technical Report and Criteria Proposals – Working Document, JRC Technical.

Dolez, P. I. and H. Benaddi, 2018. Chapter 7 – Toxicity testing of textiles. *Advanced characterization and testing of textiles.* P. Dolez, O. Vermeersch and V. Izquierdo. Cambridge, UK, Woodhead Publishing: 151–188.

Dris, R., J. Gasperi, C. Mirande, C. Mandin, M. Guerrouache, V. Langlois and B. Tassin, 2017. A first overview of textile fibers, including microplastics, in indoor and outdoor environments. *Environ. Poll.*, 221, 453–458. doi:10.1016/j.envpol.2016.12.013

Duh, B., 2002. Effect of antimony catalyst on solid-state polycondensation of poly(ethylene terephthalate). *Polymer*, 43(11), 3147–3154. doi:10.1016/S0032-3861(02)00138-6

ECHA, 2021. *Registered substances.* Retrieved from https://echa.europa.eu/information-on-chemicals/registered-substances.

ECHA and Germany, 2019. *Undecafluorohexanoic acid (PFHxA), its salts and related substances.* Retrieved from https://echa.europa.eu/sv/registry-of-restriction-intentions/-/dislist/details/0b0236e18323a25d.

Ellen MacArthur Foundation, E., 2017. *A new textiles economy: redesigning fashion's future.* A New Textiles Economy – Full Report | Shared by Fashion. Retrieved from thirdlight. com

European Commission, EC, 2003. *Integrated Pollution Prevention and Control (IPPC) reference document on best available techniques for the textiles industry.* European Commission, Brussels, Belgium.

Fred-Ahmadu, O. H., G. Bhagwat, I. Oluyoye, N. U. Benson, O. O. Ayejuyo and T. Palanisami, 2020. Interaction of chemical contaminants with microplastics: Principles and perspectives. *Sci. Total Environ.* 706, 135978. doi:10.1016/j.scitotenv.2019.135978

Glüge, J., M. Scheringer, I. T. Cousins, J. C. DeWitt, G. Goldenman, D. Herzke, R. Lohmann, C. A. Ng, X. Trier and Z. Wang, 2020. An overview of the uses of per-and polyfluoroalkyl substances (PFAS). *Environ. Sci.: Proc. Impacts*, 22(12), 2345–2373. doi:10.1039/D0EM00291G

Groh, K. J., T. Backhaus, B. Carney-Almroth, B. Geueke, P. A. Inostroza, A. Lennquist, H. A. Leslie, M. Maffini, D. Slunge, L. Trasande, A. M. Warhurst and J. Muncke, 2019. Overview of known plastic packaging-associated chemicals and their hazards. *Sci. Total Environ.*, 651, 3253–3268. doi:10.1016/j.scitotenv.2018.10.015

Harrad, S., D. S. Drage, M. Sharkey and H. Berresheim, 2020. Leaching of decabromodiphenyl ether and hexabromocyclododecane from fabrics under simulated landfill conditions. *Emerg. Contam.*, 6, 33–38. doi:10.1016/j.emcon.2019.12.005

Hartmann, N. B., T. Hüffer, R. C. Thompson, M. Hassellöv, A. Verschoor, A. E. Daugaard, S. Rist, T. Karlsson, N. Brennholt, M. Cole, M. P. Herrling, M. C. Hess, N. P. Ivleva, A. L. Lusher and M. Wagner, 2019. Are we speaking the same language? Recommendations for a definition and categorization framework for plastic debris. *Environ. Sci. Technol.*, 53(3), 1039–1047. doi:10.1021/acs.est.8b05297

Henry, B., K. Laitala and I. G. Klepp, 2019. Microfibres from apparel and home textiles: Prospects for including microplastics in environmental sustainability assessment. *Sci. Total Environ.*, 652, 483–494. doi:10.1016/j.scitotenv.2018.10.166

Hernandez, E., B. Nowack and D. M. Mitrano, 2017. Polyester textiles as a source of microplastics from households: A mechanistic study to understand microfiber release during washing. *Environ. Sci. Technol.*, 51(12), 7036–7046. doi:10.1021/acs.est.7b01750

Hill, P. J., M. Taylor, P. Goswami and R. S. Blackburn, 2017. Substitution of PFAS chemistry in outdoor apparel and the impact on repellency performance. *Chemosphere* 181, 500–507. doi:10.1016/j.chemosphere.2017.04.122

Holmquist, H., S. Schellenberger, I. van der Veen, G. M. Peters, P. E. G. Leonards and I. T. Cousins, 2016. Properties, performance and associated hazards of state-of-the-art durable water repellent (DWR) chemistry for textile finishing. *Environ. Int.*, 91, 251–264. doi:10.1016/j.envint.2016.02.035

Hope, J. A., G. Coco and S. F. Thrush, 2020. Effects of polyester microfibers on microphytobenthos and sediment-dwelling infauna. *Environ. Sci. Technol.*, 54(13), 7970–7982. doi:10.1016/j.envpol.2021.117731

Hussain, T. and A. Wahab, 2018. A critical review of the current water conservation practices in textile wet processing. *J. Cleaner Prod.*, 198, 806–819. doi:10.1016/j.jclepro.2018.07.051

Ibrahim, N. A., B. M. Eid and S. M. Sharaf, 2019. Functional finishes for cotton-based textiles: Current situation and future trends. *Tex. Clothing*, 131–190. doi:10.1002/9781119526599.ch7

Islam, S., 2020. Chapter 15 – Sustainable raw materials: 50 shades of sustainability. *Sustainable technologies for fashion and textiles*. R. Nayak. Cambridge, UK, Woodhead Publishing: 343–357.

Jahnke, A., H. P. H. Arp, B. I. Escher, B. Gewert, E. Gorokhova, D. Kühnel, M. Ogonowski, A. Potthoff, C. Rummel, M. Schmitt-Jansen, E. Toorman and M. MacLeod, 2017. Reducing uncertainty and confronting ignorance about the possible impacts of weathering plastic in the marine environment. *Environ. Sci. Technol. Lett.*, 4(3), 85–90. doi:10.1021/acs.estlett.7b00008

Jamieson, A. J., L. Brooks, W. D. Reid, S. Piertney, B. E. Narayanaswamy and T. Linley, 2019. Microplastics and synthetic particles ingested by deep-sea amphipods in six of the deepest marine ecosystems on Earth. *R. Soc. Open Sci.*, 6(2), 180667. doi:10.1098/rsos.180667

Jemec, A., P. Horvat, U. Kunej, M. Bele and A. Kržan, 2016. Uptake and effects of microplastic textile fibers on freshwater crustacean Daphnia magna. *Environ. Pollut.* 219, 201–209. doi:10.1016/j.envpol.2016.10.037

Jin, M., X. Yu, Z. Yao, P. Tao, G. Li, X. Yu, J.-L. Zhao and J. Peng, 2020. How biofilms affect the uptake and fate of hydrophobic organic compounds (HOCs) in microplastic: Insights from an In situ study of Xiangshan Bay, China. *Water Res.*, 184, 116118. doi:10.1016/j.watres.2020.116118

Joint Research Center, EC, 2014. *Environmental Improvement Potential of Textiles (IMPRO-Textiles). Reports.* Joint Research Centre, Ispra, Italy.

Kant, R., 2012. Textile dyeing industry an environmental hazard. *Nat. Sci.*, 4, 22–26. doi:10.4236/ns.2012.41004.

Kelly, B. C., M. G. Ikonomou, J. D. Blair, B. Surridge, D. Hoover, R. Grace and F. A. P. C. Gobas, 2009. Perfluoroalkyl contaminants in an arctic marine food web: Trophic magnification and wildlife exposure. *Environ. Sci. Tecnol.*, 43(11), 4037–4043. doi:10.1021/es9003894

KemI, 2013. *Hazardous chemicals in textiles – Report of a government assignment.* Swedish Chemicals Agency, Report: 3/13.

KemI, 2015. *Chemicals in textiles – Risks to human health and the environment.* Swedish Chemicals Agency, Report: 139.

Kemi, 2016. *Hazardous chemical substances in textiles – Proposals for risk management measures.* Swedish Chemicals Agency, Report: 8/16.

Kim, L., S. A. Kim, T. H. Kim, J. Kim and Y.-J. An, 2021. Synthetic and natural microfibers induce gut damage in the brine shrimp Artemia franciscana. *Aquat. Toxicol.*, 232, 105748. doi:10.1016/j.aquatox.2021.105748

Kishor, R., D. Purchase, G. D. Saratale, R. G. Saratale, L. F. R. Ferreira, M. Bilal, R. Chandra and R. N. Bharagava, 2021. Ecotoxicological and health concerns of persistent coloring pollutants of textile industry wastewater and treatment approaches for environmental safety. *J. Environ. Chem. Eng.* 9(2), 105012. doi:10.1016/j.jece.2020.105012

Koelmans, A. A., A. Bakir, G. A. Burton and C. R. Janssen, 2016. Microplastic as a vector for chemicals in the aquatic environment. Critical review and model-supported reinterpretation of empirical Studies. *Environ. Sci. Technol.*, doi:10.1021/acs.est.5b06069

Koelmans, A. A., E. Besseling, A. Wegner and E. M. Foekema, 2013. Plastic as a carrier of POPs to aquatic organisms: A model analysis. *Environ. Sci. Technol.*, 47(14), 7812–7820. doi:10.1021/es401169n

Kvasnicka, J., l. E. Cohen Huba, T. Rodgers and M. Diamond, 2021. Textile washing conveys SVOCs from indoors to outdoors: Application and evaluation of a residential multimedia model. *Environ. Sci. Technol.*, 55 (18) 12517–12527. doi:10.1021/acs.est.1c02674

Lacasse, K. and W. Baumann, 2004. Environmental considerations for textile processes and chemicals. *Textile chemicals: Environmental data and facts.* K. Lacasse and W. Baumann. Berlin, Heidelberg, Springer: 484–647.

Lacasse, K. and W. Baumann, 2012. *Textile chemicals: Environmental data and facts.* Berlin, Heidelberg, Springer Science & Business Media.

Law, C. f. I. E., 2019. *Plastic & climate: The hidden costs of a plastic planet.* Center for International Environmental Law, edited by A. Kistler and C. Muffett. Retrieved from www.ciel.org/plasticandclimate.

Lawrence, J. R., T. R. Neu, A. Paule, D. R. Korber and G. M. Wolfaardt, 2016. Aquatic biofilms: Development, cultivation, analyses, and applications. *Manual Environ. Microbiol.* 4.2.3–1–4.2.3–33.

Le Bihanic, F., C. Clérandeau, B. Cormier, J.-C. Crebassa, S. H. Keiter, R. Beiras, B. Morin, M.-L. Bégout, X. Cousin and J. Cachot, 2020. Organic contaminants sorbed to microplastics affect marine medaka fish early life stages development. *Mar. Pollut. Bull.*, 154, 111059. doi:10.1016/j.marpolbul.2020.111059

Le Guen, C., G. Suaria, R. B. Sherley, P. G. Ryan, S. Aliani, L. Boehme and A. S. Brierley, 2020. Microplastic study reveals the presence of natural and synthetic fibres in the diet of King Penguins (Aptenodytes patagonicus) foraging from South Georgia. *Environ. Int.*, 134, 105303. doi:10.1016/j.envint.2019.105303

Li, J., K. Zhang and H. Zhang, 2018. Adsorption of antibiotics on microplastics. *Environ. Poll.*, 237, 460–467. doi:10.1016/j.envpol.2018.02.050

Li, L., M. Frey and K. J. Browning, 2010. Biodegradability study on cotton and polyester fabrics. *J. Eng. Fibers Fabrics*, 5(4), 155892501000500406. doi:10.1177/155892501000500406

Li, Y., Y. Luo and Q. He, 2020. Chemical footprint of textile and apparel products: an assessment of human and ecological toxicities based on USEtox model. *J. Tex. Inst.*, 111(7), 960–971. doi:10.1080/00405000.2019.1710907

Licina, D., G. C. Morrison, G. Bekö, C. J. Weschler and W. W. Nazaroff, 2019. Clothing-mediated exposures to chemicals and particles. *Environ. Sci. Technol.*, 53(10), 5559–5575. doi:10.1021/acs.est.9b00272

Lindmark, S., 2019. *Emission of UV filter chemicals from PET fabric examining the release to water during washing*. Thesis, Umeå University, Faculty of Science and Technology, Department of Chemistry.

Lionetto, F. and C. Esposito Corcione, 2021. An overview of the sorption studies of contaminants on poly(ethylene terephthalate) microplastics in the marine environment. *J. Mar. Sci. Eng.*, 9(4), 445. doi:10.3390/jmse9040445

Liu, C., J. Li, Y. Zhang, L. Wang, J. Deng, Y. Gao, L. Yu, J. Zhang and H. Sun, 2019. Widespread distribution of PET and PC microplastics in dust in urban China and their estimated human exposure. *Environ. Int.*, 128, 116–124. doi:10.1016/j.envint.2019.04.024

Liu, J., J. Liang, J. Ding, G. Zhang, X. Zeng, Q. Yang, B. Zhu and W. Gao, 2021. Microfiber pollution: An ongoing major environmental issue related to the sustainable development of textile and clothing industry. *Environ. Dev. Sust.*, 23(8), 11240–11256. doi:10.1007/s10668-020-01173-3

Liu, J., Y. Yang, J. Ding, B. Zhu and W. Gao, 2019. Microfibers: A preliminary discussion on their definition and sources. *Environ. Sci. Poll. Res.*, 26(28), 29497–29501. doi:10.1007/s11356-019-06265-w

Llorca, M., G. Schirinzi, M. Martínez, D. Barceló and M. Farré, 2018. Adsorption of perfluoroalkyl substances on microplastics under environmental conditions. *Environ. Pollut.*, 235, 680–691. doi:10.1016/j.envpol.2017.12.075

Luongo, G., 2015. *Chemicals in textiles: A potential source for human exposure and environmental pollution*. PhD Thesis, Department of Environmental Science and Analytical Chemistry, Stockholm. ISBN: 978-91-7649-225-3

Ma, M., S. Dong, W. Jin, C. Zhang and W. Zhou, 2019. Fate of the organophosphorus pesticide profenofos in cotton fiber. *J. Environ. Sci. Health, Part B* 54(1), 70–75. doi:10.1080/03601234.2018.1505036

Markic, A., C. Niemand, J. H. Bridson, N. Mazouni-Gaertner, J.-C. Gaertner, M. Eriksen and M. Bowen, 2018. Double trouble in the South Pacific subtropical gyre: Increased plastic ingestion by fish in the oceanic accumulation zone. *Mar. Pollut. Bull.*, 136, 547–564. doi:10.1016/j.marpolbul.2018.09.031

Mateos-Cárdenas, A., J. O'Halloran, F. N. A. M. van Pelt and M. A. K. Jansen, 2021. Beyond plastic microbeads – Short-term feeding of cellulose and polyester microfibers to the freshwater amphipod Gammarus duebeni. *Sci. Total Environ.*, 753, 141859. doi:10.1016/j.scitotenv.2020.141859

Mathalon, A. and P. Hill, 2014. Microplastic fibers in the intertidal ecosystem surrounding Halifax Harbor, Nova Scotia. *Mar. Pollut. Bull.*, 81(1), 69–79. doi:10.1016/j.marpolbul.2014.02.018

Meeker, J. D., S. Sathyanarayana and S. H. Swan, 2009. Phthalates and other additives in plastics: Human exposure and associated health outcomes. *Phil. Trans. Royal Soc. B: Biol. Sci.*, 364(1526), 2097–2113. doi:10.1098/rstb.2008.0268

Mellin, P., C. Jönsson, M. Åkermo, P. Fernberg, E. Nordenberg, H. Brodin and A. Strondl, 2016. Nano-sized by-products from metal 3D printing, composite manufacturing and fabric production. *J. Cleaner Prod.*, 139, 1224–1233. doi:10.1016/j.jclepro.2016.08.141

MicrofiberConsortium, 2020. Retrieved 20 September 2020 from www.microfibre consortium.com/.

Miranda, D. A., J. P. Benskin, R. Awad, G. Lepoint, J. Leonel and V. Hatje, 2021. Bioaccumulation of Per- and polyfluoroalkyl substances (PFASs) in a tropical estuarine food web. *Sci Total Environ.*, 754, 142146. doi:10.1016/j.scitotenv.2020.142146

Mitrano, D. M., P. Limpiteeprakan, S. Babel and B. Nowack, 2016. Durability of nanoenhanced textiles through the life cycle: Releases from landfilling after washing. *Environ. Sci.: Nano*, 3(2), 375–387. doi:10.1039/C6EN00023A

Möller, A., L. Ahrens, R. Surm, J. Westerveld, F. van der Wielen, R. Ebinghaus and P. de Voogt, 2010. Distribution and sources of polyfluoroalkyl substances (PFAS) in the River Rhine watershed. *Environ. Pollut.*, 158(10), 3243–3250. doi:10.1016/j.envpol.2010.07.019

Morrison, G. C., H. V. Andersen, L. Gunnarsen, D. Varol, E. Uhde and B. Kolarik, 2018. Partitioning of PCB s from air to clothing materials in a Danish apartment. *Indoor Air*, 28(1), 188–197. doi:10.1111/ina.12411

Morrison, G. C., H. Li, S. Mishra and M. Buechlein, 2015. Airborne phthalate partitioning to cotton clothing. *Atmos. Environ.*, 115, 149–152. doi:10.1016/j.atmosenv.2015.05.051

Morrison, G. C., C. J. Weschler, G. Bekö, H. M. Koch, T. Salthammer, T. Schripp, J. Toftum and G. Clausen, 2016. Role of clothing in both accelerating and impeding dermal absorption of airborne SVOCs. *J. Exposure Sci. Environ. Epidem.*, 26(1), 113–118. doi:10.1038/jes.2015.42

Mukhtar Abdul-Bari, M., R. H. McQueen, A. Paulina de la Mata, J. C. Batcheller and J. J. Harynuk, 2020. Retention and release of odorants in cotton and polyester fabrics following multiple soil/wash procedures. *Tex. Res. J.*, 90(19–20), 2212–2222. doi:10.1177/0040517520914411

Mumtaz, M., Y. Bao, W. Li, L. Kong, J. Huang and G. Yu, 2019. Screening of textile finishing agents available on the Chinese market: An important source of per- and polyfluoroalkyl substances to the environment. *Front. Environ. Sci. Eng.*, 13(5), 67. doi:10.1007/s11783-019-1145-0

Nagy, K., R. C. Duca, S. Lovas, M. Creta, P. T. J. Scheepers, L. Godderis and B. Ádám, 2020. Systematic review of comparative studies assessing the toxicity of pesticide active ingredients and their product formulations. *Environ. Res.*, 181, 108926. doi:10.1016/j.envres.2019.108926

Napper, I. E. and R. C. Thompson, 2016. Release of synthetic microplastic plastic fibres from domestic washing machines: Effects of fabric type and washing conditions. *Mar. Pollut. Bull.*, 112, 1–2. doi.org/10.1016/j.marpolbul.2016.09.025

Nayak, R. and R. Padhye, 2014. *Antimicrobial finishes for textiles*. Cambridge, UK, Woodhead Publishing.

Nguyen, T. and M. A. Saleh, 2016. Detection of azo dyes and aromatic amines in women undergarment. *J. Environ. Sci. Health, Part A*, 51(9), 744–753. doi:10.1080/10934529.2016.1170446

Niinimäki, K., G. Peters, H. Dahlbo, P. Perry, T. Rissanen and A. Gwilt, 2020. The environmental price of fast fashion. *Nature Rev. Earth Environ.*, 1(4), 189–200. doi:10.1038/s43017-020-0039-9

Olsson, E., S. Posner, S. Roos and K. Wilson, 2010. *Mapping chemicals use in clothes.* Commission of Swedish Chemicals Agency (KemI). S. IVF. 09/52.

Palacios-Mateo, C., Y. van der Meer and G. Seide, 2021. Analysis of the polyester clothing value chain to identify key intervention points for sustainability. *Environ. Sci. Europe*, 33(1), 2. doi:10.1186/s12302-020-00447-x

Palm, C., S. E. Cornell and T. Häyhä, 2021. Making resilient decisions for sustainable circularity of fashion. *Circular Econ. Sustain.*, 1, 651–670. doi:10.1007/s43615-021-00040-1

Peters, G., M. Li and M. Lenzen, 2021. The need to decelerate fast fashion in a hot climate – A global sustainability perspective on the garment industry. *J. Cleaner Prod.* 295, 126390. doi:10.1016/j.jclepro.2021.126390

Prata, J. C., 2018. Airborne microplastics: Consequences to human health? *Environ. Poll.*, 234, 115–126. doi:10.1016/j.envpol.2017.11.043

Prokić, M. D., T. B. Radovanović, J. P. Gavrić and C. Faggio, 2018. Ecotoxicological effects of microplastics: Examination of biomarkers, current state and future perspectives. *TrAC Trends Anal. Chem.*, 111, 37–46. doi:10.1016/j.trac.2018.12.001

Qiao, R., Y. Deng, S. Zhang, M. B. Wolosker, Q. Zhu, H. Ren and Y. Zhang, 2019. Accumulation of different shapes of microplastics initiates intestinal injury and gut microbiota dysbiosis in the gut of zebrafish. *Chemosphere*, 236, 124334. doi:10.1016/j.chemosphere.2019.07.065

Qu, X., L. Su, H. Li, M. Liang and H. Shi, 2018. Assessing the relationship between the abundance and properties of microplastics in water and in mussels. *Sci. Total Environ.*, 621, 679–686. doi:10.1016/j.scitotenv.2017.11.284

Ramasamy, R. and R. B. Subramanian, 2021. Synthetic textile and microfiber pollution: A review on mitigation strategies. *Environ. Sci. Pollut. Res.*, 28, 41596–41611. doi:10.1007/s11356-021-14763-z

Rios-Fuster, B., P. Arechavala-Lopez, K. García-Marcos, C. Alomar, M. Compa, E. Álvarez, et al., 2021. Experimental evidence of physiological and behavioral effects of microplastic ingestion in *Sparus aurata. Aquatic. Toxicol.*, 231, 105737. doi:10.1016/j.aquatox.2020.105737

Robel, A. E., K. Marshall, M. Dickinson, D. Lunderberg, C. Butt, G. Peaslee, H. M. Stapleton and J. A. Field, 2017. Closing the mass balance on fluorine on papers and textiles. *Environ. Sci. Technol.*, 51(16), 9022–9032. doi:10.1021/acs.est.7b02080

Rochman, C. M., C. Brookson, J. Bikker, N. Djuric, A. Earn, K. Bucci, S. Athey, A. Huntington, H. McIlwraith, K. Munno, H. De Frond, A. Kolomijeca, L. Erdle, J. Grbic, M. Bayoumi, S. B. Borrelle, T. Wu, S. Santoro, L. M. Werbowski, X. Zhu, R. K. Giles, B. M. Hamilton, C. Thaysen, A. Kaura, N. Klasios, L. Ead, J. Kim, C. Sherlock, A. Ho and C. Hung, 2019. Rethinking microplastics as a diverse contaminant suite. *Environ. Toxicol. Chem.*, 38(4), 703–711. doi:10.1002/etc.4371

Rochman, C. M., E. HI T. Kurobe and S. J. Teh, 2013. Ingested plastic transfers hazardous chemicals to fish and induces hepatic stress. *Sci. Rep.*, 3. 3263. doi: 10.1038/srep03263

Ross, P. S., S. Chastain, E. Vassilenko, A. Etemadifar, S. Zimmermann, S.-A. Quesnel, J. Eert, E. Solomon, S. Patankar, A. M. Posacka and B. Williams, 2021. Pervasive distribution of polyester fibres in the Arctic Ocean is driven by Atlantic inputs. *Nat. Commun.*, 12(1), 106. doi:10.1038/s41467-020-20347-1

Rovira, J. and J. L. Domingo, 2019. Human health risks due to exposure to inorganic and organic chemicals from textiles: A review. *Environ. Res.* 168, 62–69. doi:10.1016/j.envres.2018.09.027

Saini, A., J. O. Okeme, J. Mark Parnis, R. H. McQueen and M. L. Diamond, 2017. From air to clothing: characterizing the accumulation of semi-volatile organic compounds to fabrics in indoor environments. *Indoor Air*, 27(3), 631–641. doi:10.1111/ina.12328

Saini, A., C. Rauert, M. J. Simpson, S. Harrad and M. L. Diamond, 2016. Characterizing the sorption of polybrominated diphenyl ethers (PBDEs) to cotton and polyester fabrics under controlled conditions. *Sci. Total Environ.*, 563–564, 99–107. doi:10.1016/j.scitotenv.2016.04.099

Sait, S. T. L., L. Sørensen, S. Kubowicz, K. Vike-Jonas, S. V. Gonzalez, A. G. Asimakopoulos and A. M. Booth, 2021. Microplastic fibres from synthetic textiles: Environmental degradation and additive chemical content. *Environ. Pollut.*, 268, 115745. doi:10.1016/j.envpol.2020.115745

Sandin, G. and G. M. Peters, 2018. Environmental impact of textile reuse and recycling – A review. *J. Cleaner Prod.*, 184, 353–365. doi:10.1016/j.jclepro.2018.02.266

Saxena, S., A. Raja and A. Arputharaj, 2017. Challenges in sustainable wet processing of textiles. *Textiles and clothing sustainability*. Singapore, Springer: 43–79.

Schecter, A., N. Shah, J. A. Colacino, S. I. Brummitt, V. Ramakrishnan, T. Robert Harris and O. Päpke, 2009. PBDEs in US and German clothes dryer lint: A potential source of indoor contamination and exposure. *Chemosphere*, 75(5), 623–628. doi:10.1016/j.chemosphere.2009.01.017

Schellenberger, S., C. Jönsson, P. Mellin, O. A. Levenstam, I. Liagkouridis, A. Ribbenstedt, A.-C. Hanning, L. Schultes, M. M. Plassmann, C. Persson, I. T. Cousins and J. P. Benskin, 2019. Release of side-chain fluorinated polymer-containing microplastic fibers from functional textiles during washing and first estimates of perfluoroalkyl acid emissions. *Environ. Sci. Technol.*, 53(24), 14329–14338. doi:10.1021/acs.est.9b04165

Schreder, E. D. and M. J. La Guardia, 2014. Flame retardant transfers from U.S. households (Dust and Laundry Wastewater) to the aquatic environment. *Environ. Sci. Technol.*, 48(19), 11575–11583. doi:10.1021/es502227h

Schür, C., C. Weil, M. Baum, J. Wallraff, M. Schreier, J. Oehlmann and M. Wagner, 2021. Incubation in wastewater reduces the multigenerational effects of microplastics in Daphnia magna. *Environ. Sci. Technol.*, 55(4), 2491–2499. doi:10.1021/acs.est.0c07911

Schwarzenbach, R. P., P. M. Gschwend and D. M. Imboden, 2016. *Environmental organic chemistry*. Hoboken, USA, John Wiley & Sons.

Scott, J. W., K. G. Gunderson, L. A. Green, R. R. Rediske and A. D. Steinman, 2021. Perfluoroalkylated Substances (PFAS) Associated with microplastics in a lake environment. *Toxics*, 9(5), 106. doi:10.3390/toxics9050106

Scott, N., A. Porter, D. Santillo, H. Simpson, S. Lloyd-Williams and C. Lewis, 2019. Particle characteristics of microplastics contaminating the mussel Mytilus edulis and their surrounding environments. *Mar. Pollut. Bull.*, 146, 125–133. doi:10.1016/j.marpolbul.2019.05.041

Selonen, S., A. Dolar, A. Jemec Kokalj, T. Skalar, L. Parramon Dolcet, R. Hurley and C. A. M. van Gestel, 2020. Exploring the impacts of plastics in soil – The effects of polyester textile fibers on soil invertebrates. *Sci. Total Environ.*, 700, 134451. doi:10.1016/j.scitotenv.2019.134451

Setyorini, L., D. Michler-Kozma, B. Sures and F. Gabel, 2021. Transfer and effects of PET microfibers in Chironomus riparius. *Sci. Total Environ.*, 757, 143735. doi:10.1016/j.scitotenv.2020.143735

Seuront, L., 2018. Microplastic leachates impair behavioural vigilance and predator avoidance in a temperate intertidal gastropod. *Biol. Lett.*, 14. doi:10.1098/rsbl.2018.0453

Sheriff, I., S. A. Debela, O. A. Kabia, C. E. Ntoutoume and M. J. Turay, 2020. The phase out of and restrictions on per-and polyfluoroalkyl substances: Time for a rethink. *Chemosphere*, 251, 126313. doi:10.1016/j.chemosphere.2020.126313

Singh, A. and C. Leppanen, 2020. Known target and nontarget effects of the novel neonicotinoid cycloxaprid to arthropods: A systematic review. *Integr. Environ. Assess. Manag.*, 16(6), 831–840. doi:10.1002/ieam.4305

Singh, S., S. Chatterji, P. T. Nandini, A. S. A. Prasad and K. V. B. Rao, 2015. Biodegradation of azo dye Direct Orange 16 by Micrococcusluteus strain SSN2. *Int. J. Environ. Sci. Technol.*, 12(7), 2161–2168. doi:10.1007/s13762-014-0588-x

Slokar, Y. M. and A. Majcen Le Marechal, 1998. Methods of decoloration of textile wastewaters. *Dyes pigm.*, 37(4), 335–356. doi:10.1016/S0143–7208(97)00075–2

Song, Y., C. Cao, R. Qiu, J. Hu, M. Liu, S. Lu, H. Shi, K. M. Raley-Susman and D. He, 2019. Uptake and adverse effects of polyethylene terephthalate microplastics fibers on terrestrial snails (Achatina fulica) after soil exposure. *Environ. Pollut.*, 250, 447–455. doi:10.1016/j.envpol.2019.04.066

Stapleton, H. M., N. G. Dodder, J. H. Offenberg, M. M. Schantz and S. A. Wise, 2005. Polybrominated diphenyl ethers in house dust and clothes dryer lint. *Environ. Sci. Technol.*, 39(4), 925–931. doi:10.1021/es0486824

Stienbarger, C. D., J. Joseph, S. N. Athey, B. Monteleone, A. L. Andrady, W. O. Watanabe, P. Seaton, A. R. Taylor and S. M. Brander, 2021. Direct ingestion, trophic transfer, and physiological effects of microplastics in the early life stages of Centropristis striata, a commercially and recreationally valuable fishery species. *Environ. Pollut.*, 285, 117653. doi:10.1016/j.envpol.2021.117653

Stone, C., F. M. Windsor, M. Munday and I. Durance, 2020. Natural or synthetic – how global trends in textile usage threaten freshwater environments. *Sci. Total Environ.*, 718, 134689. doi:10.1016/j.scitotenv.2019.134689

Stubbings, W. A., N. Kajiwara, H. Takigami and S. Harrad, 2016. Leaching behaviour of hexabromocyclododecane from treated curtains. *Chemosphere*, 144, 2091–2096. doi:10.1016/j.chemosphere.2015.10.121

Su, Y., Z. Zhang, D. Wu, L. Zhan, H. Shi and B. Xie, 2019. Occurrence of microplastics in landfill systems and their fate with landfill age. *Water Res.*, 164, 114968. doi:10.1016/j.watres.2019.114968

Sun, J., Z.-R. Zhu, W.-H. Li, X. Yan, L.-K. Wang, L. Zhang, J. Jin, X. Dai and B.-J. Ni, 2021. Revisiting microplastics in landfill leachate: Unnoticed tiny microplastics and their fate in treatment works. *Water Res.*, 190, 116784. doi:10.1016/j.watres.2020.116784

Thaysen, C., M. Sorais, J. Verreault, M. L. Diamond and C. M. Rochman, 2020. Bidirectional transfer of halogenated flame retardants between the gastrointestinal tract and ingested plastics in urban-adapted ring-billed gulls. *Sci. Total Environ.*, 730, 138887. doi:10.1016/j.scitotenv.2020.138887

Torres, F. G., D. C. Dioses-Salinas, C. I. Pizarro-Ortega and G. E. De-la-Torre, 2021. Sorption of chemical contaminants on degradable and non-degradable microplastics: Recent progress and research trends. *Sci. Total Environ.*, 757, 143875. doi:10.1016/j.scitotenv.2020.143875

Tourinho, P. S., V. Kočí, S. Loureiro and C. A. M. van Gestel, 2019. Partitioning of chemical contaminants to microplastics: Sorption mechanisms, environmental distribution and effects on toxicity and bioaccumulation. *Environ. Pollut.*, 252, 1246–1256. doi:10.1016/j.envpol.2019.06.030

Tunahan Kaya, A., M. Yurtsever and S. Çiftçi Bayraktar, 2018. Ubiquitous exposure to microfiber pollution in the air. *Eur. Phys. J. Plus*, 133(11), 488. doi:10.1140/epjp/i2018-12372-7

Unger, P. D., A. J. Salerno and M. A. Friedman, 1981. Disposition of [14C]caprolactam in the rat. *Food Cosmetics Toxicol.*, 19, 457–462. doi:10.1016/0015-6264(81)90450-8

van der Veen, I., A. C. Hanning, A. Stare, P. E. G. Leonards, J. de Boer and J. M. Weiss, 2020. The effect of weathering on per- and polyfluoroalkyl substances (PFASs) from durable water repellent (DWR) clothing. *Chemosphere*, 249, 126100. doi:10.1016/j. chemosphere.2020.126100

Velez, J. F. M., Y. Shashoua, K. Syberg and F. R. Khan, 2018. Considerations on the use of equilibrium models for the characterisation of HOC-microplastic interactions in vector studies. *Chemosphere*, 210, 359–365. doi:10.1016/j.chemosphere.2018.07.020

Verma, A. K., R. R. Dash and P. Bhunia, 2012. A review on chemical coagulation/flocculation technologies for removal of colour from textile wastewaters. *J Environ. Manage.*, 93(1), 154–168. doi:10.1016/j.jenvman.2011.09.012

Vethaak, A. D. and H. A. Leslie, 2016. Plastic debris is a human health issue. *Environ. Sci. Tech.*, 50(13), 6825–6826. doi:10.1021/acs.est.6b02569

Wang, D., G. Goldenman, T. Tugran, A. McNeil and M. Jones, 2020. *Per-and polyfluoroalkylether substances: identity, production and use.* Copenhagen, DK, Nordisk Ministerråd.

Wang, G., J. Peng, D. Zhang and X. Li, 2016. Characterizing distributions, composition profiles, sources and potential health risk of polybrominated diphenyl ethers (PBDEs) in the coastal sediments from East China Sea. *Environ. Poll.*, 213, 468–481. doi:10.1016/j. envpol.2016.02.054

Wang, L., Y. Zhang, Y. Liu, X. Gong, T. Zhang and H. Sun, 2019. Widespread occurrence of Bisphenol A in daily clothes and its high exposure risk in humans. *Environ. Sci. Technol.*, 53(12), 7095–7102. doi:10.1021/acs.est.9b02090

Wang, Z., M. Chen, L. Zhang, K. Wang, X. Yu, Z. Zheng and R. Zheng, 2018. Sorption behaviors of phenanthrene on the microplastics identified in a mariculture farm in Xiangshan Bay, southeastern China. *Sci. Total Environ.*, 628–629, 1617–1626. doi:10.1016/j. scitotenv.2018.02.146

Wang, Z., G. W. Walker, D. C. G. Muir and K. Nagatani-Yoshida, 2020. Toward a global understanding of chemical pollution: A first comprehensive analysis of national and regional chemical inventories. *Environ. Sci. Technol.*, 54(5), 2575–2584. doi:10.1021/acs.est.9b06379

Ward, J. E., S. Zhao, B. A. Holohan, K. M. Mladinich, T. W. Griffin, J. Wozniak and S. E. Shumway, 2019. Selective ingestion and egestion of plastic particles by the Blue Mussel (Mytilus edulis) and Eastern Oyster (Crassostrea virginica): Implications for using bivalves as bioindicators of microplastic pollution. *Environ. Sci. Technol.* 53(15), 8776–8784. doi:10.1021/acs.est.9b02073

Watts, A. J. R., M. A. Urbina, S. Corr, C. Lewis and T. S. Galloway, 2015. Ingestion of plastic microfibers by the Crab Carcinus maenas and its effect on food consumption and energy balance. *Environ. Sci. Technol.*, 49(24), 14597–14604. doi:10.1021/acs. est.5b04026

Weil, E. D., S. Levchik and P. Moy, 2006. Flame and smoke retardants in vinyl chloride polymers – Commercial usage and current developments. *J Fire Sci.* 24(3), 211–236. doi:10.1177/0734904106057951

Welch, C. M., 1992. Formaldehyde-free durable-press finishes. *Rev Progress Colorat Relat Topics* 22(1), 32–41. doi:10.1111/j.1478-4408.1992.tb00087.x

Welden, N. A. C. and P. R. Cowie, 2016. Environment and gut morphology influence microplastic retention in langoustine, Nephrops norvegicus. *Environ. Poll.*, 214, 859–865. doi:10.1016/j.envpol.2016.03.067

White, E. M., S. Clark, C. A. Manire, B. Crawford, S. Wang, J. Locklin and B. W. Ritchie, 2018. Ingested micronizing plastic particle compositions and size distributions within stranded post-hatchling sea turtles. *Environ. Sci. Technol.*, 52(18), 10307–10316. doi:10.1021/acs.est.8b02776

Wilding, M. A. (1995). Introduction: The structure of fibres. *Chemistry of the textiles industry.* C. M. Carr. Dordrecht, Springer Netherlands: 1–45.

Zafeiraki, E., W. A. Gebbink, R. L. A. P. Hoogenboom, M. Kotterman, C. Kwadijk, E. Dassenakis and S. P. J. van Leeuwen, 2019. Occurrence of perfluoroalkyl substances (PFASs) in a large number of wild and farmed aquatic animals collected in the Netherlands. *Chemosphere*, 232, 415–423. doi:10.1016/j.chemosphere.2019.05.200

Zambrano, M. C., J. J. Pawlak, J. Daystar, M. Ankeny, C. C. Goller and R. A. Venditti, 2020. Aerobic biodegradation in freshwater and marine environments of textile microfibers generated in clothes laundering: Effects of cellulose and polyester-based microfibers on the microbiome. *Mar. Pollut. Bull.*, 151, 110826. doi:10.1016/j.marpolbul.2019.110826

Zambrano, M. C., J. J. Pawlak, J. Daystar, M. Ankeny and R. A. Venditti, 2021. Impact of dyes and finishes on the aquatic biodegradability of cotton textile fibers and microfibers released on laundering clothes: Correlations between enzyme adsorption and activity and biodegradation rates. *Mar. Pollut. Bull.*, 165, 112030. doi:10.1016/j. marpolbul.2021.112030

Zarus, G. M., C. Muianga, C. M. Hunter and R. S. Pappas, 2021. A review of data for quantifying human exposures to micro and nanoplastics and potential health risks. *Sci. Total Environ.*, 756, 144010. doi:10.1016/j.scitotenv.2020.144010

Zhang, Q., Y. Zhao, F. Du, H. Cai, G. Wang and H. Shi, 2020. Microplastic fallout in different indoor environments. *Environ. Sci. Technol.*, 54(11), 6530–6539. doi:10.1021/acs. est.0c00087

Zhao, Y., R. Qiao, S. Zhang and G. Wang, 2021. Metabolomic profiling reveals the intestinal toxicity of different length of microplastic fibers on zebrafish (Danio rerio). *J. Hazard. Mater.*, 403, 123663. doi:10.1016/j.jhazmat.2020.123663

Zhou, H., L. Zhou and K. Ma, 2020. Microfiber from textile dyeing and printing wastewater of a typical industrial park in China: Occurrence, removal and release. *Sci. Total Environ.*, 739, 140329. doi:10.1016/j.scitotenv.2020.140329

Zhu, H. and K. Kannan, 2020. Total oxidizable precursor assay in the determination of perfluoroalkyl acids in textiles collected from the United States. *Environ. Pollut.*, 265, 114940. doi:10.1016/j.envpol.2020.114940

PART 2

Textile solutions

6

MICROFIBRE SHEDDING FROM TEXTILES DURING LAUNDERING

Different quantification methods but common findings

Imogen E. Napper and Richard C. Thompson

1 Introduction

It has been suggested that a large proportion of the microfibres found in the marine environment are released from textiles, with a key source being the washing of clothes (Belzagui, Crespi, Álvarez, Gutiérrez-Bouzán, & Vilaseca, 2019; Browne et al., 2011; De Falco, Gentile, Di Pace, Avella, & Cocca, 2018; Napper et al., 2021; Napper, Barrett, & Thompson, 2020; Napper & Thompson, 2016; Salvador Cesa, Turra, & Baruque-Ramos, 2017). Globally, Boucher and Friot (2017) estimated that of all primary microplastics in the oceans, 35% arise from laundry of textiles; an estimated 2–13 million tonnes per year (Boucher & Friot, 2017; Mishra, Rath, & Das, 2019). Approximately 63% of textile fibres produced are synthetic (e.g., polyester, nylon) (The Fibre Year, 2019). Over 42 million tonnes of synthetic fibres are produced each year by the clothing industry (Carr, 2017) with polyester dominating production (approximately 80%) (Krifa & Stewart Stevens, 2016; L'Abbate et al., 2018). Other textile fibre materials include natural (e.g., cotton, wool) and semi-synthetic or regenerated fibres (e.g., rayon, acetate). In this chapter the term microfibre will refer exclusively to fibres, including synthetic, semi-synthetic and natural, that are typically <5 mm.

The washing of clothes appears to be a key source of synthetic fibres into aquatic environments, and there is also clear evidence that several factors associated with the laundering of clothes have a key influence on fibre release (Browne et al., 2011; De Falco, Gullo, et al., 2018; Napper, Barrett, et al., 2020). Factors associated can include the type of polymer, fibre and garment that is being washed or the way it is washed (e.g. mechanical and chemical factors)

Microfibres released as a result of washing clothes exit the washing machine via the wastewater effluent and will either pass directly to watercourses or to wastewater treatment plants (WWTPs). It has been reported that the majority of

DOI: 10.4324/9781003165385-8

particles detected in WWTPs are microfibres (Gies et al., 2018; Gündoğdu, Çevik, Güzel, & Kilercioğlu, 2018; Leslie, Brandsma, van Velzen, & Vethaak, 2017). In a modern WWTP, microplastic removal from water can be up to 96% (Carr, Liu, & Tesoro, 2016; Murphy, Ewins, Carbonnier, & Quinn, 2016) before the water is released to the environment. However, even with high removal efficiency, a substantial quantity of microfibres are not captured. For example, it has been estimated that a secondary WWTP that serves a population of 650,000 (Glasgow, U.K.) with a removal efficiency of 98.41% could still release 65 million microplastic particles (including microfibres) every day (Murphy et al., 2016). Even if microfibres are intercepted during wastewater treatment, the resultant sewage sludge is often returned to the land as a fertilizer, hence microfibres are still released to the environment (Corradini et al., 2019; Gies et al., 2018; Kirchmann, Börjesson, Kätterer, & Cohen, 2017). These fibres are known to reach aquatic systems directly (Leslie, Van Velzen, & Vethaak, 2013; Parker-Jurd et al., 2020) as well as terrestrial systems via the spreading of sludge (Corradini et al., 2019; Murphy et al., 2016). Additionally, in many parts of the world, laundry is mainly done by handwashing and wastewater may not be treated at all prior to being released to aquatic environments.

Understanding the contribution of laundering to the release of microfibres into the environment is a key priority to help guide interventions. Research has focussed on evaluating and quantifying the release of microfibres during the washing of clothes and, more recently, during the everyday wearing of clothing (De Falco, Cocca, Avella, & Thompson, 2020). Different methods have been developed to evaluate the amount of microfibres shed from fabrics during washing. The first paper to highlight the extent of microfibre release from clothing was from Browne et al. (2011). Napper and Thompson (2016) then estimated that a typical wash (6 kg) could produce over 700,000 microfibres. Recent work has used ultra-fine filters to capture the microfibres released; 5 µm mesh pore size in De Falco, Gullo, et al., (2018) compared to 25 µm in Napper and Thompson (2016). Since smaller mesh size captures smaller microfibres which may bypass larger mesh pore sizes, this more recent study estimated that over 6,000,000 microfibres could be released from an average 6 kg wash (De Falco, Gullo, et al., 2018).

Fibre release can be influenced by differences in: a) presentation of the test material (whole garments vs. textile swatches); b) textile construction and material composition – i.e. fabric structure, yarn twist, fibre type and hairiness); c) load composition (mix loads, full loads, single garments); d) laundering conditions (temperature, detergent use. cycle time, water volume); and e) sampling approaches including than pore size simulated laundering vs. household appliances; model, fibre enumeration and characterization (Belzagui et al., 2019; Cesa, Turra, Checon, Leonardi, & Baruque-Ramos, 2020; Napper, Barrett, et al., 2020; Napper & Thompson, 2016). There is a consensus on the range of factors influencing release (fabric characteristics, chemical, mechanical and laundering conditions), but varying methodologies are used to quantify release.

Due to concerns about microplastics and fibres in the environment, and a need to find approaches to reduce their accumulation, research is focussing on specific pathways to the environment such as laundering clothes to identify mitigation strategies. Therefore, this chapter will examine the extent to which common conclusions and consensuses can be drawn from previous studies, despite any differences in their methodology. Additionally, the inconsistencies and knowledge gaps due to the lack of shared protocols will be discussed. Regrettably, some studies that have examined multiple factors do not present numerical (magnitude) data for all of the factors investigated and we would encourage it.

2   Fabric characteristics

Fibres from fabrics are known to be lost due to pilling. Pilling is defined as the entangling of the fabric surface during wearing or washing, resulting in formation of fibre balls (or pills) that stand proud on the surface of the fabric (Hussain, Ahmed, & Qayum, 2008). This occurs as a consequence of two processes: (i) fuzzing; the protrusion of fibres from the fabric surface, and (ii) pill formation; the persistence of formed neps (entangled masses of fibres) at the fabric surface (Naik & Lopez-Amo, 1982). The pill may be worn or pulled away from fabrics due to mechanical action during laundering or wear (Yates, 2002). However, the rate or extent to which the pilling stages occur is determined by the physical properties of the fibres which comprise the fabric (Gintis & Mead, 1959).

Therefore, different fabric characteristics used in textile manufacturing can have a major impact on how many microfibres are released during laundering. For example, factors such as the type of yarn polymer and twist and fabric structure are all influential in fibre shedding (De Falco et al., 2020). Additional characteristics include the variety of different polymer type, textile characteristics and fabric age (Table 6.1).

TABLE 6.1 Summary of research on the influence of fabric characteristics, laundering machine type, chemical factors, laundering cycle or temperature on the quantity of fibres released from garments

Factor	Description of parameters tested and percentage reductions in fibre release	Reference
Fabric Characteristics	3 independent studies showing reductions of 57%, 81% and 99% depending on polymer type or fabric construction	Napper and Thompson, 2016; Almroth et al., 2018; De Falco et al., 2020
Laundering Machine Type	1 study showing reduction of 88% depending on machine type. Fibre mass released from garments being washed was significantly greater for top-load machines in comparison to front-loading machines.	Hartline et al., 2016

(Continued)

TABLE 5.1 (Continued)

Factor	Description of parameters tested and percentage reductions in fibre release	Reference
Laundering Chemical (Detergent/ Softener)	3 independent studies showing reductions of 13%, 17%, 35% and 95% depending on which laundering detergent used.	Pirc et al., 2016; De Falco, Gullo, et al., 2018 Kelly et al., 2019
	1 study showing reductions of 35% depending on which laundering softener used.	
Laundering Cycle/ Temperature	1 study showing reduction of 58% depending on the laundering cycle or temperature used.	Kelly et al., 2019

2.1   Polymer type

Microfibres can be grouped into two main categories: (1) natural fibres (e.g. cotton or silk) that originate from natural materials and (2) man-made fibres, which can be subsequently divided into two groups depending on their polymer of origin. Semi-synthetic fibres like rayon are derived from cellulose-based materials but have been synthetically altered and are therefore considered of anthropogenic origin; they are also described as regenerated cellulosic fibres. Distinguishing regenerated cellulosic fibres from natural cellulosic fibres is challenging, as their spectra are difficult to differentiate using spectroscopy. Whereas, synthetic fibres (2b) (e.g. polyester or acrylic) originating from the extrusion of petrochemical derivatives (Dris, Gasperi, Rocher, & Tassin, 2018; Mateos-Cárdenas, O'Halloran, van Pelt, & Jansen, 2021; Stanton, Johnson, Nathanail, MacNaughtan, & Gomes, 2019) can be distinguished using Fourier-Transform Infrared Spectroscopy (FTIR).

Synthetic fibres are frequently reported in environmental samples (Miller, Watts, Winslow, Galloway, & Barrows, 2017; Napper et al., 2021; Napper, Davies, et al., 2020; Stanton, Johnson, Nathanail, MacNaughtan, & Gomes, 2020). However, there is increased evidence that suggests regenerated cellulosic fibres such as rayon, are also abundant within the environment. Rayon is often reported as a common polymer type for microplastics in both freshwater and marine samples (Lindeque et al., 2020; Nan et al., 2020; Napper et al., 2021; Park et al., 2020)

To investigate differences between polymer types and fibres released whilst laundering, Napper and Thompson (2016) tested acrylic, polyester and polyester-cotton blend jumpers; they found that both the polyester and polyester-cotton blend jumpers released less than the acrylic. However, the cause of these differences between garments was not determined and may be a consequence of the type of polymer or the yarn or fabric construction, or a combination of these factors.

2.2 Textile characteristics

Recent, research has begun to focus more on different textile characteristics of fabrics in relation to how many fibres are released during laundering. De Falco et al. (2020) investigated polyester garments with different textile characteristics including various material compositions, fabric structure, yarn twist, fibre type and hairiness. They reported compactly woven and highly twisted yarns with continuous filaments release far fewer microfibres during laundering than fabrics which have a loose structure. A polyester garment of knitted fabric structure and filament fibre type released 57% more fibres than a polyester garment with woven fabric structure and filament fibre type. Additionally, Almroth et al. (2018) observed that polyester fleece fabrics shed significantly more fibres (99%) than polyester knit fabrics (Almroth et al., 2018). Furthermore, Zambrano et al. (2019) highlighted that fabrics with lower hairiness, higher abrasion resistance and yarn strength released less microfibres. Almroth et al. (2018) found that tightly constructed yarns (i.e. with high twist) reduced microfibre release.

These differences in textile characteristics indicate some degree of consensus among the scientific community that parameters, such as the textile type, have a relatively consistent direct effect on microfibre release; despite differences in the methodological approaches used by different researchers (see Table 6.1) (De Falco et al., 2020). However, very little information is available on which specific parameters of the textile have the greatest influence and more research is needed to help guide interventions to reduce microfibre emission (De Falco et al., 2020). Consequently, focus should be placed on better understanding what permutations of textile design give rise to the lowest rate of fibre shedding. Reducing shedding through changes in fabric design will help reduce emissions during all use phases: wearing, washing and tumble drying (De Falco et al., 2020; Napper & Thompson, 2016; Pirc, Vidmar, Mozer, & Kržan, 2016). This is of key importance because any further measures down stream of production (be they in machine type, wash cycle, chemicals used or filtration and collection devices) will exert their effect on top of the reductions achieved by better design.

2.3 Fabric age

The number of microplastic fibres released during washing could additionally be impacted by the age of the garment. There has been research to suggest microfibres released from clothes are greater in the first few washes of the garment. A reduction in microfibre release from cycle one to five has been documented for the majority of garments tested by Sillanpää and Sainio (2017) and Zambrano et al. (2019) (mixture of polyester and cotton textiles).

Additionally, Napper and Thompson (2016) showed that garments had an initial peak of microfibre shedding in the first one to four washes. They reported that polyester showed a steady decrease in fibre loss overall: first wash (2.79 mg) to fifth (1.63 mg) (41% decrease). Acrylic followed a similar pattern, but the fibre loss decreased more rapidly: first wash (2.63 mg) to fourth (0.99 mg) (62% decrease). Polyester-cotton blend had the least variation, and showed little decrease between subsequent washes: first wash (0.45 mg) to fourth (0.30 mg) (Napper & Thompson, 2016) (33% decrease). It has been suggested that the initial spike in microfibre release may be from loose unbroken fibre debris from the yarn interior released in the first cycle (Kelly, Lant, Kurr, & Burgess, 2019). This subsequently links back to fabric composition and structure, which as discussed may affect microfibre release as the fabric ages.

The aging of garments may also increase fibre release. Hartline et al. (2016) conducted research on new and aged garments to determine if total recovered microfibre mass increased after aging a garment by a 24-hour no-spin agitation wash cycle (equivalent to ~24 washing cycles). On average, aging resulted in 25% more fibres released. Visual inspection of the jackets indicated that there was fraying on the aged jackets, which could lead to the increased mass of recovered fibres.

Therefore, there is consideration that a garment might shed more fibres when it is new or after aging. If more microfibres are released from the newer garments, particularly in the first cycle, this could be mitigated using a filtered prewash after garment manufacturing (Kelly et al., 2019). We suggested that additional tests on real consumer washing loads and longer-term studies are required to identify the influence of fabric aging. The majority of studies investigating fibre release have only focussed on five to ten cycles.

Taking into consideration different polymers, fabric construction and potential aging effects, there needs to be further understanding about the proportional impact each characteristic holds (see Table 6.1). The interventions in Table 6.1 should not be considered as alternatives, but rather ways of; optimizing how to use these mitigations in combination from design through washing to end of life

3   Mechanical factors

The amount of microplastics released during the washing process may also be affected by mechanical factors (De Falco, Gullo, et al., 2018; Napper & Thompson, 2016). Mechanical factors include washing machine type, rotations per minute (R.P.M.) and machine capacity and load ratio.

3.1   Washing machine type

There have been a wide range of approaches that have been used to study microfibre release during laundry, including laboratory-scale tests (e.g. using an instrument that simulates the action of a washing machine with specific modifications) (Almroth et al., 2018; De Falco, Gullo, et al., 2018; Hernandez, Nowack, & Mitrano, 2017; Jönsson et al., 2018), conventional washing machines (Browne et al., 2011; De Falco, Gullo, et al., 2018; Hartline et al., 2016; Hernandez et al., 2017; Napper, Barrett, et al., 2020; Napper & Thompson, 2016; Pirc et al., 2016) or a combination of both (De Falco, Gentile, et al., 2018; Zambrano et al., 2019). For example,

Kelly et al. (2019) developed a method for quantifying microfibre release in small-scale conditions, which qualitatively reflects the outcomes observed in full-sized domestic washing machines. The methodology accurately quantified microfibre release using a measure of lightness from black to white. Measurement of colour was preferred over microscopy to quantify microfibres as released microfibres can be very small and can form clusters on the surface of filter paper, making them difficult to count due to overlapping fibres. However, overall these methods have led to large disparities in quantity of microfibres released in the literature.

The type of washing machine used can be divided into front- and top-loading. Hartline et al. (2016) found that fibre mass released was significantly greater for top-load machines in comparison to front-loading machines. The median overall total fibre mass recovered per garment for front-load machines (median =220 mg, n = 30) was less than top-load (1906 mg, n = 40) (88% difference). It has been suggested that the central agitator of the top-load washing machine may be more abrasive on garments when compared to the rotating drum of the front-load machine, leading to the significantly higher observed shedding overall (Hartline et al., 2016). However, Kelly et al. (2019) reported that this difference could more likely be due to the front-loading machine using a much lower water-volume. Testing with additional models could improve our understanding of the influence from machine type on fibre release.

3.2   Washing duration and intensity

Other mechanical factors include the duration and intensity of washing cycles. De Falco, Gullo, et al. (2018) claimed that industrial washing could release significantly more microplastics compared to domestic washing. This is because of the differences in washing conditions and with a more aggressive way of washing in the industry. Additionally, they further suggested that when increasing the washing time, fabric will have a longer exposure time to chemical damage caused by the alkaline detergent. This will lead to an increase in water hardness and therefore an increase of abrasive damage.

Hernandez et al. (2017) also predicted that more fibres would be released from garments after increasing the time of the wash cycle. However, their results found that there was very little difference in emissions; a four-hour wash did not double the amount of fibres when compared to a two-hour wash. They found a 'fixed' amount of fibres regardless of the washing time and various mechanical stress.

4   Temperature

Several studies report a reduction in fibres at a lower temperature. For example, Napper and Thompson (2016) conducted domestic washing cycles carried out at two temperatures (30°C and 40°C). Although they found the effects of temperature to be non-significant, they reported that there were some interactive effects of temperature; polyester was often found to release more fibres than acrylic at 40°C when compared against 30°C. Additionally, De Falco, Gullo, et al. (2018) tested fabrics at 40°C and 60°C and found that higher temperatures increased microfibre release. Hernandez et al. (2017) also found higher temperature promoted the release of microfibres, especially from polyester fabric, which released significantly more microfibres when washed at 60°C than at 30°C. However, neither study presents the magnitude of effect, so it is not possible to confirm its relative importance compared to other factors. For Napper and Thompson (2016), it was clear that temperature was a less important effect than fabric type.

The latter studies reflect more industrial washing temperatures over typical household washing. Garments tend to be washed at lower temperatures, such as 30°C, due to energy costs and global warming pressures. Laundering of clothing has a large contribution to the energy expenditure of a clothing product, hence, reducing time and temperature is desirable (Cotton, Hayward, Lant, & Blackburn, 2020). So, research should aim to test temperatures around 30°C to reflect temperatures that aim to be used by the typical household.

Guidance to consumers typically focuses on having a lower temperature washing setting to mitigate fibre release. A UK-based environmental organization stated that *'a lower-temperature wash is less aggressive and therefore less likely to shake out plastic fibres'* (Byrne, 2018) and an environmental international global alliance of organizations, businesses and leaders in 75 countries stated, *'use a colder wash setting. Higher temperature can damage clothes and release more fibers'* (Plastic Pollution Coalition, 2017). However, neither statement is supported by references to previous studies or data in verification.

5 Chemical factors

The use of both detergent and fabric softener (also called fabric conditioner) when washing clothes is common practise. Detergent can come in two forms: liquid and powder.

De Falco, Gullo, et al. (2018) indicated that the use of detergents, both in liquid and powder form, induce an increase of microfibre release. They found that, for woven polyester garments, washings performed with only water produced a release of 162 ± 52 microfibres per gram of fabric, and that increased to 1,273 ± 177 when using liquid detergent and to 3,538 ± 664 when using powder detergent. Therefore, washing with no detergent could reduce fibre shedding by 95%. In particular, the powder product significantly favours the microfibre shedding more than the liquid one (De Falco, Gullo, et al., 2018). However, they also reported that powder detergent induced a significant error (underestimation) in microfibre determination since it formed a thick layer on the filtration system in which the microfibres were partially or completely embedded, thus making their numerical determination difficult (De Falco, Gullo, et al., 2018).

Almroth et al. (2018) found that washing with liquid detergent resulted in a significant increase in the amount of fibres released for three out of four fabrics they tested. Zambrano et al., (2019) also found a significant increase in microfibre mass released when the detergent solution was used as a washing agent for all fabric types tested. However, Hernandez et al. (2017), Almroth et al. (2018) and Zambrano et al. (2019) were studies which used steel balls in the washing process. The steel balls could potentially interact mechanically with detergent, causing unrealistic microfibre release; the use of steel balls is discussed in Section 3.2. In addition, some factors of detergents, including formulation (presence of oxidizing agents) and pH, also have effects on microplastic release when washing (De Falco, Gullo, et al., 2018; De Falco, Gentile, et al., 2018).

The impact of fabric softener has also been investigated. De Falco, Gullo, et al. (2018) reported that the usage of a softener during washes reduces the number of microfibres released. They found that the use of a softener during a 5 kg wash load of polyester fabrics could reduce the release of microfibres by 35% with respect to the amount released during the washing under the same conditions but only with a liquid detergent (De Falco, Gullo, et al., 2018). However, the overall use of softener did not significantly influence emission in research by Napper and Thompson (2016) and Pirc et al. (2016).

These findings indicate that the influence of detergent and fabric softener merit further exploration. Gaining a basic understanding of the impact that detergent and fabric softener have on garments, in combination with how they function within normal washing parameters (i.e., temperature and duration of cycle), is important but this may be difficult due to the number of different commercially available brands since the variety of chemical formulas used may result in different effects.

6 Sampling methodology

The majority of studies follow a similar approach to quantify microfibre release. This includes washing machines being cleaned thoroughly prior to testing and then effluent water being collected from the drain hose during the wash and rinsing process. (Cotton et al., 2020; Napper, Barrett, et al., 2020; Napper & Thompson, 2016). However, there are a variety of differences between studies. This includes load composition, sampling methods and analysis.

6.1 Load composition

The load composition used within research to understand the release of microfibres from textiles often does not reflect full mixed loads that typical households would run. Previous experiments have included mix loads, such as Napper et al. (2020), where a whole medium-sized jumper of either of 100% polyester, 100% acrylic or 60% polyester/40% cotton blend was tested. The three different synthetic fabric types were included in the washing trials to represent a typical mixed load (1.3 ± 0.2 kg), but substantially lower (81%) in weight than a typical wash (~5–7 kg).

Whereas, research by Cesa et al. (2020) tested a mix of polymer types and garment types separately, including: cotton t-shirts, polyester t-shirts, acrylic jumpers and polyamide shirts. It has been previously suggested that washing tests carried out using less garments will result in greater wettability of the fabric, which could enhance the mobility of microfibres that detach from the yarns (De Falco et al., 2020). From the best of our knowledge, no conclusion can be reached about the different effects each load will have on fibre generation.

Additionally, research has used either whole garments or textile swatches. For example, Napper and Thompson (2016) separately tested 100% polyester, 100% acrylic and 65% polyester/35% cotton blend jumpers cut into 20 × 20 cm swatches from the back panel of the garments and hemmed the edges by 0.5 cm to deter the excess loss of fibres. Kelly et al. (2019) also cut replicate t-shirts into 5 × 5 cm swatches using a laser cutter to seal the edges and prevent uncontrolled microfibre release from the cut edge (Kelly et al., 2019). Although this standardizes the garments in size and shape, it is not reflective of a typical household wash; however, this may be a preferred method to understand subtle differences in fabric construction.

Furthermore, the cutting method to make these swatches may be another factor affecting the number of microfibre released from textiles during washing (Jönsson et al., 2018). Cai et al., (2020) showed that the majority of the released microfibres during washing likely originate from edges, as opposed to the surface of the textile, so adopting cleaner cutting techniques may be important for the industry to help reduce microfibre release. The most commonly used cutting approach is mechanical cutting where knives are vertically guided to cut multiple layers of textiles (Gries, Veit, & Wulfhorst, 2014). In addition, thermal cutting is also applied during textile tailoring (Gries et al., 2014). Then, cut edges are often sewn with stiches in the later step. Many studies adopted either mechanically cut swatches with sewn edges (De Falco, Gullo, et al., 2018; Napper & Thompson, 2016) or thermally cut swatches (Almroth et al., 2018; Kelly et al., 2019) to reduce microfibre shedding from edges. However, it is still unclear whether those procedures can really prevent microfibre release from the edge and how the cutting or sewing method affects microfibre release.

There has been limited research which has used a full load of mixed fabrics within their washing tests (Galvão, Aleixo, De Pablo, Lopes, & Raimundo, 2020; Lant, Hayward, Peththawadu, Sheridan, & Dean, 2020). Therefore, further research focussing on typical realistic load conditions is needed.

6.2 Use of steel balls in washing tests

Some approaches do not reflect real domestic laundry conditions; for example, the use of steel balls during washing (Almroth et al., 2018; De Falco, Gullo, et al., 2018; Hernandez et al., 2017; Jönsson et al., 2018; Zambrano et al., 2019). In an attempt to minimize experimental variables, these methods consist of a heated water bath containing a rotating shaft that supports, radially, a number of stainless-steel canisters. The canisters contain the test sample in a liquor with a prescribed number of stainless-steel ball bearings that replicate in-wash agitation and abrasion (Tiffin, Hazlehurst, Sumner, & Taylor, 2021). However, it is clear that this approach is quite different from conditions in a conventional domestic washing machine.

It has been suggested that the steel balls magnify the effects of detergent, perhaps by forcing it into the textile weave or agitating the surfactant so that more bubbles are produced (Kelly et al., 2019). Further investigations into detergent type and their interactions with different textiles are probably warranted, but studies should use real-world conditions to keep results relevant (Kelly et al., 2019). Alternatively, formal comparisons between approaches using steel balls and conventional washing machines must be conducted in order to understand how realistic such approaches are.

6.3 Filtering and quantification

The majority of research has used a gravimetric method to quantify microfibre release (Cesa et al., 2020; Kelly et al., 2019; McIlwraith et al., 2019; Napper & Thompson, 2016). This is often partnered with a conversion formula to transfer the gravimetric results into the number of microfibres released. The gravitational method can work for the total of waste effluent or a subsample. Most studies have reported the weight of microfibres in washing machine effluent (Napper & Thompson, 2016; Pirc et al., 2016) rather than the count.

When filtering, pore size of the filter has shown to have substantial differences in the amount of microfibres captured. De Falco et al. (2018) used a 5 μm diameter filter, allowing the detection of more microfibres, compared to research with filters with a greater pore size (25 μm in Napper and Thompson, 2016; 20 and 330 μm in Hartline et al., 2016; 200 μm in Pirc et al., 2016). However, Napper et al. (2020) also used mass change from a 1 μm filter as a method to quantify the microfibre release.

Standardized filtering methodology, which can be adapted to fit different research aims, should be collaboratively developed. This includes selecting a commonly used mesh pore size. As discussed, changes in pore size when filtering can have a substantial impact on the reported abundance of released microfibres. Napper and Thompson (2016) estimated that a typical wash (6 kg) could produce over 700,000 microfibres after filtering with a mesh pore size of 25 μm. However, De Falco, Gullo, et al. (2018) estimated that over 6,000,000 microfibres could be released from an average 6 kg wash after filtering with a mesh pore size of 5 μm.

For quantification of microfibre release, optical (Hernandez et al., 2017; Jönsson et al., 2018), electron microscopy (De Falco, Gullo, et al., 2018; De Falco, Gentile, et al., 2018) and binary image analysis (Hernandez et al., 2017) have been used. Microscopy can require scaling, which assumes that microfibres are homogenously distributed across filters, potentially leading to inaccuracies. Binary image analysis (Hernandez et al., 2017) does not account for overlapping fibres, resulting in an underestimation of fibre quantities. Consequently, it is difficult to make comparisons between these studies.

7   Future work

It is important to note that whenever a new form of contamination is discovered, it is inevitable that in the early stages of research a variety of methods will be applied. The individual research questions asked will differ and scientists will likely have matched their approach to the specific question. It's also impossible to establish a standard method without trying some different approaches. So, the fact that there is a lack of a standard method and challenges in comparability should not be seen as a shortcoming of the work that has been done; rather it is a necessary reality.

As synthetic fibres released from garments during domestic washings are considered a substantial part of the microfibre contamination present in the environment (Browne et al., 2011; Kay, Hiscoe, Moberley, Bajic, & McKenna, 2018; Miller et al., 2017; Napper et al., 2021), there is an urgent need to explore the factors leading to this contamination. Increases in synthetic textiles consumption and frequency of home laundry (Laitala, Boks, & Klepp, 2011) further increase this urgency. Additionally, given the high levels of public concern about microplastics, best practices for mitigating microfibre release are increasingly being offered by industry, consumer organizations and media groups, but often without robust scientific evidence in support.

To inform effective policy, local municipalities, countries and regions seek scientific data on the effectiveness of proposed mitigation strategies for plastic pollution. Therefore, to understand the factors that affect the release of microfibres during laundry, reliable and reproducible methods for their quantification are needed.

Based on the evidence we present here, the work that has been done already indicates some key intervention points. As discussed, there is evidence of differences according to fabric characteristics, laundering conditions, mechanical factors and chemical factors for research investigating microfibre emissions from washing clothes. However, several studies now show variation in fabric characteristics has considerable influence, so prioritization of better fabric design may well be the most effective current strategy to reduce the release of fibres from clothing (see Table 6.1). While there is also evidence that factors downstream of manufacture, for example at the laundering stage, can have an influence, the evidence to guide specific interventions is less clear. In this regard, it is important to note that the interventions in Table 6.1 should not be considered as alternatives, but rather ways of optimizing how to use these mitigations in combination or as a hierarchy from design through washing to end of life.

In our view, we are now at a point where much has been learned about the factors influencing fibre release, and transition to finer scale research using a standard approach is a critical next step. Developing a clear understanding of the influence of each factor separately and in combination, with clearly defined standardization, is essential to understanding their relative importance.

The U.S.-based American Association of Textile Chemists and Colorists (AATCC) also report development of a standardized test method for microfibre shedding that will be aligned with the work of the 'The Microfibre Consortium'. However, these methods are not freely available. And this is likely to limit broad uptake, transparency and confidence.

For research to be comparable, information on laundering parameters and textile characteristics needs to be standardized, recorded and made publicly available. Parameters include:

1) **Mechanical factors**

   i   washing machine type
   ii   rotations per minute (R.P.M.)
   iii machine capacity and load ratio

2) **Laundering conditions**

   i   washing temperature
   ii   washing cycle description and duration

3) **Chemical factors**

   i   detergent use, type and general description of the product
   ii   conditioner use, type and general description of the product
   iii presence and quantity of other products used

4) **Textile material**

   i   fibre type (i.e. cross-section shape, cross-section thickness, length, composition)
   ii   yarn type (i.e. staple or filament, twists per unit length, number of filaments)
   iii fabric type (i.e. density, thickness, mass per unit area)
   iv   condition (i.e. new or worn)
   v   description of textile article, including type (e.g., garment), seaming presence, size and total weight.

5) **Testing Method**

   i   filtration system
   ii   analysis

In conclusion, different methods have been developed to evaluate the amount of microfibres shed from fabrics during laundering. This is inevitable, as the individual researchers were typically conducting different experiments with differing aims and will have likely have attempted to optimize their methods according to the question under scrutiny. The number of studies has increased dramatically, and the use of differing methods limits comparability, but it's worth keeping in mind that inter-comparability is unlikely to have been a key priority in the conception of these studies. Despite the difference in approaches there is consensus on the factors influencing microfibre release, with fabric characteristics being prominent, compared to chemical (e.g. type of detergent), mechanical (e.g. type of washing machine) and laundering conditions (e.g. temperature). This points to the need for further work to better understand the factors that lead to differences between various fabric types and how best to maximize the reduction in emissions using multiple interventions in isolation, in combination and as part of a hierarchy.

Even in the absence of consistent methodology thus far, there is sufficient evidence to indicate where the most successful intervention points are likely to lie. So while it is essential to develop standardized approaches to ensure comparability, reproducibility and transparency across studies, in our view the lack of such consistency to date does not preclude us from moving toward the intervention points that have already been identified.

References

Almroth, B. M., Åström, L., Roslund, S., Petersson, H., Johansson, M., & Persson, N. K., 2018. Quantifying shedding of synthetic fibers from textiles; A source of microplastics released into the environment. *Environmental Science and Pollution Research*, 25(2), 1191–1199. https://doi.org/10.1007/s11356-017-0528-7

Belzagui, F., Crespi, M., Álvarez, A., Gutiérrez-Bouzán, C., & Vilaseca, M., 2019. Microplastics' emissions: Microfibers' detachment from textile garments. *Environmental Pollution*, 248, 1028–1035. https://doi.org/10.1016/j.envpol.2019.02.059

Boucher, J., & Friot, D., 2017. *Primary microplastics in the oceans: A global evaluation of sources.* Retrieved 3 October 2019 from Gland, Switzerland: https://portals.iucn.org/library/sites/library/files/documents/2017-002.pdf

Browne, M. A., Crump, P., Niven, S. J., Teuten, E., Tonkin, A., Galloway, T., & Thompson, R., 2011. Accumulation of microplastic on shorelines worldwide: Sources and sinks. *Environmental Science and Technology*, 45(21), 9175–9179. https://doi.org/10.1021/es201811s

Byrne, P., 2018. *Microfibres: The plastic in our clothes.* Retrieved 23 March 2021 from https://friendsoftheearth.uk/plastics/microfibres-plastic-in-our-clothes

Cai, Y., Yang, T., Mitrano, D. M., Heuberger, M., Hufenus, R., & Nowack, B., 2020. Systematic study of microplastic fiber release from 12 different polyester textiles during washing. *Environmental Science and Technology*, 54, 4855. https://doi.org/10.1021/acs.est.9b07395

Carr, S. A., 2017. Sources and dispersive modes of micro-fibers in the environment. *Integrated Environmental Assessment and Management*, 13(3), 466–469. https://doi.org/10.1002/ieam.1916

Carr, S. A., Liu, J., & Tesoro, A. G., 2016. Transport and fate of microplastic particles in wastewater treatment plants. *Water Research*, 91, 174–182. https://doi.org/10.1016/j.watres.2016.01.002

Cesa, F. S., Turra, A., Checon, H. H., Leonardi, B., & Baruque-Ramos, J., 2020. Laundering and textile parameters influence fibers release in household washings. *Environmental Pollution*, 257, 113553. https://doi.org/10.1016/j.envpol.2019.113553

Corradini, F., Meza, P., Eguiluz, R., Casado, F., Huerta-Lwanga, E., & Geissen, V., 2019. Evidence of microplastic accumulation in agricultural soils from sewage sludge disposal. *Science of The Total Environment*, 671, 411–420. Retrieved 2 September 2019 from www.sciencedirect.com/science/article/pii/S004896971931366X

Cotton, L., Hayward, A. S., Lant, N. J., & Blackburn, R. S., 2020. Improved garment longevity and reduced microfibre release are important sustainability benefits of laundering in colder and quicker washing machine cycles. *Dyes and Pigments*, 177, 108120. https://doi.org/10.1016/j.dyepig.2019.108120

De Falco, F., Cocca, M., Avella, M., & Thompson, R. C., 2020. Microfibre release to water, via laundering, and to air, via everyday use: A comparison between polyester clothing with differing textile parameters. *Environmental Science & Technology*, 54(6), 3288–3296. https://doi.org/10.1021/acs.est.9b06892

De Falco, F., Gentile, G., Di Pace, E., Avella, M., & Cocca, M., 2018. Quantification of microfibres released during washing of synthetic clothes in real conditions and at lab scale★. *European Physical Journal Plus*, 133(7), 1–4. https://doi.org/10.1140/epjp/i2018-12123-x

De Falco, F., Gullo, M. P., Gentile, G., Di Pace, E., Cocca, M., Gelabert, L., . . . Avella, M., 2018. Evaluation of microplastic release caused by textile washing processes of synthetic fabrics. *Environmental Pollution*, 236, 916–925. https://doi.org/10.1016/J. ENVPOL.2017.10.057

Dris, R., Gasperi, J., Rocher, V., & Tassin, B., 2018. Synthetic and non-synthetic anthropogenic fibers in a river under the impact of Paris Megacity: Sampling methodological aspects and flux estimations. *Science of the Total Environment*, 618, 157–164. https://doi.org/10.1016/j.scitotenv.2017.11.009

The Fiber Year, 2019. *The fiber year 2019; World survey on textiles & nonwovens*. Retrieved from Frankfurt, Germany.

Galvão, A., Aleixo, M., De Pablo, H., Lopes, C., & Raimundo, J., 2020. Microplastics in wastewater: Microfiber emissions from common household laundry. *Environmental Science and Pollution Research*, 27(21), 26643–26649. https://doi.org/10.1007/S11356-020-08765-6

Gies, E. A., LeNoble, J. L., Noël, M., Etemadifar, A., Bishay, F., Hall, E. R., & Ross, P. S., 2018. Retention of microplastics in a major secondary wastewater treatment plant in Vancouver, Canada. *Marine Pollution Bulletin*, 133, 553–561. https://doi.org/10.1016/j.marpolbul.2018.06.006

Gintis, D., & Mead, E. J., 1959. The mechanism of pilling. *Textile Research Journal*, 29(7), 578–585. https://doi.org/10.1177/004051755902900709

Gries, T., Veit, D., & Wulfhorst, B., 2014. *Textile technology: An introduction* (2nd ed.). Cincinnati, OH: Hanser Publications. Retrieved 15 March 2021 from www.worldcat.org/title/textile-technology-an-introduction/oclc/907394165

Gündoğdu, S., Çevik, C., Güzel, E., & Kilercioğlu, S., 2018. Microplastics in municipal wastewater treatment plants in Turkey: A comparison of the influent and secondary effluent concentrations. *Environmental Monitoring and Assessment*, 190(11), 626. https://doi.org/10.1007/s10661-018-7010-y

Hartline, N. L., Bruce, N. J., Karba, S. N., Ruff, E. O., Sonar, S. U., & Holden, P. A., 2016. Microfiber masses recovered from conventional machine washing of new or aged garments. *Environmental Science and Technology*, 50(21), 11532–11538. https://doi.org/10.1021/acs.est.6b03045

Hernandez, E., Nowack, B., & Mitrano, D. M., 2017. Polyester textiles as a source of microplastics from households: A mechanistic study to understand microfiber release during washing. *Environmental Science and Technology*, 51(12), 7036–7046. https://doi.org/10.1021/acs.est.7b01750

Hussain, T., Ahmed, S., & Qayum, A., 2008. Effect of different softeners and sanforising treatment on pilling performance of polyester/viscose blended fabrics. *Coloration Technology*, 124(6), 375–378. https://doi.org/10.1111/j.1478-4408.2008.00166.x

Jönsson, C., Levenstam Arturin, O., Hanning, A.-C., Landin, R., Holmström, E., & Roos, S., 2018. Microplastics shedding from textiles – Developing analytical method for measurement of shed material representing release during domestic washing. *Sustainability*, 10(7), 2457. https://doi.org/10.3390/su10072457

Kay, P., Hiscoe, R., Moberley, I., Bajic, L., & McKenna, N., 2018. Wastewater treatment plants as a source of microplastics in river catchments. *Environmental Science and Pollution Research*, 25(20), 20264–20267. https://doi.org/10.1007/s11356-018-2070-7

Kelly, M. R., Lant, N. J., Kurr, M., & Burgess, J. G., 2019. Importance of water-volume on the release of microplastic fibers from laundry. *Environmental Science & Technology*, 53(20), 11735–11744. https://doi.org/10.1021/acs.est.9b03022

Kirchmann, H., Börjesson, G., Kätterer, T., & Cohen, Y., 2017. From agricultural use of sewage sludge to nutrient extraction: A soil science outlook. *Ambio*, 46(2), 143–154. https://doi.org/10.1007/s13280-016-0816-3

Krifa, M., & Stewart Stevens, S., 2016. Cotton utilization in conventional and non-conventional textiles – A statistical review. *Agricultural Sciences*, 07(10), 747–758. https://doi.org/10.4236/as.2016.710069

L'Abbate, P., Dassisti, M., Cappelletti, G. M., Nicoletti, G. M., Russo, C., & Ioppolo, G., 2018. Environmental analysis of polyester fabric for ticking. *Journal of Cleaner Production*, 172, 735–742. https://doi.org/10.1016/j.jclepro.2017.10.045

Laitala, K., Boks, C., & Klepp, I. G., 2011. Potential for environmental improvements in laundering. *International Journal of Consumer Studies*, 35(2), 254–264. https://doi.org/10.1111/j.1470-6431.2010.00968.x

Lant, N. J., Hayward, A. S., Peththawadu, M. M. D., Sheridan, K. J., & Dean, J. R., 2020. Microfiber release from real soiled consumer laundry and the impact of fabric care products and washing conditions. *PLoS ONE*, 15(6), e0233332. https://doi.org/10.1371/JOURNAL.PONE.0233332

Leslie, H. A., Brandsma, S. H., van Velzen, M. J. M., & Vethaak, A. D., 2017. Microplastics en route: Field measurements in the Dutch river delta and Amsterdam canals, wastewater treatment plants, North Sea sediments and biota. *Environment International*, 101, 133–142. https://doi.org/10.1016/j.envint.2017.01.018

Leslie, H. A., Van Velzen, M. J. M., & Vethaak, A. D., 2013. *Microplastic survey of the Dutch environment novel data set of microplastics in North Sea sediments, treated wastewater effluents and marine biota*. IVM Institute for Environmental Studies.

Lindeque, P. K., Cole, M., Coppock, R. L., Lewis, C. N., Miller, R. Z., Watts, A. J. R., . . . Galloway, T. S., 2020. Are we underestimating microplastic abundance in the marine environment? A comparison of microplastic capture with nets of different mesh-size. *Environmental Pollution*, 114721. https://doi.org/10.1016/j.envpol.2020.114721

Mateos-Cárdenas, A., O'Halloran, J., van Pelt, F. N. A. M., & Jansen, M. A. K., 2021. Beyond plastic microbeads – Short-term feeding of cellulose and polyester microfibers to the freshwater amphipod Gammarus duebeni. *Science of the Total Environment*, 753, 141859. https://doi.org/10.1016/j.scitotenv.2020.141859

McIlwraith, H. K., Lin, J., Erdle, L. M., Mallos, N., Diamond, M. L., & Rochman, C. M., 2019. Capturing microfibers – Marketed technologies reduce microfiber emissions from washing machines. *Marine Pollution Bulletin*, 139, 40–45. https://doi.org/10.1016/J.MARPOLBUL.2018.12.012

Miller, R. Z., Watts, A. J. R., Winslow, B. O., Galloway, T. S., & Barrows, A. P. W., 2017. Mountains to the sea: River study of plastic and non-plastic microfiber pollution in the northeast USA. *Marine Pollution Bulletin*, 124(1), 245–251. Retrieved 2 September 2019 from www.sciencedirect.com/science/article/pii/S0025326X17306094

Mishra, S., Rath, C. charan, & Das, A. P., 2019. Marine microfiber pollution: A review on present status and future challenges. *Marine Pollution Bulletin*. Elsevier Ltd. https://doi.org/10.1016/j.marpolbul.2019.01.039

Murphy, F., Ewins, C., Carbonnier, F., & Quinn, B., 2016. Wastewater Treatment Works (WwTW) as a source of microplastics in the aquatic environment. *Environmental Science and Technology*, 50(11), 5800–5808. https://doi.org/10.1021/acs.est.5b05416

Naik, A., & Lopez-Amo, F., 1982. Pilling propensity of blended textiles. *Melliand Textilbericht*, 6(416).

Nan, B., Su, L., Kellar, C., Craig, N. J., Keough, M. J., & Pettigrove, V., 2020. Identification of microplastics in surface water and Australian freshwater shrimp Paratya australiensis in Victoria, Australia. *Environmental Pollution*, 259, 113865. https://doi.org/10.1016/j.envpol.2019.113865

Napper, I. E., Baroth, A., Barrett, A. C., Bhola, S., Chowdhury, G. W., Davies, B. F. R., . . . Koldewey, H., 2021. The abundance and characteristics of microplastics in surface water in the transboundary Ganges River. *Environmental Pollution*, 116348. https://doi.org/10.1016/j.envpol.2020.116348

Napper, I. E., Barrett, A. C., & Thompson, R. C., 2020. The efficiency of devices intended to reduce microfibre release during clothes washing. *Science of The Total Environment*, 140412. https://doi.org/10.1016/j.scitotenv.2020.140412

Napper, I. E., Davies, B. F. R., Clifford, H., Elvin, S., Koldewey, H. J., Mayewski, P. A., . . . Thompson, R. C., 2020. Reaching new heights in plastic pollution – Preliminary findings of microplastics on Mount Everest. *One Earth*, 3(5), 621–630. https://doi.org/10.1016/j.oneear.2020.10.020

Napper, I. E., & Thompson, R. C., 2016. Release of synthetic microplastic plastic fibres from domestic washing machines: Effects of fabric type and washing conditions. *Marine Pollution Bulletin*, 112(1–2), 39–45. https://doi.org/10.1016/j.marpolbul.2016.09.025

Park, T. J., Lee, S. H., Lee, M. S., Lee, J. K., Lee, S. H., & Zoh, K. D., 2020. Occurrence of microplastics in the Han River and riverine fish in South Korea. *Science of the Total Environment*, 708, 134535. https://doi.org/10.1016/j.scitotenv.2019.134535

Parker-Jurd, F. N. F., Napper, I. E., Abbott, G. D., Hann, S., Wright, S. L., & Thompson, R. C., 2020. *Investigating the sources and pathways of synthetic fibre and vehicle tyre wear contamination into the marine environment.* Retrieved from http://randd.defra.gov.uk/Document.aspx?Document=14783_ExecutiveSummaryME5435Apr2020.pdf

Pirc, U., Vidmar, M., Mozer, A., & Kržan, A., 2016. Emissions of microplastic fibers from microfiber fleece during domestic washing. *Environmental Science and Pollution Research*, 23(21), 22206–22211. https://doi.org/10.1007/s11356-016-7703-0

Plastic Pollution Coalition, 2017. *15 ways to stop microfiber pollution now.* Retrieved 23 March 2021 from www.plasticpollutioncoalition.org/blog/2017/3/2/15-ways-to-stop-microfiber-pollution-now

Salvador Cesa, F., Turra, A., & Baruque-Ramos, J., 2017. Synthetic fibers as microplastics in the marine environment: A review from textile perspective with a focus on domestic washings. *Science of the Total Environment.* Elsevier B.V. https://doi.org/10.1016/j.scitotenv.2017.04.172

Sillanpää, M., & Sainio, P., 2017. Release of polyester and cotton fibers from textiles in machine washings. *Environmental Science and Pollution Research*, 24(23), 19313–19321. https://doi.org/10.1007/s11356-017-9621-1

Stanton, T., Johnson, M., Nathanail, P., MacNaughtan, W., & Gomes, R. L., 2019. Freshwater and airborne textile fibre populations are dominated by 'natural', not microplastic, fibres. *Science of The Total Environment*, 666, 377–389. https://doi.org/10.1016/j.scitotenv.2019.02.278

Stanton, T., Johnson, M., Nathanail, P., MacNaughtan, W., & Gomes, R. L., 2020. Freshwater microplastic concentrations vary through both space and time. *Environmental Pollution*, 263, 114481. https://doi.org/10.1016/j.envpol.2020.114481

Tiffin, L., Hazlehurst, A., Sumner, M., & Taylor, M., 2021. Reliable quantification of microplastic release from the domestic laundry of textile fabrics. https://doi.org/10.108 0/00405000.2021.1892305

Yates, M., 2002. *Fabrics: A guide for interior designers and architects*. New York: W.W. Norton.

Zambrano, M. C., Pawlak, J. J., Daystar, J., Ankeny, M., Cheng, J. J., & Venditti, R. A., 2019. Microfibers generated from the laundering of cotton, rayon and polyester based fabrics and their aquatic biodegradation. *Marine Pollution Bulletin*, 142, 394–407. https:// doi.org/10.1016/j.marpolbul.2019.02.062

7

WASTEWATER TREATMENT APPROACHES TO REMOVE MICROPLASTICS

Microfibre incidence and fate

Daniel Sol, Amanda Laca, Adriana Laca and Mario Díaz

Introduction and current legislation on microplastics

The increasing concern about the potential risks that microplastics (MPs) entail regarding not only environment but also human health has lately led to an increase in the number of studies on this topic. Particularly, during the last 5 years the number has increased twentyfold.

Wastewater treatment plants (WWTPs) are considered the major source of microplastics released to the environment, in particular fibres, which are the particles more commonly found in treated effluents (Ngo et al., 2019). These facilities receive a huge amount of these microcontaminants from different origins, including agricultural and industrial wastewaters, but mainly urban sewage (Figure 7.1.). WWTPs are not specifically designed for the removal of microplastics from wastewater; however, efficiencies above 90% have frequently been reported (Sol et al., 2020). The study of the different processes (physical, chemical and biological) involved in wastewater treatments can supply interesting information about the best alternatives to achieve a complete elimination of these particles from the influents.

According to the European Commission, global production of plastics has increased twentyfold since the 1960s, reaching 322 million tonnes in 2015. It is expected to double again over the next 20 years. Specifically, around 25.8 million tonnes of plastic waste are generated in Europe every year (European Commission, 2018). Different proposals and actions are being carried out by the European Union (EU) to address the environmental problems associated with the production, use and consumption of plastics. Reducing single-use plastics or boosting the recycling of plastic wastes are two of the main strategies considered to tackle these problems (Sol et al., 2020). In addition, curbing microplastics pollution is another critical issue included by the European Commission in the "European Strategy for Plastics in a Circular Economy" (European Commission, 2018).

DOI: 10.4324/9781003165385-9

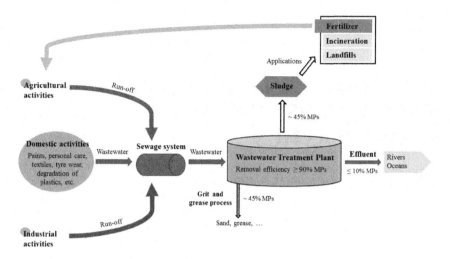

FIGURE 7.1 Emissions sources and cycle of MPs in nature considering the implication of WWTPs in the global process

It has been estimated that, in total, between 75,000 and 300,000 tonnes of microplastics are released into the environment each year in the EU (European Commission, 2020). Microplastics can be deliberately manufactured and intentionally added to certain product categories (cosmetics, personal care products, detergents and paints); these are known as primary microplastics. Microplastics can also be unintentionally released by the chemical, biological and/or physical fragmentation of plastics (secondary microplastics) (Boucher and Friot, 2017). Secondary microplastics can be dispersed during the production, transport and use of different plastic stuffs, such as tyres and synthetic clothes. Currently, this is the more common way to generate these microparticles (An et al., 2020; Hale et al., 2020).

Although primary microplastics intentionally added to products represent a relatively small proportion of these pollutants, several countries have already taken action to restrict their use in response to public concern. For instance, Canada, Ireland, UK, and the United States have banned the use of microbeads in different household products. In particular, in the United States the intentional addition of microbeads to commercial products has been banned since 2018 (The Microbead-Free Water Act of 2015, 2015). The first European country to ban the use of these particles in household and also in industrial cleaners was the UK in 2018 (at that time member of the EU) (Microbead England Regulation, 2017) and, after that, Ireland in 2020 (Microbeads (Prohibition) Act, 2019). Following this trend, the European Chemical Agency (ECHA) has made a proposal to ban the addition of microbeads to personal care and cosmetic products (ECHA, 2019). This proposal will be evaluated by the European Commission (EC) and, if it is approved, it is estimated that the release of around 400 thousand tonnes of microplastics to the environment would be avoided in the next 20-year period.

The EC also claims that more research is needed to improve the understanding of the sources and impacts of microplastics on the environment and human health, and to develop innovative solutions to prevent their dissemination. This includes ways to improve the capture of microplastics in wastewater treatment plants, as well as targeted measures for each source (European Commission, 2018).

Additionally, the European Parliament issued a proposal to introduce measures regarding the environmental problem of the presence of microplastics in treated water and sewage sludge in the context of the evaluation of the Urban Waste Water Treatment Directive (European Parliament, 2019). The approval of this proposal by the EC would imply future regulation of microplastics capture and removal in WWTPs, and member countries would have a period of 2 years to achieve the new legislative requirements.

1 Microplastics in WWTPs: origin and sampling

In addition to the intentional use of microplastics in several products, these particles can also be originated by the fragmentation (by chemical, physical and biological agents) of plastic wastes coming from maritime, agricultural, industrial and urban activities. This fragmentation together with aerial transport contribute to the dispersion of secondary microplastics in the environment (Boucher and Friot, 2017; Ogunola et al., 2018; Rhodes, 2019). Many of these MPs end up in the wastewaters received by the WWTPs. For this reason, WWTPs are considered an important source of these microparticles, especially microfibres, to the environment (An et al., 2020; Hale et al., 2020; Sol et al., 2020). Microfibres can be originated at household level (items of clothing, furnishing . . .) and also at industrial level (automotive sector, construction industry . . .) (Suaria et al., 2020), due to the use, wear and tear and the increase in the consumption of these synthetic materials (Carr, 2017; Liu et al., 2019a). Particularly, it has been reported that microfibres found in wastewaters are mainly originated by washing clothes, contributing to 35% of the global release of primary microplastics to the environment (Boucher and Friot, 2017). This value is underestimated since the release of microfibres to the atmosphere from the use of garments has not been considered (De Falco et al., 2019; De Falco et al., 2020). For example, one polyester fleece garment can emit around $1.1 \cdot 10^5$ fibres only in one wash (Almroth et al., 2018). Sillanpää and Sainio (2017) reported that polyester and cotton textiles can achieve, during the first wash, values between $2.1 \cdot 10^5$ and $1.3 \cdot 10^7$ of microfibres released per fabric kg, which means 0.12 to 0.33% w/w per fabric kg. In addition, approximately 42 million tonnes of synthetic microfibres (80% polyester) are generated by the clothing industry annually (Kelly et al., 2019). Moreover, the COVID-19 global pandemic situation has led to the implementation of the use of face masks by general public, so that, nowadays, the release of microfibres to the environment has increased due to the washing of reusable masks and/or the mismanagement of disposable masks (Aragaw, 2020; Shruti et al., 2020). Face masks are made from different polymers such as polypropylene, polyurethane, polystyrene, polycarbonate, polyethylene or polyester, among others (Fadare and Okoffo, 2020). Disposable face masks have three layers, an outer layer with water resistant nonwoven fibres, a middle layer (a melt-blown filter for virus rejection) and the inner layer made of soft fibres (Li et al., 2020a). Different processes and/or agents, such as washing, ultraviolet irradiation or alcohol disinfection and sunlight exposure, directly contribute to the release to the environment of microfibres from reusable and disposable face masks (Aragaw, 2020; Li et al., 2020a; Shruti et al., 2020). In addition, Li et al. (2020a) observed that different face masks (N95 respirator, surgical masks, cotton mask, fashion mask, nonwoven mask and activated carbon mask) can reduce the inhalation of fibres from breathing air when they are used less than 2 hours, but the inhalation of MPs from the air and from the face mask itself notably increases when the use is longer.

The presence of microplastics in the atmosphere is well known (Chen et al., 2020; Enyoh et al., 2019; Prata, 2018a). The degradation of synthetic textiles and rubber tires are important sources of MP pollution, which contribute 7% of the ocean's pollution by wind transfer (Boucher and Friot, 2017). Atmospheric microplastics have also other origins, including waste incineration, landfills and particles derived from agricultural and industrial activities, among others (Prata, 2018a). For example, the atmospheric fallout in an urban area (Paris) showed an average value of 118 particles·m^{-2} per day, being 90% fibres (Dris et al., 2015; Dris et al., 2016). These MPs can be driven into the sewage system by runoff waters, increasing the amount of these particles in the influent of WWTPs (Bayo et al., 2020a).

With the aim of analyzing microplastic occurrence at the different steps of the wastewater treatment process in WWTPs, specific devices are necessary to collect samples. There are four typical ways of sampling, i.e., container collection, automatic sample collection, surface water filtration and pumping and filtration (Alvim et al., 2020a; Sun et al., 2019). Container collection consists of a single sample of specific volume, usually between 1 and 38 L depending on the amount of organic matter present on the sample (Lares et al., 2018; Magni et al., 2019; Murphy et al., 2016). Automatic sample collection includes the sum of several samples taken at regular intervals (between 15 minutes and 2 hours) during a period of 24 hours (Talvitie et al., 2017b). According to the literature reviewed (see references included in Table 8.1.), these two previous methods have been used in 68% of WWTPs. In addition, surface water filtration can be used to collect microplastics in WWTPs with Neuston Nets or Plankton Nets (Carr et al., 2016; Sun et al., 2019). Moreover, this sampling method only allows taking samples from the surface of the water stream and the range of microplastic sampled is limited by the size of mesh, the most common being 150–330 µm. This method has been reported in 12% of the studies (see references include in Table 8.1). Approximately 20% of studies have employed the pumping and filtration as sampling method (see references included in Table 8.1). This technique consists of pumping water with an electric pump with a flexible hose so that the water stream passes through a stack of several sieves of different mesh size where microplastics and other particular matter are retained (Mason et al., 2016; Mintenig et al., 2017; Ziajahromi et al., 2017).

The method has several advantages, such as classifying microplastic by size using different meshes (20–5000 μm). In addition, long sampling times and large water volumes can be achieved, which allows for more representative and homogeneous samples. The water volume that should be passed through the sieves depends on the concentration of solids at each sampling point in the WWTPs (Elkhatib and Oyanedel-Craver, 2020; Sol et al., 2020).

2 Presence and removal of microplastics in WWTPs

2.1 Microplastics characteristics and microfibres incidence

WWTPs receive huge amounts of microplastics per day through the sewage system. For example, MP concentration between $6.10 \cdot 10^2$ and $3.14 \cdot 10^4$ particles/L was detected in raw wastewaters (Liu et al., 2021). At great extent, these MPs are removed during the treatment, being mainly concentrated in sludge (Gies et al., 2018), specially fibres (Habib et al., 1998; Zubris and Richards, 2005). Despite the high removal efficiencies, large amounts of microplastics are emitted to the environment each day in the treated water, because WWTPs are not specifically designed to remove these microparticles from the wastewater. For example, Mason et al. (2016) studied the total load of microplastics in 17 WWTPs in the United States and found that these facilities discharged in the final effluents more than 4 million microplastics daily. In addition, recent work carried out in Australia has reported that three WWTPs emitted in their effluents between $22.1 \cdot 10^6$ and $133 \cdot 10^6$ microplastics per day, even with removal efficiencies higher than 98% (Ziajahromi et al., 2021). Therefore, these facilities still represent an important hotspot for the emission of microplastics into aquatic ecosystems, and some estimations indicate that, globally, around 7.2 billion of MPs per day are discharged to rivers from WWTPs (Liu et al., 2021). Different factors such as type of treatment, operating conditions, sludge characteristics and microplastic buoyancy affect the efficiency of microplastics removal (Masiá et al., 2020; Sol et al., 2020).

Microplastics found in wastewaters can be classified according to their morphology as follows: fibres, fragments, films, pellets and foams, the first two being the most predominant with abundances of 56% and 34%, respectively, as an average value in all stages of the WWTP (Ngo et al., 2019). These percentages are usually maintained during the different steps of wastewater treatment, which implies that microfibres are the plastic particles most emitted to rivers and seas (Kay et al., 2018; Ngo et al., 2019). One of the main reasons of this fact is that the high length-to-width ratio of fibres makes them very difficult to be removed (Ngo et al., 2019). If MP size is considered, the range of 25–500 μm is the most frequently used to classify microplastics, and it has been estimated that 70% of the microplastics found in the influents of worldwide WWTPs are bigger than 500 μm in diameter, while in the effluents 90% of MPs corresponds to particles smaller than 500 μm, 60% being smaller than 100 μm (Sun et al., 2019). A characteristic of microplastics that has to be remarked is their wide variety of colours, with beige, white, black, blue and green being the colours most commonly found in wastewaters (Iyare et al., 2020; Mintenig et al., 2017; Simon et al., 2018). Finally, it is important to highlight that, regarding the microplastic nature, the predominant materials of MPs detected in WWTPs are polypropylene (PP), polyethylene (PE), polyvinyl chloride (PVC), polystyrene (PS) and polyethylene terephthalate (PET) (Xu et al., 2020). The former authors observed no clear pattern of the relative abundance of each polymer, which is determined by the origin of the wastewater.

As can be observed in Table 7.1., fibres are one of the most abundant microplastics found in WWTPs. A recent work by Liu et al. (2021) analyzed the abundance of microplastics in 38 WWTPs in 11 countries. The MP occurrence depended on several parameters, such as wastewater origin (municipal, agricultural or industrial activities) and population served (size, standard of living and lifestyle). If wastewater comes from municipal activities, the MP abundance in influent was between 0.28 and $6.10 \cdot 10^2$ particles/L, whereas if the origin is municipal and industrial this value was higher, ranging between 1.60 and $3.14 \cdot 10^4$ particles/L. Regarding the different stages of water treatment, the MP abundance after the primary treatment was 0.22–$1.26 \cdot 10^4$ particles/L, and after the secondary treatment this value was between not detected (n.d.) and $7.86 \cdot 10^3$ particles/L. Approximately, 62% of worldwide WWTPs employed a tertiary treatment (advanced oxidation or membrane filtration) and the abundance of microplastics after this stage ranged between 0.01 and $2.97 \cdot 10^2$ particles/L (Liu et al., 2021). Specifically, the MP abundance in influent was: fibres (0.22–$4.60 \cdot 10^3$ particles/L), fragments (0.25–$3.40 \cdot 10^3$ particles/L), films (0.06–$1.30 \cdot 10^3$ particles/L) and pellets (0.01–$2.21 \cdot 10^4$ particles/L). In addition, these values were notably reduced in the effluent and the predominance of MPs regarding their morphology was as follows: fibres (n.d.-35 particles/L), fragments (n.d.-80 particles/L), films (n.d.-12 particles/L) and pellets (n.d.- $1.33 \cdot 10^3$ particles/L) (Liu et al., 2021). Furthermore, Ziajahromi et al. (2021) studied three wastewater treatment plants in Australia and found that fibres contributed 76% (between $16.8 \cdot 10^6$ and $101.1 \cdot 10^6$ particles per day) of the MPs emitted in the effluents.

Additionally, the vast majority of microplastics removed from wastewater are embedded in sewage sludge and fibres appear in high numbers. For example, Corradini et al. (2019) reported 18–41 particles per gram in mixed sludge (dry weight) used in agricultural soils, and microfibres were 90% of these MPs. On the contrary, Lusher et al. (2018) found lower values of fibres in mixed sludge. Specifically, this work, which analyzed eight Norwegian WWTPs, revealed a MP abundance of 6 particles/g (dry weight), being 38% beads, 32% fragments and 29% fibres. Finally, it should be remarked that fibres are more resistant to the sludge treatment processes than other MP morphologies (Habib et al., 2020).

2.2 Evolution of microplastics and microfibres in WWTPs

In a conventional WWTP, different stages schematized in Figure 7.2. can be identified, namely pretreatment, primary, secondary and tertiary treatment. As

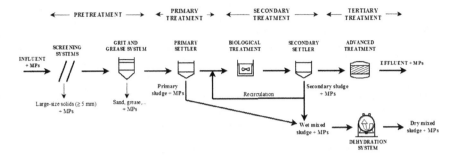

FIGURE 7.2 Schematic overview of the different stages of wastewater treatment processes found in a conventional WWTP

mentioned earlier in this chapter, concentrations and nature of microplastics received in WWTPs depend on the different activities, urban, agricultural and/or industrial, that discharge their wastewater to the sewage system. Additionally, the variability of influent flow could lead to an underestimation of microplastic concentration in raw wastewater since some of them could be retained in the sewage system by sedimentation (Masiá et al., 2020).

The pretreatment is a physical process. Firstly, different screening systems (bars, sieves . . .) with a mesh size between 1 and 6 mm, which depends on the WWTP, are employed. So, MPs bigger than the range employed in the screening systems can be removed at this stage. After that, a grit and grease system are commonly employed to remove sand by settling and grease by floating. MPs can be separated from the water together with grit and grease at this step (Masiá et al., 2020). Murphy et al. (2016) reported that 45% of MPs can be removed in the grit and grease system, but other authors claimed that more than 60% of microplastic removal in WWTP can be achieved by means of the grit and grease system (including coarse screening) (Lusher et al., 2018; Ziajahromi et al., 2021).

The primary treatment is also a physical process that removes suspended solids by settling (primary settler). In general, this process together with pretreatment has a noteworthy effect on microplastic removal (78–98%) (Prata, 2018b). The special shape of microfibres makes them very difficult to be removed from wastewater. Because of their high length-to-width ratio, fibres are able to pass through membranes or filters length wise. In addition, filters themselves can release fibres to the water due to wear and tear (Hamidian et al., 2021). However, for some particular operating conditions, they can be effectively eliminated. For example, Hidayaturrahman and Lee (2019) reported that the concentration of fibres was notably reduced (58%) from the influent to the effluent of the primary clarifier, because fibres could be more easily entrapped by solids during settling processes (Galvão et al., 2020; Hamidian et al., 2021).

The secondary treatment usually comprises an activated sludge process. Therefore, an aeration system has to be employed, which implies that some microplastic could be released to the atmosphere in the aerosols emitted (Masiá et al., 2020). After the biological treatment, there is a secondary clarifier that is used to separate the sludge from the treated water. It has been estimated that this settling process can remove 7–20% of microplastics from raw wastewater (Masiá et al., 2020). Surprisingly, Hidayaturrahman and Lee (2019) reported removal efficiencies for microfibres of around 60% in this secondary settling.

The tertiary treatment is not always present, and it is the final step in a WWTP to ensure a proper quality of effluent. This treatment usually consists of a disinfection process to reduce microbiological risks. The most common methods used are chlorination and UV irradiation, both of which have little effect on microplastics removal, e.g., a 7% can be achieved with chlorination (Liu et al., 2019b).

The use of advanced treatment systems in WWTP, like membrane bioreactor (MBR) or dynamic membrane (DM), allows removal efficiencies up to 99% (Lares et al., 2018; Lv et al., 2019; Michielssen et al., 2016; Park et al., 2020; Talvitie et al., 2017a). Table 7.1 shows an overview of existing literature from 2016 to the present on MP removal efficiencies in WWTPs, as well as the abundance of microplastics depending on its morphology in the influent and also in the effluent.

Freeman et al. (2020) indicated that certain treatments could help in the elimination of microplastics depending on their shape. For example, a primary treatment using coagulation-flocculation and subsequently sedimentation may be more effective in removing fibres, whereas skimming may remove microbeads (pellets) more effectively. In addition, a secondary treatment may be suitable to remove irregular fragments.

Primary sludge (generated in the primary settler) and secondary sludge (generated in the biological treatment) are usually managed together as "mixed sludge". Gies et al. (2018) reported that 93% of microplastics from raw wastewater were found in mixed sludge in a WWTP from Canada with a 98% of removal efficiency, so the vast majority of microplastics removed from treated water are accumulated in sludge. In this case, 73% of microplastics are retained in primary sludge, whereas 20% are embedded in secondary sludge. Several studies have reported ranges for microplastics concentration in wet and dry mixed sludge of 400–7,000 and 1,500–170,000 particles per kg, respectively (Bayo et al., 2020c; Carr et al., 2016; Edo et al., 2020; Lares et al., 2018; Leslie et al., 2017; Lusher et al., 2018; Magni et al., 2019; Mahon et al., 2017; Mintenig et al., 2017; Murphy et al., 2016). The most common microplastic found in sludge is fibres, followed by fragments, microbeads and films (Habib et al., 2020; Hamidian et al., 2021; Mahon et al., 2017; Rolsky et al., 2020). As an example, Ziajahromi et al. (2021) reported amounts of 69–79% microfibres in mixed sludge. The problem derived from the accumulation of MPs in sewage sludge is the use of this sludge as fertilizer in agriculture, which implies the release to the environment of those microplastics removed from wastewater. It has been calculated that 44,000–300,000 and 63,000–430,000 tonnes of MPs are applied on agricultural soils each year in Europe and North America, respectively (He et al., 2018; Nizzetto et al., 2016). So far, no technologies that allow the separation of microplastics from sludge are known, which implies that this would be an interesting issue for further research.

TABLE 7.1 Overview of main works from 2016 to the present on MPs removal efficiencies in WWTPs, as well as the abundance of microplastics depending on its morphology

Location of WWTP(s)	MPs size analyzed (μm)	MPs by morphology		Removal efficiency (%) and process	References
		Influent	Effluent		
Australia	25–500	Mainly fibres and granules		90	**Ziajahromi et al., 2017**
Australia	1.5–1000	Fragments (39%), Fibres (36%), Films (12%), Glitter (6%), Foams (3%), Beads (1%), Others (3%)	Fibres (58%), Fragments (25%), Films (8%), Glitter (2%), Beads (3%), Others (4%)	76.6	**Raju et al., 2020**
Australia	25–5000	WWTP – A: Fibres (84%), fragments (15%), granular (1%) WWTP – B: Fibres (82%), fragments (18%) WWTP – C: Fibres (49%), fragments (51%)	WWTP – A: Fibres (67%), fragments (33%) WWTP – B: Fibres (89%), fragments (11%) WWTP – C: Fibres (73%), fragments (27%)	≥ 98	**Ziajahromi et al., 2021**
Canada	1–65	Fibres (66%), fragments (28%), pellets (5%) and others (1%)		97–99	**Gies et al., 2018**

(Continued)

TABLE 7.1 (Continued)

Location of WWTP(s)	MPs size analyzed (μm)	MPs by morphology		Removal efficiency (%) and process	References
		Influent	Effluent		
China	> 47	Fragments (43%)	Fibres (45%)	64	**Liu et al., 2019b**
		Fibres (39%)	Fragment (45%)	Chlorination: 7	
		Microbeads (4%)	Films (6%)		
		Ellipse (6%)	Microbeads (4%)		
		Films (4%)			
		Foams (4%)			
China	43–355	Granules (50%)	Granules (36%)	79–98	**Long et al., 2019**
		Fragments (30%)	Fibres (30%)		
		Fibres (18%)	Fragments (28%)		
		Pellets (2%)	Pellets (6%)		
China	25–500	Fragments (65%), fibres (21%), films (12%) and foams (2%)		Oxidation ditch: 97	**Lu et al., 2019**
				MBR: 99.5	
China	100–5000	Fibres (55–71%)	Fragments (50–72%)	60–87	**Ruan et al., 2019**
		Fragments (25–26%)	Fibres (13–40%)		
		Sheets (3–19%)	Sheets (7–8%)		
			Beads (2–5%)		
			Foams (0–2%)		
China	50–5000	–	Microfibres (86%)	A²O: 95	**Yang et al., 2019**
			Microparticles (14%)		
China	20–5000	Fibres (38–61%), fragments (30–48%), others (3–5%)		75.7	**Jiang et al., 2020**

Country					Reference
China	0–5000	—	Fragments (36%), Pellets (24%), Fibres (39%)	—	**Zou et al., 2020**
China	75–5000	Fibres (64%), Fragments (13%), Films (14%), Particle (9%)	Fibres (40%), Films (30%), Fragments (25%), Particle (5%)	Oxidation ditch: 92.1	**Yang et al., 2021**
Czech Republic	> 1	Sand filtration: fragments (78%), fibres (22%); GAC: fragments (90%), fibres (10%)	Sand filtration: fragments (79%), fibres (21%); GAC: fragments (92%), fibres (8%)	Sand filtration: 40 GAC: 88	**Pivokonský et al., 2020**
Denmark	1–500	Mainly fragments		99.3	**Simon et al., 2018**
France	20–500	Fragments (75%), Fibres (25%)	Fragments (60%), Fibres (40%)	98.8	**Kazour et al., 2019**
Finland	20–300	Mainly fibres; Before treatment (39–81%); After advanced treatment (29–100%)		RSF: 97; Disc-filter: 40–98.5; DAF: 95; MBR: 99.9	**Talvitie et al., 2017a**
Finland	20–300	Fibres (68%), Fragments (10%), Flakes (14%), Films (8%)	Fibres (29%), Fragments (62%), Flakes (9%)	BAF: 97	**Talvitie et al., 2017b**

(Continued)

TABLE 7.1 (Continued)

Location of WWTP(s)	MPs size analyzed (µm)	MPs by morphology		Removal efficiency (%) and process	References
		Influent	*Effluent*		
Finland	250–5000	Fibres (50–90%) and fragments (10–50%)		CAS: 99 MBR: 99.4	**Lares et al., 2018**
Germany	20–5000	Fibres (61%)		97	**Mintenig et al., 2017**
Iran	3–5000	–	Fibres (76%) Films (14%) Fragments (6%) Granules (6%)	–	**Naji et al., 2021**
Israel	> 20	Fibres (74%) Particles (26%)	Fibres (90%) Particles (10%)	97	**Ben-David et al., 2021**
Italy	63–5000	Films (73%) Fragments (21%) Fibres (6%)	Fibres (41%) Films (38%) Fragments (21%)	Sand filter: 84	**Magni et al., 2019**
Italy	63–5000	Films (55%) Fragments (36%) Fibres (9%)	Fragments (67%) Films (33%)	CAS: 86 UASB + AnMBR: 94	**Pittura et al., 2021**
Korea	> 106	Fibres (50%) Fragments (50%)	Fibres (60%) Fragments (40%)	Media process: 98 A^2O: 98.4 SBR: 99.1	**Lee and Kim, 2018**
Korea	100–5000	Fragments (68%) Fibres (32%)	Fragments (82%) Fibres (18%)	99.4–99.9 (CAS, A^2O and MBR)	**Park et al., 2020**

Netherlands	20–300	Fibres, foils and spheres	11–94	Leslie et al., 2017
Scotland	> 65	Flakes (67%), fibres (19%), films (10%), beads (3%) and foams (1%)	MBR: 25 98.4	Murphy et al., 2016
South Korea	> 1.2	WWTP – A: Microbeads (18%), fibres (47%), sheets (4%), fragments (31%) WWTP – B: Microbeads (70%), fibres (15%), sheets (4%), fragments (11%) WWTP – C: Microbeads (24%), fibres (18%), sheets (4%), fragments (54%)	WWTP – A: Microbeads (79%), fibres (12%), sheets (3%), fragments (6%) WWTP – B: Microbeads (93%), fibres (5%), sheets (1%), fragments (1%) WWTP – C: Microbeads (56%), fibres (23%), fragments (21%) Coagulation-flocculation: 47–82 RSF: 74 Disc-filter: 79 Ozone: 90	Hidayaturrahman and Lee, 2019
Spain	150–5000	Fibres (90%), fragments and spheres (10%)	74.8	Alvim et al., 2020b
Spain	0.45–5000	Fragments (47%), films (34%), beads (12%), fibres (7%) and foams (0.2%)	90.3	Bayo et al., 2020a
Spain	0.45–5000	Fibres (61%), films (31%), fragments (7%) and beads (1%)	RSF: 75 MBR: 79	Bayo et al., 2020b
Spain	25–375	Primary effluent Fragments (60%) Fibres (28%) Secondary effluent Fragments (80%) Fibres (20%)	A²O: 94	Edo et al., 2020

(Continued)

TABLE 7.1 (Continued)

Location of WWTP(s)	MPs size analyzed (µm)	MPs by morphology		Removal efficiency (%) and process	References
		Influent	*Effluent*		
Spain	100–5000	Fibres (34%) Fragments (30–34%) Flakes (20–21%) Films (10–14%) Sphere (1%)	Fibres (39–41%) Fragments (30–31%) Flakes (17–18%) Films (11–12%) Sphere (0–2%)	78–97	**Franco et al., 2020**
Thailand	330–4750	Fibres (47%) Sheets (42%) Fragments (4%) Others (7%)	Fibres (50%) Fragments (30%) Sheets (15%) Others (5%)	84	**Hongprasith et al., 2020**
Turkey	> 55	Fibres (70%) Fragments (19%) Films (11%)	Fibres (60%) Fragments (20%) Films (20%)	73–76	**Gündoğdu et al., 2018**
Turkey	> 26	Fibres (79%) Soft plastics (13%) Hard plastics (8%)	Fibres (46%) Hard plastics (33%) Soft plastics (19%) Others (2%)	48–73	**Akarsu et al., 2020**
UK	60–2800	Fibres (73%), fragments (20%), films (6%) and pellets (1%)		Nitrification tanks: 96	**Blair et al., 2019**
USA	45–400	Mainly fragments		Gravity filters: 99.9	**Carr et al., 2016**
USA	20–4750	Fibres (55–62%) Fragments (23–26%) Microbeads (11–16%) Others (4%)	Fibres (61–89%) Fragments (11–33%) Others (0–6%)	CAS: 95.6 RSF: 97.2 MBR: 99.4	**Michielssen et al., 2016**
USA	> 60	Fibres (78%) and particles (22%)		75–98	**Conley et al., 2019**

2.3 Technologies for the removal of microplastics

As it has already been indicated, that although they are not specifically designed to remove microplastics, WWTPs show good removal efficiencies, especially during the pretreatment and primary treatment (Masiá et al., 2020; Sol et al., 2020). A summary of the different technologies that can be found in WWTPs and that entail a removal of MPs from wastewater is shown in Table 7.2.

All the processes included in Table 7.2 contribute, to a greater or lesser extent, to reducing the concentration of microplastics in the treated water and, subsequently, to decreasing the release of these pollutants to the environment. According to the data published so far, the most effective technique to remove microplastics is membrane bioreactor (MBR), which has been reported to achieve efficiencies close to 100% (Lares et al., 2018; Lv et al., 2019; Michielssen et al., 2016; Park et al., 2020; Talvitie et al., 2017a); fibres were the only particle detected post-treatment (Freeman et al., 2020).

TABLE 7.2 Summary of different treatment processes in WWTPs that imply the removal of MPs from wastewater and overview of the cost of the technologies employed

	Treatment process	*Removal efficiency (%)*
LOW COST	Conventional sludge activated process (CAS)	96–98
	Oxidation ditch	97
	Chlorination	7
	Coagulation-flocculation	47–82
	Sand filter	45–97
	Granular activated carbon (GAC)	88
	Nitrification tanks	96
LOW-MEDIUM COST	Anaerobic, anoxic, aerobic (A^2O)	72–98
	Sequencing batch reactor (SBR)	98
MEDIUM COST	Ultrafiltration (UF)	42
	Disc-filter	40–98
	Ozone	90
	Biological active filter (BAF)	97
	Dissolved air flotation (DAF)	95
HIGH COST	Upflow granular anaerobic sludge blanket + anaerobic membrane bioreactor (UASB + AnMBR)	94
	Reverse osmosis (RO)	90
	Dynamic membranes (DM)	99
	Membrane bioreactor (MBR)	≥ 99

Source: Table 7.1 and Sol et al. (2020)

From an economical point of view and considering that, according to literature, filter-based technologies show the best performance in removing MPs, different works have analyzed the effect of rapid sand filtration, achieving removal efficiencies up to 97%. In addition, these technologies require low operational and maintenance costs (Talvitie et al., 2017a; Michielssen et al, 2016). Nitrification tanks and oxidation ditches are other low-cost technologies that achieve removal efficiencies similar to those obtained employing rapid sand filtration. Studies on sequencing batch reactors (SBR), a low-medium cost technology, have reported values of MPs removal of 98% (Lee and Kim, 2018). Although technologies that employ membranes, such as MBR, have been described as the best alternative to remove microplastics from wastewaters (Bayo et al., 2020c), these technologies require high operating costs (Ersahin et al., 2012). Moreover, due to fouling problems, high maintenance costs are associated with these systems, which is a barrier for their general implementation in WWTPs (Liu et al., 2021; Xu et al., 2021). Additionally, Freeman et al. (2020) indicated that dissolved air flotation (DAF) is a promising technology to be employed in MP removal from wastewaters with elimination efficiencies of 95%, but the main disadvantage for its implementation is the high cost that this technology requires.

A membrane bioreactor (MBR) is the best technology to eliminate microfibres in WWTPs, since these systems can remove practically all MPs from wastewater (more than 99%) and only the 1% of the not removed MPs are microfibres (Lares et al., 2018; Lv et al., 2019; Michielssen et al., 2016; Park et al., 2020; Talvitie et al., 2017a). Nevertheless, not all MBRs are capable of reaching this removal percentage, e.g., Bayo et al. (2020b) reported 79% of MPs removal, where fibres represent 97% of microplastics released to the environment. As mentioned earlier, the high operating costs of MBRs are the main disadvantage of these systems (Ersahin et al., 2012). Among the cost-effective technologies, the best removal efficiencies (82%) are obtained by coagulation–flocculation (Hidayaturrahman and Lee, 2019). The former authors indicated that using coagulation–flocculation together with ozone, disc-filter or RSF, is possible to achieve removal efficiencies near to 100%. In these cases, microfibres represent approximately 14% of the MPs emitted in the effluent (Hidayaturrahman and Lee, 2019).

Using specific facilities that allow a total removal of MPs, especially smaller than 10–20 μm (Ngo et al., 2019; Picó et al., 2019), would avoid the emission of these microparticles in the treated water and, as mentioned earlier, technology is very close to making this objective possible. However, in-depth studies for the separation, elimination and/or valorization of microplastics from sewage sludge is still a challenge, and the release of microparticles to the environment is currently occurring when this sludge is applied to lands.

3 Processes to MP recovery

The recovery of MPs from complex matrices is a difficult task due to the presence of organic and inorganic impurities. In this section, different processes and technologies that have been developed to recover MPs at lab scale and/or in real plants are analyzed. At lab scale, the most common processes imply an oxidation (using an oxidizer to reduce the organic impurities) and a subsequently density separation process (using a saline solution to separate MPs from inorganic particles). In addition, different developing technologies to isolate microplastics are reviewed, for example, sedimentation processes, as elutriation (alone or together with flotation). Due to their hydrophobic properties, MPs can also be isolated using froth flotation or magnetic nanoparticles. Additionally, coagulation-flocculation is a process widely employed in real WWTPs to achieve an efficient liquid-solid separation, so the use of this technique to remove MPs from wastewater is remarkable. Finally, anodic oxidation should be considered as promising technology for future applications in WWTPs.

3.1 Pretreatment: oxidation of organic matter

Different processes have been studied and evaluated for the recovery of microplastics from environmental samples at laboratory scale. In general, a pretreatment is necessary to ensure the subsequent extraction of microplastics without impurities. This treatment consists of an oxidation of the organic matter present by means of different oxidizers. Hydrogen peroxide and sodium hypochlorite are the oxidizing agents most commonly employed (Okoffo et al., 2019; Stock et al., 2019), but the United States National Oceanic and Atmospheric Administration (NOAA) suggested that Fenton's reagent is the best option for aqueous samples. Employing Fenton's reagent implies a wet peroxidation (WPO), which is carried out with a solution of hydrogen peroxide (H_2O_2) and ferrous iron (iron (II) sulphate) as a catalyst. Around 87% of the organic matter is oxidized in 2 hours at room temperature without altering the physical properties of microplastics (Hurley et al., 2018; Tagg et al., 2017). Several researches have reported the use of some alternative reagents such as acids, bases or enzymes to oxidize the organic matter. However, these methods have some drawbacks, since the oxidizers can damage the microplastics and/or need long exposure times (even 13 days in the case of using enzymes) (Liu et al., 2020; Sun et al., 2019).

3.2 Density separation processes

Sedimentation is inherently common in many treatment processes. At laboratory scale, separation by utilizing MP density is the most common technique for extracting microplastics from environmental samples. Certainly, density separation is usually used to isolate microplastics from sediments and water samples. This method requires the use of a saturated saline solution, such as sodium chloride (d = 1.2 $g \cdot mL^{-1}$), zinc chloride (d = 1.5–1.7 $g \cdot mL^{-1}$) or sodium iodide (d = 1.6–1.8 $g \cdot mL^{-1}$), among others. NaCl and $ZnCl_2$ are the saline solutions most often employed (Picó et al., 2019; Ruggero et al., 2020). The NaCl solutions are cheap and environmentally friendly and can be applied to microplastics present in surface water. The major disadvantage of this solution is that it does not allow for the extraction of microplastics of high densities, such as polyvinyl chloride (d = 1.14–1.56 g·mL⁻¹) or polyethylene terephthalate (d = 1.32–1.41 g·mL⁻¹) (Alvim et al., 2020a). In this respect, zinc chloride solutions have a better chance of extracting dense microplastics; these solutions are relatively expensive and quite toxic to the environment, however. The use of sodium iodide solutions is another option to obtain microplastics with high densities, although it is even more expensive than zinc chloride, which can be reused several times without losing efficiency in microplastics extraction (Rodrigues et al., 2020). Obviously, employing one or another brine solution depends mainly on the origin of samples. For example, turbulent waters contain a homogeneous distribution of microplastics of several densities, whereas sludge contains heavy MPs, which would require high density saline solutions to extract the totality of microplastics (Alvim et al., 2020a; Bayo et al., 2020c; Sol et al., 2020).

The elutriation system is another methodology designed at lab scale for separating particles based on their size, shape and density by means of using a stream flow (gas or liquid) in a direction usually opposite to the direction of sedimentation (Prata et al., 2019; Ruggero et al., 2020; Sol et al., 2020; Zarfl, 2019). This process is employed to isolate microplastics from sediment samples. It consists of a column, whose size is between 147 and 186 cm in height and 10 and 15 cm in width, where a flow of liquid (usually water) is injected through the bottom of the elutriation column. At the top of the column there is the filtration device, and particles go upwards in the column so that microplastics are retained in the meshes of the filtration device. The optimization of the different parameters, such as temperature or flow stream, allows the separation of MPs from the impurities (Kedzierski et al., 2016; Kedzierski et al., 2017; Kedzierski et al., 2018; Zhu, 2015).

Claessens et al. (2013) studied the separation of microplastics in two steps. The first one comprises an elutriation system using a water flow and, subsequently, in the second step, NaCl and NaI solutions are employed to separate MPs by density. These authors reported that 75% of microfibres (of different sizes) was extracted from the sample when NaCl solution was used in the second step, whereas a higher percentage was achieved (98%) when the NaI solution was employed.

Other systems that use density separation processes are Munich Plastic Sediment Separator (MPSS) and Sediment-Microplastic Isolation (SMI). MPSS is a specific elutriation system that combines sedimentation and flotation processes. This device consists of a sediment container, a conical standpipe and a dividing chamber with a ball valve and a filter holder. Zinc chloride solution is introduced using the bottom valve situated at the bottom of the device. Then, a solid sample is slowly added while the rotor is stirring during 15 minutes, after that the first separation is carried out during 1 to 2 hours (MPs float and solids settle). After this time, the dividing chamber is employed to separate the MPs. This device was designed to treat marine sediments and the recovery efficiency of microplastics reported in literature is very variable, with ranges between 96 and 100% (Imhof et al., 2012) and 13 and 39% (Zobkov and Esiukova, 2017). Sediment-Microplastic Isolation (SMI) is a portable and small-scale device of PVC employed to isolate microplastics from sediments at laboratory scale. It comprises of a two-pipe system connected by a ball valve, then the sample and zinc chloride solution are introduced into the device, stirred, so that sediments settle into the lower pipe. The valve is closed and the content of the upper pipe is filtered through a mesh. Coppock et al. (2017) recovered a 92–98% of microplastics, the vast majority being fibres. MPSS is suitable for 5–6 kg of sample, whereas the SMI device is applied for small samples (30–50 g).

3.3 Coagulation-flocculation

Coagulation-flocculation processes are employed in tertiary treatments in WWTPs to eliminate colloidal particles by settling. Certain chemicals are added to the water stream to favour the formation of flocs (Ma et al., 2018; Te et al., 2016). Different parameters, such as temperature, pH or the quantity of chemicals, can be optimized to improve the efficiency of the process. The coagulants used most frequently are $FeCl_3$ and $AlCl_3$. The Al-salts offer better performance in terms of removing pollutants in water, but the elimination of MPs from the water stream requires high quantities of Al-salts that could be harmful to human health (Li et al., 2020b). Hidayaturrahman and Lee (2019) reported that coagulation-flocculation processes can achieve removal efficiencies of microplastics between 47 and 82% in WWTPs. Although this treatment is more effective to reduce microbeads and fragments, with average values of removal of 71 and 60%, respectively, it also can reduce the concentration of microfibres with removal efficiencies between 44 and 57%. In WWTPs, treatments that combined coagulation-flocculation with a subsequent treatment, such as ozone, membrane disc-filter or rapid sand filtration, were reported to give microfibre removals of 93, 79 and 76%, respectively (Hidayaturrahman and Lee, 2019). Additionally, a study carried out by Wang et al. (2020a) in one of the largest drinking water treatment plants in China found that the coagulation-flocculation process removed 51–61% of fibres. Fibres larger than 10 μm have a greater tendency to be trapped and agglomerated in flocs in comparison to other MP morphologies. Additionally, Katrivesis et al. (2019) analyzed different parameters in coagulation-flocculation processes to obtain potable water and, in accordance with results reported by Wang et al. (2020a), the best removal efficiency percentages (51–61%) were achieved for microfibres particles. Considering the mentioned data, coagulation-flocculation treatments are interesting technologies that are been already used, but a wider implementation could be carried out in WWTPs for the removal of MPs in general, and fibres in particular, and further investigations on this matter should be carried out to improve the WWTPs performance regarding the elimination of microplastics.

3.4 Froth flotation

Froth flotation is a physical process to separate materials based upon whether they are hydrophobic or hydrophilic (Crawford and Quinn, 2017). This technique has been used at laboratory level to separate MPs from sediments, which are introduced through the top of a reactor vessel containing water, while air is introduced through the bottom. A stirrer homogenizes the air bubbles, which interact with microplastics. Air and MPs are both hydrophobic, so MPs and air bubbles go upwards to the surface and the supernatant is collected in a container, whereas hydrophilic particles remain in the liquid phase. Imhof et al. (2012) used a range of MP size between 1 and 5 mm, achieving a removal efficiency of 55% with this technique. This percentage is variable since, due to their hydrophobic properties, microplastics can adsorb different chemical pollutants, which can negatively affect the separation of MPs by froth flotation (Crawford and Quinn, 2017; Fraunholcz, 2004).

Considering the conventional treatment in WWTPs, a similar process occurs during the activated sludge treatment. When air is injected in the bottom, microplastics can be trapped in air bubbles that carry them to the surface of the bioreactor.

3.5 Bioremediation

Bioremediation is an emerging technology with potential applications to degrade and/or separate microplastics present in the environment. Two approaches can be considered: the first one involves the use of microorganisms, such as bacteria, fungi or algae, to biodegrade the plastics found in different ecosystems (Shahnawaz et al., 2019). The main disadvantage of this technology is that the biodegradation process needs long time periods, so it is not a practical method to be applied in WWTPs yet (Caruso, 2015). The second approach implies the use of eukaryotic species, which are able to bioaccumulate specific microplastics, so that MPs can be recovered selectively. For example, Courtene-Jones et al. (2019) reported that specific species of echinoderms, like *Ophiomusium lymani*, have the particular characteristic of accumulating MP fragments and fibres (between 1.96 ± 0.66 and 3.43 ± 1.35 MPs/g). A recent work has suggested that some eukaryotes like annelids, echinoderms or seagrasses could be promising organisms to be employed for removing microplastics in WWTPs (Masiá et al., 2020). Therefore, further research on this topic should be carried out, specifically in the recovery of fibres.

3.6 Other processes

The extensive research over the last few years on the removal of microplastics has led to the emergence of new techniques to separate microplastics from different matrices. In that sense, Grbic et al. (2019) have proposed a method based on the magnetic properties of microplastics, where hydrophobic iron nanoparticles interact with MPs by means of a magnetization process. This technique has been employed with microplastics of different nature, namely, polyethylene, polystyrene, polyurethane, polyethylene terephthalate, polyvinyl chloride and polypropylene. Particles between 200 μm and 1 mm showed removal efficiencies of 78–84%, whereas 93% of particles bigger than 1 mm were recovered. In particular, 92% of particles of polyethylene and polystyrene whose size was between 10 and 20 μm were removed from the samples. According to these authors, future studies using this method should be focused on recovering microfibres, due to the prevalence of these particles in the microplastics released to the environment (usually 80–90%) (Cesa et al., 2017; Gago et al., 2018).

A recent promising strategy to degrade polystyrene microbeads in water has been described by Kiendrebeogo et al. (2021). Specifically, microplastics can be degraded by anodic oxidation without generation of toxic byproducts. The effect of different parameters on the process has been analyzed, i.e., current intensity, type of oxygen-intensive anodes (Boron-doped diamond (BDD), mixed metal oxide (MMO) and iridium oxide (IrO_2)), area of the anode surface and type and concentration of electrolyte (Na_2SO_4, NaCl, and $NaNO_3$). Results showed that, employing the optimum conditions (BDD, an intensity of 9 A and a supporting electrolyte of 0.03M Na_2SO_4), after 2 hours of electrooxidation, a degradation of 89% of microplastics was achieved. Thus, the electrooxidation process could be a viable alternative to be applied in real wastewater treatment plants. However, more in-depth research on different aspects of the methodology, such as the pollution derived from the use of the anode, another type of MPs like fibres, as well as the potential interference that water contaminants may cause, should be carried out.

The separation of microplastics can also be carried out in solid matrices. Felsing et al. (2018) have employed a hamos KWS type separator based on the electrostatic behaviour of materials to isolate all the types of MPs from sediments such as sand. The sample is dried and sieved, and then it is introduced into a rotating metal drum where particles are electrostatically charged using a corona electrode. Microplastics are non-conductive materials, so that particles are separated in different containers depending on their conductive capacity. MP recovery is very high, achieving values of 99%, even for small particles (63 μm). Additionally, these kinds of electrostatic separators can process several tonnes of sample per hour.

4   Some future prospects

The ubiquitous presence of microplastics in the environment, as well as the potential risk that they entail, requires a move forward by the searching alternatives that reduce their release into nature. Microfibres are the morphology of MPs most frequently found in natural ecosystems, being the 80–90% of the total MPs released to the environment (Cesa et al., 2017; Gago et al., 2018). The presence of fibres has been reported far and wide in the nature, namely, in wastewaters (Gatidou et al., 2019; Iyare et al., 2020; Sol et al., 2020), oceans (Boucher and Friot, 2017; Eriksen et al., 2014), sea-ice (Obbard, et al., 2014; González-Pleiter et al., 2020), deep-sea (Sanchez-Vidal et al., 2018; Woodall et al., 2014), rivers (Besseling et al., 2017; Wang et al., 2017), sediments (Lots, et al., 2017; Masiá et al., 2019; Masiá et al., 2021), foodstuffs (Cox et al., 2019; Iñiguez et al., 2017; Van Cauwenberghe et al., 2014), drinking water (Eerkes-Medrano et al., 2019; O'mann, 2021), living beings (Lu et al., 2019; Wang et al., 2020b), terrestrial lands (Hurley and Nizzetto,

2018; Xu et al., 2019) and the atmosphere (Dris et al., 2015; Dris et al., 2016). For example, it has been described that 3–10 tonnes of microfibres are deposited in Paris each year by atmospheric fallout (Dris et al., 2016), whereas washing synthetic textiles (mainly fibres) contribute 35% to primary MP emission to the ocean MP pollution (Boucher and Friot, 2017).

It is necessary to focus the implementation of new technologies for the large-scale recovery of microplastics in the WWTPs since these facilities represent an important point of emission of MPs to aquatic ecosystems. Processes of water treatment have to be improved, so that the emission of MPs in the effluents would be negligible. Different technologies, such as bioremediation, electrostatic separators, magnetic nanoparticles or froth flotation, could be potentially employed to achieve this aim, but they still need to be optimized to be applied at large scale.

Moreover, treated wastewater frequently contains small MPs (between 10 and 300 μm) and a high proportion of fibres. There are no cost-effective technologies to remove or degrade these, specifically MPs. Considering the technologies currently applied in WWTPs, primary settling and coagulation/flocculation processes could be the most efficient technologies to eliminate fibres and small MPs. Process conditions in primary clarifier (retention time, temperature, dimensions and shape of clarifier, etc.) and in coagulation/flocculation treatments (temperature, reagents, etc.) should be optimized to achieve the highest removal efficiency of microplastics, and especially microfibres in WWTPs. If this optimization is combined with other technologies applied in tertiary treatments, like ozonation, membrane filters or rapid sand filtration, the total removal efficiency of MPs could be approximately 97%, whereas 93% of microfibres could be eliminated from wastewater.

The removal of microplastics present in wastewaters, together with implementing new technologies to recover the microplastics retained in the sewage sludge, represents a great future challenge to comply with the legislation that foreseeably will regulate the performance of WWTPs regarding these microparticles.

Finally, it also should be considered that new procedures have to be developed to recycle and/or valorize the microplastics isolated through the wastewater treatment process in order to achieve a circular economy in the global field of plastic waste management.

References

Akarsu, C., Kumbur, H., Gökdağ, K., Kıdeyş, A.E., Sanchez-Vidal, A., 2020. Microplastics composition and load from three wastewater treatment plants discharging into Mersin Bay, north eastern Mediterranean Sea. *Mar. Pollut. Bull.*, 150, 110776. doi:10.1016/j.marpolbul.2019.110776.

Almroth, B.M.C., Åström, L., Roslund, S., Petersson, H., Johansson, M., Persson, K., 2018. Quantifying shedding of synthetic fibers from textiles; a source of microplastics released into the environment. *Environ. Sci. Pollut. Res.*, 25, 1191–1199. doi:10.1007/s11356-017-0528-7.

Alvim, C.B., Bes-Piá, M.A., Mendoza-Roca, J.A., 2020b. Separation and identification of microplastics from primary and secondary effluents and activated sludge from wastewater treatment plants. *Chem. Eng. J.*, 402, 126293. doi:10.1016/j.cej.2020.126293.

Alvim, C.B., Mendoza-Roca, J.A., Bes-Piá, A., 2020a. Wastewater treatment plant as microplastics release source – Quantification and identification techniques. *J. Environ. Manage.*, 255, 109739. doi:10.1016/j.jenvman.2019.109739.

An, L., Liu, Q., Deng, Y., Wu, W., Gao, Y., Ling, W., 2020. Sources of microplastics in the environment. In: He, D., Lu, Y. (Eds.), *Microplastics in Terrestrial Environments: The Handbook of Environmental Chemistry*, Vol. 95. Springer, Cham, 143–159. doi:10.1007/698_2020_449.

Aragaw, T.A., 2020. Surgical face masks as a potential source for microplastic pollution in the COVID-19 scenario. *Mar. Pollut. Bull.*, 159, 111517. doi:10.1016/j.marpolbul.2020.111517.

Bayo, J., López-Castellanos, J., Olmos, S., 2020b. Membrane bioreactor and rapid sand filtration for the removal of microplastics in an urban wastewater treatment plant. *Mar. Pollut. Bull.*, 156, 111211. doi:10.1016/j.marpolbul.2020.111211.

Bayo, J., Olmos, S., López-Castellanos, J., 2020a. Microplastics in an urban wastewater treatment plant: The influence of physicochemical parameters and environmental factors. *Chemosphere*, 238, 124593. doi:10.1016/j.chemosphere.2019.124593.

Bayo, J., Olmos, S., López-Castellanos, J., 2020c. Removal of microplastics from wastewater. In: Rocha-Santos, T., Costa, M., Mouneyrac, C. (Eds.), *Handbook of Microplastics in the Environment. Removal of Microplastics from Wastewater*. Springer, Cham, 1–20. doi:10.1007/978-3-030-10618-8_33–1.

Ben-David, E.A., Habibi, M., Haddad, E., Hasanin, M., Angel, D.L., Broth, A.M., Sabbah, I., 2021. Microplastic distributions in a domestic wastewater treatment plant: Removal efficiency, seasonal variation and influence of sampling technique. *Sci. Total Environ.*, 752, 141880. doi:10.1016/j.scitotenv.2020.141880.

Besseling, E., Quik, J.T., Sun, M., Koelmans, A.A., 2017. Fate of nano-and microplastic in freshwater systems: A modeling study. *Environ. Pollut.*, 220, 540–548. doi:10.1016/j.envpol.2016.10.001.

Blair, R.M., Waldron, S., Gauchotte-Lindsay, C., 2019. Average daily flow of microplastics through a tertiary wastewater treatment plant over a ten-month Period. *Water Res.*, 163, 114909. doi:10.1016/j.watres.2019.114909.

Boucher, J., Friot, D., 2017. *Primary Microplastics in the Oceans: A Global Evaluation of Sources.* Gland, Switzerland: IUCN. doi:10.2305/IUCN.CH.2017.01.en.

Carr, S.A., 2017. Sources and dispersive modes of micro-fibers in the environment. *Integr. Environ. Asses. Manag.*, 13, 466–469. doi:10.1002/ieam.1916.

Carr, S.A., Liu, J., Tesoro, A.G., 2016. Transport and fate of microplastic particles in wastewater treatment Plants. *Water Res.*, 91, 174–182. doi:10.1016/j.watres.2016.01.002.

Caruso, G., 2015. Plastic degrading microorganisms as a tool for bioremediation of plastic contamination in aquatic environments. *J. Pollut. Eff. Cont.*, 3(3), doi:10.4172/2375-4397.1000e112.

Cesa, F.S., Turra, A., Baruque-Ramos, J., 2017. Synthetic fibers as microplastics in the marine environment: A review from textile perspective with a focus on domestic washings. *Sci. Total Environ.*, 598, 1116–1129. doi:10.1016/j.scitotenv.2017.04.172.

Chen, G., Feng, Q., Wang, J., 2020. Mini-review of microplastics in the atmosphere and their risks to humans. *Sci. Total Environ.*, 703, 135504. doi:10.1016/j.scitotenv.2019.135504.

Claessens, M., Van Cauwenberghe, L., Vandegehuchte, M.B., Janssen, C.R., 2013. New techniques for the detection of microplastics in sediments and field collected organisms. *Mar. Pollut. Bull.*, 70(1–2), 227–233. doi:10.1016/j.marpolbul.2013.03.009.

Conley, K., Clum, A., Deepe, J., Lane, H., Beckingham, B., 2019. Wastewater treatment plants as a source of microplastics to an urban estuary: Removal efficiencies and loading per capita over one year. *Water Res. X*, 3, 100030. doi:10.1016/j.wroa.2019.100030.

Coppock, R.L., Cole, M., Lindeque, P.K., Queirós, A.M., Galloway, T.S., 2017. A small-scale, portable method for extracting microplastics from marine sediments. *Environ. Pollut.*, 230, 829–837. doi:10.1016/j.envpol.2017.07.017.

Corradini, F., Meza, P., Eguiluz, R., Casado, F., Huerta-Lwanga, E., Geissen, V., 2019. Evidence of microplastic accumulation in agricultural soils from sewage sludge disposal. *Sci. Total Environ.*, 671, 411–420. doi:10.1016/j.scitotenv.2019.03.368.

Courtene-Jones, W., Quinn, B., Ewins, C., Gary, S.F., Narayanaswamy, B.E., 2019. Consistent microplastic ingestion by deep-sea invertebrates over the last four decades (1976–2015), a study from the North East Atlantic. *Environ. Pollut.*, 244, 503–512. doi:10.1016/j.envpol.2018.10.090.

Cox, K.D., Covernton, G.A., Davies, H.L., Dower, J.F., Juanes, F., Dudas, S.E., 2019. Human consumption of microplastics. *Environ. Sci. Technol.*, 53(12), 7068–7074. doi:10.1021/acs.est.9b01517.

Crawford, C.B., Quinn, B., 2017. Chapter 9: Microplastic pollutants. In: *Microplastic Separation Techniques*. Elsevier Science, Amsterdam, Netherlands, 203–218. doi:10.1016/B978-0-12-809406-8.00009-8.

De Falco, F., Cocca, M., Avella, M., Thompson, R.C., 2020. Microfiber release to water, via laundering, and to air, via everyday use: A comparison between polyester clothing with differing textile parameters. *Environ. Sci. Technol.*, 54(6), 3288–3296. doi:10.1021/acs.est.9b06892.

De Falco, F., Di Pace, E., Cocca, M., Avella, M., 2019. The contribution of washing processes of synthetic clothes to microplastic pollution. *Sci. Rep.*, 9, 6633. doi:10.1038/s41598-019-43023-x.

Dris, R., Gasperi, J., Rocher, V., Saad, M., Renault, N., Tassin, B., 2015. Microplastic contamination in an urban area: A case study in Greater Paris. *Environ. Chem.*, 12, 592–599. doi:10.1071/EN14167.

Dris, R., Gasperi, J., Saad, M., Mirande, C., Tassin, B., 2016. Synthetic fibres in atmospheric fallout: A source of microplastics in the environment? *Mar. Pollut. Bull.*, 104, 290–293. doi:10.1016/j.envpol.2018.02.016.

ECHA, 2019. *Annex XV Restriction Report. Proposal for a Restriction*. Available at: https://echa.europa.eu/documents/10162/05bd96e3-b969-0a7c-c6d0-441182893720.

Edo, C., González-Pleiter, M., Leganés, F., Fernández-Piñas, F., Rosal, R., 2020. Fate of microplastics in wastewater treatment plants and their environmental dispersion with effluent and sludge. *Environ. Pollut.*, 259, 113837. doi:10.1016/j.envpol.2019.113837.

Eerkes-Medrano, D., Leslie, H.A., Quinn, B., 2019. Microplastics in drinking water: A review and assessment. *Curr. Opin. Environ. Sci. Health.*, 7, 69–75. doi:10.1016/j.coesh.2018.12.001.

Elkhatib, D., Oyanedel-Craver, V., 2020. A critical review of extraction and identification methods of microplastics in wastewater and drinking water. *Environ. Sci. Technol.*, 54, 7037–7049. doi:10.1021/acs.est.9b06672.

Enyoh, C.E., Verla, A.W., Verla, E.N., Ibe, F.C., Amaobi, C.E., 2019. Airborne microplastics: A review study on method for analysis, occurrence, movement and risks. *Environ. Monit. Assess.*, 191, 668. doi:10.1007/s10661-019-7842-0.

Eriksen, M, Lebreton, L.C.M., Carson, H.S., Thiel, M., Moore, C.J., Borerro, J.C., Galgani, F., Ryan, P.G., Reisser, J., 2014. Plastic pollution in the world's oceans: More than 5 Trillion plastic pieces weighing over 250,000 tons afloat at sea. *PLoS ONE*, 9(12), e111913. doi:10.1371/journal.pone.0111913.

Ersahin, M.E., Ozgun, H., Dereli, R.K., Ozturk, I., Roest, K., van Lier, J.B., 2012. A review on dynamic membrane filtration: Materials, applications and future perspectives. *Bioresour. Technol.*, 122, 196–206. doi:10.1016/j.biortech.2012.03.086.

European Commission, 2018. *Communication from the Commission to the European Parliament, the Council, the European Economic and Social Committee of the Regions: A European Strategy for Plastics in a Circular Economy*. COM/2018/028 final. Available at: https://eur-lex. europa.eu/resource.html?uri=cellar:2df5d1d2-fac7-11e7-b8f5-01aa75ed71a1.0001.02/ DOC_1&format=PDF.

European Commission, 2020. *Communication from the Commission to the European Parliament, the Council, the European Economic and Social Committee of the Regions: A new Circular Economy Action Plan; For a cleaner and more competitive Europe*. COM (2020) 98 final. Available at: https://eur-lex. europa.eu/resource.html?uri=cellar:9903b325-6388-11ea-b735-01aa75ed71a1.0017.02/ DOC_1&format=PDF.

European Parliament, 2019. *Minimum Requirements for Water Reuse*. Available at: www.europarl. europa.eu/RegData/seance_pleniere/textes_adoptes/provisoire/2019/02-12/0071/ P8_TA-PROV(2019)0071_EN.pdf.

Fadare, O.O., Okoffo, E.D., 2020. Covid-19 face masks: A potential source of microplastic fibers in the environment. *Sci. Total Environ.*, 737, 140279. doi:10.1016/j. scitotenv.2020.140279.

Felsing, S., Kochleus, C., Buchinger, S., Brennholt, N., Stock, F., Reifferscheid, G., 2018. A new approach in separating microplastics from environmental samples based on their electrostatic behavior. *Environ. Pollut.*, 234, 20–28. doi:10.1016/j.envpol.2017.11.013.

Franco, A.A , Arellano, J.M., Albendín, G., Rodríguez-Barroso, R., Zahedi, S., Quiroga, J.M., Coello, Mª.D., 2020. Mapping microplastics in Cadiz (Spain): Occurrence of microplastics in municipal and industrial wastewaters. *J. Water Process. Eng.*, 38, 101596. doi:10.1016/j.jwpe.2020.101596.

Fraunholcz, N., 2004. Separation of waste plastics by froth flotation – a review, part I. *Miner. Eng.*, 17, 261–268. doi:10.1016/j.mineng.2003.10.028.

Freeman, S., Booth, A.M., Sabbah, I., Tiller, R., Dierking, J., Klun, K., Rotter, A., Ben-David, E., Javidpour, J., Angel, D.L., 2020. Between source and sea: The role of wastewater treatment in reducing marine microplastics. *J. Environ. Manage.*, 226, 110642. doi:10.1016/j.jenvman.2020.110642.

Gago, J., Carretero, O., Filgueiras, A., Viñas, L., 2018. Synthetic microfibers in the marine environment: A review on their occurrence in seawater and sediments. *Mar. Pollut. Bull.*, 127, 365–376. doi:10.1016/j.marpolbul.2017.11.070.

Galvão, A., Aleixo, M., De Pablo, H., Lopes, C., Raimundo, J., 2020. Microplastics in wastewater: Microfiber emissions from common household laundry. *Environ. Sci. Pollut. Res.*, 27, 26643–26649. doi:10.1007/s11356-020-08765-6.

Gatidou, G., Arvaniti, O.S., Stasinakis, A.S., 2019. Review on the occurrence and fate of microplastics in sewage treatment plants. *J. Hazard. Mater.*, 367, 504–512. doi:10.1016/j. jhazmat.2018.12.081.

Gies, E.A., LeNoble, J.L., Noel, M., Etemadifar, A., Bishay, F., Hall, E.R., Ross, P.S., 2018. Retention of microplastic in a major secondary wastewater treatment plant in Vancouver, Canada. *Mar. Pollut. Bull.*, 133, 553–561. doi:10.1016/j. marpolbul.2018.06.006.

González-Pleiter, M., Velázquez, D., Edo, C., Carretero, O., Gago, J., Barón-Sola, A., Hernández, L.E., Yousef, I., Quesada, A., Leganés, F., Rosal, R., Fernández-Piñas, F., 2020. Fibers spreading worldwide: Microplastics and other anthropogenic litter in an Arctic freshwater lake. *Sci. Total Environ.*, 722, 137904. doi:10.1016/j. scitotenv.2020.137904.

Grbic, J., Nguyen, B., Guo, E., You, J.B., Sinton, D., Rochman, C.M., 2019. Magnetic extraction of microplastics from environmental samples. *Environ. Sci. Technol. Lett.*, 6(2), 68–72. doi:10.1021/acs.estlett.8b00671.

Gündoğdu, S., Çevik, C., Güzel, E., Kilercioğlu, S., 2018. Microplastics in municipal wastewater treatment plants in Turkey: A comparison of the influent and secondary effluent concentrations. *Environ. Monit. Assess.*, 190, 626. doi:10.1007/s10661-018-7010-y.

Habib, D., Locke, D.C., Cannone, L.J., 1998. Synthetic fibers as indicators of municipal sewage sludge, sludge products, and sewage treatment plant effluents. *Water Air Soil Pollut.*, 103, 1–8. doi:10.1023/A:1004908110793.

Habib, R.Z., Thiemann, T., Al Kendi, R., 2020. Microplastics and wastewater treatment plants – A review. *J. Water Resource Prot.*, 12(1), 1–35. doi:10.4236/jwarp.2020.121001.

Hale, R.C., Seeley, M.E., La Guardia, M.J., Mai, L., Zeng, E.Y., 2020. A global perspective on microplastics. *J. Geophys. Res. Oceans*, 125(1), 1–40. doi:10.1029/2018JC014719.

Hamidian, A.H., Ozumchelouei, E.J., Feizi, F., Wu, C., Zhang, Y., Yang, M., 2021. A review on the characteristics of microplastics in wastewater treatment plants: A source of toxic chemicals. *J. Clean. Prod.*, 295, 126480. doi:10.1016/j.jclepro.2021.126480.

He, D., Luo, Y., Lu, S., Liu, M., Song, Y., Lei, L., 2018. Microplastics in soils: Analytical methods, pollution characteristics and ecological risks. *Trends Anal. Chem.*, 109, 163–172. doi:10.1016/j.trac.2018.10.006.

Hidayaturrahman, H., Lee, T-G., 2019. A study on characteristics of microplastic in wastewater of South Korea: Identification, quantification, and fate of microplastics during treatment process. *Mar. Pollut. Bull.*, 146, 696–702. doi:10.1016/j.marpolbul.2019.06.071.

Hongprasith, N., Kittimethawong, C., Lertluksanaporn, R., Eamchotchawalit, T., Kittipongvises, S., Lohwacharin, J., 2020. IR microspectroscopic identification of microplastics in municipal wastewater treatment plants. *Environ. Sci. Pollut. Res.*, 27, 18557–18564. doi:10.1007/s11356-020-08265-7.

Hurley, R.R., Lusher, A.L., Olsen, M., Nizzetto, L., 2018. Validation of a method for extracting microplastics from complex, organic-rich, environmental matrices. *Environ. Sci. Technol.*, 52(13), 7409–7417. doi:10.1021/acs.est.8b01517.

Hurley, R.R., Nizzetto, L., 2018. Fate and occurrence of micro(nano)plastics in soils: Knowledge gaps and possible risks. *Curr. Opin. Environ. Sci. Health.*, 1, 6–11. doi:10.1016/j.coesh.2017.10.006.

Imhof, H.K., Schmid, J., Niessner, R., Ivleva, N.P., Laforsch, C., 2012. A novel, highly efficient method for the separation and quantification of plastic particles in sediments of aquatic environments. *Limnol. Oceanogr. Methods*, 10, 524–537. doi:10.4319/lom.2012.10.524.

Iñiguez, M.E., Conesa, J.A., Fullana, A., 2017. Microplastics in Spanish table salt. *Sci. Rep.*, 7, 8620. doi:10.1038/s41598-017-09128-x.

Iyare, P.U., Ouki, S.K., Bond, T., 2020. Microplastics removal in wastewater treatment plants: A critical review. *Environ. Sci. Water. Res. Technol.*, 6, 2664. doi:10.1039/D0EW00397B.

Jiang, J., Wang, X., Ren, H., Cao, G., Xie, G., Xing, D., Liu, B., 2020. Investigation and fate of microplastics in wastewater and sludge filter cake from a wastewater treatment plant in China. *Sci. Total Environ.*, 746, 141378. doi:10.1016/j.scitotenv.2020.141378.

Katrivesis, F.K., Karela, A.D., Papadakis, V.G., Paraskeva, C.A., 2019. Revisiting of coagulation-flocculation processes in the production of potable water. *J. Water Process Eng.*, 27, 193–204. doi:10.1016/j.jwpe.2018.12.007.

Kay, P., Hiscoe, R., Moberley, I., Bajic, L., Mckenna, N., 2018. Wastewater treatment plants as a source of microplastics in river catchments. *Environ. Sci. Pollut. Res.*, 25, 20264–20267. doi:10.1007/s11356-018-2070-7.

Kazour, M., Terki, S., Rabhi, K., Jemaa, S., Khalaf, G., Amara, R., 2019. Sources of microplastics pollution in the marine environment: Importance of wastewater treatment plant and coastal landfill. *Mar. Pollut. Bull.*, 146, 608–618. doi:10.1016/j.marpolbul.2019.06.066.

Kedzierski, M., Le Tilly, V., Bourseau, P., Bellegou, H., César, G., Sire, O., Bruzaud, S., 2016. Microplastics elutriation from sandy sediments: A granulometric approach. *Mar. Pollut. Bull.*, 107(1), 315–323. doi:10.1016/j.marpolbul.2016.03.041.

Kedzierski, M., Le Tilly, V., Bourseau, P., Bellegou, H., César, G., Sire, O., Bruzaud, S., 2017. Microplastics elutriation system. Part A: Numerical modeling. *Mar. Pollut. Bull.*, 119(2), 151–161. doi:10.1016/j.marpolbul.2017.04.060.

Kedzierski, M., Le Tilly, V., Bourseau, P., César, G., Sire, O., Bruzaud, S., 2018. Microplastics elutriation system. Part B: Insight of the next generation. *Mar. Pollut. Bull.*, 133, 9–17. doi:10.1016/j.marpolbul.2018.05.011.

Kelly, M.R., Lant, N.J., Kurr, M., Burgess, J.G., 2019. Importance of water-volume on the release of microplastic fibers from laundry. *Environ. Sci. Technol.*, 53(20), 11735–11744. doi:10.1021/acs.est.9b03022.

Kiendrebeogo, M., Estahbanati, M.R.K., Mostafazadeh, A.K., Drogui, P., Tyagi, R.D., 2021. Treatment of microplastics in water by anodic oxidation: A case study for polystyrene. *Environ. Pollut.*, 269, 116168. doi:10.1016/j.envpol.2020.116168.

Lares, M., Ncibi, M.C., Sillanpää, M., 2018. Occurrence, identification and removal of microplastic particles and fibers in conventional activated sludge process and advanced MBR technology. *Water Res.*, 133, 236–246. doi:10.1016/j.watres.2018.01.049.

Lee, H., Kim, Y., 2018. Treatment characteristics of microplastics at biological sewage treatment facilities in Korea. *Mar. Pollut. Bull.*, 137, 1–8. doi:10.1016/j.marpolbul.2018.09.050.

Leslie, H.A., Brandsma, S.H., van Velzen, M.J.M., Vethaak, A.D., 2017. Microplastics en route: Field measurements in the Dutch river delta and Amsterdam canals, wastewater treatment plants, North Sea sediments and biota. *Environ. Int.*, 101, 133–142. doi:10.1016/j.envint.2017.01.018.

Li, L., Zhao, X., Li, Z., Song, K., 2020a. COVID-19: Performance study of microplastic inhalation risk posed by wearing masks. *J. Hazard. Mater.*, 411, 124955. doi:10.1016/j.jhazmat.2020.124955.

Li, L., Liu, D., Song, K., Zhou, Y., 2020b. Performance evaluation of MBR in treating microplastics polyvinylchloride contaminated polluted surface water. *Mar. Pollut. Bull.*, 150, 110724. doi:10.1016/j.marpolbul.2019.110724.

Liu, J., Yang, Y., Ding, J., Zhu, B., Gao, W., 2019a. Microfibers: A preliminary discussion on their definition and sources. *Environ. Sci. Pollut. Res. Int.*, 26, 29497–29501. doi:10.1007/s11356-019-06265-w.

Liu, M., Lu, S., Chen, Y., Cao, C., Bigalke, M., He, D., 2020. Analytical methods for microplastics in environments: Current advances and challenges. In: He, D., Luo, Y. (Eds.), *The Handbook of Environmental Chemistry*. Springer, Berlin, Heidelberg, 1–22. doi:10.1007/698_2019_436.

Liu, W., Zhang, J., Liu, H., Guo, X., Zhang, X., Yao, X., Cao, Z., Zhang, T., 2021. A review of the removal of microplastics in global wastewater treatment plants: Characteristics and mechanisms. *Environ. Int.*, 146, 106277. doi:10.1016/j.envint.2020.106277.

Liu, X., Yuan, X., Di, M., Li, Z., Wang, J., 2019b. Transfer and fate of microplastics during the conventional activated sludge process in one wastewater treatment plant of China. *Chem. Eng. J.*, 362, 176–182. doi:10.1016/j.cej.2019.01.033.

Long, Z., Pan, Z., Wang, W., Ren, J., Yu, X., Lin, L., Lin, H., Chen, H., Jin, X., 2019. Microplastic abundance, characteristics, and removal in wastewater treatment plants in a coastal city of China. *Water Res.*, 155, 255–265. doi:10.1016/j.watres.2019.02.028.

Lots, F.A.E., Behrens, P., Vijver, M.G., Horton, A.A., Bosker, T., 2017. A large-scale investigation of microplastic contamination: Abundance and characteristics of microplastics in European beach sediment. *Mar. Pollut. Bull.*, 123(1–2), 219–226. doi:10.1016/j.marpolbul.2017.08.057.

Lu, L., Luo, T., Zhao, Y., Cai, C., Fu, Z., Jin, Y., 2019. Interaction between microplastics and microorganism as well as gut microbiota: A consideration on environment animal and human health. *Sci. Total Environ.*, 667, 94–100. doi:10.1016/j.scitotenv.2019.02.380.

Lusher, A.L., Hurley, R., Vogelsang, C., Nizzetto, L., Olsen, M., 2018. *Mapping Microplastics in Sludge*. Report No. M907 for the Norwegian Institute for Water Research (NIVA). NIVA, Oslo. Available at: http://hdl.handle.net/11250/2493527.

Lv, X., Dong, Q., Zuo, Z., Liu, Y., Huang, X., Wu, W.M., 2019. Microplastics in a municipal wastewater treatment plant: Fate, dynamic distribution, removal efficiencies, and control strategies. *J. Clean. Prod.*, 225, 579–586. doi:10.1016/j.jclepro.2019.03.321.

Ma, B., Li, W., Liu, R., Liu, G., Sun, J., Liu, H., Qu, J., van der Meer, W., 2018. Multiple dynamic Al-based floc layers on ultrafiltration membrane surfaces for humic acid and reservoir water fouling reduction. *Water Res.*, 139, 291–300. doi:10.1016/j.watres.2018.04.012.

Magni, S., Binelli, A., Pittura, L., Avio, C.G., Della Torre, C., Parenti, C.C., Gorbi, S., Regoli, F., 2019. The fate of microplastics in an Italian wastewater treatment plant. *Sci. Total Environ.*, 652, 602–610. doi:10.1016/j.scitotenv.2018.10.269.

Mahon, A.M., O'Connell, B., Healy, M.G., O'Connor, I., Officer, R., Nash, R., Morrison, L., 2017. Microplastics in sewage sludge: Effects of treatment. *Environ. Sci. Technol.*, 51, 810–818. doi:10.1021/acs.est.6b04048.

Masiá, P., Ardura, A., Gaitán, M., Gerber, S., Rayon-Viña, F., Garcia-Vazquez, E., 2021. Maritime ports and beach management as sources of coastal macro-, meso-, and microplastic pollution. *Environ. Sci. Pollut. Res.*, 28, 30722–30731. doi:10.1007/s11356-021-12821-0.

Masiá, P., Ardura, A., Garcia-Vazquez, E., 2019. Microplastics in special protected areas for migratory birds in the Bay of Biscay. *Mar. Pollut. Bull.*, 146, 993–1001. doi:10.1016/j.marpolbul.2019.07.065.

Masiá, P., Sol, D., Ardura, A., Laca, A., Borrell, Y.J., Dopico, E., Laca, A., Machado-Schiaffino, G., Díaz, M., Garcia-Vazquez, E., 2020. Bioremediation as a promising strategy to microplastics removal in wastewater treatment plants. *Mar. Pollut. Bull.*, 156, 111252. doi:10.1016/j.marpolbul.2020.111252.

Mason, S.A., Garneau, D., Sutton, R., Chu, Y., Ehmann, K., Barnes, J., Fink, P., Papazissimos, D., Rogers, D.L., 2016. Microplastic pollution is widely detected in US municipal wastewater treatment plant effluent. *Environ. Pollut.*, 218, 1045–1054. doi:10.1016/j.envpol.2016.08.056.

Michielssen, M.R., Michielssen, E.R., Ni, J., Duhaime, M.B., 2016. Fate of microplastics and other small anthropogenic litter (SAL) in wastewater treatment plants depends on unit processes employed. *Environ. Sci. Water Res. Technol.*, 2(6), 1064–1073. doi:10.1039/C6EW00207B.

Microbead England Regulation, 2017. *Implementation of the Environmental Protection (Microbeads) (England) Regulations 2017*. Available at: www.legislation.gov.uk/ukia/2017/178/pdfs/ukia_20170178_en.pdf

The Microbead-Free Waters Act of 2015, 2015. Available at: www.congress.gov/114/crpt/hrpt371/CRPT-114hrpt371.pdf.

Microbeads (Prohibition) Act, 2019. Available at: www.irishstatutebook.ie/eli/2019/act/52/enacted/en/pdf.

Mintenig, S.M., Int-Veen, I., Löder, M.G.J., Primpke, S., Gerdts, G., 2017. Identification of microplastic in effluents of waste water treatment plants using focal plane array-based micro-Fourier-transform infrared imaging. *Water Res.*, 108, 365–372. doi:10.1016/j.watres.2016.11.015.

Murphy, F., Ewins, C., Carbonnier, F., Quinn, B., 2016. Wastewater Treatment Works (WwTW) as a source of microplastics in the aquatic environment. *Environ. Sci. Technol.*, 50(11), 5800–5808. doi:10.1021/acs.est.5b05416.

Naji, A., Azadkhah, S., Farahani, H., Uddin, S., Khan, F.R., 2021. Microplastics in wastewater outlets of Bandar Abbas city (Iran): A potential point source of microplastics into the Persian Gulf. *Chemosphere*, 262, 128039. doi:10.1016/j.chemosphere.2020.128039.

Ngo, P.L., Pramanik, B.K., Shah, K., Roychand, R., 2019. Pathway, classification and removal efficiency of microplastics in wastewater treatment plants. *Environ. Pollut.*, 255(2), 113326. doi:10.1016/j.envpol.2019.113326.

Nizzetto, L., Futter, M. and Langaas, S., 2016. Are agricultural soils dumps for microplastics of urban origin? *Environ. Sci. Technol.*, 50, 10777–10779. doi:10.1021/acs.est.6b04140.

O'mann, B.E., 2021. Microplastics in drinking water? Present state of knowledge and open questions. *Curr. Opin. Food Sci.*, 41, 44–51. doi:10.1016/j.cofs.2021.02.011.

Obbard, R.W., Sadri, S., Wong, Y.Q., Khitun, A.A., Baker, I., Thompson, R.C., 2014. Global warming releases microplastic legacy frozen in Arctic Sea ice. *Earths Future*, 2, 315–320. doi:10.1002/2014EF000240.

Ogunola, O.S., Onada, O.A., Falaye, A.E., 2018. Mitigation measures to avert the impacts of plastics and microplastics in the marine environment (a review). *Environ. Sci. Pollut. Res.*, 25(10), 9293–9310. doi:10.1007/s11356-018-1499-z.

Okotto, E.D., O'Brien, S., O'Brien, J.W., Tscharke, B.J., Thomas, K.V., 2019. Wastewater treatment plants as a source of plastics in the environment: A review of occurrence, methods for identification, quantification and fate. *Environ. Sci. Water Res. Technol.*, 5(11), 1908–1931. doi:10.1039/C9EW00428A.

Park, H.J., Oh, M.J., Kim, P.G., Kim, G., Jeong, D.H., Ju, B.K., Lee, W.S., Chung, H.M., Kang, H.J., Kwon, J.H., 2020. National reconnaissance survey of microplastics in municipal wastewater treatments plants in Korea. *Environ. Sci. Technol.*, 54(3), 1503–1512. doi:10.1021/acs.est.9b04929.

Picó, Y., Alfarhan, A., Barceló, D., 2019. Nano- and microplastic analysis: Focus on their occurrence in freshwater ecosystems and remediation technologies. *Trends Anal. Chem.*, 113, 409–425. doi:10.1016/j.trac.2018.08.022.

Pittura, L., Foglia, A., Akyol, Ç, Cipolletta, G., Benedetti, M., Regoli, F., Eusebi, A.L., Sabbatini, S., Tseng, L.Y., Katsou, E., Gorbi, S., Fatone, F., 2021. Microplastics in real wastewater treatment schemes: Comparative assessment and relevant inhibition effects on anaerobic processes. *Chemosphere*, 262, 128415. doi:10.1016/j.chemosphere.2020.128415.

Pivokonský, M., Pivokonská, L., Novotná, K., Čermáková, L., Klimtová, M., 2020. Occurrence and fate of microplastics at two different drinking water treatment plants within a river catchment. *Sci. Total Environ.*, 741, 140236. doi:10.1016/j.scitotenv.2020.140236.

Prata, J.C., 2018a. Airborne microplastics: Consequences to human health? *Environ. Pollut.*, 234, 115–126. doi.org/10.1016/j.envpol.2017.11.043.

Prata, J.C., 2018b. Microplastics in wastewater: State of the knowledge on sources, fate and solutions. *Mar. Pollut. Bull.*, 129(1), 262–265. doi:10.1016/j.marpolbul.2018.02.046.

Prata, J.C., da Costa, J.P., Duarte, A.C., Rocha-Santos, C., 2019. Methods for sampling and detection of microplastics in water and sediment: A critical review. *Trends Anal. Chem.*, 110, 150–159. doi:10.1016/j.trac.2018.10.029.

Raju, S., Carbery, M., Kuttykattil, A., Senthirajah, K., Lundmark, A., Rogers, Z., SCB, S., Evans, G., Palanisami, T., 2020. Improved methodology to determine the fate and transport of microplastics in a secondary wastewater treatment plant. *Water Res.*, 173, 115549. doi:10.1016/j.watres.2020.115549.

Rhodes, C.J., 2019. Solving the plastic problem: From cradle to grave, to reincarnation. *Sci. Prog.*, 102(3), 218–248. doi:10.1177/0036850419867204.

Rodrigues, M.O., Gonçalves, A.M.M., Gonçalves, F.J.M., Abrantes, N., 2020. Improving cost-efficiency for MPs density separation by zinc chloride reuse. *MethodsX*, 7, 100785. doi:10.1016/j.mex.2020.100785.

Rolsky, C., Kelkar, V., Driver, E., Halden, R.U., 2020. Municipal sewage sludge as a source of microplastics in the environment. *Curr. Opin. Environ. Sci. Health*, 14, 16–22. doi:10.1016/j.coesh.2019.12.001.

Ruan, Y., Zhang, K., Wu, C., Wu, R., Lam, P.K.S., 2019. A preliminary screening of HBCD enantiomers transported by microplastics in wastewater treatment plants. *Sci. Total Environ.*, 674, 171–178. doi:10.1016/j.scitotenv.2019.04.007.

Ruggero, F., Gori, R., Lubello, C., 2020. Methodologies for microplastics recovery and identification in heterogeneous solid matrices: A review. *J. Polym. Environ.*, 28, 739–748. doi:10.1007/s10924-019-01644-3.

Sanchez-Vidal, A., Thompson, R.C., Canals, M., de Haan, W.P., 2018. The imprint of microfibres in southern European deep seas. *PLoS ONE*, 13, e0207033. doi:10.1371/journal.pone.0207033.

Shahnawaz, M., Sangale, M.K., Ade, A.B., 2019. Case studies and recent update of plastic waste degradation. In: *Bioremediation Technology for Plastic Waste*. Springer, Singapore, 31–43. doi:10.1007/978-981-13-7492-0_4.

Shruti, V.C., Pérez-Guevara, F., Elizalde-Martínez, I., Kutralam-Muniasamy, G., 2020. Reusable masks for COVID-19: A missing piece of the microplastic problem during the global health crisis. *Mar. Pollut. Bull.*, 161, 111777–111782. doi:10.1016/j.marpolbul.2020.111777.

Sillanpää, M., Sainio, P., 2017. Release of polyester and cotton fibers from textiles in machine washings. *Environ. Sci. Pollut. Res.*, 24, 19313–19321. doi:10.1007/s11356-017-9621-1.

Simon, M., van Last, N., Vollertsen, J., 2018. Quantification of microplastic mass and removal rates at wastewater treatment plants applying Focal Plane Array (FPA)-based Fourier Transform Infrared (FT-IR) imaging. *Water Res.*, 142, 1–9. doi:10.1016/j.watres.2018.05.019.

Sol, D., Laca, A., Laca, A., Díaz, M., 2020. Approaching the environmental problem of microplastics: Importance of WWTP treatments. *Sci. Total Environ.*, 740, 140016. doi:10.1016/j.scitotenv.2020.140016.

Stock, F., Kochleus, C., Bänsch-Baltruschat, B., Brennholt, N., Reifferscheid, G., 2019. Sampling techniques and preparation methods for microplastic analyses in the aquatic environment – A review. *Trends Anal. Chem.*, 113, 84–92. doi:10.1016/j.trac.2019.01.014.

Suaria, G., Achtypi, A., Perold, V., Lee, J.R., Pierucci, A., Bornman, T.G., Aliani, S., Ryan, P.G., 2020. Microfibers in oceanic surface waters: A global characterization. *Sci. Adv.*, 6(23), eaay8493. doi:10.1126/sciadv.aay8493.

Sun, J., Dai, X., Wang, Q., van Loosdrecht, M.C.M., Ni, B.J., 2019. Microplastics in wastewater treatment plants: Detection, occurrence and Removal. *Water Res.*, 152, 21–37. doi:10.1016/j.watres.2018.12.050.

Tagg, A.S., Harrison, J.P., Ju-Nam, Y., Sapp, M., Bradley, E.L., Sinclair, C.J., Ojeada, J.J., 2017. Fenton's reagent for the rapid and efficient isolation of microplastics from wastewater. *Chem. Commun.*, 53, 372. doi:10.1039/C6CC08798A.

Talvitie, J., Mikola, A., Koistinen, A., Setälä, O., 2017a. Solutions to microplastic pollution – Removal of microplastics from wastewater effluent with advanced wastewater treatment technologies. *Water Res.*, 123, 401–407. doi:10.1016/j.watres.2017.07.005.

Talvitie, J., Mikola, A., Setälä, O., Heinonen, M., Koistinen, A., 2017b. How well is microlitter purified from wastewater? – A detailed study on the stepwise removal of microlitter in a tertiary level wastewater treatment Plant. *Water Res.*, 109, 164–172. doi:10.1016/j. watres.2016.11.046.

Te, C.Y., Budiman, P.M., Shak, K.P.Y., Wu, T.Y., 2016. Recent advancement of coagulation – Flocculation and its application in wastewater treatment. *Ind. Eng. Chem. Res.*, 55(16), 4363–4389. doi:10.1021/acs.iecr.5b04703.

Van Cauwenberghe, L.V., Janssen, C.R., 2014. Microplastics in bivalves cultured for human consumption. *Environ. Pollut.*, 193, 65–70. doi:10.1016/j.envpol.2014.06.010.

Wang, J., Peng, J., Tan, Z., Gao, Y., Zhan, Z., Chen, Q., Cai, L., 2017. Microplastics in the surface sediments from the Beijiang River littoral zone: Composition, abundance, surface textures and interaction with heavy metals. *Chemosphere*, 171, 248–258. doi:10.1016/j.chemosphere.2016.12.074.

Wang, W., Ge, J., Yu, X., 2020b. Bioavailability and toxicity of microplastics to fish species: A review. *Ecotoxicol. Environ. Saf.*, 189, 109913. doi:10.1016/j.ecoenv.2019.109913.

Wang, Z., Lin, T., Chen, W., 2020a. Occurrence and removal of microplastics in an advanced drinking water treatment plant (ADWTP). *Sci. Total Environ.*, 700, 134520. doi:10.1016/j.scitotenv.2019.134520.

Woodall, L.C., Sanchez-Vidal, A., Canals, M., Paterson, G.L., Coppock, R., Sleight, V., Calafat, A., Rogers, A.D., Narayanaswamy, B.E., Thompson, R.C., 2014. The deep sea is a major sink for microplastic debris. *R. Soc. Open Sci.*, 1, 140317. doi:10.1098/rsos.140317.

Xu, B., Liu, F., Cryder, Z., Huang, D., Lu, Z., He, Y., Wang, H., Lu, Z., Brookes, P.C., Tang, C., Gan, J., Xu, J., 2019. Microplastics in the soil environment: Occurrence, risks, interactions and fate – A review. *Crit. Rev. Env. Sci. Tec.*, 50(21), 2175–2222. doi:10.10 80/10643389.2019.1694822.

Xu, S., Ma, J., Ji, R., Pan, K., Miao, A.J., 2020. Microplastics in aquatic environments: Occurrence, accumulation, and biological effects. *Sci. Total Environ.*, 703, 134699. doi:10.1016/j.scitotenv.2019.134699.

Xu, Z., Bai, X., Ye, Z., 2021. Removal and generation of microplastics in wastewater treatment plants: A review. *J. Clean. Prod.*, 291, 125982. doi:10.1016/j. jclepro.2021.125982.

Yang, L., Li, K., Cui, S., Kang, Y., An, L., Lei, K., 2019. Removal of microplastics in municipal sewage from China's largest water reclamation Plant. *Water Res.*, 155, 175–181. doi:10.1016/j.watres.2019.02.046.

Yang, Z., Li, S., Ma, S., Liu, P., Peng, D., Ouyang, Z., Guo, X., 2021. Characteristics and removal efficiency of microplastics in sewage treatment plant of Xi'an City, northwest China. *Sci. Total Environ.*, 771, 145377. doi:10.1016/j.scitotenv.2021.145377.

Zarfl, C., 2019. Promising techniques and open challenges for microplastic identification and quantification in environmental matrices. *Anal. Bioanal. Chem.*, 411, 3743–3756. doi:10.1007/s00216-019-01763-9

Zhu, X., 2015. Optimization of elutriation device for filtration of microplastic particles from sediment. *Mar. Pollut. Bull.*, 92(1–2), 69–72. doi:10.1016/j.marpolbul.2014.12.054.

Ziajahromi, S., Neale, P.A., Rintoul, L., Leusch, F.D.L., 2017. Wastewater treatment plants as a pathway for microplastics: Development of a new approach to sample wastewater-based microplastics. *Water Res.*, 112, 93–99. doi:10.1016/j.watres.2017.01.042.

Ziajahromi, S., Neale, P.A., Silveira, I.T., Chua, A., Leusch, F.D.L., 2021. An audit of microplastic abundance throughout three Australian wastewater treatment plants. *Chemosphere*, 263, 128294. doi:10.1016/j.chemosphere.2020.128294.

Zobkov, M.B., Esiukova, E.E., 2017. Evaluation of the Munich Plastic Sediment Separator efficiency in extraction of microplastics from natural marine bottom sediments. *Limnol. Oceanogr. Methods*, 15, 967–978. doi:10.1002/lom3.10217.

Zou, Y., Ye, C., Pan, Y., 2020. Abundance and characteristics of microplastics in municipal wastewater treatment plan effluent: A case study of Guangzhou, China. *Environ. Sci. Pollut. Res.*, 28, 11572–11585. doi:10.1007/s11356-020-11431-6.

Zubris, K.A.V., Richards, B.K., 2005. Synthetic fibers as an indicator of land application of sludge. *Environ. Pollut.*, 138(2), 201–211. doi:10.1016/j.envpol.2005.04.013.

8

DEGRADATION OF FIBROUS MICROPLASTICS IN THE MARINE ENVIRONMENT

Christian Lott, Andreas Eich and Miriam Weber

1 Introduction

Fibrous microparticles or microfibres enter the marine environment by advective transport via the atmosphere (air and rain, e.g. Dris et al., 2016; Allen et al., 2019; Brahney et al., 2020; Frank et al., 2021), by flowing water through rivers (e.g. Lechner et al., 2014) or let in directly from shore e.g. via wastewater (e.g. Browne et al., 2011). Microfibres are also formed at the coast or at sea by fragmentation of fibrous materials in use. Fibres have been reported from marine samples since the middle of the last century and characterized as of natural origin (manila, coir, jute) by Atkins (1954) or described as strongly coloured (red, blue, orange) by Buchanan (1971). In environmental studies (e.g. Browne et al., 2011, review by Hidalgo-Ruz et al. and refs. therein), fibres from natural materials, especially cellulose and its derivatives, received little attention (cf. Stanton et al., 2019) or were explicitly excluded from the analysis of environmental samples (e.g. Cózar et al., 2014; Kanhai et al., 2020) and the focus was on synthetic fibres, seen as micro-*plastics*. Only recently, the high abundance of coloured fibres which have been identified (e.g. by FTIR and Raman spectroscopy) as cellulosic or cellulose-like have been taken into account (Sanchez-Vidal, 2018; Stanton et al., 2019; Suaria et al., 2020) and led to the question of how their obvious environmental persistence could be explained. Although not plastic, the natural polymer cellulose and its man-made derivatives (as a base material for many applications) are included in this chapter in the considerations of degradation in the marine environment for their abundance amongst microfibres and their obvious persistence in some cases. We generally use the term polymer to refer to macro- and microplastic and cellulosic (micro-)fibres.

DOI: 10.4324/9781003165385-10

2 Sources and materials of microfibres

2.1 Applications of fibres at sea as a source

In addition to the widely discussed use in apparel (Henry et al., 2019) fibrous technical materials are also applied at the shore, on and in the water. Monofilaments, twine, fibre loft, non-woven (felt-like) or woven fabrics such as sails, flags, tarpaulins, awnings, shades, covers, as well as rope, knotted and knitted protection, bonded and knotted nets are used in various applications for leisure and commercial applications. Banks of waterways and coasts are being stabilized by fibrous construction materials, so-called geotextiles (Wiewel and Lamoree, 2016), sand bags and barrier tubes. Fisheries and aquaculture widely rely on the use of fibres (GLAUKOS report, Lusher et al./FAO, 2017), many of which are abandoned, lost at sea (Gilman et al./FAO, 2016, Viool et al./EU, 2018) or, in the case of so-called dolly ropes, sacrificially abraded to protect the actual net.

2.2 Litter as a source

Further contributions come from the fragmentation of litter items of fibrous nature: of the over 5,200 billion cigarettes consumed annually (British American Tobacco), it is estimated that 4.5 trillion cigarette butts per year are being littered (e.g. Slaughter et al., 2010), rendering cigarette butts one of the most abundant item found in beach litter (Addamo et al./EU, 2017). In a bottom trawl at 60 m depth off Barcelona, Spain a large part of the litter catch consisted of cleansing wipes and sanitary towels followed by plastics and textiles (Canals et al., 2021). Menstruation products (pads and tampons) are flushed to waterways and the sea, e.g. diapers made up for 21% on average (max. 31%) of waste found on river banks in Indonesia (World Bank, 2018). Face masks were boosted to global distribution by the Covid-19 pandemic and find their way to the ocean in masses, estimated from 0.15 to 0.39 Mt/year (Chowdhury et al., 2021). All these items are made of or contain fibres that may eventually be released and distributed in the marine environment. Fibres were found to be the most prevalent microplastic particles in global river waters and sediments, and a large share originates from the degradation of non-woven synthetic textiles (Martinez Silva and Nanny, 2020). Over 86% of all anthropogenic particles in Northern American lakes and Arctic marine sediments were found to be microfibres (Athey et al., 2020). Packaging items made from fibres, such as rice bags and vegetable nets, packing straps and binders also end up in the sea through littering, loss during operation and lack of proper waste management. Whereas many fibrous items are made from one single base polymer with small amounts of additives (e.g. polyester rope), other items of daily (single) use, such as diapers, are highly engineered objects containing several different materials of synthetic and non-synthetic origin, some of which are fibrous.

2.3 Polymers used

The material composition of marine plastic debris follows the share of polymers produced. The global plastic demand was 368 Mt in 2019 (Plastics Europe, 2020), and is dominated by seven families of synthetic polymers considered non-biodegradable and often referred to as conventional polymers: polyethylene (PE), polypropylene (PP), polyvinylchloride (PVC), polyethylene terephthalate (PET), polyurethane (PUR), polyamide (PA) and polystyrene (PS), all of which except PS are also used for outdoor and marine fibre applications in fisheries, aquaculture, shipping and sailing, but expanded (foamed) PS being of large abundance in floating debris. In 2020, 111 Mt fibres were produced, of which 52% were PE, 5.6% were PA, 23% were cotton and 6.4% were MCF (man-made cellulosic fibres: 79% Viscose, 4.3% Lyocell, 2.8% Modal, >1% Cupro), and 13% cellulose acetates, 1% wool, <1% down and 11.4% others (Textile Exchange, 2021). With a global market of 1.227 Mt (2020) and a share of only 0.3% of all plastic produced, synthetic *biodegradable* polymers are still rare and only a few dedicated applications in or at sea exist so far. Assuming the same material flow as for conventional plastics, the percentage of biodegradable plastic items littered or lost to the open environment is expected to be (still) limited. However, the market of biodegradable plastic is expected to grow by 50% from 2019 to 2025 (European Bioplastics, 2020). The most important classes of biodegradable polymers and their market share in detail are thermoplastic starch (TPS, 32.2%), polylactic acid (PLA, 32.2%), polybutylene-co-adipate-co-terephthalate (PBAT, 23.2%), polybutylene succinate (PBS, 7.1%), polyhydroxyalkanoates (PHA, 2.9%) and others: 2.4%, (European Bioplastics, 2020), from which starch is not used for fibres as such.

3 Abiotic mechanisms of (micro-)plastic/fibre degradation

Once an item is introduced to the marine environment it is subjected to potentially intense physical, chemical and biological agents (e.g. Albertsson et al., 2020; Meereboer et al., 2020; Wang et al., 2021; Chamas et al., 2020). All these contribute to the degradation with time, depending on the conditions in the receiving environment, during transport or at the final sink. Therefore, (bio-)degradation of a solid polymer or plastic object in the open environment is a process that has to be seen in the context of material properties *and* the prevailing environmental conditions. In the following paragraphs we consider the fate of a polymer exposed to natural physical, chemical and biological conditions, and the processes leading to the degradation of a virgin item to its degradation products.

3.1 Mechanical impact

Any movement caused by wind or waves results in strong mechanical impact on the object that may cause smashing and shattering into smaller pieces. Abrasion of plastics in contact with mineral grains and rocks in the shoreline further disintegrate the object. Mechanical action by animals also contributes to the physical disintegration: grazing from snails, crabs and fish, picking by birds, biting and chewing by fish, turtles and mammals can be regularly observed on marine debris and items intentionally used in the sea such as rope, nets, buoys, floats, etc. Mechanical degradation results in deformation, disintegration and fragmentation.

3.1   Solar radiation

Plastic items exposed to atmospheric conditions either at the sea surface or on a beach experience solar irradiation, which may cause degradation of the polymeric structure. Dark-coloured plastic materials heat up substantially in the sun, reaching temperatures of 60°C and above, leading to a weakening of intermolecular forces between the polymer strands. As heat conductivity of plastics is rather low, this effect is most intense at the material surface. Volatile compounds such as plasticizers may evaporate, and the remaining plastic gradually changes composition over time. Volume loss can lead to tensions within the material and, eventually, micro-fissures at the surface. Cracks can progress and eventually lead to plastic fragmentation and disintegration of the item.

Photodegradation, i.e. the alteration of the chemical structure of the material especially by ultraviolet (UV) light, is caused by the absorption of photons in the polymer by the transfer of their energy to electrons in the target molecule, leading to the promotion of the electrons to an excited state. Excited-state molecules are chemically more reactive, and in the presence of oxygen (or water) can be oxidized (or hydrolyzed) more readily, which leads to the cleavage of chemical bonds and the scission of the polymer chain, and thus the production of shorter chain-length molecules and a decrease of bulk molecular weight. This process is called photochemical degradation.

3.2   Oxygen

In air and with strong light, reactive oxygen species, so-called 'photochemically produced reactive intermediates' can be formed, which include $OH°$, superoxide and singlet O_2. These oxidants may introduce carbonyl groups into the polymers which themselves may act as photosensitizers, thereby triggering additional reactions that lead to bond cleavage. These may occur, for instance, in polyolefins such as PE, PP, as well as PVC and polystyrene, which have a pure carbon-carbon backbone. The oxidation eventually results in chain scission and a shift in the molecular weight distribution of the polymer strands to smaller average molecular weights.

3.3   Water and ions

In the presence of water, soluble compounds such as additives and molecular degradation products (oligomers, monomers) can leach out of the plastic item. Polyesters, polyamides and polyurethanes are slightly hygroscopic and under certain environmental conditions take up water. Water sorption causes swelling of the amorphous regions of PET and internal stress between amorphous and crystalline regions, leading to the formation of microcavities (Bastioli et al., 1990). At lower temperatures saturation was observed, but above the glass transition temperature (T_g(PET) = 67°C), water sorption increased and was attributed to hydrolysis. Nylon 6 (PA 6) immersed at 25°C to equilibrium showed 8% water uptake after two weeks. PA 6.6 absorbed less water and took much longer to equilibrate (Monson et al., 2007). In a natural scenario with changing humidity, e.g. at a beach, swollen materials subsequently drying will shrink and internal material stress will lead to weakening and eventual cracking. Besides the physical effect of water on the polymer, hydrolysis, i.e. the addition of a water molecule to break down chemical bonds, can occur. Plastic samples aged under water showed the smallest degradation effects for vinyl polymers (PE, PP, PS), whereas polyesters, such as PET and PLA, showed higher sensitivity to the weathering due to hydrolysis (Fambri et al., 2020). If the diffusion of water into the polymer is faster than the degradation of polymer bonds, the polymer will undergo bulk degradation, because degradation is not confined to the polymer surface. If, however, the reaction of water molecules with hydrolysable bonds is faster than the diffusion of water, the water will be consumed by the hydrolysis of bonds on the polymer surface and will thus be prevented from diffusion into the bulk. Degradation processes are then strictly confined to the material surface and, in an ideal case, i.e. when the degradation products are reasonably water soluble, represent a surface-eroding polymer (Burkersroda et al., 2002). In natural scenarios, a transition between bulk and surface degradation is likely. The non-hydrolysable polyolefins PE and PP, and also PVC and PS, are apolar, thus 'hydrophobic' and practically impermeable for water. Here, degradation is rather driven by oxidation and progressing from the surface of the material.

3.4   Surface to volume ratio

Besides surface erosion from the outside to the interior or increased fragmentation by bulk degradation, items can be mechanically stressed (see earlier in this chapter) which is further promoting deterioration. The smaller the particles of the original bulk material become, the higher the reactive surface and the higher also the potential gross degradation rate (Chinaglia et al., 2018).

Summarized, the combination of these physical and chemical factors alone can lead to substantial degradation of a polymeric item: on a macroscopic level, discoloration, surface roughening, embrittlement, cracking and measurable loss of tensile properties, strength and elongation occur. At molecular level, chain scission, decrease in average molecular weight, change in crystallinity and 'carbonyl index', oxidized and/or hydrolyzed chain ends and the appearance of first lower-molecular weight intermediates result. In sum, this eventually leads to the fragmentation of the materials, the formation of (micro-)particles and an increase in surface-to-volume ratio of the plastic item. Shedding of particles, plastic dust, flakes and microfibres occur. This concert of mainly physical and chemical, i.e. *abiotic*, processes is also called ageing or weathering.

4 Biotic processes

4.1 Plastic as microhabitat

Any solid surface exposed to the marine environment will immediately be colonized by bacteria, archaea and fungi, which adhere to the substrate (Harrison et al., 2014) and excrete extracellular polymeric substances (EPS), consisting of mostly polysaccharides and proteins that eventually embed the microbial community in a mucous layer, the so-called biofilm (Zobell, 1943; Dexter, 1979; Lobelle and Cunliffe, 2011; Eich et al., 2015, see also Ye and Andrady, 1991 and references therein). Although also conventional plastics have been shown to be heavily colonized the presence of microbes does not necessarily mean that they are effectively able to bio-degrade the plastic and to use the polymeric carbon for their metabolism (Jacquin et al., 2021). After the formation of a microbial film, higher organisms, such as protists and microalgae, algal spores and animal larvae arrive and, in a battle for space and nutrition but also in a cooperative manner, overgrow each other, creating a microhabitat, dynamic over time, a process called 'fouling' (Pauli et al., 2017). The material properties themselves affect the biofilm formation and fouling processes (Patil and Anil, 2005; Jones et al., 2007; Eich et al., 2015; Pauli et al., 2017; Jacquin et al., 2021; Vaksmaa et al., 2021). Due to fouling, an originally floating item might increase in bulk density, causing it to eventually sink (Ye & Andrady, 1991). This process is influenced by a complex and changing interaction between material composition and environmental conditions (Barrows et al., 2018; Barnes et al., 2009; Cole et al., 2011; Kooi et al., 2017; Thompson et al., 2004). For small particles such as microfibres, the material density is less important to keep them afloat or make them sink as viscous forces within the water dominate (Kukulka et al., 2012). Field experiments have shown that biofouled plastic debris undergoes defouling when submerged, causing the plastic to return to the surface (Ye and Andrady, 1991; Kooi et al., 2017). Changes of the external environmental factors such as temperature or light when a particle is sinking to greater depth also lead to changes of the chemical conditions in the microhabitat (Karthäuser et al., 2021), or even to a change in community composition from phototrophs to heterotrophs. The biofilm forms a selective barrier between outer environment and the polymer. The metabolic processes within this microhabitat of the 'plastisphere' (Zettler et al., 2013; Amaral-Zettler et al., 2020) eventually determine the physical and chemical conditions at the polymer surface and may differ greatly from the environmental conditions in the surrounding water or sediment. Oxygen can be consumed but also produced within the fouling community when the polymer is exposed to light. In very clear (sea)water, UV light can penetrate several tens of meters (Fleischmann, 1989), but is quickly attenuated by scattering and absorption in turbid water, depending on particles and coloured compounds (Markager and

Vincent, 2000) such as chlorophyll or other dissolved organic matter. A matured biofilm in the light will contain photosynthetic organisms such as cyanobacteria and microalgae, which will use the light themselves and, thanks to their pigments, (partially) shield the polymer surface below from (harsh) irradiation (Nelson et al., 2021). Under high light exposure, natural biofilms may become over-saturated with oxygen (Polerecky et al., 2008) and reactive oxygen species may form, largely enhancing the degradation process chemically. The biofilm and fouling community at the plastic surface may accelerate (Andrady, 1990; Flemming, 1998) or delay its (bio-)degradation in the sea (Nelson et al., 2021). These studies indicate that both effects are likely to occur, and it depends on the dominating organisms which effect prevails. At night or in low light conditions, i.e. once a plastic piece or microfibre is covered by biofilm or with sediment, or ends up otherwise out of reach of UV light, all the abiotic processes directly linked to photochemical reactions will cease. Now, the aerobic respiration of the organisms, i.e. the consumption of oxygen, can result in hypoxic or anoxic conditions within the microhabitat and microbial metabolism shifts from aerobic to anaerobic. Typical anaerobic metabolic processes such as fermentation, sulphate reduction and nitrate reduction are likely to occur and may impact the degradation processes of the polymer.

4.2 Uptake

Bacteria, archaea and fungi cannot take up solid particles, and thus also very large molecules such as plastic polymers through their cell membranes to be metabolized internally. To make organic particles accessible and usable as carbon and an energy source, microbes have evolved means to chemically attack (natural) polymers by excreting enzymes onto the target, subsequently taking up the usable lower molecular weight degradation products (Riedel and Grunau, 2011). As a rule of thumb, a molecular weight of about several hundred Dalton (g mol^{-1}) (e.g. Nikaido and Vaara, 1985 and refs. therein) is seen as the maximum size to be taken up by the microorganism. Once taken up, the intermediates are further degraded and eventually channelled into the cell's metabolic pathways, either to produce ATP (i.e. the energy-rich 'fuel' of a living cell) or used as building blocks for cell growth and reproduction (biomass).

4.3 Biomass formation and mineralization

If the carbon originating from the polymer is used for energy metabolism, it results in the final products of biodegradation carbon dioxide (in the presence of oxygen), or carbon dioxide, and/or methane (if there is no oxygen available), and water. If the original polymer also contained other elements besides C, H, and O, mineral salts are formed such as nitrate, nitrite and ammonium in case of nitrogen compounds or phosphates in the case of phosphorous compounds present in the original polymer. Mineralization is a very slow process under natural conditions because a part of the polymer undergoing biodegradation will initially be turned into biomass (Andrady,

1994). Typically the carbon use efficiency for microbes is 50% at most, meaning 50% of the polymer carbon is converted to CO_2 and 50% into biomass (cf. Manzoni et al., 2018), but for polymers with no N and P it is expected to be lower. Therefore, complete biodegradation and not mineralization is the measurable goal when assessing removal from the environment (Van der Zee, 2020).

To follow this cascade of biodegradation, the budget can be made:

$$C_{POLYMER} = C_{BIOMASS} + C_{CO2} + C_{CH4} + C_{INTERMEDIATES}$$

In case of a complete mineralization, no residuals are left over.

4.4 Degradation rate

The extent to which a polymer is degraded and at which rate is strongly dependent on the ensemble of the environmental conditions it is facing, thus the habitat it becomes part of or is transiting. If a plastic item or microfibre is not *biodegrad*-able, degradation will remain incomplete and stop at the level of fragmentation, i.e. solid particles of the original polymer or of intermediates with higher molecular weight are left behind, e.g. in the form of micro- and nanoplastics (cf. Arp et al., 2021). The deeper in the sea a microfibre is exposed, the less prominent are physical factors such as UV light and heat, and also mechanical forces acting on the material. In the deep, chemical and biological factors dominate. Again, if the material is not prone to chemical or biological attack, no further degradation is to be expected in a reasonable (human) time scale. Plastic fragments, thus also microfibres, eventually will arrive at the seafloor (Van Cauwenberghe et al., 2013), of which 80% is covered with sediment, forming the biggest sink for (micro-)plastic (Woodall et al., 2014). The most abundant marine sediments are mud and sand. Apart from the seafloor surface of coastal areas, marine sediments are dark zones, by the majority low in organics and low in microbial activity, under high pressure and with cold temperatures. However, the microbial communities living in marine sediments can degrade a series of complex polymeric compounds, such as cellulose, lignin and chitin (Wu et al., 2008). The abundance of microbes is very different between different marine compartments. In the open water (pelagic), there are about 10^5 to 10^6 cells per ml. At the seafloor (benthic), for sediments 10^9 cells per ml were reported (e.g. Schmidt et al., 1998). Experiments on several biodegradable polymers show much faster biodegradation in the benthic than in the pelagic coastal habitat at the same location (Lott et al., 2021). Microbial abundance may be one factor, but given the dominance of the biofilm over the surrounding environment, also the usually much higher availability of nutrients such as N-containing compounds (nitrate, nitrite, ammonium), P-containing compounds (phosphates), silica and essential metals at the seafloor sediments might play an important role (Ratto et al., 2001; Wu et al., 2008). The physiological background of this consideration is that even easily biodegradable polymers such as cellulose consist of C, H and O only. For microbes to grow and to build up biomass (e.g. proteins and DNA), N and P are crucial and often the limiting factors for growth in natural microbial communities (Sala et al., 2001). Depending on the sediment grain size, the hydrodynamic conditions and the natural organic carbon input, usually only the upper few millimetres to centimetres of the sediment are oxygenated, compared to the deeper sediment (Weber et al., 2007; Köster et al., 2008). For microbial activity, two contrasting scenarios can be distinguished. Oxic and anoxic 'worlds' are divided by the thermodynamic limitations in the absence or presence of oxygen as the terminal electron acceptor for metabolic reactions. This is also represented by the activity of enzymes that do function only in one of the two situations and are inhibited in the other. Whether a biodegradable polymer might be biodegraded faster in the presence or absence of oxygen cannot generally be answered (Lott et al., 2020). Furthermore, the (bio-)degradation rate of polymers does not only differ by material, but also depends on the habitat and climate zone (Lott et al., 2021).

4.5 Biodegradation of synthetic conventional polymers

Biodegradation studies of conventional plastic polymers PE, PP, PS, PET, PVC and PUR have been published for many decades (e.g. Albertsson et al., 1978). Most of these studies subjected the polymers to artificial weathering, thus *abiotic* degradation before testing *bio*degradation. Substantial biodegradation of conventional plastic was measured only in artificially pre-treated materials (see e.g. reviews by Eubeler et al., 2009 and 2010; Krueger et al., 2015; Danso et al., 2018) or on unusually low-crystalline grades (e.g. Yoshida et al., 2016). Laboratory studies reported degradation effects of microorganisms on many types of polymers, usually by enzymatic hydrolysis or oxidation, and produced a wealth of data with highly heterogeneous experimental and analytical approaches which make it difficult to verify and compare the results. Several studies claim to have observed or measured substantial biodegradation of un-weathered or otherwise pre-treated plastics based only on indirect measures such as material loss, changes in material properties on the macro (e.g. tensile properties) or micro (e.g. molecular chain length distribution) level. Only a few studies followed the carbon from the original polymer to the metabolic end products CO_2, CH_4 and microbial biomass (e.g. Albertsson, 1978; Albertsson and Ljungqvist, 1986). The enzymes involved and mechanisms associated with these observed phenomena are still unclear (Restrepo-Flórez et al., 2014). Degradation of *weathered* PE increased with UV irradiation time and extracellular enzymes of microbes seem able to attack weathered PE slowly and partly (see review by Eubeler et al., 2010). If *abiotic* degradation to molecular weights below 5000 Da occurs, *bio*degradation seems to be happening relatively fast; however, the production of wax-like plastic-derived substances by artificial weathering does not reflect scenarios likely in nature. None of the studies reviewed by Danso et al. (2019) revealed biochemical mechanisms and enzymes involved in PE and PP breakdown, no detailed biochemical characterization was performed, and no amino acid sequence of the enzyme or the corresponding gene was deposited. Insight into the possible biological mechanisms underlying PE bio-degradation is extremely limited, since most studies published so far remained on the observational level (Krueger et al., 2015). Enzymes reported to be involved in the biodegradation of (pre-treated) PE and PP include lignin-degrading enzymes such as fungal laccases, manganese peroxidases and lignin peroxidases (Wei and Zimmermann, 2017). However, no defined enzymes that act on the polymer have been identified at the level of amino acid or DNA sequences (Danso et al., 2019), and an efficient biodegradation of unweathered PE cannot be expected (Krueger et al., 2015), especially not in an open environment scenario. Research into the biodegradation of PP is rather scarce and only low rates of weight loss of the pre-treated polymer *in vitro* and *in situ* are reported (Krueger et al., 2015). Otake et al. (1995) examined PVC and PS buried for 32 years in soil and found no apparent biodegradation. Danso et al. (2019) state that although several studies claim the observation of biodegradation of PVC and PP, it is likely that these reports were in part misled by the degradation of the chemical additives or lower molecular weight of PVC oligomers rather than the polymer. Consequently, no defined enzymes or pathways that are responsible for the degradation of either of these two high-molecular weight polymers are known. In a preliminary study (Krueger et al., 2015), a terrestrial brown-rot fungus was found to degrade PS in a hydrochinone-driven Fenton reaction.

Acrylics or PAN (Poly Acryl Nitrile), also marketed as Dralon®, Orlon® and Dolan®, are a diverse family of polymers with a C-C backbone, some of which are used as (non-fibrous) super absorbent polymers in hygiene products. Others are used also in textiles and regularly found in environmental microfibre studies. Marketed as ideally suited for use in boat covers, sunshades, biminis, upholstery and cushion fabrics for the marine sector, in addition to high weathering resistance, PANs are promoted also as resistant to rotting by moulds and fungi and as having high strength and abrasion resistance (DOLAN GmbH), with a higher light stability, acid and alkaline resistance than other common fibre materials (DRALON GmbH). Enzymatic reactions on the nitrile group have been described from fungi and bacterial isolates (Fischer-Colbrie et al., 2006 and references therein), but the further biodegradation of the C-C backbone has not been shown so far. Given the desired and marketed properties, these materials are likely to be highly recalcitrant.

PET as a polyester is generally hydrolysable. Bacteria, archaea and fungi possess a wide range of hydrolases such as cutinases, lipases, carboxylesterases and tannases, targeting natural polyester biopolymers. PETases are the best-studied, plastic-degrading enzymes, and more than 800 potential PET hydrolases in bacteria and archaea are known (Danso et al., 2018). PETase-like enzymes were found to be active also on PBAT, a biodegradable aliphatic-aromatic co-polymer (Meyer-Cifuentes et al., 2020) (see further in this chapter). Only experiments with low–crystallinity PET or at elevated temperature showed substantial biodegradation (Müller et al., 2005; Ronkvist et al., 2009; Wei and Zimmermann, 2017; Yoshida et al., 2016). PET of a low crystallinity of 1.9% was used as major energy and carbon source by some bacteria (Yoshida et al., 2016 with response from Yang et al.,

2016). Ioakeimidis et al. (2016) studied the degradation potential of PET bottles exposed for more than 15 years in the marine environment with an ATR-FTIR-based approach and found the surface of the older PETs was altered. Cutinases from terrestrial fungi were also found to degrade PET of low crystallinity (Krueger et al., 2015). However, PET grades used for beverage bottles and polyester fibres usually have a crystallinity of 30 to over 60% and are highly recalcitrant to enzymatic degradation (Krueger et al., 2015).

Polyurethanes (PUR) can be divided in two principal sub-groups: polyester and polyether polyurethanes. Bacteria and fungi, mainly from soil environments, were found to use lipases, hydrolases from the cutinase family, metallo-hydrolases, esterases and proteases to cleave ester and urethane bonds of ester-linked PUR (e.g. Eubeler et al., 2010). Despite polyether PURs being regarded as more recalcitrant than polyester PURs, Álvarez-Barragán et al. (2016) found high weight loss of polyether PUR when incubated with fungal isolates. Rutkowska et al. (2002) found substantial degradation for polyester PUR and no degradation for polyether PUR in Baltic Sea water after 12 months. PUR fibres are marketed as, for example, Elastane, Lycra or Spandex.

Technical polyamides (PA) are the synthetic analogues to proteins such as collagen, wool or silk. Biodegradation of a polyamide is strongly dependent on its exact composition and resulting physical-chemical properties. Nylons are composed of aliphatic constituents and nylon-6,6 (or PA 6.6) is the most common synthetic polyamide used in plastic production.

So far, there are some indications, but no direct evidence, for PA biodegradation, and no enzymes able to degrade the intact high-molecular-weight polymer were identified. Hydrolases and aminotransferases are involved in the degradation of oligomers (see reviews by Krueger et al., 2015; Danso et al., 2019). Terrestrial fungi were found to generate oxidative degradation products (e.g. Deguchi et al., 1997, 1998), and a lignin-modifying enzymatic system of the fungi, with a manganese-containing enzyme was found to be involved in nylon biodegradation. Nylon 6 as sole source of nitrogen for mycelial growth was reported (Friedrich et al., 2007; Klun et al., 2003). Nylon 4 has been found to biodegrade rather fast in soil (Hashimoto et al., 1994) and activated sludge from wastewater treatment (Tokiwa et al., 2009).

To summarize the knowledge on biodegradation of conventional plastic polymers, there is a wealth of claims based on observations and indirect measurements, but the direct proof for the biodegradation of conventional synthetic plastic polymers is still missing. No specific enzymes with a hydrolytic or oxidative activity towards PE, PS, PP or PVC have been characterized, and the mechanisms of cleavage of the covalent bonds in carbon-carbon backbone petro-polymers are unknown. Thus, there is no evidence for biodegradation of unweathered conventional plastic polymers in the open environment at a substantial rate compared to human timescale. In their review, Krueger et al. (2015) state that published research is strongly biased to successes obtained under optimized conditions, thus painting an overly optimistic picture with limited transferability to real environments.

Despite these obvious incongruencies, data from such studies are taken without further validation to calculate degradation rates and half-lives of conventional plastics in the environment (e.g. Chamas et al., 2020). Such scientific practice is raising great concern about wrong conclusions that might be drawn based on doubtful results and emphasizes the need for the development and implementation of multiple well-defined standard metrics to quantify the rates of polymer degradation in the environment (SAPEA Report, Albertsson et al., 2020; Albright and Chai, 2021).

4.6 Synthetic and natural biodegradable polymers

In addition to traditional natural polymer fibres such as cellulose (jute, hemp, cotton) and wool, several biodegradable plastic materials have been introduced to the market since the 1970s, mainly recruiting base materials from a small group of polymer classes: starch (mainly as thermoplastic starch TPS) of plant origin, polyhydroxyalkanoates (PHAs) produced by bacteria as an internal storage and several synthetic polyesters such as polylactic acid (PLA) engineered from sugars, poly-ε-caprolactone (PCL) from fossil oil and various polymeric combinations of 1,4-butanediol or 1,2-ethylene glycol with dicarboxylic acids (see further in this chapter). Most of these materials are used already for fibre applications and development is ongoing.

In PLA, chemical hydrolysis takes place already at high humidity at elevated temperatures such as in industrial composting plants with an observed differentiation between amorphous and crystalline regions. In distilled water, substantial degradation due to hydrolysis occurred only at higher temperatures of 40 and 50°C (Deroiné et al., 2014a). Under environmental temperatures, PLA is considered as slowly (bio-)degradable. No substantial degradation was observed in seawater field tests (Lott et al., 2018), in marine and freshwater lab tests (Narancic et al., 2018; Greene et al., 2012), and lab tests with marine sand (De Falco et al., 2021). Mid- (e.g. five years) to long-term (e.g. few decades) experiments under marine conditions are still to be conducted. Efforts are being made to use the assumed co-metabolization of PLA blended with an easier biodegradable compound to tune the overall biodegradability of a PLA-based plastic item in the open environment (Pelegrini et al., 2016). Also, co-polymerization is used to slightly alter the properties of PLA and achieve substantial biodegradation rates under, for example, marine conditions (Martin et al., 2014).

Copolymers of 1,4-**b**utanediol or 1,2-**e**thylene glycol with **s**uccinic acid, **se**bacic acid, **a**dipic acid and **t**erephthalic acid to PBS, PES, PBSe, PBSeT, PBAT and PBSAT comprise a group of base materials used for biodegradable plastic manufacturing (Künkel et al., 2016). Various possible combinations allow the tailoring of functionalities in a wide range from packaging and agricultural film to fibre applications. The biodegradation rates of each combination are expected to be different, which allows to meet requirements on function during the use phase and biodegradation performance in the open environment. However, extrapolations from one material to another should be avoided and biodegradation rates rather assessed for the specific case. Several fungi and bacteria from pure cultures and soil isolates were found to degrade PBS (Tokiwa et al., 2009), and exposure to marine matrices resulted in the biodegradation of PBS (Sekiguchi et al., 2011; Kim et al., 2016), PBSA (Cocca et al., 2017; De Falco et al., 2021), PBSe (Briassoulis et al., 2019; Lott et al., 2021), PBSeT (Briassoulis et al., 2019; Lott et al., 2021), PBAT (Wang et al., 2018; Meyer-Cifuentes et al., 2020) and PBSAT (Grimaldo et al., 2020; Su et al., 2019; Kim et al., 2020). Zumstein et al. (2018) showed mineralization and incorporation of PBAT carbon into the biomass of bacteria and fungi in experiments with agricultural soil at 25°C via stable isotope labelling.

Polyhydroxyalkanoates (PHAs) are known with about 90 different combinations of hydroxyalkanoic acids with different chain lengths and positions of their hydroxyl groups forming this class of polyesters. The most common representatives are poly(3-hydroxybutyrate) (PHB), poly(4-hydroxybutyrate) (P(4-HB)), poly(3-hydroxybutyrate-co-valerate) (PHBV), poly(3-hydroxybutyrate-co-hexanoate) (PHBH) and poly(3-hydroxybutyrate-co-4-hydroxybutyrate) (P(3-HB-co-4HB) (Künkel et al., 2016). PHAs are also generally considered biodegradable under marine conditions (for an overview see Dilkes-Hoffman et al., 2019; Sekiguchi et al., 2011; Tosin et al., 2012; Deroiné et al., 2014b; Cocca et al., 2017; Narancic et al., 2018; Lott et al., 2020 and 2021; De Falco et al., 2021; Eich et al., 2021).

Poly-ε-caprolactone (PCL) is a fossil-based polymer with good biodegradability in lab tests with freshwater and marine matrices (e.g. Tsuji and Suzuyoshi, 2002; Narancic et al., 2018), in tanks with deep-sea marine water (Ebisui et al., 2006; Sekiguchi et al., 2011) and marine sand (Cocca et al., 2017; De Falco et al., 2021). PCL-degrading bacteria were isolated from deep-sea sediments (Sekiguchi et al., 2010).

Starch is a polysaccharide and, as the natural storage compound of many plants, it is well biodegradable (Narancic et al., 2018). TPS is not used as fibre material *per se* but in composites with other polymers.

Cellulose is a polysaccharide and as the key structural element of plants, cellulose is the most abundant biopolymer in the open environment. Technically, cellulose is used for many applications in its pure form (e.g. as cotton, hemp or jute fibre) or as regenerated material. Cellulose can be dissolved in strong bases or organic solvents and then extruded to fibres or film. Rayon, or also synonymous viscose, usually refers to regenerated cellulose fibres where different names such as Modal, Lyocell, Cupro refer to different processing methods. Chemically, regenerated cellulose is identical to its natural base material, but the regenerated polymer has lower molecular weight and crystallinity. In nature, all organisms that produce cellulose (plants, algae, but also some bacteria, fungi, protists and a group of animals called tunicates) also must be capable of cellulolysis via cellulases. Many microbes use cellulose as nutrition and thus also possess these enzymes (for details see e.g. Thapa et al., 2020). Different grades of cellulose raw materials, e.g. for paper manufacturing, are biodegraded at different rates in aquatic environments (Hofsten and Edberg, 1972). In standard biodegradation tests, cellulose in the form of pure filter paper or as microcrystalline powder is often used as a biodegradable reference material, i.e. as positive biodegradation control (e.g. ASTM 6691, ISO 22404).

Chemical derivatives of cellulose include nitrocellulose (which was the first man-made plastic in 1855), also known from early photographic film celluloid, and cellulose acetate (CA) which replaced celluloid and is used, among other applications, for cigarette filters.

Different grades of CA are described by the degree of polymerization (number of acetylated glucose subunits in a chain) and the number of acetyl groups per monomer, which is given as degree of substitution (DS) (Haske-Cornelius et al., 2017). Cellulose acetates with DS ≤ 2.5 were readily mineralized in a controlled composting test and the biodegradation rate was lower the higher the degree of substitution (Van der Zee et al., 1998, review by Puls et al., 2010). No biodegradation was measured in tests in water with an inoculum from activated sludge. The biodegradation of CA 2.5 from cigarette filters was measured in anaerobic mesophilic digestion conditions (37°C; ISO 15985, ASTM D5511), freshwater inoculated with activated sludge (ISO 14851), seawater (ASTM D6691) and soil (ISO 17556) (Hölter and La Personne, 2017). Yadav and Hakkarainen (2021) summarize current knowledge and point out the challenge of finding a balance between the high degree of acetylation being crucial for good thermoplastic properties, which at the same time lowers the biodegradation rate.

4.7   Cellulosic fibres and the cellulose enigma

Given the good biodegradability of cellulose and its chemically identical regenerates on the one hand and the high abundance of (micro-)fibres characterized as cellulose-like or cellulosic found in the environment on the other hand, there is a possible explanation for this 'cellulose enigma'. Fibres used for textile applications can undergo dozens of treatments from the base polymer until the final product arrives at the customer (Hauser, 2015; Richards, 2015). Bleaching, strong acids and bases are applied, often at high temperatures. Fixation occurs, e.g. with formaldehyde. Dyeing with different dyestuffs, some of which enter the fibre, others form an external layer, and coatings e.g. with silicones, polyurethanes, PVC and PTFE are common. Treatments with chrome dyes, zinc mordants and organo-tin compounds are, or at least historically were, applied adding heavy metals to the fibre. Biocides, e.g. nano-silver or organic chemicals, are used as anti-microbial treatment of fibres and textiles.

A strong indication for a good preservation by the various treatments during the finishing process is the high abundance of coloured fibres with a cellulosic FTIR signature (e.g. Suaria et al., 2020; Sanchez-Vidal et al., 2018; Athey et al., 2020). In forensics, the identification of dyestuffs in fibres on top of the FTIR spectrum with Raman spectroscopy is a valuable tool (Lepot et al., 2008; Groves et al., 2018). However, in published environmental research, information beyond the generic base material fingerprint is rare (e.g. Remy et al., 2015; Athey et al., 2020; Comnea-Stancu et al., 2017). Although a delayed or strongly inhibited biodegradation of finished cellulosic textile fibres can be assumed, from the textile engineering perspective the underlaying mechanisms are largely unexplored and the lifetime of such treated natural fibres in the environment is unknown. This demonstrates not only a gap in knowledge, but also a lack of communication between disciplines. Lykaki et al. (2021) found only a slight negative effect on the biodegradability of cotton and viscose fibres treated with two different types of reactive dyes and a softener, but a much slower biodegradation rate when the fibres were treated with an antimicrobial agent. The crucial treatment steps that render cellulosic fibres to persist for a longer time period in the open (marine) environment have yet to be identified.

5 Biodegradability as a desired/engineered property

Given its ubiquity in the open environment, plastic is predicted to become a stratigraphic marker of the Anthropocene (Zalasiewicz et al., 2016; Waters et al., 2016, cf. Krause et al., 2020). Biodegradation is discussed as a possible solution for the global plastic pollution and often the desired time frame mentioned is unrealistically short. Especially for littered plastic, the wish that as soon as a plastic item has terminated its use phase it might miraculously disappear seems not to consider the properties of the material it was designed for to fulfil its function. Polymers need to meet the functionality during use.

Additionally, there are many applications where biodegradability in a certain environment is a desired key function (e.g. biodegradable mulch films, slow-release fertilizer capsules and seed coating in agriculture, knitted and non-woven fibres for geotextiles in landscaping, feeding pipes and mussel nets in aquaculture). Plastics are also made to be used in marine applications (fisheries, boating, aquaculture, shore protection, etc.) where the stability during the use phase has to be put in balance with an eventual biodegradation of lost parts or particles e.g. as fibre loss from rope.

As biodegradability in the environment does not only depend on the material properties, a prediction of the biodegradation rate or lifetime in the open environment is difficult. Therefore the urgent and timely question is about rates and extents of biodegradation in different environments. Unless one knows the exact pathways with transition times and sinks, one cannot predict the corresponding environmental conditions an item is facing during its journey through the environment from source to sink. This demonstrates that claims about a material to be 'biodegradable in the open environment' are too generic and that there is the requirement to describe the specific environmental conditions for which a claim is valid.

Polymer degradation processes can also be mediated by catalysts, substances that lower the activation energy of a chemical reaction (McKeown et al., 2020). Various technologies emerged to enhance the molecular degradation of conventional plastic (Vazquez et al., 2019) by the addition of metal salts to render polymers such as PE, PP and PET more susceptible to photo and thermal activation once these materials are exposed to UV light and oxygen at the end of their use phase, e.g. if littered. These technologies are commercially advertised as a solution to mitigate environmental plastic pollution. The technologies are referred to as 'oxo-(bio)degradable' additives or 'biotransformation' technology. In recent years several brands proposed similar technologies, also to the textile and fashion industry, but little information is disclosed on the exact mechanisms involved in the polymer breakdown. In order to make these technologies work as desired and claimed, special conditions are required which cannot be guaranteed in the open environment. A pre-treatment with high UV light, and/or heat in a lab experiment is not reflecting a real-world scenario for a fibre or plastic item that might fall directly into a river or the sea or be buried under dust or soil. To our knowledge, no independent scientific studies exist (cf. Deconink and De Wilde, 2013, 2014) to prove the claimed performance under *unconditioned* natural circumstances. As data on material composition, experimental conditions or biodegradation rates usually are not openly accessible, peer-review and independent evaluation is difficult or impossible (cf. Wiesinger et al., 2020). There is an ongoing debate and lobbying whether or not this kind of technology brings benefit or is misleading industry, public and private decision-makers and consumers. For the packaging sector, 'oxo-(bio-)degradable' plastic is banned in the European Union (European Union, 2019), but allowed or even (exclusively) privileged by law in other regions of the world, mainly Asia and Africa (Deconink and De Wilde, 2013; European Commission et al., 2016). For the textile and fashion industry, the decision so far is up to the apparel manufacturers and brand owners to engage in such technology or to refuse.

On a research level, there are attempts to use natural enzymes directly in the plastic manufacturing process, to modulate biodegradability of polymers and to explore a possible route for biochemical recycling, e.g. of PET (Tournier et al., 2020). DelRe et al. (2021) found that a nano-dispersion of enzymes in the polyesters PCL and PLA led to greatly accelerated depolymerization. However, in the polymers with C-C backbone tested (PE and PS), no material changes were observed. As a solution for the global environmental plastic pollution, such technology so far seems irrelevant or even dangerous when claims are false.

6 Preservation of polymers in nature – learning from archaeology and palaeontology

Biodegradation is a natural process but, also for natural materials, has its limits as it can drastically be seen in the geological record of lifeforms that date back millions of years. Long-term preservation of remains of humans in archaeology and the fossilization of natural polymers as studied in palaeontology impressively show the character of *environmental* biodegradability as a system property: it is the interplay of material and habitat, i.e. the environmental conditions that determine whether at all and, if so, at which rate biodegradation is occurring.

In a natural scenario, there are several possibilities for how a polymer can end up. In extremes, the material abruptly is deposited in a place where all the agents mentioned earlier are not present or very weak. Examples of well preserved, i.e. little degraded natural fibres, are twisted flax fibres in a dry cave from 30,000 years ago (Kvavadze et al., 2009) or dyed fabric at the coast of Peru (6,000 years, Splitstoser et a., 2016) or in the Negev desert (3,000 years, Sukenik et al., 2021). Without water and light, keratin from fur clothing and human tissue in deserts (no water) and ice mummies (no liquid water, no light, low temperature) like Ötzi (O'Sullivan et al., 2016) did not biodegrade for several hundreds to thousands of years. Melanin as the eye pigment of fish was found in fossils from 4.5 million years ago (Lindgren et al., 2012), presumably once buried in anoxic mud without light nor oxygen. Lee et al. (2017) detected collagen in dinosaur bones from 195 million years ago.

Also in modern times, there are various examples of fibres and textiles that were well-preserved under marine conditions for decades or even centuries. Ropes and sails were retrieved from the iconic shipwreck Vasa (sunk in 1628) conserved in the harbour of Stockholm for 333 years (Bengtsson, 1975). A felt hat made from animal hair and a cotton waist coat were found in a New England wreck sunken in 1798 (Putman, 2013), and dyed fibres were little degraded after 130 years aboard the deep-sea shipwreck SS Central America at 2200 m depth (Chen and Jakes, 2001).

7 Perspective

The biodegradation of plastics as a general mitigation of global marine plastic pollution is unrealistic. Biodegradation of conventional polymers in favourable settings is too slow and may not happen at all in human time scale in most scenarios. There is no natural remedy for (marine) plastic pollution to be expected. All other means to reduce littering and any other unwanted introduction of plastic into the oceans and the natural environment in general must be strongly intensified. However, for applications in which plastics are used in the natural environment such as in fisheries and aquaculture, and applications with a high probability of plastics ending up in the environment, such as from abrasion of car tires or shedding microfibres from textiles, biodegradable materials could contribute to decreasing the accumulation of plastics. Environmental biodegradability as an option, even as a legal requirement for high-loss applications, should be further evaluated. As examples, with the known high share of littered cigarette butts globally, or the insufficient management for contaminated waste, such as the 'dirty third' (some of which contain fibrous materials such as hygiene products), strictly applied full environmental biodegradability would have a measurable positive impact on the reduction of persistent plastic pollution in nature. This could accompany measures of reduction at the source at higher levels of the waste hierarchy. Although the acute effects of biodegradable plastics may be similar, at least they would not last 'forever' and could lead to a (much) slower accumulation.

The emerging knowledge on the mechanisms of biodegradation of some synthetic polymers in nature brings about the ideas of an engineered cure for plastic accumulation, e.g. by the release of PET-degrading microbes to heavily polluted zones. With uncalculated risks being expected to be associated with such operations, these considerations lack any technical and economic feasibility and may rather remain ephemeral at the level of news headlines.

For material development, several challenges exist. Besides the question of how to match the requirements for functionality during the use phase with the risk of loss and the desired or even designed biodegradability, knowledge gaps have still to be overcome to achieve a re-design of high-risk applications. Methods for the assessment of pathways of plastic into and through the natural environment, of the lifetime or half-life of a specific material in a certain compartment as well as a solid assessment of environmental benefit, risk and impact are still under development.

In recent years, solid scientific evidence on the performance of the few groups of environmentally biodegradable polymers known so far is becoming available. However, questions on the underlying mechanisms of biodegradation, the active microbial players and biodegradation rates in the variety of marine habitats, but also in freshwater and soil, still must be answered. A comprehensive catalogue covering the combinations of materials and environmental conditions would be extremely helpful for all stakeholder groups to base decisions on. Complications arise from the further treatment of base materials during processing until in use as a finished product (e.g. coated cup, printed bag, dyed fabric).

Looking for solutions, research-driven innovations need to be harmonized with regulatory efforts, e.g. in the debate about the EU single-use plastics directive (European Parliament, 2019) and its respective Guideline (European Commission, 2021).

For this complex topic, certainly a transdisciplinary approach is needed and transparent communication based on scientific evidence rather than guessing, ambiguity or *a-priori* prohibition seems expedient.

8   Acknowledgements

We thank Michael Sander, ETH Zurich for valuable discussions and comments on the manuscript.

References

Addamo A, Laroche P, Hanke G, 2017. *Top Marine Beach Litter Items in Europe*. EUR 29249 EN. Publications Office of the European Union, Luxembourg. https://doi.org/10.2760/496717. https://publications.jrc.ec.europa.eu/repository/handle/JRC108181

Albertsson A-C, 1978. Biodegradation of synthetic polymers. II. A limited microbial conversion of ^{14}C polyethylene to $^{14}CO_2$ by some soil fungi. *J. Appl. Polymer Sci.*, 22, 3419–3433. https://doi.org/10.1002/app.1978.070221207

Albertsson A-C, Bødtker G, Boldizar A, Filatova T, Prieto Jimenez MA, Loos K, Poortinga W, Sander M, Seppälä J, Thompson R, Weber M, 2020. *Biodegradability of Plastics in the Open Environment*. SAPEA, Science Advice for Policy by European Academies, Evidence Review Report No. 8. Berlin, 231p. https://doi.org/10.26356/biodegradabilityplastics

Albertsson A-C, Ljungquist O, 1986. Degradable polymers. I. Synthesis, characterization, and long-term in vitro degradation of a ^{14}C-Labeled aliphatic polyester. J. Macromol. Sci.: Part A – *Chem.*, 23(3), 393–409. https://doi.org/10.1080/00222338608063402

Albright VC, Chai Y, 2021. Knowledge gaps in polymer biodegradation research. *Environ. Sci. Technol.*, 55(17), 11476–11488. doi:10.1021/acs.est.1c00994

Allen S, Deonie A, Vernon RP, Gaël LR, Pilar DJ, Anaëlle S, Stéphane B, Didier G, 2019. Atmospheric transport and deposition of microplastics in a mountain catchment. *Nat. Geosci.*, 12, 339–344. https://doi.org/10.1038/s41561-019-0335-5

Álvarez-Barragán J, Domínguez-Malfavón L, Vargas-Suárez M, González-Hernández R, Aguilar-Osorio G, Loza-Tavera H, 2016. Biodegradative activities of selected environmental fungi on a polyester polyurethane varnish and polyether polyurethane foams. *Appl. Environ. Microbiol.*, 82, 5225–5235. https://doi.org/10.1128/AEM.01344-16.

Amaral-Zettler LA, Zettler ER and Mincer TJ, 2020. Ecology of the plastisphere. *Nat. Rev. Microbiol.* https://doi.org/10.1038/s41579-019-0308-0

Andrady AL, 1990. Environmental degradation of plastics under land and marine exposure conditions. In: *Proceedings of the Second International Conference on Marine Debris, 2–7 April 1989, Honolulu, Hawaii.* U.S. Dep. Comer. NOM Tech. Memo. NHFS. NOM-TH-NHFS-SWFSC-154

Andrady AL, 1994. Assessment of environmental biodegradation of synthetic polymers. *J. Macromolecul. Sci., Part C: Polymer Rev.*, 34(1), 25–76. doi:10.1080/15321799408009632

Arp HPH, Kühnel D, Rummel C, MacLeod M, Potthoff A, Reichelt S, Rojo-Nieto E, Schmitt-Jansen M, Sonnenberg J, Toorman E, Jahnke A, 2021. Weathering plastics as a planetary boundary threat: Exposure, fate, and hazards. *Environ. Sci. Technol.*, 55, 7246–7255. https://doi.org/10.1021/acs.est.1c01512

ASTM D5511, 2018. *Standard Test Method for Determining Anaerobic Biodegradation of Plastic Materials Under High-Solids Anaerobic-Digestion Conditions.* ASTM International, West Conshohocken, PA. https://doi.org/10.1520/D5511-18

ASTM D6691-17, 2017. *Standard Test Method for Determining Aerobic Biodegradation of Plastic Materials in the Marine Environment by a Defined Microbial Consortium or Natural Sea Water Inoculum.* ASTM International, West Conshohocken, PA. https://doi.org/10.1520/D6691-17

Athey SN, Adams JK, Erdle LM, Jantunen LM, Helm PA, Finkelstein SA, Diamond ML, 2020. The widespread environmental footprint of indigo denim microfibers from blue jeans. Environ. Sci. Technol. Lett., 7(11), 840–847. https://doi.org/10.1021/acs.estlett.0c00498

Atkins WRG, FRS, Jenkins PG, Warren FJ, 1954. The suspended matter in sea water and its seasonal changes as affecting the visual range of the Secchi disc. *J. Mar. Biol. Ass. UK*, 33, 497–509. https://doi.org/10.1017/S0025315400008493

Barnes DKA, Galgani F, Thompson RC, Barlaz M, 2009. Accumulation and fragmentation of plastic debris in global environments. *Philos. Trans. R. Soc. B*, 364, 1985–1998. https://doi.org/10.1098/rstb.2008.0205

Barrows APW, Cathey SE, Petersen CW, 2018. Marine environment microfibre contamination: Global patterns and the diversity of microparticle origins. *Environ. Pollut.*, 237, 275e284 https://doi.org/10.1016/j.envpol.2018.02.062

Bastioli C, Guanella I, Romano G, 1990. Effects of water sorption on the physical properties of PET, PBT and their long fibre composites. *Polym. Compos.*, 11(1). https://doi.org/10.1002/pc.750110102

Bengtsson S, 1975. Preservation of the 'Wasa' sails. *Stud. Conserv.*, 20(suppl 1), 33–35. https://doi.org/10.1179/sic.1975.s1.006

Brahney J, Hallerud M, Heim E, Hahnenberger M, Sukumaran S, 2020. Plastic rain in protected areas of the United States. *Science*, 368(6496), 1257–1260. https://doi.org/10.1126/science.aaz5819

Briassoulis D, Pikasi A, Briassoulis C, Mistriotis A, 2019. Disintegration behaviour of bio-based plastics in coastal zone marine environments: A field experiment under natural conditions. *Sci. Total Environ.*, 688, 208–223. https://doi.org/10.1016/j.scitotenv.2019.06.129

British American Tobacco, 2021. www.bat.com/group/sites/UK__9D9KCY.nsf/vwPagesWebLive/DO9DCKFM, accessed 20 Feb 2021.

Browne, MA, Crump, P, Niven, SJ, Teuten, E, Tonkin, A, Galloway, T, Thompson, R, 2011. Accumulation of microplastic on shorelines woldwide: Sources and sinks. *Environ. Sci. Technol.*, 45(21), 9175–9179. https://doi.org/10.1021/es201811s

Buchanan JB, 1971. Pollution by synthetic fibres. *Mar. Pollut. Bull.*, 2, 23. https://doi.org/10.1016/0025-326X(71)90136-6

Burkersroda F von, Schedl L, Göpferich A, 2002. Why degradable polymers undergo surface erosion or bulk erosion. *Biomaterials*, 23(21), 4221–4231. https://doi.org/10.1016/s0142-9612(02)00170-9

Canals M, et al., 2021. The quest for seafloor macrolitter: A critical review of background knowledge, current methods and future prospects. *Environ. Res. Lett.*, 16, 023001. https://doi.org/10.1088/1748-9326/abc6d4

Chamas A, Moon H, Zheng J, Qiu Y, Tabassum T, Jang JH, Abu-Omar M, Scott SL, and Suh S, 2020. Degradation rates of plastics in the environment. *ACS Sustain. Chem. Eng.*, 8(9), 3494–3511. https://doi.org/10.1021/acssuschemeng.9b06635

Chen R, Jakes KA, 2001. Cellulolytic biodegradation of cotton fibres from a deep-ocean environment. *J. Am. Inst. Conserv.*, 40(2), 91–103. doi.org/10.1179/019713601806113076

Chinaglia S, Tosin M, Degli Innocenti F, 2018. Biodegradation rate of biodegradable plastics at molecular level. *Polym. Degrad. Stabil.*, 147, 237–244. https://doi.org/10.1016/j.polymdegradstab.2017.12.011

Chowdhury H, Chowdhury T, Sait SM, 2021. Estimating marine plastic pollution from COVID-19 face masks in coastal regions, *Mar. Poll. Bull.*, 168, 112419. https://doi.org/10.1016/j.marpolbul.2021.112419.

Cocca M, De Falco F, Gentile G, Avolio R, Errico ME, Di Pace E, Avella M, 2017. Degradation of biodegradable plastic buried in sand. In: Cocca M, et al. (eds.), *Proceedings of the International Conference on Microplastic Pollution in the Mediterranean Sea*. Springer Water Book Series. Springer, Cham, pp. 205–209. https://doi.org/10.1007/978-3-319-71279-6_28

Cole M, Lindeque P, Halsband C, Galloway TS, 2011. Microplastics as contaminants in the marine environment: A review. *Mar. Pollut. Bull.*, 62, 2588–2597. https://doi.org/10.1016/j.marpolbul.2011.09.025.

Comnea-Stancu IR, Wieland K, Ramer G, Schwaighofer A, Lendl B, 2017. On the identification of Rayon/Viscose as a major fraction of microplastics in the marine environment: Discrimination between natural and manmade cellulosic fibres using Fourier transform infrared spectroscopy. *Appl. Spectrosc.*, 71(5), 939–950. https://doi.org/10.1177/0003702816660725

Cózar A, Echevarría F, González-Gordillo JI, Irigoien X, Úbeda B, Hernández-León S, Palma AT, Navarro S, García-de-Lomas J, Ruiz A, Fernández-de-Puelles ML, Duarte CM, 2014. Plastic debris in the open ocean. *Proc. Natl. Acad. Sci. USA*, 111(28), 10239–10244 www.pnas.org/cgi/doi/10.1073/pnas.1314705111

Danso D, Chow J, Streit WR, 2019. Plastics: Environmental and biotechnological perspectives on microbial degradation. *Appl. Environ. Microb.*, 85, e01095–19. https://doi.org/10.1128/AEM.01095–19.

Danso D, Schmeisser C, Chow J, Zimmermann W, Wei R, Leggewie C, Li X, Hazen T, Streit WR, 2018. New insights into the function and global distribution of polyethylene terephthalate (PET)-degrading bacteria and enzymes in marine and terrestrial metagenomes. *Appl. Environ. Microb.*, 84, e02773–17. https://doi.org/10.1128/AEM.02773-17.

Deconink S, De Wilde B, 2013. *Benefits and Challenges of Bio- and Oxo-Degradable Plastics. A Comparative Literature Study*. Final Report, Plastics Europe, Brussels, 118 p. www.ows.be/wp-content/uploads/2013/10/Final-Report-DSL-1_Rev02.pdf, accessed 20 Dec 2020.

Deconink S, De Wilde B, 2014. *Review of Information on Enzyme-Mediated Degradable Plastics*. Study EUBP-2. Organic Waste Systems, Ghent, Belgium, 16p. www.ows.be/wp-content/uploads/2014/08/Report_Rev01.pdf, accessed 20 Dec 2020.

De Falco F, Avolio R, Errico ME, Di Pace E, Avella M, Cocca M, Gentile G, 2021. Comparison of biodegradable polyesters degradation behaviour in sand. *J. Hazard. Mater.*, 416, 126231. https://doi.org/10.1016/j.jhazmat.2021.126231

Deguchi T, Kakezawa M, Nishida T, 1997. Nylon biodegradation by lignin-degrading fungi. *Appl. Environ. Microb.*, 63, 329–331. https://doi.org/10.1128/aem.63.1.329–331.1997.

Deguchi T, Kitaoka Y, Kakezawa M, Nishida T, 1998. Purification and characterization of a nylon-degrading enzyme. *Appl. Environ. Microb.*, 64, 1366–1371. https://doi.org/10.1128/AEM.64.4.1366–1371.1998.

DelRe C, Jiang Y, Kang P, Kwon J, Hall A, Jayapurna I, . . . Xu T, 2021. Near-complete depolymerization of polyesters with nano-dispersed enzymes. *Nature*, 592(7855), 558–563. doi:10.1038/s41586-021-03408-3

Deroiné M, Duigou AL, Corre Y-M, Gac P-YL, Davies P, César G, Bruzaud S, 2014a. Accelerated ageing of polylactide in aqueous environments: Comparative study between distilled water and seawater. *Polym. Degrad. Stabil.*, 108, 319–329. https://doi.org/10.1016/j.polymdegradstab.2014.01.020.

Deroiné M, Duigou AL, Corre Y-M, Gac P-YL, Davies P, César G, Bruzaud S, 2014b. Seawater accelerated ageing of poly(3-hydroxybutyrate-co-3-hydroxyvalerate). *Polym. Degrad. Stabil.*, 105, 237–247. http://doi.org/10.1016/j.polymdegradstab.2014.04.026.

Dexter SC, 1979. Influence of substratum critical surface tension on bacterial adhesion – in situ studies. *J. Colloid Interf. Sci.*, 70, 346–354. https://doi.org/10.1016/0021-9797(79)90038-9

Dilkes-Hoffman LS, Lant PA, Laycock B, Pratt S, 2019. The rate of biodegradation of PHA bioplastics in the marine environment: A meta-study. *Mar. Pollut. Bull.*, 142, 15–24. https://doi.org/10.1016/j.marpolbul.2019.03.020

DOLAN GmbH, 2021. www.dolan-gmbh.de/index.html, accessed 15 Feb 2021.

DRALON GmbH, 2021. www.dralon.com/, accessed 15 Feb 2021.

Dris R, Gasperi J, Saad M, Mirande C, Tassin B, 2016. Synthetic fibres in atmospheric fallout: A source of microplastics in the environment? *Mar. Pollut. Bull.*, 104(1–2), 290–293. https://doi.org/10.1016/j.marpolbul.2016.01.006

Ebisui A, Murakami H, Oyaizu Y, Enoki M, Kanehiro H, Wakabayashi S, Watanabe T, 2006. Biodegradation of poly (ε-caprolactone) monofilament fibres in deep seawater at near 0°C. *Deep Ocean Water Res.*, 7(2), 31–36

Eich A, Mildenberger T, Laforsch C, Weber M, 2015. Biofilm and diatom succession on polyethylene (PE) and biodegradable plastic bags in two marine habitats: early signs of degradation in the pelagic and benthic zone? *PLoS ONE*, 2015, 10(9), e0137201. https://doi.org/10.1371/journal.pone.0137201

Eich A, Weber M, Lott C, 2021. Disintegration half-life of biodegradable plastic films on different marine beach sediments. *PeerJ*, 9, e11981. https://doi.org/10.7717/peerj.11981

Eubeler JP, Bernhard M, Zok S, Knepper TP, 2009. Environmental biodegradation of synthetic polymers. I. Test methodologies and procedures. *Trend. Anal. Chem.*, 28, 1057–1072. https://doi.org/10.1016/j.trac.2009.06.007

Eubeler JP, Bernhard M, Zok S, Knepper TP, 2010. Environmental biodegradation of synthetic polymers. II. Biodegradation of different polymer groups. *Trend. Anal. Chem.*, 29, 84–100 https://doi.org/10.1016/j.trac.2009.06.007

European Bioplastics, 2020. https://docs.european-bioplastics.org/conference/Report_Bioplastics_Market_Data_2020_short_version.pdf, accessed 13 Mar 2021.

European Commission, 2021. Commission guidelines on single-use plastic products in accordance with Directive (EU) 2019/904 of the European Parliament and of the Council on the reduction of the impact of certain plastic products on the environment. Commission Notice 2021/ C 216/01. *Official Journal of the European Union*, 7.6.2021, C216/1. https://eur-lex.europa.eu/legal-content/EN/TXT/HTML/?uri=CELEX:52 021XC0607(03)&from=EN

European Commission, GD Environment, Hogg D, Gibbs A, Ettlinger S, et al., 2016. The impact of the use of "oxo-degradable" plastic on the environment: Final report, Publications Office, 2016, https://data.europa.eu/doi/10.2779/992559

European Parliament, 2019. Directive 2019/904 of the European Parliament and of the Council of 5 June 2019 on the reduction of the impact of certain plastic products on the environment. *Official Journal of the European Union*, 12.6.2019, L155/1–19. https://eur-lex.europa.eu/eli/dir/2019/904/oj

European Union, 2019. Directive (EU) 2019/904 of the European Parliament and of the Council of 5 June 2019 on the reduction of the impact of certain plastic products on the environment. *Official Journal of the European Union*, L155/1, 12.6.2019. https://eur-lex.europa.eu/legal-content/EN/TXT/PDF/?uri=CELEX:32019L0904&from=EN [accessed 13.10.2021]

Fambri L, Caria R, Atzori F, Ceccato R, Lorenzi D, 2020. Controlled aging and degradation of selected plastics in marine environment: 12 months of follow-up. In: Cocca M, et al. (eds.), *Proceedings of the International Conference on Microplastic Pollution in the Mediterranean Sea*. Springer Water Book Series. Springer, Cham, pp. 89–100. https://doi.org/10.1007/978-3-030-45909-3_16

Fischer-Colbrie G, Herrmann M, Heumann S, Puolakka A, Wirth A, Cavaco-Paulo A, Guebitz GM, 2006. Surface modification of polyacrylonitrile with nitrile hydratase and amidase from *Agrobacterium tumefaciens*. *Biocatal. Biotransfor.*, 24(6), 419–425. https://doi.org/10.1080/10242420601033977

Fleischmann M, 1989. The measurement and penetration of ultraviolet radiation into tropical marine water. *Limnol. Oceanogr.*, 34(8), 1623–1629. https://doi.org/10.4319/lo.1989.34.8.1623

Flemming HC, 1998. Relevance of biofilms for the biodeterioration of surfaces of polymeric materials. *Polym. Degrad. Stabil.*, 59, 309–315. https://doi.org/10.1016/S0141-3910(97)00189-4

Frank YA, Vorobiev ED, Vorobiev DS, Trifonov AA, Antsiferov DV, Soliman Hunter T, Wilson SP, Strezov V, 2021. Preliminary screening for microplastic concentrations in the surface water of the Ob and Tom rivers in Siberia, Russia. *Sustainability*, 13, 80. https://doi.org/10.3390/su13010080

Friedrich J, Zalar P, Mohorčič M, Klun U, Kržan A, 2007. Ability of fungi to degrade synthetic polymer nylon-6. *Chemosphere*, 67, 2089–2095. https://doi.org/10.1016/j.chemosphere.2006.09.038.

Gilman E, Chopin F, Suuronen P, Kuemlangan B, 2016. *Abandoned, Lost and Discarded Gillnets and Trammel Nets: Methods to Estimate Ghost Fishing Mortality, and the Status of Regional Monitoring and Management*. FAO Fisheries and Aquaculture Technical Paper No. 600. Rome. Italy.

GLAUKOS, 2021. *Circular Solutions for the Textile Industry*. Report on Market Studies, Status March 2021. https://glaukos.fvaweb.eu/wp-content/uploads/2021/03/Glaukos-Report-on-market-studies_for-publication.pdf

Greene J, 2012. PLA and PHA biodegradation in the marine environment. *Report CalRecycle*, Sacramento, CA: State of California, Department of Resources Recycling and Recovery. https://www2.calrecycle.ca.gov/Publications/Download/1006

Grimaldo E, Herrmann B, Jacques N, Vollstad J, Su B, 2020. Effect of mechanical properties of monofilament twines on the catch efficiency of biodegradable gillnets. *PLoS ONE*, 15(9), e0234224. https://doi.org/10.1371/journal.pone.0234224

Groves Eotorizedd, Palenik CS, 2018. A generalised approach to forensic dye identification: development and utility of reference libraries. *J. AOAC Int.*, 101(5), 1385–1396. https://doi.org/10.5740/jaoacint.18–0052

Harrison JP, Schrazberger M, Sapp M, Osborn AM, 2014. Rapid bacterial colonization of low-density polyethylene microplastics in coastal sediment microcosms. *BMC Microbiol.*, 14, 232. https://doi.org/10.1186/s12866-014-0232-4

Hashimoto K, Hamano T, Okada M, 1994. Degradation of several polyamides in soil. *J. Appl. Polymer Sci.*, 54, 1579–1583

Haske-Cornelius O, Alessandro Pellis A, Tegl G, Wurz S, Saake B, Ludwig R, Sebastian A, Nyanhongo GS, Guebitz GM, 2017. Enzymatic systems for cellulose acetate degradation. *Catalysts*, 7, 287. https://doi.org/10.3390/catal7100287

Hauser P, 2015. Chapter 18: Fabric finishing: Pretreatment/textile wet processing. In: Sinclair R (ed.), *Textiles and Fashion: Materials, Design and Technology*. Woodhead Publishing Series in Textiles, Number 126. Elsevier, Cambridge. http://doi.org/10.1016/B978-1-84569-931-4.00018-0

Henry B, Laitala K, Klepp IG, 2019. Microfibres from apparel and home textiles: Prospects for including microplastics in environmental sustainability assessment. *Sci. Total Environ.*, 652, 483–494. https://doi.org/10.1016/j.scitotenv.2018.10.166

Hidalgo-Ruz V, Gutow L, Thompson RC, Thiel M, 2012. Microplastics in the marine environment: A review of the methods used for identification and quantification. *Environ. Sci. Technol.*, 46(6), 3060–3075. https://doi.org/10.1021/es2031505

Hofsten B von, Edberg N, 1972. Estimating the rate of degradation of cellulose fibres in water. *OIKOS*, 23, 29–34.

Hölter D, La Personne P, 2017. *New Aspects of Cellulose Acetate Biodegradation.* Conference Presentation CORESTA SSPR, Kitzbühel, Austria 2017. www.coresta.org/sites/default/files/abstracts/2017_ST13_Holter.pdf, accessed 25 Apr 2021

Ioakeimidis C, et al., 2016. The degradation potential of PET bottles in the marine environment: An ATR-FTIR based approach. *Sci. Rep.*, 6, 23501. https://doi.org/10.1038/srep23501.

ISO 14851, 2019. *Determination of the Ultimate Aerobic Biodegradability of Plastic Materials in an Aqueous Medium – Method by Measuring the Oxygen Demand in a Closed Respirometer.* https://doi.org/10.31030/3026665

ISO 15985, 2014. *Plastics – Determination of the Ultimate Anaerobic Biodegradation under High-Solids Anaerobic-Digestion Conditions – Method by Analysis of Released Biogas.* https://doi.org/10.31030/2800532

ISO 17556, 2019. *Plastics – Determination of the Ultimate Aerobic Biodegradability of Plastic Materials in Soil by Measuring the Oxygen Demand in a Respirometer or the Amount of Carbon Dioxide Evolved.* https://doi.org/10.31030/3072096

ISO 22404, 2019. *Plastics – Determination of the Aerobic Biodegradation of Non-Floating Materials Exposed to Marine Sediment – Method by Analysis of Evolved Carbon Dioxide.* https://doi.org/10.31030/3252690

Jacquin J, Callac N, Cheng J, Giraud C, Gorand Y, Denoual C, Pujo-Pay M, Conan P, Meistertzheim A-L, Barbe V, Bruzaud S and Ghiglione J-F, 2021. Microbial diversity and activity during the biodegradation in seawater of various substitutes to conventional plastic cotton swab sticks. *Front. Microbiol.*, 12, 604395. https://doi.org/10.3389/fmicb.2021.604395

Jones PR, Cottrell MT, Kirchman DL, Dexter SC, 2007. Bacterial community structure of biofilms on artificial surfaces in an estuary. *Microbial Ecol.*, 53, 153–162. https://doi.org/10.1007/s00248-006-9154-5

Kanhai LDK, Gardfeldt K, Krumpen T, Thompson RC, O'Connor I, 2020. Microplastics in sea ice and seawater beneath ice floes from the Arctic Ocean. *Sci. Rep.,* 10(1). https://doi.org/10.1038/s41598-020-61948-6

Karthäuser C, Ahmerkamp S, Marchant HK, et al., 2021. Small sinking particles control anammox rates in the Peruvian oxygen minimum zone. *Nat. Commun.*, 12, 3235. https://doi.org/10.1038/s41467-021-23340-4

Kim S, Kim P, Jeong S, Lee K, 2020. Assessment of the physical characteristics and fishing performance of gillnets using biodegradable resin (PBS/PBAT and PBSAT) to reduce ghost fishing. *Aquat. Conserv.*, 2020, 1–17. https://doi.org/https://doi.org/10.1002/aqc.3354

Kim S, Kim P, Lim J, An H, Suuronen P, 2016. Use of biodegradable driftnets to prevent ghost fishing: physical properties and fishing performance for yellow croaker. *Anim. Conserv.* https://doi.org/10.1111/acv.12256

Klun U, Friedrich J, Kržan A, 2003. Polyamide-6 fibre degradation by a lignolytic fungus. *Polym. Degrad. Stabil.*, 79, 99–104. doi.org/10.1016/S0141-3910(02)00260-4

Kooi M, Nes EHV, Scheffer M, Koelmans AA, 2017. Ups and downs in the ocean: Effects of biofouling on vertical transport of microplastics. *Environ. Sci. Technol.*, 51(14), 7963–7971. https://doi.org/10.1021/acs.est.6b04702

Köster M, Wardenga R, Blume M, 2008. Microscale investigations of microbial communities in coastal surficial sediments. *Mar. Ecol.*, 29, 89–105 https://doi.org/10.1111/j.1439-0485.2007.00219.x

Krause S, Molari M, Gorb EV, Gorb SN, Kossel E, Haeckel M, 2020. Persistence of plastic debris and its colonization by bacterial communities after two decades on the abyssal seafloor. *Sci. Rep.*, 10, 9484. https://doi.org/10.1038/s41598-020-66361-7

Krueger MC, Harms H, Schlosser D, 2015. Prospects for microbiological solutions to environmental pollution with plastics. *Appl. Microbiol. Biotechnol.*, 99, 8857–8874. https://doi.org/10.1007/s00253-015-6879-4

Kukulka T, Proskurowski G, Morét-Ferguson S, Meyer DW, Law KL, 2012. The effect of wind mixing on the vertical distribution of buoyant plastic debris. *Geophys. Res. Lett.*, 39(7), L07601. https://doi.org/10.1029/2012GL051116

Künkel A, Becker J, Börger L, Hamprecht J, Koltzenburg S, Loos R, Schick MB, Schlegel K, Sinkel C, Skupin G, Yamamoto M, 2016. Polymers, biodegradable. In: *Ullmann's Encyclopedia of Industrial Chemistry.* https://doi.org/10.1002/14356007.n21_n01.pub2

Kvavadze E, Bar-Yosef O, Belfer-Cohen A, Boaretto E, Jakeli N, Matskevich Z, Meshveliani T, 2009. 30 000-year-old wild flax fibres. *Science*, 325. https://doi.org/10.1126/science.1175404

Lechner A, Keckeis H, Lumesberger-Loisl F, Zens B, Krusch R, Tritthart M, Glas M, Schludermann E, 2014. The Danube so colourful: A potpourri of plastic litter outnumbers fish larvae in Europe's second largest river. *Environ. Pollut.*, 188, 177–181. https://doi.org/10.1016/j.envpol.2014.02.006.

Lee YC, Chiang CC, Huang PY, Chung CY, Huang TD, Wang CC, Chen CI, Chang RS, Liao CH, Reisz RR, 2017. Evidence of preserved collagen in an Early Jurassic sauropodomorph dinosaur revealed by synchrotron FTIR microspectroscopy. *Nat. Commun.*, 8, 14220. https://doi.org/10.1038/ncomms14220.

Lepot L, De Wael K, Gason F, Gilbert B, 2008. Application of Raman spectroscopy to forensic fibre cases. *Sci. Justice*, 48, 109–117. https://doi.org/10.1016/j.scijus.2007.09.013

Lindgren J, Uvdal P, Sjövall P, Nilsson DE, Engdahl A, Schultz BP, Thiel V, 2012. Molecular preservation of the pigment melanin in fossil melanosomes. *Nat. Commun.*, 3, 824. https://doi.org/10.1038/ncomms1819

Lobelle D, Cunliffe M, 2011. Early microbial biofilm formation on marine plastic debris. *Mar. Pollut. Bull.*, 62, 197–200. https://doi.org/10.1016/j.marpolbul.2010.10.013

Lott C, Eich A, Makarow D, Unger B, van Eekert M, Schuman E, Reinach MS, Lasut MT, Weber M, 2021. Half-life of biodegradable plastics in the marine environment depends on material, habitat, and climate zone. *Front. Mar. Sci.*, 8, 662074. https://doi.org/10.3389/fmars.2021.662074

Lott C, Eich A, Unger B, Makarow D, Battagliarin G, Schlegel K, Lasut MT, Weber M, 2020. Field and mesocosm methods to test biodegradable plastic film under marine conditions. *PLoS ONE*, 15(7), e0236579. https://doi.org/10.1371/journal.pone.0236579

Lott C, Eich A, Unger B, Makarow D, Lasut MT, Weber M, 2017. *Performance of Bio-Degradable Plastic in the Marine Environment.* Poster presented at MICRO2018 Conference, Lanzarote, Spain. www.hydramarinesciences.com/.cm4all/uproc.php/0/Lott%20et%20al-Biodegradable_Marine_Poster20181113-MICRO2018_1.pdf?cdp=a&_=1672cda212e, accessed 12 Dec 2020.

Lusher AL, Hollman PCH, Mendoza-Hill JJ, 2017. *Microplastics in Fisheries and Aquaculture: Status of Knowledge on their Occurrence and Implications for Aquatic Organisms and Food Safety.* FAO Fisheries and Aquaculture Technical Paper No. 615. Rome, Italy.

Lykaki M, Zhang Y-Q, Markiewicz M, Brandt S, Kolbe S, Schrick J, Rabe M, Stolte S, 2021. The influence of textile finishing agents on the biodegradability of shed fibres. *Green Chem.*, 23, 5212–5221. https://doi.org/10.1039/D1GC00883H

Manzoni S, Čapek P, Porada P, Thurner M, Winterdahl M, Beer C, . . . Way D, 2018. Reviews and syntheses: Carbon use efficiency from organisms to ecosystems – definitions, theories, and empirical evidence. *Biogeosciences,* 15(19), 5929–5949. https://doi.org/10.5194/bg-15-5929-2018

Markager S, Vincent WF, 2000. Spectral light attenuation and the absorption of UV and blue light in natural waters. *Limnol. Oceanogr.*, 45(3), 642–650. https://doi.org/10.4319/lo.2000.45.3.0642

Martin RT, Camargo LP, Miller SA, 2014. Marine-degradable polylactic acid. *Green Chem.*, 16, 1768–1773. https://doi.org/10.1039/C3GC42604A

Martinez Silva P, Nanny MA, 2020. Impact of microplastic fibres from the degradation of nonwoven synthetic textiles to the Magdalena river water column and river sediments by the City of Neiva, Huila (Colombia). *Water*, 12(4), 1210. https://doi.org/10.3390/w12041210

McKeown P, Kamran M, Davidson MG, Jones MD, Román-Ramírez LA, Wood J, 2020. Organocatalysis for versatile polymer degradation. *Green Chem.*, 22(12), 3721–3726. https://doi.org/10.1039/D0GC01252A

Meereboer KW, Misra M, Mohanty AK, 2020. Review of recent advances in the biodegradability of polyhydroxyalkanoate (PHA) bioplastics and their composites. *Green Chem.*, 22, 5519. https://doi.org/10.1039/d0gc01647k

Meyer-Cifuentes IE, Werner J, Jehmlich N, Will SE, Neumann-Schaal M, Öztürk B, 2020. Synergistic biodegradation of aromatic-aliphatic copolyester plastic by a marine microbial consortium. *Nat. Commun.*, 11, 5790. https://doi.org/10.1038/s41467-020-19583-2

The Microfibre Consortium, 2020. https://static1.squarespace.com/static/5aaba1998f513028aeec604c/t/5efb08cc84a29a2018664c86/1593510092204/TMC_Definitions+Website+Page_May+2020.pdf, accessed 15 Jan 2021.

Monson L, Braunwarth M, Extrand CW, 2007. Moisture absorption by various polyamides and their associated dimensional changes. *J. Appl. Polymer Sci.*, 107, 355–363. https://doi.org/10.1002/app.27057

Müller RJ, Schrader H, Profe J, Dresler K, Deckwer W-D, 2005. Enzymatic degradation of poly(ethylene terephthalate): Rapid hydrolyse using a hydrolase from *T. fusca. Macromole. Rapid Commun.*, 26(17), 1400–1405. https://doi.org/10.1002/marc.200500410

Narancic T, Verstichel S, Chaganti SR, Morales-Gamez L, Kenny ST, De Wilde B, Padamati RB, O'Connor KE, 2018. Biodegradable plastic blends create new possibilities for end-of-life management of plastics but they are not a panacea for plastic pollution. *Environ. Sci. Technol.*, 52(18), 10441–10452. https://doi.org/10.1021/acs.est.8b02963

Nelson TF, Reddy CM, Ward CP, 2021. Product formulation controls the impact of biofouling on consumer plastic photochemical fate in the ocean. *Environ. Sci. Technol.*, 55(13), 8898–8907. https://doi.org/10.1021/acs.est.1c02079

Nikaido H, Vaara M, 1985. Molecular basis of bacterial outer membrane permeability. *Microbiol. Rev.*, 49(1), 1–32. https://doi.org/10.1128/mr.49.1.1-32.1985

O'Sullivan NJ, Teasdale MD, Mattiangeli V, Maixner F, Pinhasi R, Bradley DG, Zink A, 2016. A whole mitochondria analysis of the Tyrolean Iceman's leather provides insights into the animal sources of Copper Age clothing. *Sci. Rep.*, 6, 31279. https://doi.org/10.1038/srep31279

Otake Y, Kobayashi T, Asabe H, Murakami N, Ono K, 1995. Biodegradation of low-density polyethylene, polystyrene, polyvinyl chloride, and urea formaldehyde resin buried under soil for over 32 years. *J. Appl. Polymer Sci.*, 56, 1789–1796 https://doi.org/10.1002/app.1995.070561309

Patil JS, Anil AC, 2005. Biofilm diatom community structure: Influence of temporal and substratum variability. *Biofouling*, 21, 189–206. https://doi.org/10.1080/08927010500256757

Pauli N-C, Petermann JS, Lott C, Weber M, 2017. Macrofouling communities and the degradation of plastic bags in the sea: An in situ experiment. *R. Soc. Open Sci.*, 4, 170549. http://doi.org/10.1098/rsos.170549

Pelegrini MK, Donazzolo I, Brambilla V, Grisa AMC, Piazza D, Zattera AJ, 2016. Degradation of PLA and PLA in composites with triacetin and buriti fibre after 600 days in a simulated marine environment. *J. Appl. Polymer Sci.*, 133(15), 43290. https://doi.org/10.1002/app.43290.

Plastics Europe, 2020. *Plastics – The Facts 2019.* www.google.com/url?sa=t&rct=j&q=&esrc=s&source=web&cd=&cad=rja&uact=8&ved=2ahUKEwj0o77yu7HzAhUx8bsIHYwsCE0QFnoECAIQAQ&url=https%3A%2F%2Fwww.plasticseurope.org%2Fapplication%2Ffiles%2F5716%2F0752%2F4286%2FAF_Plastics_the_facts-WEB-2020-ING_FINAL.pdf&usg=AOvVaw2LyT7fMqnV7o4l2AIBfTls, accessed 20 Jan 2021.

Polerecky L, Lott C, Weber M, 2008. In situ measurement of gross photosynthesis using a microsensor-based light-shade shift method. *Limnol. Oceanogr.-Meth.*, 6, 373–383. https://doi.org/10.4319/lom.2008.6.373

Puls J, Wilson SA, Hölter D, 2010. Degradation of cellulose acetate-based materials: A review. *J. Polym. Environ.*, 19(1), 152–165. https://doi.org/10.1007/s10924-010-0258-0

Putman TR, 2013. Textile artifacts from H.M. Sloop De Braak. *The Military Collector & Historian: Journal of the Company of Military Historians*, 65(1), 75–88. www.tylerruddputman.com, accessed 20 Jan 2021.

Ratto JA, Russo J, Allen A, Herbert J, Wirsen C, 2001. Chapter 20: Biodegradable polymers in the marine environment: A tiered approach to assessing microbial degradability. In Gross R (ed.), *Biopolymers from Polysaccarides and Agroproteins*. ACS Symposium Series. American Chemical Society, Washington, DC.

Remy F, Collard F, Gilbert B, Compere P, Eppe G, Lepoint G, 2015. When microplastic is not plastic: The ingestion of artificial cellulose fibres by macrofauna living in seagrass macrophytodetritus. *Environ. Sci. Technol.*, 49, 11158–11166. https://doi.org/10.1021/acs.est.5b02005

Restrepo-Flórez J-M, Bassi A, Thompson MR, 2014. Microbial degradation and deterioration of polyethylene e – A review. *Int. Biodeter. Biodegr.*, 88, 83e90. http://doi.org/10.1016/j.ibiod.2013.12.014

Richards PR, 2015. Chapter 19: Fabric finishing: Dyeing and colouring. In: Sinclair R (ed.), *Textiles and Fashion. Materials, Design and Technology*. Woodhead Publishing Series in Textiles, Number 126. Elsevier, Cambridge, pp. 475–505. https://doi.org/10.1016/B978-1-84569-931-4.00019-2

Riedel K, Grunau A, 2011. Exoenzymes. In: Reitner J, Thiel V (eds.), *Encyclopedia of Geobiology. Encyclopedia of Earth Sciences Series*. Springer, Dordrecht. https://doi.org/10.1007/978-1-4020-9212-1_85

Ronkvist ÅM, Xie W, Lu W, Gross RA, 2009. Cutinase-catalyzed hydrolysis of poly(ethylene terephthalate). *Macromolecules*, 42(14), 5128–5138. https://doi.org/10.1021/ma9005318

Rutkowska M, Kraskowska K, Heimowska A, Steinka I, Janik H, 2002. Degradation of polyurethanes in sea water. *Polym. Degrad. Stabil.*, 76, 233–239 https://doi.org/10.1016/S0141-3910(02)00019-8

Sala MM, Karner M, Arin L, Marrasé C, 2001. Measurement of ectoenzyme activities as an indication of inorganic nutrient imbalance in microbial communities. *Aquat. Microb. Ecol.*, 23, 301–311. https://doi.org/10.3354/ame023301

Sanchez-Vidal A, Thompson RC, Canals M, de Haan WP, 2018. The imprint of microfibres in southern European deep seas. *PLoS ONE*, 13(11), e0207033. https://doi.org/10.1371/journal. pone.0207033

Schmidt J, Deming JW, Jumars PA, Keil RG, 1998. Constancy of bacterial abundance in surficial marine sediments. *Limnol. Oceanogr.*, 43(5), 976–982 https://doi.org/10.4319/lo.1998.43.5.0976

Sekiguchi T, Saika A, Nomura K, Watanabe T, Watanabe T, Fujimoto Y, Enoki M, Sato T, Kato C, Kanehiro H, 2011. Biodegradation of aliphatic polyesters soaked in deep seawaters and isolation of poly(ε-caprolactone)-degrading bacteria. *Polym. Degrad. Stabil.*, 96, 1397–1403. https://doi.org/10.1016/j. polymdegradstab.2011.03.004

Sekiguchi T, Sato T, Enoki M, Kanehiro H, Uematsu K, Kato C, 2010. Isolation and characterization of biodegradable plastic degrading bacteria from deep-sea environments. *JAMSTEC Rep. Res. Dev.*, 11, 33–41.

Slaughter E, Gersberg RM, Watanabe K, Rudolph J, Stransky C, Novotny TE, 2011. Toxicity of cigarette butts, and their chemical components, to marine and freshwater fish. *Tob. Control*, 20(Suppl 1), i25ei29. https://doi.org/10.1136/tc.2010.040170

Splitstoser JC, Dillehay TD, Wouters J, Claro A, 2016. Early pre-Hispanic use of indigo blue in Peru. *Sci. Adv.*, 2, e1501623. https://doi.org/10.1126/sciadv.1501623

Stanton T, Johnson M, Nathanail P, MacNaughtan W, Gomes RL, 2019. Freshwater and airborne textile fibre populations are dominated by "natural", not microplastic, fibres. *Sci. Total Environ.*, 666, 377–389. https://doi.org/10.1016/j.scitotenv.2019.0

Su B, Føre HM, Grimaldo E, 2019. A comparative study of the mechanical properties of biodegradable PBSAT and PA gillnets in Norwegian coastal waters. *OMAE 2019*, 95350 2019.

Suaria G, Achtypi A, Perold V, Lee JR, Pierucci A, Bornman TG, Aliani S, Ryan PG, 2020. Microfibres in oceanic surface waters: A global characterization. *Sci. Adv.*, 6, eaay8493. https://doi.org/10.1126/sciadv.aay8493

Sukenik N, Iluz D, Amar Z, Varvak A, Shamir O, Ben-Yosef E, 2021. Early evidence of royal purple dyed textile from Timna Valley (Israel). *PLoS ONE*, 16(1), e0245897. https://doi.org/10.1371/journal.pone.0245897

Textile Exchange, 2021. https://textileexchange.org/wp-content/uploads/2020/06/Textile-Exchange_Preferred-Fiber-Material-Market-Report_2020.pdf, accessed 20 Feb 2021.

Thapa S, Mishra J, Arora N, et al., 2020. Microbial cellulolytic enzymes: Diversity and biotechnology with reference to lignocellulosic biomass degradation. *Rev. Environ. Sci. Biotechnol.*, 19, 621–648. https://doi.org/10.1007/s11157-020-09536-y

Thompson RC, Olsen Y, Mitchell RP, Davis AR, John AW, McGonigle D, Russell AE, 2004. Lost at sea: Where is all the plastics? *Science*, 304, 838. https://doi.org/10.1126/science.1094559

Tokiwa Y, Calabia BP, Ugwu CU, Aiba S, 2009. Biodegradability of plastics. *Int. J. Mol. Sci.*, 10, 3722–3742. https://doi.org/10.3390/ijms10093722

Tosin M, Weber M, Siotto M, Lott C, Degli Innocenti F, 2012. Laboratory test methods to determine the degradation of plastics in marine environmental conditions. *Front. Microbiol.*, 3, 225. https://doi.org/10.3389/fmicb.2012.00225

Tournier V, Topham CM, Gilles A, et al., 2020. An engineered PET depolymerase to break down and recycle plastic bottles. *Nature*, 580, 216–219. doi.org/10.1038/s41586-020-2149-4

Tsuji H, Suzuyoshi K, 2002. Environmental degradation of biodegradable polyesters 1. Poly(ε-caprolactone), poly[(R)-3-hydroxybutyrate], and poly(L-lactide) films in controlled static seawater. *Polym. Degrad. Stabil.*, 75, 347–355

Vaksmaa A, Knittel K, Abdala Asbun A, Goudriaan M, Ellrott A, Witte HJ, Vollmer I, Meirer F, Lott C, Weber M, Engelmann JC and Niemann H, 2021. Microbial communities on plastic polymers in the Mediterranean Sea. *Front. Microbiol.*, 12, 673553. https://doi.org/10.3389/fmicb.2021.673553

Van Cauwenberghe L, Vanreusel A, Mees J, Janssen CR, 2013. Microplastic pollution in deep-sea sediments. *Environ. Pollut.*, 182, 495–499. https://doi.org/10.1016/j.envpol.2013.08.013

Van der Zee M, 2020. Methods for evaluating the biodegradability of environmentally degradable polymers. In Bastioli C (ed.), *Handbook of Biodegradable Polymers*. De Gruyter, Berlin, Boston. https://doi.org/10.1515/9781501511967

Van der Zee M, Stoutjesdijk JH, Feil H, Feijen J, 1998. Relevance of aquatic biodegradation tests for predicting degradation of polymeric material during biological solid waste treatment. *Chemosphere*, 36(3), 461–473. https://doi.org/10.1016/s0045-6535(97)1001

Vazquez, YV, Ressia JA, Cerrada ML, Barbosa SE, Vallés EM, 2019. Prodegradant additives effect onto commercial polyolefins. *J. Polym. Environ.* https://doi.org/10.1007/s10924-018-01364-0

Viool V, Oudmaijer S, Walser B, Claessens R, van Hoof L, Strootman WJ, 2018. *Study to Support Impact Assessment for Options to Reduce the Level of ALDFG, Final Report 22–02–2018*. European Commission, Brussels https://webgate.ec.europa.eu/maritimeforum/en/system/files/Final%20Report%20Plastics%20from%20Fishing%20Gear%20Delivered.pdf, accessed 20 Mar 2021.

Wang G-X, Huang D, Ji J-H, Völker C, Wurm FR, 2021. Seawater-degradable polymers – Fighting the marine plastic pollution. *Adv. Sci.*, 8, 2001121. https://doi.org/10.1002/advs.202001121

Wang X-W, Wang G-X, Huang D, Lu B, Zhen Z-C, Ding Y, Ren Z-L, Wang P-L, Zhang W, Ji J-H, 2018. Degradability comparison of poly(butylene adipate terephthalate) and its composites filled with starch and calcium carbonate in different aquatic environments. *J. Appl. Polymer Sci.*, e46916. https://doi.org/10.1002/app.46916

Waters CN, Zalasiewicz J, Summerhayes C, Barnosky AD, Poirier C, Galuszka A, . . . Wolfe AP, 2016. The Anthropocene is functionally and stratigraphically distinct from the Holocene. *Science*, 351(6269), aad2622–aad2622. https://doi.org/10.1126/science.aad2622

Weber M, Färber P, Meyer V, Lott C, Eickert G, Fabricius K, de Beer D, 2007. In situ applications of a new diver-operated motorised microsensor profile. *Environ. Sci. Technol.*, 41, 6210–6215. https://doi.org/10.1021/es070200b

Wei R, Zimmermann W, 2017. Microbial enzymes for the recycling of recalcitrant petroleum-based plastics: How far are we? *Microb. Biotechnol.*, 10(6), 1308–1322 https://doi.org/10.1111/1751–7915.12710

Wiesinger H, Klotz M, Wang Z, Zhao y, Haupt M, Hellweg S, 2020. *The Identity of Oxo-Degradable Plastics and their Use in Switzerland*. Project Report Commissioned by the Federal Office for the Environment. ETH Zürich, 74 p. www.bafu.admin.ch/dam/bafu/en/dokumente/chemikalien/externe-studien-berichte/the-identity-of-oxo-degradable-plastics-and-their-use-in-switzerland.pdf.download.pdf/ETHZ_Report_oxo-degradable_plastics.pdf

Wiewel BV, Lamoree M, 2016. Geotextile composition, application and ecotoxicology – A review. *J. Hazard. Mater.* http://doi.org/10.1016/j.jhazmat.2016.04.060

Woodall LC, Sanchez-Vidal A, Canals M, Paterson GLJ, Coppock R, Sleight V, Calafat A, Rogers AD, Narayanaswamy BE, Thompson RC, 2014. The deep sea is a major sink for microplastic debris. *R. Soc. Open Sci.*, 1, 140317. http://doi.org/10.1098/rsos.140317

World Bank, 2018. *Indonesia Marine Debris Hotspots Rapid Assessment*. http://documents1.worldbank.org/curated/en/983771527663689822/pdf/Indonesia-Marine-Debris-hotspot-rapid-assessment-synthesis-report.pdf, accessed 20 Feb 2021.

Wu L, Kellogg L, Devol AH, Tiedje JM, Zhou J, 2008. Microarray-based characterization of microbial community functional structure and heterogeneity in marine sediments from the Gulf of Mexico. *Appl. Environ. Microbiol.*, 74, 4516–4529. https://doi.org/10.1128/AEM.02751–07

Yang Y, Yang J, Jiang L, 2016. Comment on "A bacterium that degrades and assimilates poly(ethylene terephthalate)." *Science*, 353(6301), 759. doi:10.1126/science.aaf8305

Yadav N, Hakkarainen M, 2021. Degradable or not? Cellulose acetate as a model for complicated interplay between structure, environment and degradation. *Chemosphere*, 265, 128731. https://doi.org/10.1016/j.chemosphere.2020.128731

Ye S, Andrady AL, 1991. Fouling of floating plastic debris under Biscayne Bay exposure conditions. *Mar. Pollut. Bull.*, 22, 608–613. https://doi.org/10.1016/0025–326X(91)90249-R

Yoshida S, Hiraga K, Takehana T, Taniguchi I, Yamaji H, Maeda, Y, . . . Oda, K, 2016. A bacterium that degrades and assimilates poly(ethylene terephthalate). *Science*, 351(6278), 1196–1199. https://doi.org/10.1126/science.aad6359

Zalasiewicz J, Waters CN, Ivar do Sul JA, Corcoran PL, Barnosky AD, Cearreta A, . . . Yonan Y, 2016. The geological cycle of plastics and their use as a stratigraphic indicator of the Anthropocene. *Anthropocene*, 13, 4–17. https://doi.org/10.1016/j.ancene.2016.01.0

Zettler ER, Mincer TJ, Amaral-Zettler LA, 2013. Life in the "Plastisphere": Microbial communities on plastic marine debris. *Environ. Sci. Technol.*, 47, 7137–7146. https://doi.org/10.1021/es401288x

Zobell CE, 1943. The effect of solid surfaces upon bacterial activity. *J. Bacteriol.*, 46, 39–56.

Zumstein MT, Schintlmeister A, Nelson TF, Baumgartner R, Woebken D, Wagner M, Kohler H-PE, McNeill K, Sander M, 2018. Biodegradation of synthetic polymers in soils: Tracking carbon into CO_2 and microbial biomass. *Sci. Adv.*, 4(7), eaas9024. https://doi.org/10.1126/sciadv.aas9024

9

SOURCING AND RE-SOURCING END-OF-USE TEXTILES

Wolfgang Ipsmiller and Andreas Bartl

1 Introduction

1.1 Brief historical outline

The skill of making textiles is one of the oldest crafts of humankind. The wearing of clothing represents an important difference between humans and animals. There is evidence that already 30,000 years ago flax was processed into textile structures (Kvavadze et al., 2009). Over the millennia, textile production was carried out on a very small scale based on fibres derived from crops or animal fur. In the 18th century, the industrial revolution changed textile production massively, and an increasing mechanization and acceleration of the manufacturing process, such as the flying shuttle in 1733 by John Kay, took place (O'Brian, 2019). Despite all the technological advances in textile production, textiles were based exclusively on natural fibres until the 20th century (CIRFS, 2020). The first attempt to produce a man-made fibre, yet never used on an industrial scale, was made by Comte de Chardonnet in 1884 with cellulose nitrate (Liebert, 2010). The solubility of cellulose xanthate in aqueous sodium hydroxide solution was discovered in 1891, but it was not before 1904 when the process was used to finally produce fibres (Liebert, 2010). Still today, the cellulose xanthate route (viscose process) is used for the production of fibres.

It took until the 1930s before fibres based on synthetic polymers were developed and produced on an industrial scale. Polyamide was the first embodiment from this category. In the United States, polyamide 6.6 fibres were marketed by DuPont (Nylon) in the late 1930s. Only a little later in Germany, I. G. Farbenindustrie started the production of polyamide 6 fibres (Carothers, 1937; Kohan, 1986; Matthies & Seydl, 1986). The first developments in polyester, now the most important polymer for fibres, arose in the early 1930s (Carothers & Hill, 1932). However, it

DOI: 10.4324/9781003165385-11

was not before 1941 when a patent was filed on polyesters comprising polyethylene terephthalate (Whinfield & Dickson, 1946), whose property profile was suitable for fibre production. In the following decades, synthetic polymers for fibre production became more and more important. In the mid-90s, the production of synthetic polymer fibres surpassed that of cotton, and today this fibre category accounts for around three quarters of total fibre production (CIRFS, 2016).

1.2   Fibre definitions

Considering the fact that fibres are an important raw material and indispensable for the production of everyday goods, as well as becoming more and more important, some definitions are provided here. BISFA (Bureau International pour la Standardisation des Fibres Artificielles) defines 'fibre' as a morphological term for substances characterized by their flexibility, fineness and high ratio of length to cross-sectional area (BISFA, 2017).

BISFA further discerns subcategories of fibres with regard to their morphology as specified in Table 9.1. On the one hand, the definitions concern fibres intentionally produced for textiles or other purposes. On the other hand, designations are also given for objects, subsumed under the term 'dust', that can occur unintentionally and unavoidably in connection with fibres or fibre-containing products. It stands to reason that the second category has a high risk of entering the environment and therefore should be considered a potential source of microplastics.

TABLE 9.1 BISFA definitions of fibre-related terms

Fibres (intentionally produced)	
Filament	A fibre of very great length; considered as continuous
Staple fibre	A textile fibre of limited but spinnable length
Flock	Very short fibres intentionally produced for other purposes than spinning
Dust (fibre dust)	
Fibre fly	Airborne fibres or parts of fibres (light enough to fly), visible as fibres to the human eye
Particulates from fibres	Airborne particles, not visible as fibres to the naked eye. May or may not be of the polymer material of the fibre or have fibre shape under microscopic view
Fibril	A subdivision of a fibre; can be attached to the fibre or loose
Respirable fibre-shaped particulates (RFP)	Airborne particulates fulfilling the following dimensional conditions: length > 5 μm and diameter < 3 μm and length/diameter ratio of > 3:1

Source: (BISFA, 2017)

1.3 Fibre market

Textiles are primarily made of fibres (EC, 2011) and so the amount of fibres produced gives a very good indication of how many textile products are entering the market. World fibre production has been massively increasing over the last few decades. Within only ten years (2009 to 2019), total fibre production increased by more than 60% from 66 to $107 \cdot 10^6$ t (IVC, 2020; USDA, 2021) as plotted in Figure 9.1. A closer look reveals that growth is mainly due to increase in synthetic fibre production. Between 2009 and 2019, cotton manufacture stagnated between 21 and $28 \cdot 10^6$ t (USDA, 2021). In the same period, both the yield of synthetic (40 to $74 \cdot 10^6$ t) and cellulosic fibres (3.8 to $7.0 \cdot 10^6$ t), increased by 85% (IVC, 2020).

1.4 Fibre materials

It has already been mentioned that until the 20th century fibres were derived from crops or animal fur. These fibres are therefore referred to as natural fibres. Natural fibres consist of bio-based polymers that existed on earth for millions of years. Nature has therefore developed mechanisms to metabolize these materials, i.e. to biodegrade them. For example, cellulose-based fibres (e.g. cotton, hemp, linen, etc.) can be broken down into the constituting monomers by cellulases (Vasconcelos & Cavaco-Paulo, 2006) or protein fibres (e.g. wool) by proteases (Quartinello et al., 2018). These fibres are therefore not a primary source of microplastics.

Starting from the beginning of the 20th century, fibres have been produced also through technical processes, yielding so-called man-made fibres (CIRFS, 2020).

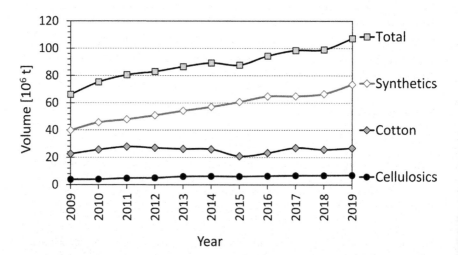

FIGURE 9.1 World production volume of textile fibres (man-made cellulosic and synthetic fibres, cotton) from 2009 to 2019

Source: (IVC, 2020; USDA, 2021).

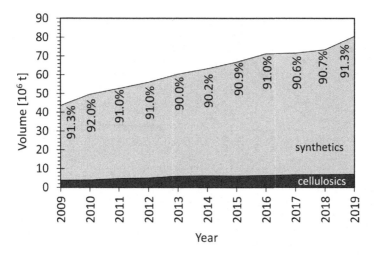

FIGURE 9.2 Production volumes of cellulosic and synthetic man-made fibres. The percent values indicate the annual share of synthetics in the total man-made fibre market

Source: (IVC, 2020)

However, these fibres can be made of both synthetic and natural polymers (mainly cellulose, resulting in cellulose derivatives). Among man-made fibres, those based on synthetic polymers are of paramount importance and exhibit a share of greater than 90% as plotted in Figure 9.2. Within the past decade, the relationship between the two types has not changed in favour of cellulosic man-made fibres, despite the strong overall increase in production volume.

A closer look at synthetic polymer fibres shows that today the PET (Polyethylene terephthalate) fibre is the most abundant synthetic fibre by far. Its production volume increased from $3.4 \cdot 10^6$ t (1975) to $53.7 \cdot 10^6$ t (2017). Despite the distinct increase of total fibre production from $10.6 \cdot 10^6$ t (1975) to $71.6 \cdot 10^6$ t (2017), the share of PET grew from 32% to 83% in the same period (IVC, 2018b, 2020), as sketched in Figure 9.3 (left chart). The loser in this development was PA (Polyamide), which increased in volume from 2.5 to $5.7 \cdot 10^6$ t between 1975 and 2017, but shrank in share from 23% to 8% (IVC, 2018a, 2020), plotted in the right chart of Figure 9.3. PET and PA fibres together dominate the market, contributing with 83% to the synthetic fibre market.

Man-made fibres need not necessarily be based on polymers derived from fossil resources but can, in principle, be produced from bio-based resources. However, petroleum-based polymers are of major importance; 91% or $73.5 \cdot 10^6$ t of $80.7 \cdot 10^6$ t are based on fossil resources. Among natural polymers, only cellulose, predominantly derived from wood, plays an appreciable role. With a production level of $7.0 \cdot 10^6$ t (IVC, 2020), they accounted for 8.7% of the total man-made fibres market. Other bio-based polymers exhibit a volume of $240 \cdot 10^3$ t only and just hold a share of 0.3% (CIRFS, 2020; EUPB, 2021).

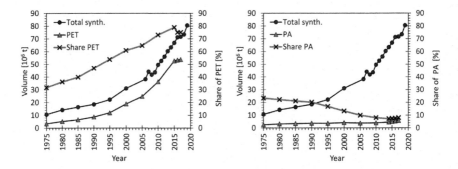

FIGURE 9.3 Production volumes of PET (left chart), PA (right chart) and synthetic fibres in total in 10^6 t and respective share of PET and PA compared to overall production of synthetic fibres over time

Source: (IVC, 2018a, 2018b, 2020)

Bio-based polymers are not necessarily biodegradable. Clearly, cellulose is unequivocally biodegradable. Derivatives, such as cellulose acetate, are non-bio-degradable but play an unimportant role in the fibre sector (EUPB, 2021) and will therefore not be the main target group for the evaluation of fibre release into the environment.

Vice versa, fossil-based synthetic polymers are not necessarily non-biodegradable. However, the polymers mainly used in practice (PET, PA, etc.) indeed do fall into this category (EUPB, 2021). Other – and for that matter biodegradable – polymers within this type of fibres are completely unusual to the market. Hence, it is evident that this type of man-made fibres, while posing the largest amount in fibre production share as mentioned earlier, represents a potential source for the release of microplastics into the environment.

2 From cradle to product

2.1 The textile processing chain

Textiles require a long and complex chain of production and processing steps. As most fibres are based on synthetic polymers, petroleum as a fossil resource is of major importance. However, in practice, natural fibres also depend on non-renewable resources for both, crop cultivation (e.g. fuels for harvesters) and all the more for the subsequent processing chain. Figure 9.4 shows a rough scheme of the textile processing chain and highlights the main processes and (intermediate) products. These processes are described in more detail in the following sections. The sketch, however, does not contain all streams. It is clear that all production steps will require energy, some of them water and will also generate waste and fibre emissions into the environment. An estimation of that can be found in the individual sections.

2.2 Raw material

For the purposes of this section, raw materials are understood to mean the extraction and production of precursors, which are then used for the manufacture of fibres and these raw materials are either based on fossil or bio-based resources.

Figure 9.4 indicates the route in which fibres can be directly derived from renewable resources, chiefly cotton fibres, which amount to around $27 \cdot 10^6$ t (in 2019 (USDA, 2021)). Other materials gathered from bio-based resources are of minor importance. Table 9.2 provides a non-exhaustive overview of possible materials.

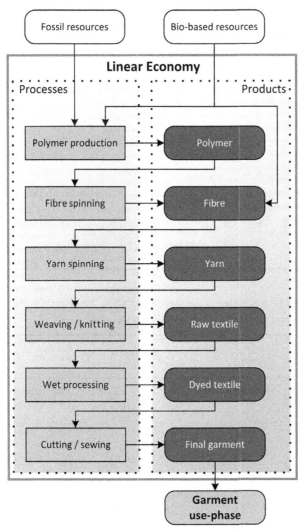

FIGURE 9.4 Simplified scheme of the (linear) textile processing chain from resources to final garment. The sketch does not include all streams, e.g., energy is required for all steps

The second possible route (polymer production, as specified in Figure 9.4) is producing fibres from an intermediate polymer that can originate from fossil and bio-based materials. Table 9.3 summarizes energy use, water consumption and greenhouse gas (GHG) emissions for the production for three synthetic polymers relevant for fibre manufacture. For a comprehensive evaluation of the environmental impact, it is necessary to consider the water consumption that can vary dependent upon processes, materials, and whether they are bio- or fossil-based. Energy consumption can be as high as 129 GJ/t (for PA6.6 (PlasticsEurope, 2014b)) which

TABLE 9.2 Examples of raw materials derived from bio-based resources

Process	Crop/Animal	Product
Cultivation of fibre plants	Cotton	Cotton fibre (Dochia, Sirghie, Kozłowski, & Roskwitalski, 2012)
	Jute	Jute fibre (Roy & Lutfar, 2012)
Livestock farming	Sheep	Wool (Jamshed, 2012)
	Silkworm	Silk (Babu, 2019)
Forestry	Beech	Cellulose (Seisl & Hengstmann, 2021)
Aquaculture or collection	Seaweeds	Alginate (Qin, 2008)
Cultivation/use of plants/ plant parts for energy	Trees, annual plants	Biofuel (ethanol) (Hosseini, 2019)
Cultivation of plants for feedstock	Corn	1,3-Propanediol (Kurian, 2005)
	Castor beans	11-Aminoundecanoic acid (Martino et al., 2014)

TABLE 9.3 Energy use, water consumption and GHG emissions for the production of selected polymers relevant for fibre production

Polymer	Energy [GJ/1 t]	Water [m³/1 t]	GHG [t CO2e/1 t]	Reference
PET	68.6–80.5	48.8	2.19–3.30	(PlasticsEurope, 2017; van der Velden et al., 2014)
PET bio-based	51.0–58.7			(Chen & Patel, 2012)
PA	119–129	1.1–1362	6.42–6.52	(PlasticsEurope, 2014a, 2014b)
PA bio-based	36.7		-0.36	(Pelt, 2016)
PP	71.3–77.9	27.6	1.63–2.18	(Mannheim & Simenfalvi, 2020; PlasticsEurope, 2016)
PP bio-based	41–43		-0.2 to -0.3	(Chen & Patel, 2012)

corresponds to about 3 t of crude oil assuming a caloric value of 42.7 GJ/t (range between 41.0 and 44.4 GJ/t (Fein, Wilson, & Sherman, 1953)). PET as the most relevant polymer for fibre manufacture exhibits an energy consumption between 70 and 80 GJ/t (PlasticsEurope, 2017; van der Velden, Patel, & Vogtländer, 2014) for polymerization (i.e. approx. 2 t crude oil). GHG emissions more or less reflect energy consumption.

One conclusion that can be drawn from the data is the fact that bio-based material can significantly decrease the energy consumption and, in consequence, lower GHG emissions. Due to the deductions for biogenic carbon embedded in polymers, the nominal value can be negative.

2.3 Fibre production

The process 'fibre production' means the conversion of a polymer into fibre. Frequently, this process is referred to as spinning, fibre spinning, or (primary) spinning. The term spinning is ambiguous and can also mean the (secondary) spinning of fibres into a yarn (Section 2.4). In principle, a distinction can be made between two main types of (primary) spinning processes:

- The simplest form is melt-spinning which is feasible for thermoplastic polymers (e.g. PET). In these processes, the polymer is melted and extruded through a spinneret (Murase & Nagai, 1994). During fibre formation, only heat needs to be dissipated. It is reported that the energy consumption for PET and PP (Polypropylene) is just below 100 GJ/t and GHG emissions in the range between 2.8 to 4.1 t CO_{2e}/t (Kalliala & Nousiainen, 1999; Shen & Patel, 2010; Shen, Worrell, & Patel, 2010a, 2010b). The water demand is reported to be between 17.2 and 125 m^3/t (Kalliala & Nousiainen, 1999; Shen & Patel, 2010; Shen et al., 2010a, 2010b). If desired, the fibres can also be textured (i.e. to give man-made fibres a natural-like feel) for which an energy consumption of 15.2–17.5 GJ/t is reported (Kim, Grady, & Hersh, 1983).
- In the case that the polymer is not meltable, a solvent-spinning process will be applied. It is necessary to dissolve the polymer in a suitable solvent. The process can be subdivided into dry spinning (i.e. solvent is evaporated) and wet spinning (i.e. coagulation of the polymer usually takes place in a spinning bath) (Tsurumi, 1994). Solvent spinning requires the use (and recirculation) of a solvent and possibly the use of chemicals for the spinning bath. PAN (Polyacrylonitrile) as a representative of synthetic polymers in this group exhibits higher energy consumption (133 GJ/t), analogously higher GHG emissions (5.4 t CO_{2e}/t) and in particular higher water consumption (3600 m^3) compared to melt spinning (Yacout, Abd El-Kawi, & Hassouna, 2016). In addition, viscose or lyocell fibres, which are based on the natural polymer cellulose, demand a solvent spinning process. The energy consumption is in the range between 70 to 106 GJ/t (Shen & Patel, 2010). Depending on the share of renewable energy, GHG emissions can vary between 1.5 and 5.3 t CO_{2e}/t (Shen & Patel,

2010). Water consumption (300–400 m³/t) of cellulose-based man-made fibres is moderate (Shen & Patel, 2010).

- Cotton fibres, like all other natural fibres, do not require a technical manufacturing process. However, the cultivation of the crops and the extraction of the fibres from them require the use of resources. For cotton, the energy requirement is between 55 and 61 GJ/t and the GHG emissions are between 3.7 to 4.5 t CO_{2e}/t (Chapagain, Hoekstra, Savenije, & Gautam, 2005; Kalliala & Nousiainen, 1999; Shen & Patel, 2010). Cotton is characterized by its extremely high water consumption, which can be up to 22,000 m³/t (Kalliala & Nousiainen, 1999).

2.4 Yarn production

The term yarn production is also called secondary spinning (Section 2.3). BISFA defines yarn as '*a textile product of substantial length and relatively small cross section, composed of fibres with or without twist. This general term covers all the specific types of yarns, e.g. single yarn, multiple wound yarn, filament yarn, spun yarn*' (BISFA, 2017). In practice, yarns are classified according to their physical characteristics as well as performance properties (Alagirusamy & Das, 2015).

Yarn production comprises the several sub-processes (Angelova, Velichkova, Sofronova, Ganev, & Stankov, 2020) and more or less uses electric energy (Palamutcu, 2010) only. The reported values for energy consumption may deviate significantly as they depend upon several circumstances such as spinning system or yarn properties (linear density, twist), but less so upon the fibre material (Angelova et al., 2020). Generally, the specific energy consumption increases with decreasing yarn titre and yarns for weaving (which demand higher twisting) require more energy than such as used for knitting (Hasanbeigi & Price, 2012). In fact, the reported energy consumption may be as low as 5 GJ/t (37 tex yarn) or even up to 81 GJ/t (4.5 tex yarn) (Kim et al., 1983; Koç & Kaplan, 2007; Palamutcu, 2010; van der Velden et al., 2014; Zhang, Liu, Xiao, & Yuan, 2015).

2.5 Fabric production

During this step, a textile fabric is produced which needs further processing to obtain a final product. Regulation (EU) No 1007/2011 states that a '*textile product means any raw, semi-worked, worked, semi- manufactured, manufactured, semi-made-up or made-up product which is exclusively composed of textile fibres, regardless of the mixing or assembly process employed*' (EC, 2011).

On the one hand, yarns are the input material (see Section 2.4) which can be processed into woven or knitted fabric (see Table 9.4). Obviously, nonwoven production will circumvent the energy uptake for yarn formation – if not for special processes such as melt blowing – yet if used as a fabric, quality demands for the nonwoven fabrics require distinct processing steps (Sayed & Parte, 2015) that

TABLE 9.4 Basic types of textile fabrics and their definitions

Term	Definition	Reference
Woven fabric	A fabric produced by interlacing (by weaving on a loom or a weaving machine) a set of warp threads and a set of weft threads, normally at right angles to each other	(ISO, 1976; Stankard, 2015)
Knitted fabric	Generic name applied to textile fabrics in which at least one system of threads is formed into knitted loops and the knitted loops are intermeshed into stitches	(ISO, 1998; Power, 2015)
Nonwovens	Engineered fibrous assembly, primarily planar, which has been given a designed level of structural integrity by physical and/or chemical means, excluding weaving, knitting or papermaking	(ISO, 2019; Mao & Russell, 2015)

TABLE 9.5 Specific energy consumption for weaving and knitting

Process	Yarn titre		Reference
	30 tex	4.5 tex	
Weaving	18 GJ/t	120 GJ/t	(Koç & Çinçik, 2010; van der Velden et al., 2014)
Knitting	0.5 GJ/t	2 GJ/t	(van der Velden et al., 2014)

exhibit energy requirements of their own. Hence, resource needs for nonwoven technologies are not necessarily lower than for yarn formation and weaving or knitting.

Similar to yarn production, there are also large differences in the literature regarding energy consumption of weaving and knitting. On the one hand, knitting is less energy consuming than weaving. On the other hand, the weight of a fabric (grammage), expressed in g/m^2 (ISO, 1997), is a crucial parameter affecting not only density, thickness or strength of the fabric but also energy demand for production. In general, the thinner the textile (i.e. lower grammage), the higher the specific energy consumption, as demonstrated by Table 9.5. The titre of the yarn used has a significant influence on the grammage and is often the only specification.

2.6   Dyeing and finishing

Obtaining suitable properties in a textile fibre or fabric typically necessitates processing steps to introduce colour, remove undesired colour nuances from the natural colour of the material, and to equip surfaces with substances to make the final textile or garment ready for use for the planned purpose. This step comprises processes such as mercerization, dyeing, bleaching, printing or finishing (Global-Standard, 2020b; TextileGuide, 2021).

In addition, during processing it is often mandatory to apply certain chemicals, allowing for reduction of mechanical friction or electrical charge during yarn formation and fabric crafting. Typically, processes such as sizing, desizing or scouring are applied (GlobalStandard, 2020b; TextileGuide, 2021).

While for the first purpose fixation or removal of substances must be permanent, for the second purpose, easy removability after no longer needed is beneficial. Many of these treatment steps are carried out in an aqueous – or other solvent – solution or dispersion, hence are categorized as 'wet processing' (GlobalStandard, 2020b).

Wet processing requires the intensive use of energy (26–108 GJ/t) and resources such as water (100–200 m^3/t) as well as chemicals and significantly emits GHG (1.4–6.8 t CO_{2e}/t) (Dey & Islam, 2015; Kant, 2012; van der Velden et al., 2014; Woolridge, Ward, Phillips, Collins, & Gandy, 2006). In literature it is reported that thousands of different substances are used and that up to 20% of industrial wastewater pollution is caused by these processes (Kant, 2012). It should also be considered that, similar to washing operations, these processes release fibres from the textiles into the environment.

It should be mentioned that many of the used substances are reported harmful or toxic (Kant, 2012; Verma, 2008), which is opposed to positive notions in using sustainably produced and/or bio-degradable natural polymers in fibre production. Thus, efforts are being taken in setting up standards for certification of inoffensive dyestuff, sizing and finishing agents, for example (GlobalStandard, 2020a).

2.7 Textile production

The term 'textile production' in this context means the manufacture of final products such as apparel or home-textiles. The items have to undergo all production steps as described earlier. In practice, the production might deviate from the described order, for instance dyeing can already take place on yarn level instead of fabric level (Liu et al., 2020).

In total the energy consumption adds up to 313 to 960 GJ/t (Steinberger, Friot, Jolliet, & Erkman, 2009), causing GHG emissions between 50 to 123 t CO_{2e}/t (Nolimal, 2018). In the latter case, this means the consumption is equivalent to about 22 t oil per t garment.

2.8 Résumé

Textile production is coupled with a considerable uptake of resources and energy, as has been highlighted in Sections 2.1–2.7. Dependent upon fibre material and processing technology, differences can be noteworthy and it may be necessary to look into particular processes to derive accurate estimations. A general statement can be provided considering the following:

- Textile production is a multiple stage process.
- The individual steps within this chain are closely linked, but for the individual steps, a high variation can be found dependent upon material composition, textile structure and finishing steps.
- Energy consumption for yarn and fabric production is indirectly proportional to the fineness of the structures and also increases with complexity (referring to material and geometric conditions). Energy consumption can vary by one order of magnitude.
- Ecological relevance may originate from the emissions of fibres and/or fibrous dust throughout the entire production chain, use phase as well as the end-of-life phase.
- Naturally, non-bio-degradable polymers (frequently synthetic) will penetrate ecological habitats, accumulate and affect these on a large scale, if no counter-measures are taken.
- Non obviously, the natural fibres and man-made fibres based on natural polymers (i.e. mainly cellulose) that have been found in the environment might impose unknown impact

(Suaria et al., 2020).

The textile production sequence is quite strict. Therefore, any intermediate from recycling processes designated for the manufacture of new textiles is bound to be introduced at a certain level and will need to undergo each step lying ahead to yield the textile, i.e., adding resource uptake to that of the recycling process. A sustainability assessment for a particular end-of-use textile treatment process designed in that way should thus incorporate an estimation of the savings potential based upon the considerations in this section.

It should be pointed out that certain textile applications require processing steps not generally part of the textile production chain. In particular, fibre or textile 'functionalization' may be necessary, meaning the fibres and/or fabrics are equipped with certain properties that they do not otherwise inherit by the fibre material or processing conditions. Bearing in mind the principle of spinning a man-made fibre out of a molten or (physically) dissolved polymer, it is conceivable that one option to implement that is adding functional additives to the spinning mass, such as flame retardants for inherent flame retardancy (Weil & Levchik, 2017) or others (Mohan, 2015; Schill+Seilacher, 2021; Songwon, 2021). Where typical applications lie in work safety and potential shares of those additives are considerable, fibres for consumer textiles, if at all, will contain much lower amounts, and yet are produced in higher quantities. However, additives may be added on the fibre's or fabric's surface in subsequent processing steps, and may be necessary for other purposes such as increasing surface smoothness to reduce friction during processing. It is obvious that additives and their production require resources and may contribute to the emission of non-desired substances, too, and may thus pose certain risks when released during fibre or textile processing or product use.

However, for the abundance of additives and their related profile of production and application, and for the applied quantities differing greatly, it is not expedient to provide a gross estimation of that impact, let alone that data would hardly be contrastable. A consideration in an environmental or economic assessment of production, re-use or recycling processes should be carried out separately and according to presence.

3 End-of-life options

3.1 Fundamentals

Basically, one can distinguish between two types of textile waste.

- Post-industrial
  The term post-industrial waste denotes materials that are generated during the textile manufacturing process. This can take place during yarn formation, spinning and knitting, dyeing and finishing as well as garment making. As textile production frequently takes place in emerging and developing countries, the major amount of post-industrial textile waste is generated there. This means that stringent waste legislation of developed countries is not applicable and little is known about this type of textile waste (Tomovska, Jordeva, Trajković, & Zafirova, 2017). It is estimated that 75% of offcuts are collected (Payne, 2015), but concrete information about the whereabouts of the textile waste is not available. In principle, recycling of post-industrial textile waste is easier than post-consumer textile waste, as producers know which materials they use. The most important key factors are ease and costs of sorting and the impediments to sorting (Tomovska et al., 2017).

- Post-consumer
  The term post-consumer stands for textiles that are disposed of by consumers after use. Any re-use or recycling option requires a separate collection of end-of-life textiles. In contrast to post-industrial waste, post-consumer textile waste consists of various types of textiles composed of numerous fibre types. The fibre composition does not fully reflect the use of polymers for fibre production (Figure 9.1). A study from 2015 (Ward, Hewitt, & Russell, 2013) reports that cotton shows a share of about 55%, which is much higher than its share in total fibre production (24% in 2015 (CIRFS, 2020)). PET, which covered 59% of total fibre production in 2015 (CIRFS, 2020; IVC, 2018b), exhibits only a share of about 23% in collected post-consumer textiles (Ward et al., 2013). The proportion of acrylic, viscose, wool or polyamide fibres is in the single digits. Polypropylene and other polymer types were grouped under 'other fibres' in the study and together accounted for less than 3%. The study further states that almost 64% of the collected garments consisted of a single fibre material (Ward et al., 2013).

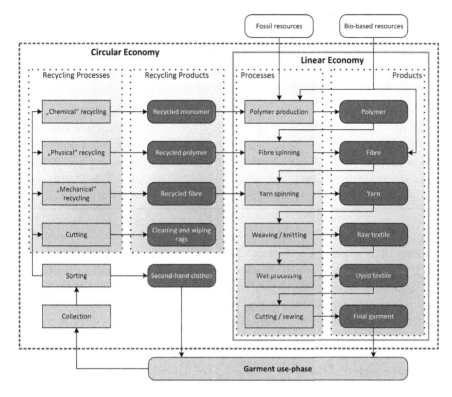

FIGURE 9.5 Simplified scheme of the textile processing chain and possible routes for re-use, recycling and recovery

The sketch shown in Figure 9.5 considers post-consumer textile waste. It shows the most important routes to feed back end-of-life textiles into the value chain. It is evident that for all the alternative processes, collection and sorting are inevitable.

3.2 Legal background

The management of waste has developed over the last few decades. In Europe, modern waste management began in the 1970s with the first directive on waste. Since then numerous laws and regulations on waste have been introduced and, as a matter of fact, the share of waste bound for landfill has decreased and the proportion of recycled waste has increased (Bartl, 2014). However, textiles have not been in the focus of EU legislation until recently. It was only in 2018 that the Directive (EU) 2018/852 considered end-of-use textiles as part of municipal waste (EC, 2018). Amongst other aims, it requires that by 2025 a separate collection of textiles will be mandatory, as well as initiatives to promote repair and re-use of textiles to be launched.

TABLE 9.6 Amount of separately collected post-consumer textiles in relation to amount put on market for selected countries

Country	Year	Collected Amount of End-of-Life Clothing			References
		[1000 t]	[Mass %]	[kg/Capita]	
Germany	2018	1,271	78	15.3	(bsve, 2020)
Denmark	2016	37	43	6.4	(Nørup, Pihl, Damgaard, & Scheutz, 2018)
Netherlands	2018	136	45	7.9	(Miljøstyrelsen, 2020)
France	2018	249	38	3.7	(Re_fashion, 2020a)
Austria	2015	29	27	3.4	(BMLRT, 2017)

Even if it is not yet foreseeable how the legal framework conditions will look like in detail and which recycling processes will be available in the future, an efficient collection and sorting system is a basic prerequisite for the re-use and recycling of end-of-life textiles. A corresponding financing system such as Extended Producer Responsibility (EPR) or deposit systems will be inevitable in order to shift the costs, which will be higher than at present, from the general public (disposal via municipal waste) to the polluter (as is already the case in the packaging sector) (Lindhqvist & Lifset, 1998). It is also clear that the financing system to be implemented must not only finance collection and sorting, but should also create incentives for avoidance, longer useful life, repair or re-use. This has also already been called for by the Commission in Directive (EU) 2018/851 (EC, 2018) and COM(2020) 98 (EC, 2020). In the EU, France was a forerunner and already introduced an EPR system in December 2008 (Re_fashion, 2020a).

3.3 Collection

Post-consumer textiles arise in many areas and must be collected separately (Table 9.6). In the event that textiles are mixed with municipal waste, they become contaminated and are thus unsuitable for a re-use or recycling processes. Today, in most cases, this separate collection takes place on a volunteer basis and is financed by the sales of second-hand clothing. Actually, collectors will only focus on re-usable items and other products are not target of textile collection. As mentioned earlier, this will change in the near future.

3.4 Sorting

Just as separate collection of end-of-life textiles is essential, the collected textiles must be sorted according to their re-use and recycling possibilities. In principle, three main fractions are generated (Nørup et al., 2018):

(a) Re-use
(b) Recycling
(c) Waste

The fraction feasible for re-use (a) can be further subdivided. On the one hand, good-quality items can be sold in Europe (even up to 26% (Karigl, Bernhardt, & Hauer, 2019)). However, the report does not further specify the general situation in Europe, and textiles collected in Austria or Germany, for example, can only be resold locally in the low single-digit percentage range. Most of the re-useable items are exported to emerging and developing markets. The more precisely the sorting is matched to the customer's needs, the more items can be set for high-quality and high-price re-use. It is reported that in Germany on average 154, sometimes even up to 350, sub-fractions are generated (Korolkow, 2014).

A comparison of the energy consumed for garment production reveals that the sorting process only consumes minor amounts. In total, for electricity (machinery, lighting, etc.), gas (heating) and fuel (trucks), merely 0.1 GJ/t of energy are required with sorting (Nørup et al., 2018). Furthermore, baling packaging (2.6–3.3 kg/1 t sorted textiles) and baling wire (0.7–0.8 kg/1 t sorted textiles) are used in quite low amounts.

In order to identify and select reusable items, especially those suitable for sale in the EU, manual sorting employing skilled workforce is essential (Botticello, 2012). Despite minor resource consumption for operation, in view of high labour costs in Europe, sorting is a costly process and is preferably located in EU countries (e.g., Lithuania) with lower wage levels. In 2016, for example, sorting 1 t of end-of-life textiles in Vilnius cost €161, with labour costs alone accounting for 91% (i.e. €147 (Nørup et al., 2018)).

In recent years, technologies for automatic sorting have been evolving and currently some systems are on the verge of market introduction. Most of the systems are based on near infrared (NIR). Using NIR, textiles can be sorted into different fractions according to their fibre composition. Thus, pure fractions (e.g., 100% cotton, 100% polyester, etc.) and mixed fractions (e.g., cotton/polyester) can be generated. However, it must be kept in mind that small amounts of fibres in the textile may fall below the detection limit. For example, in practice, it is usually not possible to detect spandex in the range of less than 3% as it yet often occurs in textiles (Miljøstyrelsen, 2020; Re_fashion, 2020b).

Figure 9.6 shows the share of the generated fractions from manual sorting. Nowadays, sorting is primarily aimed at generating fractions for re-use, as recycling technologies are poorly developed and hardly profitable. The share of re-useable items ranges between 60 and 70%. The share of recycling ranges between 20 and 30% (cleaning and wiping rags – C&W rags – account for recycling) whereas it is not further specified which technologies are used. Finally, around 10% of the collected textiles are not feasible for re-use and recycling, and are either recovered (i.e., incineration with energy recovery) or, if legally permitted, landfilled.

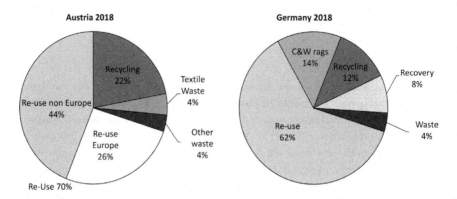

FIGURE 9.6 Main fractions of end-of-life textiles after sorting processes

Source: (bsve, 2020; Karigl et al., 2019)

3.5   Re-use

Re-use in the sense of Directive 98/2008/EC (EC, 2008) requires that the items are used for the same purpose they were intended for, which means the use as clothing, here second-hand (SHC). SHC feasible for high-income countries demand that they are more or less unworn, correspond to current fashion trends and are ideally from well-known brands. Considering a selling price of €1–2 (Allwood, Laursen, Malvido de Rodríguez, & Bocken, 2006) for a shirt (a few 100 g) earns revenues of 10,000 €/t. However, as already mentioned earlier, only a small share can be re-sold on the spot (Hawley, 2006).

The major fraction of SHC is sold whereat the revenues are used to fund collection, sorting and disposal. Charity organizations will use the surplus for a good purpose. In recent years, the financing model has reached its limits. Prices already dropped from 250–350 €/t in 2015 to 200–260 €/t in 2019 (Germany, (bsve, 2020)). However, in March 2020 Kenya has imposed an import ban on SHC, justified by protective measures against COVID-19 (KEBS, 2020). Higher collection volumes during COVID-19 lockdowns in several countries and dwindling sales markets have brought the system to a standstill (Schaart & Guillot, 2020).

The pros and cons of exporting SHC to Africa have been the subject of controversial debate for several years. The fact is that from the 1980s to the 2000s, the Kenyan textile industry collapsed while Kenya imported more and more second-hand clothes (Frazer, 2008). The extent, to which there is a causal relationship, is not clear. The East African Community (Burundi, Kenya, Rwanda, South Sudan, Tanzania and Uganda) started to introduce an increasing taxation on second-hand clothes. On the one hand, this offers the chance to promote domestic textile production in Africa but, on the other hand, might affect people who cannot afford prices for new clothing (Bryan, 2019; Kagome Wetengere, 2018).

It remains to be seen how SHC exports to Africa will develop in the future. Although the effects of the SARS-CoV-2 pandemic on textile trade will revert with a normalizing situation, new EU legislation will also have a massive impact, and it is not yet clear whereto the matter will develop.

3.6 Recycling

The utilization and treatment of textiles at the end of their useful life is complex, let alone ambiguous definitions of what is or is not categorized as textile waste. In most cases, the composition of textile waste may vary within a wide range, yet there are many possibilities to try to tackle the issue. Wang in 2010 already provided an insight into types of waste and treatment technologies with a focus on carpets, yet with a global depiction (Wang, 2010). It is the aim of this section to discuss the technologies or methods in a slightly different way, focusing on fabrics, and providing an insight in what, in our view, will be the most important and/or widely used technologies in the future or which recent developments could establish a more thorough reclamation of valuable (EURATEX, 2004) components.

3.6.1 Cutting

The term 'cutting' in this context means that end-of-life textiles are cut into pieces of suitable size and are used as cleaning and wiping (C&W) rags. During this procedure, the physical and the chemical constitution of the textile is largely maintained. As the resulting product is not used for the same purpose it was conceived for, this practice will not account for re-use (EC, 2008).

Textiles to be cut into C&W rags need to consist largely of hydrophilic fibres (cotton, linen, viscose, etc.). The size of the rags should be in the range of 20 cm × 30 cm, and components other than textiles such as fastenings, eyelets or zippers must be removed (DIN, 2005). The process is based on manual labour and therefore costly. It is reported that long-term unemployed and special education graduates with developmental delays and other impairments are involved in the manufacture of C&W rags (Sperger, 2021b). Prices are reported to range around 2,000 €/t (Sperger, 2021a).

The so-produced C&W rags are single use products and have to be compared with multi-use rags made from virgin resources in terms of their environmental impact. Hardly any literature is available on this topic. However, a study of MIPS (Material Input Per Unit of Service (Ritthoff, Rohn, & Liedtke, 2002)) claims advantages of single-use C&W rags from end-of-life textiles over multiuse rags from virgin materials (Irgang & Leiler, 2003).

C&W rags will not comply with efforts to implement closed-loop recycling options or multi-cascade use, as it adds one step to the product life cycle only.

3.6.2 Mechanical disintegration

The term 'disintegration' in this context means that the fabric is broken down into its basic constituent, namely fibres. The process starts with a pre-opening (i.e., cutting) of the end-of-life textiles in a shredder followed by a unit that opens the fabric, a so-called tearing line. The unit consists of a set of drums (e.g., two to six opening sections, (Laroche, 2021)) that are equipped with hardened metal pins and carrier rollers. With each pass through a section, the fibres in the fabric are loosened and individual fibres are released. However, due to the mechanical stress, fibre lengths are reduced and a considerable fraction of dust occurs (Gulich, 2006).

In principle, the so-reclaimed fibres can be used for a de-novo yarn formation and subsequent weaving or knitting. However, as the input stream is frequently not well defined (i.e., various fibre materials, different colours) and massively damaged, the quality of the recycling yarns is quite low. As a matter of fact, in Germany, about 95% of reclaimed fibres are not processed into yarns but directly into non-woven material (Gulich, 2006).

3.6.3   Grinder-cutting

In this context, the term 'grinder-cutting' means that textile waste is processed in a cutting mill and flock (Table 9.1) is produced. The process can also work a broad spectrum of input materials such as damaged or dirty garment or fluff, either from tire recycling or shredder light fraction (Bartl, 2011).

Ground flock can be used as additive in construction materials (Bahardoust, Marini, Neubacher, Mihalyi, & Bartl, 2006; Bartl, Wistuba, Marini, Spiegl, & Blab, 2010; Reinthaller, Bartl, Marini, & Haner, 2011). Even if the production of ground flock corresponds to a (one-stage) cascade utilization rather than recycling, it is favourable over incineration.

3.6.4   Recycling options on polymer level

Processes falling in this category use melting or dissolution of the textile material, either with or without intermediate production (granules, etc.). Because cellulose dissolution is complex, most approaches refer to synthetic polymers, apart from ionic liquids where literature holds several research projects (e.g. (Haslinger, Hummel, Anghelescu-Hakala, Määttänen, & Sixta, 2019)). Conditions are set as to maintain the polymer structure, and the prepared secondary polymer materials can be processed into fibres in melt- or solvent-spinning processes as described in Section 2.3. Currently, the typical application is bottle-to-fibre, using PET bottles as a polymer source (PCI, 2013; Rengel, 2017). However, the methods are not widely used in textile recycling, as they necessitate pure materials. The tolerance for impurities out of molten masses or polymer solutions is limited to the capacity of filtration units and thus directly linked to effort for operation, changeover time and, eventually, operating costs. This means that high shares of materials other than the main component will render these processes unfeasible, which rules out the direct feed of multi-material textiles. In the end, if multi-material textiles contain components not separable by melting or dissolution, process options of this kind will generally fail, due to (mostly undesired and permanent) mixing of materials.

One positive example is the recycling of cotton into high-quality lyocell fibres which is already carried out on an industrial scale and marketed under the brand REFIBRA™ (Lenzing, 2018). However, the process demands pure cotton waste and thus currently only post-industrial textile wastes (cutting from garment making) are a feasible input stream.

However, recently, sophisticated processes have been described using switching hydrophilicity solvents to extract PET from a textile blend (Yousef et al., 2020), possibly one way of reducing the separation problems for certain material combinations in dissolution processes.

3.6.5   Preparation of disintegrated cellulose

In literature, several attempts can be found distinctively concerning the disintegration of cellulose, mainly from cotton fibres from pure cotton fabric or blended fabrics also containing cotton as well as lignocellulosic biomass. There are efforts to use methods to treat the latter – although substrates are different, yet all contain cellulose – for fibrous waste treatment. The processes already discussed generally use catalytic procedures (Hou, Ling, Shi, & Yan, 2019) and/or thermo-baric steam treatment or 'steam explosion', hitherto known mainly from bio-refinery applications (Pavlov, Denisova, Makarova, Budaeva, & Sakovich, 2015; Ruiz et al., 2020), where the cellulose polymer structure is maintained for the most part, but the external structure is made void. This leads to a powder-like cellulose polymer substance known as microcrystalline cellulose that is reported to be used in the pharmaceutical industry (Uesu, Pineda, & Hechenleitner, 2000).

3.6.6   Recycling options on monomer level (including feedstock recycling)

Where processes for direct fibre retrieval or recycling on polymer level are not possible, hydrolytic or, more general, lytic methods using thermal, chemical, biochemical operations or combinations thereof can be applied and processes can comprise catalysts (Sinha, Patel, & Patel, 2010). The physical as well as the chemical constitution of the input material are being altered. In most cases, this means depolymerization into constituting monomers, if the processes applied are selective, or any low-molecular-weight substances, if the processes are unselective.

Embodying the latter, textile wastes may be subjected to pyrolysis reactions (Miranda, Bustos, & Vasile, 2007) or gasification, yielding pyrolysis gasses or fuels, however, all these operations are somewhat exempt from genuine recycling options as the products generated cannot be re-fed into the textile production chain as discussed in Section 3.1. Increasing selectivity of depolymerization processes will enable the production of synthesis gas, base chemicals such as alcohols, polyalcohols (Guo, Lindqvist, & de la Motte, 2018; Nikles & Farahat, 2005), amines or ionic liquids (Asaadi et al., 2016). A relatively new process principle in textile recycling, exhibiting remarkably high selectiveness – or even component-exclusivity – is enzymatic hydrolysis that has been common for some time in textile and detergent industry for surface modification and reduction of pilling during washing (Galante & Formantici, 2003). These processes use certain classes of enzymes as biocatalysts to hydrolyze a substrate selectively under comparably mild reaction conditions. Typically, a range of enzymes needs to act synergistically, as described, for example, for cellulosic material (Yang, Dai, Ding, & Wyman, 2011).

Today, research & development in the use of enzymes for textile recycling processes is concretizing, and projects are proposing methods for the conversion of polymers into monomers for subsequent use as a feedstock for fine chemicals or re-polymerization into precursors for fibre production. Research covers technologies for the depolymerization of synthetic polymers such as PET (e.g. (Kawai, Kawabata, & Oda, 2019)), protein fibres (Quartinello et al., 2018) or cellulosic material yielding glucose monomer (e.g. (Vecchiato et al., 2018)). In that, the latter seem the most developed, for ready-to-use enzyme preparations are commercially available (Novozymes, 2021).

3.6.7 Textile recycling cascades

In the view of legal developments outlined in Section 3.2, not least due to known environmental concerns, discussion gains momentum in how to set up routines that would facilitate the recycling of textiles, reintroducing substitutes comparable to virgin materials comprising material blends (Rengel, 2017). Obviously, since using treatment methods yielding an entry point lower within the textile processing chain will eventually reduce the overall savings potential (for the consumption of resources, energy, water, emissions and other parameters), it is generally advisable to deploy those processes with the most reasonable relation of cost-benefit and environmental impacts. Yet, using single recycling processes with product output streams situated at the head of the processing chain often leads to recycling products of inferior quality, thus reducing the overall effectiveness and sustainability of the recycling attempt (Gould, 2015; Payne, 2015; Wang, 2010). Frequently, prior to those attempts, the quality of the fabric to be recycled still is within a high range, since textiles, if disposed of due to appearance of visible defects in the fabric (cracks, abrasions, holes, etc.), did not experience overall loss of functions or integrity.

In fact, fibres or contained additives stay functional largely if, for example, recycling in this regard needs to consider the textile as conjunction of various functions rather than an entity itself. Using this approach, a detour via the implementation of a treatment cascade of the options discussed in the previous sections, although reducing the savings potential for one compound, may increase the net surplus.

Researchers noticing that suggest that elaborate chemical recycling steps may be implemented beneficially as pre-treatment methods, concerning blended fabrics in particular. One project recently suggested is the alkaline hydrolysis of polyester from cotton/PET blends to obtain a pure cotton fraction (Palme, Peterson, de la Motte, Theliander, & Brelid, 2017). Two other studies attempted the opposite by enzymatic hydrolysis (Li, Hu, Du, & Lin, 2019) or acidic hydrolysis with mechanical agitation (Ouchi, Toida, Kumaresan, Ando, & Kato, 2010) of cotton and reclaiming PET from a blended textile. A third study used ionic liquids to bring cellulose from a post-consumer cotton/PET blend into solution, liberating the PET share and spinning the cellulose into micro-fibres (Haslinger et al., 2019). Reducing one component by the reduction to monomers can thus enable the preparation of a second component for possible re-introduction into the textile processing chain. Yet another project applied enzymatic hydrolysis on a bi-component fabric comprising a synthetic and a flame-retardant cellulose derivative fibre (a protection textile), reclaiming the additive and synthetic fibre in a mechanical approach (Ipsmiller et al., 2019). Once again, enzymatic processes are highly selective, which provides two advantages. One, the risk of damage to other components not to be altered is low. Second, the de-polymerization products within the reaction solution are pure and suitable for various downstream processes such as fermentation (Vecchiato et al., 2019), provided that the solution can be used as such or separation steps will allow for a concentration.

4   Summary and conclusions

This communication is essentially divided into two parts. On the one hand, the route from cradle to final textiles is described in Section 2. It is evident that large amounts of resources are consumed and significant quantities of GHG are emitted. Unfortunately, the literature often lacks information on important details such as fibre fineness, which limits the comparability of the data. This lack on information seems to be the reason for large deviations between various studies. The cumulative energy requirement for the final garment ranges between approximately 170 GJ/t (van der Velden et al., 2014) and 960 GJ/t (Steinberger et al., 2009). The difference in the cumulative energy requirement of textiles made of various fibre materials is, however, rather limited (van der Velden et al., 2014). Cotton exhibits a share of 25% compared to total fibre production (IVC, 2020; USDA, 2021) but its proportion is 55% in post-consumer textile waste (Ward et al., 2013). Despite this large deviation, it is evident that man-made fibres will gain importance over cotton, which is demonstrated by the growth rates shown in Table 9.7. In the future, the share of cotton will further decrease at the expense of man-made fibres.

Even though the environmental impact of cotton and impact of man-made fibres are in a similar range, cotton has a clear advantage in terms of biodegradability. Man-made synthetic fibres are almost exclusively based on fossil resources, and the most-used polymers (PET, PA, PAN and PP) are not biodegradable. Textiles made thereof represent a potential source of fibre emissions

TABLE 9.7 Production of man-made fibres (synthetics and cellulosics) and cotton in 2009 and 2019, and average growth rate within the period

	Synthetics	Cellulosics	Cotton
Production in 2009 [10^6 t]	39.8	3.8	22.5
Production in 2019 [10^6 t]	73.5	7.0	26.8
Average growth 2009 to 2019 [%]	5.9	8.8	1.2

Source: (IVC, 2020; USDA, 2021)

into the environment and can even be found on Mount Everest (Napper et al., 2020). Even though the growth of man-made cellulosic fibres has been considerable over the last decade, the ratio between cellulosic and synthetic fibres has remained constant (Figure 9.2). Not least because of the rapidly growing overall fibre market, textiles pose an increasing problem in terms of microfiber emissions to nature. While during the sewage process in wastewater treatment plants the release of fibrous fragments in the millimetre (i.e. length) range can effectively be avoided, no barrier will prevent the effluents of factories or laundries from carrying such fibrous debris into the environment when wastewater treatment is not implemented. Emissions in the lower millimetre or sub-millimetre range, however, will pose a problem, in particular when airborne. Due to the extreme surface-to-volume ratio and adding the fact that fibre densities are typically low, fibres, quite in contrast to 'classical' particles, are greatly susceptible to wind drag, which can lead to their spreading over a remarkably large area or volume (Piribauer, Laminger, Ipsmiller, Koch, & Bartl, 2019). These issues apply whenever fibre release from worn textiles – or, more generally, textiles exposed to the open – can be expected which is usually the case, and therefore need to be taken into account.

On the other hand, Section 3 summarizes the state-of-the-art methods and points out possible development perspectives to feed back materials from end-of-life textiles into the value chain. As recycling technologies are still in their infancy, little information is available about their environmental impact. It was thus not possible to compare virgin products with recycled products in terms of energy consumption or GHG emission. Nevertheless, it can be shown which approaches exist today for the recycling of textiles. Massive changes are expected in this area in the coming years.

Even if recycling will gain more importance in the near future, it is evident that this approach will only fight the symptoms. Waste prevention must indeed be implemented, also in the field of textiles. However, currently the fast fashion business model counteracts these efforts, and despite positive developments in facilitating recycling to reroute valuable components into the production chain, actions have to be taken to reduce the ever growing amount of textiles put on the market (West, Saunders, & Willet, 2021).

List of Abbreviations

Abbreviation	Explanation
C&W (rags)	Cleaning and wiping (rags)
EPR	Extended producer responsibility
GHG	Greenhouse gasses
MIPS	Material input per unit of service
PA	Polyamide
PA6	Polyamide (25038–54–4) derived from caprolactam
PA66	Polyamide (32131–17–2) derived from hexamethylenediamine and adipic acid
PAN	Polyacrylonitrile (25014–41–9)
PET	Polyethylene terephthalate (25038–59–9)
PP	Polypropylene (9003–07–0)
SHC	Second-hand clothes

References

Alagirusamy, R., Das, A., 2015. Chapter 8 – Conversion of fibre to yarn: An overview. In R. Sinclair (Ed.), *Textiles and Fashion* (pp. 159–189). Cambridge, UK: Woodhead Publishing.

Allwood, J.M., Laursen, S., Malvido de Rodríguez, C., Bocken, N., 2006. *Well Dressed? The Present and Future Sustainability of Clothing and Textiles in the United Kingdom.* Cambridge, UK: Institute for Manufacturing, University of Cambridge.

Angelova, R.A., Velichkova, R., Sofronova, D., Ganev, I., Stankov, P., 2020. Consumption of electric energy in the production of cotton textiles and garments. *ICTTE 2020*, 1031, 012030. https://doi.org/10.1088/1757-899X/1031/1/012030

Asaadi, S., Hummel, M., Hellsten, S., Härkäsalmi, T., Ma, Y., Michud, A., Sixta, H., 2016. Renewable high-performance fibers from the chemical recycling of cotton waste utilizing an ionic liquid. *ChemSusChem*, 9(22), 3250–3258. https://doi.org/10.1002/cssc.201600680

Babu, K.M., 2019. Chapter 1 – Introduction to silk and sericulture. In K. M. Babu (Ed.), *Silk* (2nd ed., pp. 1–29). Cambridge, UK: Woodhead Publishing.

Bahardoust, M.H., Marini, Ingo, Neubacher, F., Mihalyi, B., Bartl, A., 2006. *Verfahren zur Verwertung von Polymerarmierten Elastomerprodukten.* Austrian Patent AT413355B.

Bartl, A., 2011. From fluff to stuff: An economic solution? *Waste Manag. World*, 12, 14–18.

Bartl, A., 2014. Moving from recycling to waste prevention: A review of barriers and enables. *Waste Manag. Res.*, 32(9_suppl), 3–18. https://doi.org/10.1177/0734242X14541986

Bartl, A., Wistuba, M., Marini, I., Spiegl, M., Blab, R., 2010. *Method for Producing an Aggregate for Producing Building Materials.* European Patent EP2146938B1.

BISFA, 2017. *Terminology of Man-Made Fibres.* Bureau International pour la Standardisation des Fibres Artificielles, Brussels/BE.

BMLRT, 2017. *Federal Waste Management Plan 2017 Part 2.* Retrieved from Vienna/AT: www.bmk.gv.at/dam/jcr:4c825332-43bc-4989-bb9b-b46bd0d35bd1/Federal_Waste_Management_Plan_2017_Part_2.pdf

Botticello, J., 2012. Between classification, objectification, and perception: Processing secondhand clothing for recycling and reuse. *Textile*, 10(2), 164–183. https://doi.org/10.2752/175183512X13315695424356

Bryan, C., 2019. *Secondhand Clothing Import Ban in the EAC.* Retrieved from https://borgenproject.org/secondhand-clothing-import-ban-in-the-eac/

bsve., 2020. *Demand, Consumption, Reuse and Recycling of Clothing and Textiles in Germany.* Retrieved from Bonn/DE: www.bvse.de/dateien2020/2-PDF/02-Presse/06-Textil/2020/bvse-Textilstudie_2020_eng.pdf

Carothers, W.H., 1937. US Patent No. US2071250 U. P. Office.

Carothers, W.H., Hill, J.W., 1932. Studies on polymerization and ring formation. XV. Artificial fibers from synthetic linear condensation superpolymers. *J. Am. Chem. Soc.*, 54(4), 1579–1587. https://doi.org/10.1021/ja01343a051

Chapagain, A., Hoekstra, A., Savenije, H., Gautam, R., 2005. *The Water Footprint of Cotton Consumption.* Integrated Assessment. Value of Water Research Report Series No. 18, UNESCO-IHE Delft, Delft/NL.

Chen, G.-Q., Patel, M.K., 2012. Plastics derived from biological sources: Present and future: A technical and environmental review. *Chem. Rev.*, 112(4), 2082–2099. https://doi.org/10.1021/cr200162d

CIRFS, 2016. *Information on Man-made Fibres.* Brussels, BE: European Man-Made Fibres Association.

CIRFS, 2020. *Information on Man-made Fibres* (Vol. 55th). Brussels, BE: European Man-Made Fibres Association.

Dey, S., Islam, A., 2015. A review on textile wastewater characterization in Bangladesh. *Resources and Environment*, 5(1), 15–44.

DIN, 2005. *Putzlappen.* DIN 61650:2005–04. Berlin/DE: Deutsches Institut für Normung e.V.

Dochia, M., Sirghie, C., Kozłowski, R.M., Roskwitalski, Z., 2012. Chapter 2 – Cotton fibres. In R.M. Kozłowski (Ed.), *Handbook of Natural Fibres* (Vol. 1, pp. 11–23). Cambridge, UK: Woodhead Publishing.

EC, 2008. Richtlinie 2008/98/EG des Europäischen Parlaments und des Rates vom 19. November 2008 über Abfälle und zur Aufhebung bestimmter Richtlinien. *Official Journal of the European Union*, 51(L 312), 3–30.

EC, 2011. Verordnung (EU) Nr. 1007/2011 des Europäischen Parlaments und des Rates vom 27. September 2011 über die Bezeichnungen von Textilfasern und die damit zusammenhängende Etikettierung und Kennzeichnung der Faserzusammensetzung von Textilerzeugnissen und zur Aufhebung der Richtlinie 73/44/EWG des Rates und der Richtlinien 96/73/EG und 2008/121/EG des Europäischen Parlaments und des Rates Text von Bedeutung für den EWR. *Amtsblatt der Europäischen Union*, L 272. https://doi.org/10.3000/19770642.L_2011.272.deu

EC, 2018. Richtlinie (EU) 2018/851 des Europäischen Parlaments und des Rates vom 30. Mai 2018 zur Änderung der Richtlinie 2008/98/EG über Abfälle Official. *Journal of the European Union*, 61(L 150), 109–140.

EC, 2020. *A New Circular Economy Action PlanFor a Cleaner and More Competitive Europe.* Communication from the Commission to the European Parliament, the European Council, the Council, the European Economic and Social Committee and the Committee of the Regions, COM(2020) 98 final.

EUPB, 2021. *Bioplastics Market Data.* Retrieved from www.european-bioplastics.org/market/

EURATEX, 2004. *European Technology Platform for the Future of Textiles and Clothing: A Vision for 2020.* Brussels, BE: Euratex – European Apparel and Textile Organisation.

Fein, R.S., Wilson, H.I., Sherman, J., 1953. Net heat of combustion of petroleum hydrocarbons. *Ind. Eng. Chem.*, 45(3), 610–614.

Frazer, G., 2008. Used-clothing donations and apparel production in Africa. *Eco. J.*, 118(532), 1764–1784. https://doi.org/10.1111/j.1468-0297.2008.02190.x

Galante, Y.M., Formantici, C., 2003. Enzyme applications in detergency and in manufacturing industries. *Curr. Org. Chem.*, 7(13), 1399–1422. https://doi.org/10.2174/138527 2033486468

GlobalStandard, 2020a. *Global Organic Textile Standards (GOTS)*. Version 6. Retrieved from www.global-standard.org/images/resource-library/documents/standard-and-manual/gots_version_6_0_en1.pdf

GlobalStandard, 2020b. *Wet-Processing*. Retrieved from https://global-standard.org/certification-and-labelling/who-needs-to-be-certified/wet-processing

Gould, H., 2015. Waste is so last season: Recycling clothes in the fashion industry. *The Guardian*. Retrieved from www.theguardian.com/sustainable-business/sustainable-fashion-blog/2015/feb/26/waste-recycling-textiles-fashion-industry

Gulich, B., 2006. Development of products made of reclaimed fibres. In Y. Wang (Ed.), *Recycling in Textiles* (pp. 117–136). Cambridge, UK: Woodhead Publishing Limited.

Guo, Z., Lindqvist, K., de la Motte, H., 2018. An efficient recycling process of glycolysis of PET in the presence of a sustainable nanocatalyst. *J. Appl. Polym. Sci.*, 135(21), 46285. https://doi.org/10.1002/app.46285

Hasanbeigi, A., Price, L., 2012. A review of energy use and energy efficiency technologies for the textile industry. *Renew. Sust. Energ. Rev.*, 16(6), 3648–3665. https://doi.org/10.1016/j.rser.2012.03.029

Haslinger, S., Hummel, M., Anghelescu-Hakala, A., Määttänen, M., Sixta, H., 2019. Upcycling of cotton polyester blended textile waste to new man-made cellulose fibers. *Waste Manage.*, 97, 88–96. https://doi.org/10.1016/j.wasman.2019.07.040

Hawley, J., 2006. Textile recycling: A system perspective. In Y. Wang (Ed.), *Recycling in Textiles* (pp. 7–24). Cambridge, UK: Woodhead Publishing Limited.

Hosseini, M., 2019. Chapter 1 – A perspective on bioprocessing for biofuels, bio-based chemicals, and bioproducts. In M. Hosseini (Ed.), *Advanced Bioprocessing for Alternative Fuels, Biobased Chemicals, and Bioproducts* (pp. 1–11). Cambridge, UK: Woodhead Publishing.

Hou, W., Ling, C., Shi, S., Yan, Z., 2019. Preparation and characterization of microcrystalline cellulose from waste cotton fabrics by using phosphotungstic acid. *Int. J. Biol. Macromol.*, 123, 363–368. https://doi.org/10.1016/j.ijbiomac.2018.11.112

Ipsmiller, W., Piribauer, B., Vecchiato, S., Andreas, B., Gübitz, G., Ruppert, G., 2019. Circular economy solution for flame-retardant protective clothing. *Tech. Text.*, 62(3), 185–188.

Irgang, G., Leiler, W., 2003. Erfolg mit Altkleidern Warum in manchen Fällen Einweg ressourceneffizienter sein kann alsMehrweg. In F. Schmidt-Bleek (Ed.), *Der ökologische Rucksack: Wirtschaft für eine Zukunft mit Zukunft* (pp. 87–90). Stuttgart, Germany: Verlag, Hirzel.

ISO, 1976. *Textiles – Weaves – Definitions of General Terms and Basic Weaves* (Vol. ISO 3572). Vernier, Geneva/CH: International Organization for Standardization.

ISO, 1997. *Textiles – Fabrics – Determination of Mass Per Unit Area Using Small Samples* (Vol. ISO 12127). Vernier, Geneva/CH: International Organization for Standardization.

ISO, 1998. *Knitted Fabrics – Types – Vocabulary* (Vol. ISO 8388). Vernier, Geneva/CH: International Organization for Standardization.

ISO, 2019. *Nonwovens – Vocabulary* (Vol. ISO 9092). Vernier, Geneva/CH: International Organization for Standardization.

IVC, 2018a. Production of polyamide fibers worldwide from 1975 to 2017. *Statista*. Retrieved from www.statista.com/statistics/649908/polyamide-fiber-production-worldwide/

IVC, 2018b. Production of polyester fibers worldwide from 1975 to 2017. *Statista*. Retrieved from www.statista.com/statistics/912301/polyester-fiber-production-worldwide/

IVC, 2020. Worldwide production volume of chemical and textile fibers from 1975 to 2019. *Statista*. Retrieved from www.statista.com/statistics/271651/global-production-of-the-chemical-fiber-industry/

Jamshed, M., 2012. Factors affecting wool quality and quantity in sheep. *Afr. J. Biotechnol.*, 11. https://doi.org/10.5897/AJBX11.064

Kagome Wetengere, K., 2018. Is the banning of importation of second-hand clothes and shoes a panacea to industrialization in East Africa? *Af. J. Econ. Rev.*, 6, 119–141. Retrieved from http://ageconsearch.umn.edu/record/274747/files/166029-428047-1-SM.pdf

Kalliala, E.M., Nousiainen, P., 1999. Environmental profile of cotton and polyester-cotton fabrics. *Autex Res. J.*, 1(1), 8–20. Retrieved from www.scopus.com/inward/record. uri?eid=2-s2.0-3242796595&partnerID=40&md5=62e77a06b3aacd49a431250ea2501239

Kant, R., 2012. Textile dyeing industry an environmental hazard. *Nat. Sci.*, 4, 22–26. https://doi.org/ 10.4236/ns.2012.41004

Karigl, B., Bernhardt, A., Hauer, W., 2019. *Verwertung von gesammelten Alttextilien. Ermittlung der Anteile von Altkleidern und Altschuhen zur Weiterverwendung, zum Recycling und zur Beseitigung von HUMANA People to People Österreich.* Vienna/AT: Umweltbundesamt GmbH.

Kawai, F., Kawabata, T., Oda, M., 2019. Current knowledge on enzymatic PET degradation and its possible application to waste stream management and other fields. *Appl. Microbiol. Biotechnol.*, 103(11), 4253–4268. https://doi.org/10.1007/s00253-019-09717-y

KEBS, 2020. *Public Notice to Importers of Used/Second-Hand Garments and Used Shoes (MITUMBA).* Retrieved from www.kebs.org/index.php?option=com_content&view=article&id=655:public-notice-to-importers-of-used-second-hand-garments-and-used-shoes-mitumba&catid=23&Itemid=180

Kim, S.Y., Grady, P.L., Hersh, S.P., 1983. Energy consumption and conservation in the fibre-producing and textile industries. *Text. Prog.*, 13(3), 1–14. https://doi.org/10.1080/00405168308688996

Koç, E., Çinçik, E., 2010. Analysis of energy consumption in woven fabric production. *Fibres Text. East. Eur.*, 18(2), 14–20.

Koç, E., Kaplan, E., 2007. An investigation on energy consumption in yarn production with special reference to ring spinning. *Fibres Text. East. Eur.*, 15(4), 18–24.

Kohan, M.I., 1986. *The History and Development of Nylon-66.* Paper presented at the High Performance Polymers: Their Origin and Development, Proceedings of the Symposium on the History of High Performance Polymers at the American Chemical Society Meeting, New York/USA, April 15–18, 1986.

Korolkow, J., 2014. *Konsum, Bedarf und Wiederverwendung von Bekleidung und Textilien in Deutschland.* Berlin/DE: bvse-Bundesverband Sekundärrohstoffe und Entsorgung e. V.

Kurian, J.V., 2005. A new polymer platform for the future – Sorona® from Corn Derived 1,3-Propanediol. *J. Environ. Polym. Degrad.*, 13(2), 159–167. https://doi.org/10.1007/s10924-005-2947-7

Kvavadze, E., Bar-Yosef, O., Belfer-Cohen, A., Boaretto, E., Jakeli, N., Matskevich, Z., Meshveliani, T., 2009. 30,000-year-old wild flax fibers. *Science*, 325(5946), 1359. https://doi.org/10.1126/science.1175404

Laroche, 2021. *Cadette.* Retrieved from www.laroche.fr/en/domaines-dactivites/recycling.html?qt-qt_recyclage_en=4#qt-qt_recyclage_en

Lenzing, 2018. *TENCEL™ Lyocell Fibers Produced with REFIBRA™ Technology – Development of Circular Flow Mode.* Lenzing Group Sustainability Report 2017 Non-Financial Statement, Lenzing/AT, p. 74.

Li, X., Hu, Y., Du, C., Lin, C.S.K., 2019. Recovery of glucose and polyester from textile waste by enzymatic hydrolysis. *Waste Biomass Valorizat.*, 10(12), 3763–3772. https://doi.org/10.1007/s12649-018-0483-7

Liebert, T., 2010. Cellulose solvents – Remarkable history, bright future. In *Cellulose Solvents: For Analysis, Shaping and Chemical Modification: 1033* (pp. 3–54). Washington, DC: American Chemical Society.

Lindhqvist, T., Lifset, R., 1998. Getting the goal right: EPR and DfE. *J. Ind. Ecol.*, 2(1), 6–8. https://doi.org/10.1162/jiec.1998.2.1.6

Liu, Y., Zhu, L., Zhang, C., Ren, F., Huang, H., Liu, Z., 2020. Life cycle assessment of melange yarns from the manufacturer perspective. *Int. J. Life Cycle Assess.*, 25(3), 588–599. https://doi.org/10.1007/s11367-019-01705-8

Mannheim, V., Simenfalvi, Z., 2020. Total life cycle of polypropylene products: Reducing environmental impacts in the manufacturing phase. *Polymers*, 12(9). https://doi.org/10.3390/polym12091901

Mao, N., Russell, S.J., 2015. Chapter 13 – Fibre to fabric: Nonwoven fabrics. In R. Sinclair (Ed.), *Textiles and Fashion* (pp. 307–335). Cambridge, UK: Woodhead Publishing.

Martino, L., Basilissi, L., Farina, H., Ortenzi, M.A., Zini, E., Di Silvestro, G., Scandola, M., 2014. Bio-based polyamide 11: Synthesis, rheology and solid-state properties of star structures. *Eur. Polym. J.*, 59, 69–77. https://doi.org/10.1016/j.eurpolymj.2014.07.012

Matthies, P., Seydl, W.F., 1986. *History and Development of Nylon 6*. Paper presented at the High Performance Polymers: Their Origin and Development, Proceedings of the Symposium on the History of High Performance Polymers at the American Chemical Society Meeting, New York/USA, April 15–18, 1986.

Miljøstyrelsen, 2020. *Towards 2025: Separate Collection and Treatment of Textiles in Six EU Countries* (Vol. Environmental Project No 2140). København, DK: The Danish Environmental Protection Agency.

Miranda, R., Bustos, D., Vasile, C., 2007. Pyrolysis of textile wastes: I. Kinetics and yields. *J. Anal. Appl. Pyrolysis*, 80(2), 489–495.

Mohan, J., 2015. Technical textiles. *HSME Magazine*. Retrieved from www.hsmemagazine.com/article/technical-textiles-1207/

Murase, Y., Nagai, A., 1994. Chapter 2 – Melt spinning. In T. Nakajima, K. Kajiwara, J. E. McIntyre (Eds.), *Advanced Fiber Spinning Technology* (pp. 25–64). Cambridge, UK: Woodhead Publishing.

Napper, I.E., Davies, B.F.R., Clifford, H., Elvin, S., Koldewey, H.J., Mayewski, P.A., . . . Thompson, R.C., 2020. Reaching new heights in plastic pollution – Preliminary findings of microplastics on Mount Everest. *One Earth*, 3(5), 621–630. https://doi.org/10.1016/j.oneear.2020.10.020

Nikles, D.E., Farahat, M.S., 2005. New motivation for the depolymerization products derived from poly(ethylene terephthalate) (PET) waste: A review. *Macromol. Mater. Eng.*, 290(1), 13–30. https://doi.org/10.1002/mame.200400186

Nolimal, S., 2018. Life cycle assessment of four different sweaters. *DePaul Discoveries*, 7(1). Retrieved from https://via.library.depaul.edu/depaul-disc/vol7/iss1/9

Nørup, N., Pihl, K., Damgaard, A., Scheutz, C., 2018. Development and testing of a sorting and quality assessment method for textile waste. *Waste Manage.*, 79, 8–21. https://doi.org/10.1016/j.wasman.2018.07.008

Novozymes, 2021. *Beautiful Biology, Enzymes and Microorganisms that We Find in Nature Make Everyday Products More Sustainable*. Retrieved from www.novozymes.com/en/biology

O'Brian, P., 2019. *The Precocious Mechanization of a Global Industry: English Cotton Textile Production from the Flying Shuttle (1733) to the Self-Acting Mule (1825): A Bibliographical Survey and Critique*. Retrieved from London/UK: http://eprints.lse.ac.uk/100321/1/WP295.pdf

Ouchi, A., Toida, T., Kumaresan, S., Ando, W., Kato, J., 2010. A new methodology to recycle polyester from fabric blends with cellulose. *Cellulose*, 17(1), 215–222. https://doi.org/10.1007/s10570-009-9358-1

Palamutcu, S., 2010. Electric energy consumption in the cotton textile processing stages. *Energy*, 35(7), 2945–2952. https://doi.org/10.1016/j.energy.2010.03.029

Palme, A., Peterson, A., de la Motte, H., Theliander, H., Brelid, H., 2017. Development of an efficient route for combined recycling of PET and cotton from mixed fabrics. *Text. Cloth. Sust.*, 3(1), 4. https://doi.org/10.1186/s40689-017-0026-9

Pavlov, I.N., Denisova, M.N., Makarova, E., Budaeva, V., Sakovich, G., 2015. Versatile thermobaric setup and production of hydrotropic cellulose therein. *Cellul. Chem. Technol.*, 49, 847–852.

Payne, A., 2015. Chapter 6 – Open- and closed-loop recycling of textile and apparel products. In S.S. Muthu (Ed.), *Handbook of Life Cycle Assessment (LCA) of Textiles and Clothing* (pp. 103–123). Cambridge, UK: Woodhead Publishing.

PCI, 2013. New yarns from old bottles. *Fibers Filam*, 16, 12–23.

Pelt, M.V., 2016. *Bio-based Polyamides: Environmental Impact and Applicability in Soccer Shoe Outsoles*. Master Thesis, Utrecht University, Faculty of Geosciences Theses, Utrecht/NL.

Piribauer, B., Laminger, T., Ipsmiller, W., Koch, D., Bartl, A., 2019. Assessment of microplastics in the environment – Fibres: The disregarded twin? *Detritus*, 9, 201–212.

PlasticsEurope, 2014a. *Polyamide 6 (PA6)*. Retrieved from www.plasticseurope.org/download_file/804/0

PlasticsEurope, 2014b. *Polyamide 6.6 (PA6.6)*. Retrieved from www.plasticseurope.org/download_file/817/0

PlasticsEurope, 2016. *Polypropylene (PP)*. Retrieved from www.plasticseurope.org/download_file/766/0

PlasticsEurope, 2017. *Polyethylene Terephthalate (PET) – (Bottle Grade)*. Retrieved from www.plasticseurope.org/download_file/754/0

Power, E.J., 2015. Chapter 12 – Yarn to fabric: Knitting. In R. Sinclair (Ed.), *Textiles and Fashion* (pp. 289–305). Cambridge, UK: Woodhead Publishing.

Qin, Y., 2008. Alginate fibres: An overview of the production processes and applications in wound management. *Polym. Int.*, 57(2), 171–180. https://doi.org/10.1002/pi.2296

Quartinello, F., Vecchiato, S., Weinberger, S., Kremser, K., Skopek, L., Pellis, A., Guebitz, G.M., 2018. Highly selective enzymatic recovery of building blocks from wool-cotton-polyester textile waste blends. *Polymers*, 10(10), 1107. https://doi.org/10.3390/polym10101107

Re_fashion, 2020a. *Annual Report #2019*. Retrieved from https://refashion.fr/pro/sites/default/files/fichiers/ECO_TLC_EN_BD.pdf

Re_fashion, 2020b. *Technical Monitoring on Optical Sorting and Textile Recognition Technologies at a European Level*. Retrieved from https://refashion.fr/pro/sites/default/files/fichiers/Terra_summary_study_on_textile_material_sorting_VUK_300320.pdf

Reinthaller, C., Bartl, A., Marini, I., Haner, A.S., 2011. *Zuschlagstoff für die Herstellung von Baumaterialien*. Austrian Patent AT508898B1.

Rengel, A., 2017. *Recycled Textile Fibres and Textile Recycling, an Overview of the Market and its Possibilities for Public Procurers in Switzerland*. Federal Office for the Environment (FOEN), Economics and Innovation Division, Green Public Procurement Service, Bern/CH.

Ritthoff, M., Rohn, H., Liedtke, C., 2002. *MIPS berechnen: Ressourcenproduktivität von Produkten und Dienstleistungen*. Wuppertal, DE: Wuppertal-Inst. für Klima, Umwelt, Energie.

Roy, S., Lutfar, L.B., 2012. Chapter 3 – Bast fibres: Jute. In R. M. Kozłowski (Ed.), *Handbook of Natural Fibres* (Vol. 1, pp. 24–46). Cambridge, UK: Woodhead Publishing.

Ruiz, H.A., Conrad, M., Sun, S.N., Sanchez, A., Rocha, G.J.M., Romaní, A., . . . Meyer, A.S., 2020. Engineering aspects of hydrothermal pretreatment: From batch to continuous operation, scale-up and pilot reactor under biorefinery concept. *Bioresour. Technol.*, 299. doi:10.1016/j.biortech.2019.122685

Sayed, U., Parte, S., 2015. Recycling of non woven waste. *Int. J. Adv. Sci. Eng.*, 1(4), 67–71.

Schaart, E., Guillot, L., 2020. *Because of Coronavirus, Europe is Drowning in Second-hand Clothes.* Retrieved from www.politico.eu/article/coronavirus-europe-drowning-second-hand-clothes/

Schill+Seilacher, 2021. *Chemicals for Technical Textiles.* Retrieved from www.schillseilacher. de/en/products/chemicals-for-technical-textiles

Seisl, S., Hengstmann, R., 2021. Manmade Cellulosic Fibers (MMCF) – A historical introduction and existing solutions to a moresustainable production. In A. Matthes, K. Beyer, H. Cebulla, M. G. Arnold, A. Schumann (Eds.), *Sustainable Textile and Fashion Value Chains: Drivers, Concepts, Theories and Solutions* (pp. 3–22). Cham: Springer International Publishing.

Shen, L., Patel, M.K., 2010. Life cycle assessment of man-made cellulose fibres. *Lenzinger Berichte*, 88, 1–59. Retrieved from www.sciencedirect.com/science/article/pii/S092134491000217X

Shen, L., Worrell, E., Patel, M.K., 2010a. Environmental impact assessment of man-made cellulose fibres. *Resour. Conserv. Recycl.*, 55(2), 260–274. https://doi.org/10.1016/j.resconrec.2010.10.001

Shen, L., Worrell, E., Patel, M.K., 2010b. Open-loop recycling: A LCA case study of PET bottle-to-fibre recycling. *Resour. Conserv. Recycl.*, 55(1), 34–52. https://doi.org/10.1016/j.resconrec.2010.06.014

Sinha, V., Patel, M.R., Patel, J.V., 2010. Pet waste management by chemical recycling: A review. *J. Environ. Polym. Degrad.*, 18(1), 8–25. https://doi.org/10.1007/s10924-008-0106-7

Songwon, 2021. *Textile and Fibers, Structuring the Fabric of the Future.* Retrieved from www.songwon.com/industries/textile-fibers

Sperger, 2021a. *Putzlappen – Probebestellung.* Retrieved from www.putzlappen.at/php/musterbestell.php

Sperger, 2021b. *Sammeln und sortieren . . .* Retrieved from www.putzlappen.at/herstellung.htm

Stankard, S., 2015. Chapter 11 – Yarn to fabric: Weaving. In R. Sinclair (Ed.), *Textiles and Fashion* (pp. 255–287). Cambridge, UK: Woodhead Publishing.

Steinberger, J.K., Friot, D., Jolliet, O., Erkman, S., 2009. A spatially explicit life cycle inventory of the global textile chain. *Int. J. Life Cycle Assess.*, 14(5), 443–455. https://doi.org/10.1007/s11367-009-0078-4

Suaria, G., Achtypi, A., Perold, V., Lee, J., Pierucci, A., Bornman, T., . . . Ryan, P., 2020. Microfibers in oceanic surface waters: A global characterization. *Sci. Adv.*, 6, eaay8493. https://doi.org/10.1126/sciadv.aay8493

TextileGuide, 2021. *The Textile Process.* Retrieved from https://textileguide.chemsec.org/find/get-familiar-with-your-textile-production-processes/

Tomovska, E., Jordeva, S., Trajković, D., Zafirova, K., 2017. Attitudes towards managing post-industrial apparel cuttings waste. *J. Text. Inst.*, 108(2), 172–177. https://doi.org/10.1080/00405000.2016.1160764

Tsurumi, T., 1994. Chapter 3 – Solution spinning. In T. Nakajima, K. Kajiwara, J. E. McIntyre (Eds.), *Advanced Fiber Spinning Technology* (pp. 65–104). Cambridge, UK: Woodhead Publishing.

Uesu, N.Y., Pineda, E.A.G., Hechenleitner, A.A.W., 2000. Microcrystalline cellulose from soybean husk: effects of solvent treatments on its properties as acetylsalicylic acid carrier. *Int. J. Pharm.*, 206(1), 85–96. https://doi.org/10.1016/S0378-5173(00)00532-9

USDA, 2021. *Cotton: World Markets and Trade.* Retrieved from https://apps.fas.usda.gov/psdonline/circulars/cotton.pdf

van der Velden, N.M., Patel, M.K., Vogtländer, J.G., 2014. LCA benchmarking study on textiles made of cotton, polyester, nylon, acryl, or elastane. *Int. J. Life Cycle Assess.*, 19(2), 331–356. https://doi.org/10.1007/s11367-013-0626-9

Vasconcelos, A., Cavaco-Paulo, A., 2006. Enzymatic removal of cellulose from cotton/polyester fabric blends. *Cellulose*, 13(5), 611–618. https://doi.org/10.1007/s10570-006-9063-2

Vecchiato, S., Skopek, L., Jankova, S., Pellis, A., Ipsmiller, W., Aldrian, A., . . . Guebitz, G.M., 2018. Enzymatic recycling of high-value phosphor flame-retardant pigment and glucose from rayon fibers. *ACS Sustain. Chem. Eng.*, 6(2), 2386–2394. https://doi.org/10.1021/acssuschemeng.7b03840

Vecchiato, S., Skopek, L., Rußmayer, H., Steiger, M., Aldrian, A., Beer, B., . . . Guebitz, G., 2019. Microbial production of high value molecules using rayon waste material as carbon-source. *Nat. Biotechnol.*, 51. https://doi.org/10.1016/j.nbt.2019.01.010

Verma, Y., 2008. Acute toxicity assessment of textile dyes and textile and dye industrial effluents using Daphnia magna bioassay. *Toxicol. Ind. Health*, 24(7), 491–500. https://doi.org/10.1177/0748233708095769

Wang, Y., 2010. Fiber and textile waste utilization. *Waste Biomass Valorizat.*, 1(1), 135–143. https://doi.org/10.1007/s12649-009-9005-y

Ward, G.D., Hewitt, A.D., Russell, S.J., 2013. Fibre composition of donated post-consumer clothing in the UK. *Proc. Inst. Civ. Eng.: Waste Resour. Manag.*, 166(1), 29–37. https://doi.org/10.1680/warm.12.00014

Weil, E.D., Levchik, S.V., 2017. Phosphorus flame retardants. In Kirk-Othmer (ed.), *Encyclopedia of Chemical Technology* (pp. 1–34). Hoboken, NJ: John Wiley & Sons.

West, J., Saunders, C., Willet, J., 2021. A bottom up approach to slowing fashion: Tailored solutions for consumers. *J. Clean. Prod.*, 296, 126387. https://doi.org/10.1016/j.jclepro.2021.126387

Whinfield, J.R., Dickson, J.T., 1946. GB Patent No. GB578079 B. P. Office.

Woolridge, A.C., Ward, G.D., Phillips, P.S., Collins, M., Gandy, S., 2006. Life cycle assessment for reuse/recycling of donated waste textiles compared to use of virgin material: An UK energy saving perspective. *Resour. Conserv. Recycl.*, 46(1), 94–103. https://doi.org/10.1016/j.resconrec.2005.06.006

Yacout, D.M.M., Abd El-Kawi, M.A., Hassouna, M.S., 2016. Cradle to gate environmental impact assessment of acrylic fiber manufacturing. *Int. J. Life Cycle Assess.*, 21(3), 326–336. https://doi.org/10.1007/s11367-015-1023-3

Yang, B., Dai, Z., Ding, S.-Y., Wyman, C.E., 2011. Enzymatic hydrolysis of cellulosic biomass. *Biofuels*, 2(4), 421–449. https://doi.org/10.4155/bfs.11.116

Yousef, S., Tatariants, M., Tichonovas, M., Kliucininkas, L., Lukošiūtė, S.-I., Yan, L., 2020. Sustainable green technology for recovery of cotton fibers and polyester from textile waste. *J. Clean. Prod.*, 254, 120078. https://doi.org/10.1016/j.jclepro.2020.120078

Zhang, Y., Liu, X., Xiao, R., Yuan, Z., 2015. Life cycle assessment of cotton T-shirts in China. *Int. J. Life Cycle Assess.*, 20(7), 994–1004. https://doi.org/10.1007/s11367-015-0889-4.

10

INNOVATIVE APPROACHES TO MITIGATE MICROFIBRE POLLUTION

Francesca De Falco and Mariacristina Cocca

1 Introduction

The release of microfibres (MFs) from synthetic garments represents an environmental problem affecting not only the marine or general aquatic environments, but all the environmental compartments and ecosystems, i.e., terrestrial and atmospheric ones. During the last few years, it was clarified that MFs can be released not only to water due to laundry, but also to air, due to wearing. Different studies reported the presence of MFs in indoor and outdoor environments (Dris et al., 2016; Dris et al., 2017; Kaya et al., 2018; Brahney et al., 2020). A quantification of MFs released to air from polyester garments worn by volunteers, performing a sequence of movements in a decontaminated closed room, was recently reported (De Falco et al., 2020). The amount of MFs released to air was found close to that released from the same garments to water during washings. In detail, it was estimated that one person could annually release 2.98×10^8 MFs to water by washing polyester garments, and 1.03×10^9 MFs to air by wearing polyester garments. Nowadays, it is clear that MFs can be released from textiles to the environment during production, laundry, drying, wearing and end-of-life disposal. Therefore, it is becoming more and more pressing to identify solutions to mitigate this source of pollution.

This chapter provides an overview of some mitigation actions that can be applied on textile at production and laundry levels. Several scientific papers have been focused on the identification of the influence of textile and washing parameters on the release of MFs and on the testing of the technologies and devices available up to now to mitigate MFs pollution. Each study adopted a different methodology: some simulated washing by using laboratory simulators, others used real household washing machines; some used standard or purposely produced fabrics, others tested real garments. Also, several methods have been applied to quantify MFs released:

DOI: 10.4324/9781003165385-12

almost all works filtered the washing effluents but some analyzed the filter surfaces by using microscopic techniques to evaluate the number of MFs released, others used gravimetric approaches to evaluate the amount of MFs released; some analyzed aliquots of the wastewater, others filtered all the washing waters (see Chapter 6). Of course, the application of different methodologies across the current scientific literature mines the comparison of the results but, nevertheless, some common outcomes can be gathered and are reported in the following sections along with technologies and devices that have been developed.

2 Mitigation actions for textile production

2.1 Textile design and manufacturing

In 2019, the global fibre production reached about 111 million metric tons (Mt), whose 62.9% was composed of synthetic fibres (TextileExchange, 2020). Since 1975, fiber global production has been constantly increasing and it is estimated that 146 million Mt will be produced in 2030 (TextileExchange, 2020).

These data allow us to understand that the prevention of MF release from textiles is a major issue that requires dedicated solutions. Several studies have already pointed out that textile parameters influence MF release, so changes in textile design and manufacturing processes (i.e. finishing) should be considered to mitigate MF pollution (Carney Almroth et al., 2018; De Falco et al., 2019a; Cai et al., 2020b).

Figure 10.1 reports three steps of garment production. The first step is related to the selection of raw materials and production of fibres, such as natural fibres or synthetic fibres. Fibres can be of two types: continuous filaments (e.g. fibres of indefinite length) or staple fibres (e.g. fibre of comparatively short length) (Spencer, 2001). Then, textile industry produces yarns, assemblies of fibres in a lengthways direction of substantial length and relatively small cross-section, with or without twist (Spencer, 2001; Wilson, 2000). Twist is defined as the number of turns present in a unit length of the yarn, and it is used for different purposes such as to induce structural integrity in staple spun yarns or to prevent fraying in multifilament yarns (Gandhi, 2012). Fabrics are produced by interlacing yarns to form woven structures (the warp yarn runs in a lengthways direction and the weft in a

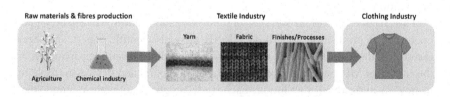

FIGURE 10.1 Textile manufacturing supply chain

Source: Elaborated by the authors from De Falco et al. (2020), Niinimäki et al. (2020), Wilson (2000), Palacios-Mateo et al. (2021)

widthway direction) or knitted ones (loops of yarn are interlaced) (Wilson, 2000). At this point, processes/finishes are applied to improve or impart particular properties to the fabric. Such processes include preparatory ones (scouring, desizing, bleaching, etc.),[1] dyeing (actually this can be performed also directly on fibres or yarns), printing, finishing treatments (antimicrobial, flame-retardant, water repellant, etc.) (Wilson, 2000). Finally fabrics are cut and sewed into final garments according to a specific design. More details on the main steps of textile manufacturing are reported in Chapter 9.

A recent report tried to estimate the quantity of MFs that could be released during the textile manufacturing phase (WRAP, 2019). Considering activities such as fibre processing, spinning,[2] weaving, knitting and garment construction, it was estimated that for 1,130,000 tons of clothing consumed in the UK annually, 168,452 tons of textile mass is lost and most of this mass could potentially be in the form of MFs. However, consistent estimations of the contribution of textile manufacturing to MF release are difficult to make at the current state of knowledge. Analyses and data are needed at the different production stages to assess the quantity of MF released. Up to now, different studies have highlighted the presence of MFs in the wastewater of textile production plants. Xu et al. (2018) sampled and analyzed water coming from a Chinese textile industry wastewater treatment plant (WWTP), calculating that it was releasing 4.89×10^8 MFs to water every day. Deng et al. (2020) also examined water and sediment samples collected from a textile industrial area in Shaoxing City, China. They found that fibers were the most abundant type of microplastics found in both water (95%) and sediment (79%), with polyester as the main polymer detected. Finally, Chan et al. (2020) analyzed industrial wastewater effluents from a typical textile wet-processing mill in China. Their results showed the presence of an average of 361.6 ± 24.5 MFs/L in the effluent, whose 92% of all fibres were shorter than 1000 μm. Such findings point out that mitigation actions should be also applied at textile production plants to reduce the release of MFs to water and possibly to air at this stage. Nevertheless, more data and studies are needed to effectively identify the best mitigation solutions to apply.

2.2 Influence of textile parameters on MF release

Several studies have identified how textile structure and characteristics affect MF release by testing different textiles/garments in real or simulated washings. In a recent work, Cesa et al. (2020) discussed that more investigations on the role of textile parameters are still needed. For instance, they point out that if on one hand parameters linked to fibre mass (i.e. linear density or yarn count, fabric thickness and fabric weight per unit area) make fibres more available to external stresses, on the other hand those related to fibre cohesion (i.e. yarn twist, fabric interlacing, fabric density, fibers size and regularity) hold them, thus avoiding propagation. In addition, another parameter to take into account is fibre tenacity that indicates its resistance to be broken.

The influence of textile structure and characteristics on the release of MFs mainly for polyester fabrics was deeply investigated (De Falco et al., 2018a, 2019a, 2020). Standard fabrics were tested in laboratory washing simulations, finding that woven polyester made of short staple fibres released more MFs than knitted polyester made of continuous filaments. The authors correlated this result to the length of the fibres composing the yarns (De Falco et al., 2018a). Polyester commercial garments were tested at real scale using a commercial washing machine, with a washing load of 2–2.5 kg (De Falco et al., 2019a). The lowest quantity of MFs (48.6 ± 2.2 mg/kg) was released during the washing of a blouse manufactured with woven fabric with highly twisted yarns made of continuous filaments and with low hairiness. The highest amount of MFs was obtained during washing of a top having the front part made of polyester and the back of a blend of cotton/modal (307.6 ± 21.8 mg/kg). In this last case, the thermogravimetric analysis performed on the released MFs allow the conclusion that around 80% of MFs were of cellulosic composition. A similar result was obtained in the investigation on the release of MFs to water and to air from polyester garments during washing and wearing (De Falco et al., 2020). Single garments with different textile characteristics underwent washing tests in a commercial washing machine and wearing test in simulations of real-life activities thank to volunteers that wore the garments. The results of both types of tests showed that polyester/cotton blends release great quantities of MFs during washing (around 400 MFs/gram of fabric) and wearing tests (around 4000 MFs/gram of fabric), but such MFs were mostly cotton ones. In both media, the lowest release was obtained for a fabric with a very compact structure, woven with highly twisted yarns made of continuous filaments, features preferred to looser structures (knitted, short staple fibers, lower twist).

Zambrano et al. (2019) tested fabrics produced on purpose for the experiments, having the same textile characteristics (i.e. knitted with staple fibres) but different chemical composition (100% cotton, 100% rayon, 100% polyester and 50%/ 50% polyester/cotton fabrics). The fabrics underwent accelerated and home laundering experiments, in a laboratory simulator and a washing machine, respectively. All three cellulose-based fabrics released more microfibers (0.2–4 mg/g fabric) than polyester (0.1–1 mg/g fabric) during the accelerated experiments. The authors hypothesized that MF shedding depends on fuzz formation (a fibre with a loose end that extend out of the fabric) and the consequent breaking of these fibres by mechanical actions during washing. They correlate such hypothesis with their results by analyzing some mechanical properties of the tested fabrics, finding that the polyester fabric had a higher abrasion resistance and yarn breaking strength which led to a lower fuzz formation and MF release.

Yang et al. (2019) performed washing experiments in two types of laundry machines (platen and pulsator) using commercial fabrics such as polyester, polyamide and acetate. In all the washing conditions tested, polyester released lower quantities of MFs than the other two fabrics. The authors ascribed such trend to the low weight per unit area of polyester, lower pilling resistance of acetate and to the compactness of the textile structures. However, clear info on the influence of pilling resistance and tear strength on the release could not be gathered since polyester had the same pilling resistance of polyamide and a tear strength similar to acetate.

Carney Almroth et al. (2018) studied the release of MFs from polyester (polyethylene terephthalate), polyacrylic (polyacrylonitrile) and polyamide fabrics manufactured *ad hoc* to be tested using a laboratory simulator of real washing processes. The polyester fabrics presented different textile parameters such as knitting factors like gauge (number of loop-forming needles per inch), type of fibres (filaments or short staple) and mechanical finishing (i.e. napping to produce fleece). Their outcomes showed that polyester fleece fabrics released more fibres, with an average of 7360 fibers/m^{-2}/L^{-1} in one wash, compared with the other polyester fabrics which released 87 fibers/m^{-2}/L^{-1}. Moreover, the polyester fabric with yarns made of short staple fibres released significantly more MFs than other three polyester fabrics with similar knitting factors but composed by filaments. Other important findings were that loose textile constructions cause a greater release and highly twisted yarns should be preferred to reduce MF shedding. Regarding the polymer composition of the fibres, no significant differences were found among the three types of synthetic fibres tested.

Similarly, other works by Pirc et al. (2016) and Sillanpää et al. (2017) reported high values of MF release from polyester fleece fabrics. The tendency of fleece fabrics to release MFs was also observed in two works of Cai et al. (2020a, 2020b). In their study of 12 different polyesters, they found a MF release ranging from 210 to 72,000 MFs/g of textile per wash, with the highest MF release values from textiles with mechanically processed surfaces (i.e., fleece) (Cai et al., 2020a). The trend was confirmed in the other study in which they developed a MF extraction method to investigate representative products along the textile production line (Cai et al., 2020b). In addition, they also found an influence on MF shedding of the cutting method used in textile production, pointing out that scissor-cut fabric samples released 3−21 times greater numbers of MFs than laser-cut ones (Cai et al., 2020a, 2020b). The role of sewing was investigated by Dalla Fontana et al. (2021) by washing polyester fabrics sewed with double heat-sealing or with a polyester thread using an overlock machine, finding that the heat-sealing caused a lower MF release.

The studies reported earlier differ in terms of methodologies and procedures applied both for the washing tests and the evaluation of MF release. Therefore, direct comparisons could be challenging as well as drawing final conclusions. However, despite such differences, it is possible to identify key textile structures and parameters that could have a role in reducing the release of MFs:

- Yarns composed by **continuous filaments** shed less MFs than those made of short staple fibres. A possible explanation is that staple fibres, for their smaller length, could slip away from the yarn more easily due to the mechanical stresses induced by processes like washing and wearing.
- **Compact textile structures** (i.e. woven, high twist) release less MFs than looser structures (i.e. knitted, low twist). In this case, the compactness of the

structure resulted in a low relaxation state that led to a more close structure of the garment, making it more difficult for the MFs to slip away.

- Structures like **fleece** cause a great release of MFs due to the fuzzy texture of fleece obtained by napping and shearing processes
- **Cutting and sewing** processes that involve **heating** (i.e. laser, heat-sealing) reduce MF shedding compared to conventional ones (i.e. scissor, sewing with thread).

Concerning the effect of the fiber chemical composition on the MF release, a clear conclusion cannot be drawn yet, but data seem to converge on the fact that cellulose-based fibers (either natural or man-made) release far more MFs than synthetic ones. This could be due to several reasons: cotton fibres are always short staple ones; synthetic fibres like polyester have a greater resistance to breaking and abrasion; cellulose fibres are more hydrophilic so swell in water, possibly facilitating MF detachment (Palacios-Mateo et al., 2021). This is an aspect that should be deeply investigated together with the possible impact of natural fibres on natural ecosystems (Suaria et al., 2020).

The definition of guidelines and best practices for the textile industry and the improvement of the awareness of the general people on which textile features and processes can mitigate MF release should represent a priority in the collaboration among textile and garment manufacturer, research institutes and academia.

2.3 Development of finishing treatments to mitigate MF release

A possible mitigation action at the manufacturing level is represented by the application of innovative finishing treatments. The Life+ project MERMAIDS "Mitigation of microplastics impact caused by textile washing processes", LIFE13 ENV/IT/001069, introduced this solution that consists in the application of a protective coating on the surface of the fabric (EU MERMAIDS, 2015a). The idea at the basis of this approach was to use a polymeric coating on fabric surfaces to protect them from mechanical and chemical stresses during a washing process. The MERMAIDS project tested different finishing treatments based on conventional and commercial textile auxiliaries including polyurethane and acrylic resins, silicon emulsion and acid cellulase. The polymeric dispersions were applied at lab scale on polyester fabrics using padding (the fabric is impregnated in a textile auxiliary bath and then squeezed between two squeeze rollers) or exhaustion (the fabric is immersed in the bath solution by setting a certain temperature and time of cycle). The best results in terms of MF reduction were obtained using an amino-functional elastomeric silicon macro-emulsion on polyester fabrics. The finishing was also applied at pilot scale.

However, the use of conventional synthetic auxiliaries as finishing materials can jeopardize the overall environmental benefits provided by the application of the coating, since the coating itself can become a source of pollution. Therefore, starting from the results of the MERMAIDS project, further research has investigated

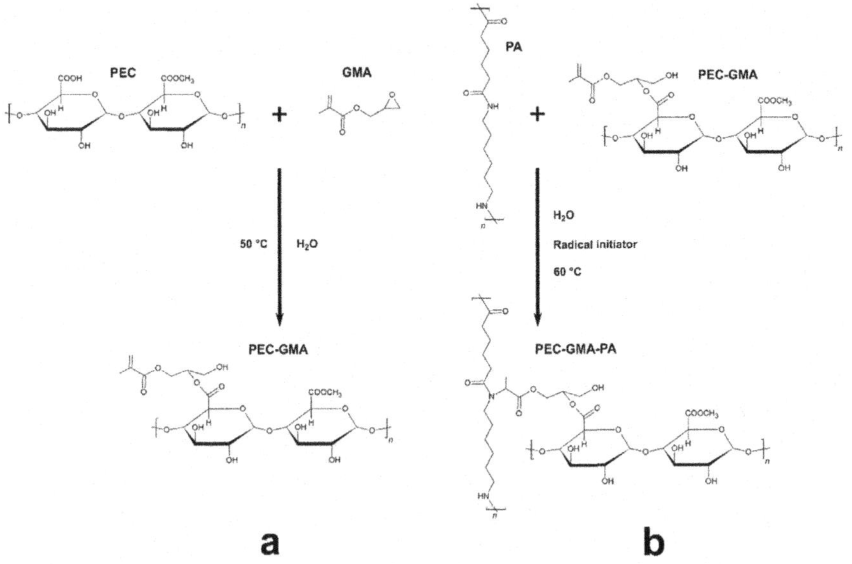

FIGURE 10.2 Reaction schemes of the pectin-based finishing treatment: (a) synthesis of pectin-GMA (PEC-GMA), (b) grafting of PEC-GMA on polyamide 6.6. (PA)[3]

alternative materials to the conventional finishing auxiliaries like natural polysaccharides (De Falco et al., 2018b), repetitive polypeptides (Pena-Francesch & Demirel, 2019) or biodegradable polymers like poly (lactic acid), PLA, and poly (butylene succinate-co-butylene adipate), PBSA, (De Falco et al., 2019b; De Falco F. et al., 2019c).

An eco-sustainable finishing treatment of polyamide 6.6 fabrics based on pectin, a natural polysaccharide present in plant cell, was developed using a two-step synthetic route with water as solvent (Figure 10.2) (De Falco et al., 2018b). In the first step, pectin was chemically modified by reaction with a monomer, glycidyl methacrylate (GMA) to introduce vinyl groups in the pectin chain. Such groups were then exploited in the second reaction step to graft pectin-GMA on the polyamide chain by free radical polymerization. The reaction was optimized (i.e. reagent ratios, concentration, etc.) to obtain a thin homogeneous coating that did not affect key textile properties (i.e. the hand of the fabric). The effectiveness of the treatment in mitigating MF release was evaluated by washing untreated and treated fabric samples using a laboratory simulator. Results shown that untreated polyamide fabrics released 3966 ± 1425 MFs/gram of washed fabric, while the pectin treated fabric released only 463 ± 37 MFs/gram. Therefore, the pectin treatment was able to reduce by almost 90% the number of MFs released and was resistant to one washing cycle.

Tandem repeat proteins inspired by squid ring teeth (SRT) were used to create coatings on textiles (Pena-Francesch & Demirel, 2019). In detail, a homogeneous film of this protein-based material was obtained on synthetic microfibre cloths

(87% polyester, 13% polyamide) and its resistance was tested in abrasion tests. SRT-coated fibers did not break or detach from the textile after the test, suggesting that the coating could provide mechanical stability to the fibres, preventing their release. Notwithstanding such encouraging results, the resistance and stability of the coating during washing processes was not tested yet.

Using an electrofluidodynamic (EFD) method, two coatings made of biodegradable polymers were deposited on polyamide 6.6 (De Falco et al., 2019c). The method is based on the use of electrical forces (applied between the needle of a syringe and a metallic collector) to reach liquid atomization of the solution contained in the syringe that is deposited on the substrate laid on the collector. Usually, by modifying the parameters involved in the process (i.e. voltage, distance needle–collector, feed rate, solution viscosity, etc.) the method allows for the deposit of submicron fibres (e.g. electrospinning) or particles (e.g. electrospraying). Firstly, the process parameters were optimized to develop a nonconventional EFD method to modify and functionalize textile surfaces, succeeding in depositing a continuous uniform polymeric layer on fabric surface (De Falco et al., 2019b). Then, the methodology was used to treat polyamide 6.6 fabrics with two different biodegradable polymers, PLA and PBSA (De Falco F. et al., 2019c). PLA was chosen as it is a polymer widely applied in electrofluidodynamics, while PBSA has showed a good degradation rate in marine environment (De Falco et al., 2021a). For both polymers, the coatings obtained had nanometric dimensions in the range of 100–150 nm, thus not altering fabric properties like the hand and wettability. On the contrary, the tear strength of the polyamide fabric was improved by both treatments, passing from 64.6 ± 1.0 N to 96.6 ± 2.8 N and 91.6 ± 5.3 when coated with PLA and PBSA, respectively. This is an aspect that could lead to a general greater resistance of the fabric to the mechanical stresses induced by its use, possibly preventing MFs release. The coated fabrics underwent five subsequent washing tests to assess their durability and mitigation action. After the first wash cycle, both coatings proved to be able to reduce about 90% of the quantity of MF released, in comparison with uncoated polyamide. After five washing cycles, scanning electron microscopy, Fourier Transform Infrared spectroscopy and tear strength analyses of the coated fabrics revealed a good durability of the PLA coating that remained almost unaltered after washings, while the PBSA one showed some damages and a lower resistance to the washing process.

In terms of industrial scale-up, among the treatments mentioned earlier, the one that holds the greatest potential is the pectin-based treatment. Its application process is similar to the padding process already used for finishing treatments at industrial level. In detail, padding comprises two steps: 1) the fabric is immersed in the liquor to achieve a good impregnation (e.g. immersion in the pectin-GMA solution) and 2) it is passed between two rollers to squeeze it. Moreover, such treatment allows for the application of circular economy concepts, since pectin, a cheap and abundantly product, is a waste product of agricultural/food manufacturing and can be easily extracted, for example, from citrus peel and apple pomace (Voragen et al., 2009).

However, all the treatments described, and in general the technology of the protective coating, still need more research and testing. It is of crucial importance to better assess the effectiveness and durability of such treatments, their application on different types of fabrics, influence on textile properties and compatibility with other processes of the textile manufacturing chain (i.e. dying). Only after these key aspects are thoroughly investigated it will be possible to estimate their implementation costs for the textile industry.

3 Mitigation actions for textile laundry

3.1 Influence of washing conditions on MF release

Mitigation actions can be applied also at the textile washing stage by favouring certain washing conditions that can help prevent MF release. As for textile parameters, also in this case the indications come from data reported in recent scientific literature. However, there is still no univocal conclusion of the assessments among the scientific community, and this is mainly due to the fact that each scientific study develops and applies a different methodology to quantify the release of microfibres during washing (as discussed in Chapter 6). Therefore, direct comparison among different works is tricky but, nevertheless, some factors of influence have undoubtedly an effect on the release and are worth mentioning and being further investigated.

For instance, most research works agree that the use of detergent increase the release of microfibres compared to washings with only water (Hernandez et al., 2017; Carney Almroth et al., 2018; De Falco et al., 2018a; Yang et al., 2019; Zambrano et al., 2019); only one study found a decreasing effect (Cesa et al., 2020) while few detected no significant influence (Pirc et al., 2016; Kelly et al., 2019; Lant et al., 2020) or one that is not so clear (Napper & Thompson, 2016). In general, detergents decrease the surface tension and act as dispersing agents, probably favouring the release and transport of microfibres (Carney Almroth et al., 2018). Of course, it is not possible to avoid the usage of detergent for obvious reasons related to the effectiveness of the cleaning process, but some choices can be recommended.

The effect of liquid and powder detergents on the release of MFs from three synthetic fabrics (woven and knitted polyester, woven polypropylene) was analyzed in comparison with washing with only water (De Falco et al., 2018a). With respect to the washing tests with water, independently from the fabric chemical composition, the usage of liquid detergent during washing tests increased the MF release by about ten times with respect to the washing tests with water. Instead, the usage of a powder detergent increased the release by around 20–30 times. This worsening effect of the powder detergent was related to the presence in its formulation of inorganic compounds insoluble in water, like zeolites, that could cause friction and abrasion on the surface of the fabrics, favouring MF shedding.

In addition, the effect on woven polyester of different laundry additives such as softener, bleaching and oxidizing products was also evaluated (De Falco et al., 2018a). The outcomes showed that the use of the softener could decrease MF release by 35%, in comparison to washing in the same conditions but using a liquid detergent. Such effect was ascribed to the ability of the softener to reduce the friction among fibres, allowing microfibrils to lay parallel to the fibre bundle, and thus decreasing damaging and breaking phenomena. However, an unclear trend concerning softener was previously recorded by Napper and Thompson (2016). Pirc et al. (2016) and Lant et al. (2020) detected no significant effect of the softener, but the latter called for more studies since even if the softener may not have a direct impact on MF shedding, it could still have an indirect influence by extending the lifetime of textiles and reducing in this way the consumption and purchase of new items. The difference in the reported results could be ascribed not only to the different washing method used, but also to the washing load tested. Recently, it was highlighted an increase of MF release when decreasing the washing load, i.e. the amount of released MFs increased by around five times by decreasing the washing load (Volgare et al., 2021). The higher water volume to fabric ratio and mechanical stress to which the fabric is subjected to, in the case of a low washing load, hinder the determination of the role of other washing parameters, like the type of detergent and laundry additives used, on the release.

Other typical parameters of common washing programs that have been investigated are temperature, time and mechanical action. Hartline et al. (2016) performed washing tests using two types of commercial washing machines, top-load (vertical-axis machine) and front-load (horizontal-axis machine) that are common in the United States. Their results showed that a greater MF mass was released when using top-load since its central agitator could be more abrasive on textiles as compared to the rotating drum of the front-load machine. De Falco et al. (2018a) tested woven polyester using a laboratory simulator in six different combinations of temperature, time, water hardness and mechanical action (simulated by adding steel balls in the containers of the simulator). They found that higher temperature, washing time and mechanical action induced an increase of MF release, but no statistically significant differences were detected among the different conditions. Lant et al. (2020) washed real soiled consumer loads in a washing machine using liquid detergent and testing two types of washing programs: "Cotton Short" (40°C, 85 minutes, 1600 rpm spin speed) or "Cold Express" (a quick cycle using unheated water at 15°C, 30 minutes, 1600 rpm). They found that passing to the colder and quicker program is possible to significantly reduce 30% of the MF release. Moreover, these washing conditions also reduced dye transfer and soil redisposition. Other findings on the influence of washing temperature were reported by Yang et al. (2019), who detected that polyester, acetate and polyamide fabrics released more MFs when passing from 30°C to 40°C and then 60°C. A similar trend was also observed by Zambrano et al. (2019), in laboratory simulations of the washing of four different fabrics (cotton, polyester, rayon, polyester/cotton), testing two temperatures, 25°C and 44 °C. In general, for all the tested fabrics the mass of MFs released increased with temperature, but significant differences were found only for cotton and polyester cotton blend. Dalla Fontana et al. (2020) also observed that more stressing washing conditions (e.g. higher temperature, longer time, stronger centrifugation) may cause a greater release of MFs. On the contrary, Hernandez et al. (2017) and Kelly et al. (2019) reported no influence of temperature, time and mechanical action, while Napper and Thompson (2016) could not obtain a consistent trend related to the influence of temperature on the release.

Comparing the results of the works discussed earlier, they align and confirm with the mitigation measures reported by "The good practice guide" produced during the Mermaids project as reported in Figure 10.3 (EU MERMAIDS, 2015b). Moreover, washings at lower temperature and for lower time also have the effect of reducing the colour loss and dye transfer in the wastewater with consequent environmental consequences (Cotton et al., 2020). In general, these washing parameters could potentially help a better maintenance of clothes, extending their lifetime, with sustainability benefits like lower consumption and purchase of new garments.

However, more research is needed to gather more and conclusive data on the parameters that influence the release of MFs during laundry. In particular, as for

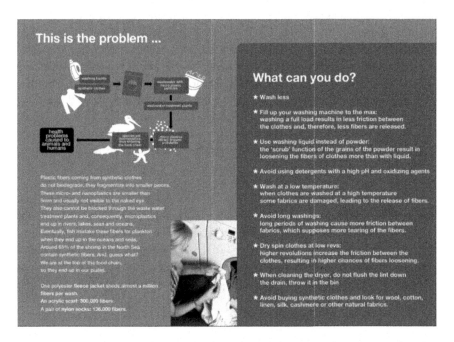

FIGURE 10.3 Good practice guide produced in the framework of the Mermaids Life+ project (LIFE13 ENV/IT/001069).

Source: EU MERMAIDS, 2015b

textile parameters, standardized methodologies are needed to study and single out the parameters that can best reduce MF shedding.

3.2 Development of capturing devices and filtration systems

The problem of MF pollution has also inspired enterprises to develop commercial solutions. The main focus has been the development of devices for washing machines to prevent/reduce the release of MFs and their entrance into the wastewater. Most of these devices are already in commerce but there is still a lack of consistent information available on their effectiveness, mainly due to the absence of standardized methods to test them. Here are summarized solutions currently available or in development phase, categorized as capturing devices or filtration systems.

Up to now, only two capturing devices have been proposed and commercialized, and they are both added directly in the drum of the washing machine. The first is Cora Ball (Cora Ball, 2021), a device whose design is inspired by the structure of corals, a ball with stalks that have small hooks on the ends which should collect entangled fibres. According to the indications of the developers, the use of this ball, made of 100% recycled and 100% recyclable plastic, should be avoided with delicate fabrics like lace, knits, tassels, chunky or wide-knit, crocheted sections or fraying threads. They recommend to clean the ball not necessarily after every wash, but only when big entanglements of fibres are visible, by hand-removing them and throwing them in the rubbish. Of course, such indications may raise some doubts on the efficiency of the device in capturing the smallest fraction of MFs. Two independent research studies tested the efficiency of the ball in reducing MF release. The first evaluated the effectiveness of the device in reducing the quantity of MFs, both in term of number of MFs and in weight. The Cora Ball reduced the number of microfibers per L of effluent by an average of 26% but only a 5% reduction by weight of MFs released was observed (McIlwraith et al., 2019). The second study found an efficiency of 31% in terms of reduced weight of MFs released (Napper et al., 2020).

The second capturing device is the Guppyfriend washing bag (Guppyfriend, 2021a), a polyamide 6.6 50×74 cm bag where the clothes to be washed are put inside, filling the bag up to two thirds since the textiles need to move inside the bag. According to the developers, the bag can easily be recycled at the end of its lifecycle and the structure of the filter surface (50 μm pore size) is optimized to obtain a smooth surface able to protect the garments, to avoid pilling and to reduce fibre loss. The washing bag should be cleaned by removing the released microfibers from hems inside it and disposing of them properly in a closed container. The bag was tested by the Fraunhofer Institute UMSICHT and the German Textile Research Centre North-West DTNW, reporting a reduction of the amount of fibre released of 79% for partly synthetic clothes, and 86% from completely synthetic textiles; the bag remained intact after 50 washes and did not release fibres itself (Guppyfriend, 2021b). An independent test was also performed by Napper et al. (2020), who found it able to reduce MF release to wastewater by around 54%.

Most of the filtration systems developed are intended to be installed in line with the external drain pipe of the washing machine. This is a type of solution that is not of easy design since it must be able to retain fibres of micro dimensions without blocking the flux of water.

The company Environmental Enhancements (Environmental Enhancements, 2021) proposed two filters to remove not only general lint produced by washings, but also MFs: the Lint LUV-R Septic SAV-R made of stainless steel mesh with hole diameters of 1,580 μm and to be cleaned every ten to 15 loads of laundry; the MicroPlastics LUV-R made of stainless steel mesh with hole diameters of 150 μm and to be cleaned every two to three loads of laundry. According to the company, the filters have a dynamic action, meaning that as the filter collects lint, it becomes more efficient since the trapped lint acts as a filter itself and has a 65% (Lint LUV-R) or 87% (MicroPlastics LUV-VR) initial efficiency capture of microfibers, reaching 100% at saturation. Different versions of the Lint LUV-R (it is not always clear the correspondence with the products presented on the website) were tested in three independent researches. The first by McIlwraith et al. (2019) tested a Lint LUV-R with a stainless-steel mesh filter with a pore size of 150 μm and reported an efficiency of 80% in terms of weight reduction of MFs released by a 100% polyester fleece blanket. The work by Napper et al. (2020) tested a Lint LUV-R with a mesh of two pore size of 285 μm and 175 μm, and results showed an efficiency of 29% also in terms of weight reduction of MFs emitted by a mixed washing load composed by 100% polyester, 100% acrylic or 60% polyester/40% cotton blend jumpers. Finally, Browne et al. (2020) used a Lint LUV-R filter testing two different meshes of 2 mm and 150 μm, which had an efficiency of 65% and 74%, respectively, in reducing the amount in weight of MFs released by polyester t-shirts.

The Slovenian company PlanetCare Ltd. presents two filtration solutions on their website: a household microfiber filter to be installed externally at the domestic washing machine (PlanetCare, 2021a); a commercial microfiber filter for the service industry using a larger washing machine (i.e. launderettes, smaller hotels, sports facilities, etc.) (PlanetCare, 2021b). Both of them have exchangeable cartridges that retain MFs with an efficiency of 90% in the case of the household filter. For this latter, a full cartridge needs to be replaced after approximately 20 wash cycles. The used cartridges are to be sent back to PlanetCare for refurbishment.

The household filter was tested in four different independent researches during its developing phase performed by the Slovenian National Institute of Chemistry (MFs retained efficiency of 79%) (Slovenian National Institute, 2017); an unnamed major machine producer (MFs retained efficiency of 80%) (PlanetCare, 2018); the Swedish Environmental Protection Agency (2018), Napper et al. (2020) (efficiency of 25%, pore size of the filter observed of 200μm).

Recently, the effectiveness of two prototypes developed by PlanetCare for capturing microfibres was evaluated. The optimization of the filter design was found to be essential to improve its effectiveness in retaining MFs. In fact, the optimized filtration system was able to retain 64% of MFs released during washing of commercial polyester T-shirts. Moreover, the analysis of the retained MFs dimensions indicated that it was effective to also capture smaller MFs with an average length of 308±157 μm (De Falco et al., 2021b).

Another external system is Filtrol™, a re-usable inline filter developed by Wexco Environmental to be externally installed at washing machines (Filtrol, 2021). It uses a reusable mesh filter that should be cleaned every eight to ten washings. Its use in combination with fabric softener or excessive amount of laundry detergent is discouraged since it can cause a slimy residue and restrict the filtering process. It was tested by the University of Toronto (2020), which found an efficiency of 89% in weight of MFs removed.

A different approach has been proposed by the company Xeros Technology Group (UK), that has developed and patented a prototype filter named XFiltra that should be included directly within the washing machine, removing the need for the user to purchase, install and operate an external filter unit (Xeros Technology Group, 2021). The filter is designed to perform three actions: filtration, pump and de-watering. The fibres collected are spun into a drier state to allow easy removal and disposal by the user. According to tests performed by the company, the filter can remove more than 90% of MFs from the effluent (Xeros Technology Group, 2021). Napper et al. (2020) tested this device and found that its filter with a pore size of 60 μm was able to reduce by 78% the quantity in weight of MFs released, proving to be the most efficient device out of six devices they tested, probably because the pore size dimension of 60 μm allows to remove the majority of MFs emitted during a washing process (De Falco et al., 2019a). This device is not in commerce yet, but the company has signed an agreement with a global leader in commercial laundry solutions with the aim of incorporating XFiltra into their commercial washing machines.

In order to spread and encourage the application of these solutions, it is essential to create standard methods to test these devices in order to ensure a certification of their effectiveness, compatibility with washing machines, compatibility with the washing and cleaning process of textiles. The studies that have already tested some of these devices, each one using a different methodology, tested different garments and did not perform multiple tests changing all the relevant parameters (i.e. type of textile, washing program, detergent, type of machine, etc.). The promising results pointed out by these independent researches represent the starting point to develop hierarchical and structured testing/certification methods that could have multiple advantages of assuring the correct functioning of the device, avoiding false claims by the producers, giving clear and trustable information to the consumers. Other issues that should be addressed are the cleaning and disposal processes of the device and of the MFs collected, respectively. The developers of some of these devices (especially for the capturing ones) recommend cleaning them when fibres or entanglements are visible, but MFs have a wide dimensional range so the smallest ones cannot be visible with the naked eye. Therefore, these devices can be maybe more effective in capturing MFs of bigger dimensions. The dimensional range of the MFs retained by filter devices also need further researches. The correct disposal of the MFs retained by these devices is essential to avoid the release of these MFs, for instance to the air, due to incorrect handling of the material filtered. The adoption of filters for washing machines also needs endorsement and assurance from the washing machine producers that these devices do not affect the correct functioning of the machines. Collaborations between filter and washing machine producers is essential. Further tests are also needed to check if capturing in-drum devices do not affect the quality of the cleaning function of the washing process.

4   Support to the textile industry

Up to now, two main initiatives have been developed to support the textile industry to improve its sustainability by considering and treating MF pollution.

The Microfibre Consortium (TMC) (TMC, 2021) aims to develop practical solutions for the textile industry to minimize fibre fragmentation and release to the environment from textile manufacturing and product life cycle. TMC was legally registered in the UK (2018) as a Company Ltd (The Outdoor Microfibre Consortium Ltd) by Guarantee, operating as a non-profit. In 2017, TMC started developing a standard test method to determine fibres released from fabric during domestic laundering. The method is based on the use of lab scale equipment and a gravimetric approach. In 2021, TMC announced the public release of its test method that determines the level of MFs shed from fabrics during domestic laundering. The Wear Off Microfibers Alliance (WOMA) was recently launched by Plastic Soup Foundation (PSF, The Netherlands), in cooperation with the Institute for Polymers, Composites and Biomaterials of the National Research Council of Italy (IPCB-CNR) (WOMA, 2021). Starting from their long-standing cooperation and experience on the MF topic established during the Mermaids Project, a method to quantify MFs was patented (submitted request for European patent extension n. EP21188664.3 30/07/2021, pending) and the WOMA started. WOMA aims to widespread, among textile industries, the application of the developed methodology to test MF release from textiles during washings. In addition, WOMA aims to increase the awareness of the textile consumers by clearly identifying the textile products on the basis of their MFs release by applying a label (trademark n. 018416847, 04/03/2021). In detail, the WOMA methodology is able to quantify and certify MF release from the washing of textiles employing two types of tests: one at lab-scale by using a lab simulator, and another one at real scale by using a washing machine. The cross-comparison of the outputs of the two types of procedures allows for the determination of the level of MF release. According to the different levels of microfiber release, the textile items will receive a label that will indicate the level of release. The results, from best (green) to worst (red), are reported in Figure 10.4.

FIGURE 10.4 The WOMA label will report a symbol of a washing machine with a coloured window representing the level of the release as indicated here: Green = low; Yellow = Medium, Orange = High; Red= very high

Source: Reproduced from WOMA (2021)

5 Conclusions

A key aspect that emerges from the actions that involve textile production and laundry is the lack of standardized methodologies to quantify MF shedding and, consequently, assess the influence of different parameters on the release and the effectiveness of technologies and devices in mitigating MF release. This problem is thoroughly addressed and discussed in Chapter 6.

Regarding the actions for textile production, a change in the mentality surrounding this industry is needed. Garments and fabrics should be designed keeping in mind their sustainability, trying to create a garment that is functional but also has the lowest possible environmental impact. This can be achieved by dedicated regulations that make the application of mitigation measures for MF release mandatory. In this way, each company can modify its design and manufacturing processes in order to reduce not only its "microfibre footprint", but also its general environmental impact.

At textile laundry level, an important point to implement mitigation measures is to spread knowledge and awareness among consumers. Dedicated campaigns are needed that can involve environmental NGOs, but also political bodies. The environmental consequences of MF pollution, particularly on humans, should be highlighted to urge for a change in washing habits. These measures also imply other environmental benefits like lower energy and water consumption and associated carbon footprint.

In general, no easy solution can be applied to mitigate MF pollution and a multilevel approach is needed. Beside mitigation actions for textile production and laundry, additional measures should be applied to develop new sustainable materials for textiles and improve WWTPs (Chapter 7). Of course, to build and put into action such a multilevel approach, a strong and reliable collaboration is needed among all the players involved like academia, research institutes, textile manufacturers, fashion designers, consumers, policymakers and so on. Without a deep interconnection of all the fields and expertise involved, effective solutions are unlikely to be developed and implemented.

Notes

1 Scouring is a pre-treatment to remove fats and other impurities; desizing removes sizing agents used in the weaving process; bleaching improves the optical brightness of the fabric.
2 Spinning is the twisting of fibres to form yarn.
3 Reprinted from Carbohydrate Polymers, 198, Francesca De Falco, Gennaro Gentile, Roberto Avolio, Maria Emanuela Errico, Emilia Di Pace, Veronica Ambrogi, Maurizio Avella, Mariacristina Cocca, Pectin based finishing to mitigate the impact of microplastics released by polyamide fabrics, 175–180, Copyright (2018), with permission from Elsevier.

References

Brahney, J., Hallerud, M., Heim, E., Hahnenberger, M., Sukumaran, S., 2020. Plastic rain in protected areas of the United States. *Science*, 368(6496), 1257–1260. doi:10.1126/science.aaz5819

Browne, M., Ros, M., & Johnston, L., 2020. Pore-size and polymer affect the ability of filters for washing-machines to reduce domestic emissions of fibres to sewage. *PLoS ONE*, 15(6), 0234248. doi:10.1371/journal.pone.0234248

Cai, Y., Mitrano, D., Heuberger, M., Hufenus, R., & Nowack, B., 2020b. The origin of microplastic fiber in polyester textiles: The textile production process matters. *J. Clean. Prod.*, 267, 121970. doi:10.1016/j.jclepro.2020.121970

Cai, Y., Yang, T., Mitrano, D., Heuberger, M., Hufenus, R., & Nowack, B., 2020a. Systematic study of microplastic fiber release from 12 different polyester textiles during washing. *Environ. Sci. Technol.*, 54, 4847–4855. doi:10.1021/acs.est.9b07395

Carney Almroth, B., Åström, L., Roslund, S., & Petersson, H., 2018. Quantifying shedding of synthetic fibers from textiles: A source of microplastics released into the environment. *Environ. Sci. Pollut. Res.*, 25, 1191. doi:10.1007/s11356-017-0528-7

Cesa, F. S., Turra, A., Checon, H. H., Leonardi, B., Baruque-Ramos, J., 2020. Laundering and textile parameters influence fibres release in household washings. *Environ. Pollut.*, 257, 113553. doi:10.1016/j.envpol.2019.113553

Chan, C. K., Park, C., Chan, K., Mak, D., Fang, J., Mitrano, D., 2020. Microplastic fibre releases from industrial wastewater effluent: A textile wet-processing mill in China. *Environ. Chem.*, 18(3), 93–93. doi:10.1071/en20143

Cora Ball, 2021. *Cora Ball website*. Retrieved on 24/03/2021 from https://coraball.com/

Cotton, L., Hayward, A., Lant, N., Blackburn, R., 2020. Improved garment longevity and reduced microfibre release are important sustainability benefits of laundering in colder and quicker washing machine cycles. *Dyes and Pigments*, 177, 108120. doi:10.1016/j.dyepig.2019.108120

Dalla Fontana, G., Mossotti, R., Montarsolo, A., 2020. Assessment of microplastics release from polyester fabrics: The impact of different washing conditions. *Environ. Pollut.*, 264, 113960. doi:10.1016/j.envpol.2020.113960

Dalla Fontana, G., Mossotti, R., Montarsolo, A., 2021. Influence of sewing on microplastic release from textiles. *Water Air Soil Pollut.*, 232, 50. doi:10.1007/s11270-021-04995-7

De Falco, F., Avolio, R., Errico, M. E., Di Pace, E., Avella, M., Cocca, M., Gentile, G., 2021a. Comparison of biodegradable polyesters degradation behavior in sand. *J. Hazard. Mater.*, 416, 126231. doi:10.1016/j.jhazmat.2021.126231.

De Falco, F., Cocca, M., Avella, M., & Thompson, R., 2020. Microfiber release to water, via laundering, and to air, via everyday use: A comparison between polyester clothing with differing textile parameters. *Environ. Sci. Technol.*, 54, 3288–3296. doi:10.1021/acs.est.9b06892

De Falco, F., Cocca, M., Guarino, V., Gentile, G., Ambrogi, V., Ambrosio, L., Avella, M., 2019c. Novel finishing treatments of polyamide fabrics by electrofluidodynamic porcess to reduce microplastic release during washings. *Polym. Degrad. Stab.*, 165, 110−116. doi:10.1016/j.polymdegradstab.2019.05.001

De Falco, F., Di Pace, E., Avella, M., Gentile, G., Errico, M.E., Krzan, A., ElKhiar H., Zupan, M., Cocca, M., 2021b. Development and performance evaluation of a filtration system for washing machines to reduce microfiber release in wastewater. *Water Air Soil Pollut.*, 232, 406. doi:10.1007/s11270-021-05342-6

De Falco, F., Di Pace, E., Cocca, M., Avella, M., 2019a. The contribution of washing processes of synthetic clothes to microplastic pollution. *Sci. Rep.*, 9, 6633. doi:10.1038/s41598–019–43023-x

De Falco, F., Gentile, G., Avolio, R., Errico, M. E., Di Pace, E., Ambrogi, V., Avella, M., Cocca, M., 2018b. Pectin based finishing to mitigate the impact of microplastics released by polyamide fabrics. *Carbohydr. Polym.*, 198, 175−180. doi:10.1016/j.carbpol.2018.06.062

De Falco, F., Guarino, V., Gentile, G., Cocca, M., Ambrogi, V., Ambrosio, L., Avella, M., 2019b. Design of functional textile coatings via non-conventional electrofluidodynamic processes. *J. Colloid Interface Sci.*, 541, 367–375. doi:10.1016/j.jcis.2019.01.086

De Falco, F., Gullo, M. P., Gentile, G., Di Pace, E., Cocca, M., Gelabert, L., Brouta-Agnesa, M., Rovira, A., Escudero, R., Villalba, R., Mossotti, R., Montarsolo, A., Gavignano, S., Tonin, C., Avella, M., 2018a. Evaluation of microplastic release caused by textile washing processes of synthetic fabrics. *Environ. Pollut.*, 236, 916−925. doi:10.1016/j.envpol.2017.10.057

Deng, H., Wei, R., Luo, W., Hu, L., Li, B., Di, Y., 2020. Microplastic pollution in water and sediment in a textile industrial area. *Environ. Pollut.*, 258, 13658. doi:10.1016/j.envpol.2019.113658

Dris, R., Gasperi, J., Mirande, C., Mandin, C., Guerrouache, M., Langlois, V., Tassin, B., 2017. A first overview of textile fibres, including microplastics, in indoor and outdoor environments. *Environ. Pollut.*, 221, 453−458. doi:10.1016/j.envpol.2016.12.013

Dris, R., Gasperi, J., Saad, M., Mirande, C., Tassin, B., 2016. Synthetic fibres in atmospheric fallout: a source of microplastics in the environment? *Mar. Pollut. Bull.*, 104, 290−293. doi:10.1016/j.marpolbul.2016.01.006

Environmental Enhancements, 2021. *Environmental enhancements website.* Retrieved on 24/03/2021 from https://environmentalenhancements.com/store/

EU MERMAIDS Life+ project LIFE13 ENV/IT/001069, 2015a. *Report of the reduction of fibres loss by the use of textiles auxiliaries.* Retrieved on 24/03/2021 from https://life-mermaids.eu/en/deliverables-mermaids-life-2/

EU MERMAIDS Life+ project LIFE13 ENV/IT/001069, 2015b. *Good practice guidelines.* Retrieved on 24/03/2021 from https://life-mermaids.eu/en/deliverables-mermaids-life-2/

Filtrol, 2021. *Filtrol website.* Retrieved on 24/03/2021 from https://filtrol.net/

Gandhi, K., 2012. *Woven textiles principles, technologies and applications* (1st ed.). New Delhi: Woodhead Publishing.

Guppyfriend, 2021a. *Guppyfriend washing bag website.* Retrieved on 24/03/2021 from https://en.guppyfriend.com/

Guppyfriend, 2021b. *Guppyfriend FAQ.* Retrieved on 24/03/2021 from https://en.guppyfriend.com/products/guppyfriend-waschbeutel-kaufen#tab3

Hartline, N., Bruce, N., Karba, S., Ruff, E., Sonar, S., Holden, P., 2016. Microfiber masses recovered from conventional machine washing of new or aged garments. *Environ. Sci. Technol.*, 50, 11532−11538. doi:10.1021/acs.est.6b03045

Hernandez, E., Nowack, B., Mitrano, D., 2017. Polyester textiles as a source of microplastics from households: A mechanistic study to understand microfiber release during washing. *Environ. Sci. Technol.*, 51(12), 7036–7046. doi:10.1021/acs.est.7b01750

Kaya, A. T., Yurtsever, M., & Bayraktar, S. C., 2018. Ubiquitous exposure to microfibre pollution in the air. *Eur. Phys. J. Plus.*, 133, 133−488. doi:10.1140/epjp/i2018−12372 7

Kelly, M., Lant, N. J., Kurr, M., Grant Burgess, J., 2019. Importance of water-volume on the release of microplastic fibers from laundry. *Environ. Sci. Technol.*, 53(20), 11735–11744. doi:10.1021/acs.est.9b03022

Lant, N. J., Peththawadu, M., Sheridan, K., Dean, J., 2020. Microfiber release from real soiled consumer laundry and the impact of fabric care products and washing conditions. *PLoS ONE*, 15(6), e0233332. doi:10.1371/journal.pone.0233332

McIlwraith, H. K., Lin, J., Erdle, L. M., Mallos, N., Diamond, M. L., & Rochman, C. M., 2019. Capturing microfibres – Marketed technologies reduce microfibre emissions from washing machines. *Mar. Pollut. Bull.*, 139, 40−45. doi:10.1016/j.marpolbul.2018.12.012

Napper, I. E., Barrett, A., Thompson, R., 2020. The efficiency of devices intended to reduce microfibre release during clothes washing. *Sci. Total Environ.*, 738, 140412. doi:10.1016/j.scitotenv.2020.140412

Napper, I. E., Thompson, R. C., 2016. Release of synthetic microplastic plastic fibres from domestic washing machines: Effects of fabric type and washing conditions. *Mar. Pollut. Bull.*, 112, 39–45. doi:10.1016/j.marpolbul.2016.09.025

Niinimäki, K., Peters, G., Dahlbo, H., Perry, P., Rissanen, T., Gwilt, A., 2020. The environmental price of fast fashion. *Nat. Rev. Earth Environ.*, 1, 189–200. doi:10.1038/s43017-020-0039-9

Palacios-Mateo, C., van der Meer, Y., & Seide, G., 2021. Analysis of the polyester clothing value chain to identify key intervention points. *Environ. Sci. Eur.*, 33, 2. doi:10.1186/s12302-020-00447-x

Pena-Francesch, A., Demirel, M. C., 2019. Squid-inspired tandem repeat proteins: Functional fibers and films. *Front. Chem.*, 7, 69. doi:10.3389/fchem.2019.00069

Pirc, U., Vidmar, M., Mozer, A., Kržan, A., 2016. Emissions of microplastic fibers from microfiber fleece during domestic washing. *Environ. Sci. Pollut. Res.*, 23, 22206–22211. doi:10.1007/s11356-016-7703-0

PlanetCare, 2018. *Planet care independent test results.* Retrieved on 24/03/2021 from https://cdn.shopify.com/s/files/1/0088/0145/2087/files/RB_retention_summary.pdf?v=1615717148

PlanetCare, 2021a. *Planetcare microfiber filter.* Retrieved on 24/03/2021 from https://planet-care.org/products/microfiber-filter

PlanetCare, 2021b. *Planetcare commercial filtering solutions.* Retrieved on 24/03/2021 from https://planetcare.org/pages/commercial-filtering-solutions

Sillanpää, M., Sainio, P., 2017. Release of polyester and cotton fibres from textiles in machine washings. *Environ. Sci. Pollut. Res.,* 24, 19313–19321. doi:10.1007/s11356-017-9621-1

Slovenian National Institute, 2017. *Planet care independent test results.* Retrieved on 24/03/2021 from https://cdn.shopify.com/s/files/1/0088/0145/2087/files/NIC_study_report_PLANETCARE_Sept_2017.pdf?v=1615717147

Spencer, D., 2001. *Knitting technology* (3rd. ed.). Cambridge: Woodhead Publishing.

Suaria, G., Achtypi, A., Perold, V., Lee, J. R., Pierucci, A., Bornman, T. G., Aliani, S., 2020. Microfibers in oceanic surface waters: A global characterization. *Sci. Adv.,* 6(23), eaay8493. doi: 10.1126/sciadv.aay8493

Swedish Environmental Protection Agency, 2018. *PlanetCare Independent test results.* Retrieved on 24/03/2021 from https://cdn.shopify.com/s/files/1/0088/0145/2087/files/Swedish_EPA_filter_report_dec_2018.pdf?v=1615717146

TextileExchange, 2020. *Preferred fiber & materials market report.* Retrieved on 22/03/2021 from https://textileexchange.org/wp-content/uploads/2020/06/Textile-Exchange_Preferred-Fiber-Material-Market-Report_2020.pdf

TMC, 2021. *The microfibre consortium website.* Retrieved on 26/07/2021 from www.microfibreconsortium.com/

University of Toronto, 2020. *The filtrol catch rate.* Retrieved on 24/03/2021 from https://rochmanlab.files.wordpress.com/2019/01/microfiber-policy-brief-2019.pdf

Volgare, M., De Falco, F., Avolio, R., Castaldo, R., Errico, M.E., Gentile, G., Ambrogi, V., Cocca, M., 2021. Washing load influences the microplastic release from polyester fabrics by affecting wettability and mechanical stress. *Sci. Rep.,* 11, 19479. doi:10.1038/s41598-021-98836-6

Voragen, A. G., Coenen, G., Verhoef, R. P., & Schols, H. A., 2009. Pectin, a versatile polysaccharide present in plant cell walls. *Struct. Chem.,* 20, 263–275. doi:10.1007/s11224-009-9442-z

Wilson, J., 2000. *Handbook of textile design: Principles, processes and practice.* Cambridge, UK: Woodhead Publishing Ltd and CRC Press LLC.

WOMA, 2021. *Ocean clean wash website: Label & benchmark.* Retrieved on 26/07/2021 from www.oceancleanwash.org/label-benchmark/

WRAP, 2019. *Textile derived microfibre release: Investigating the current evidence base.* Banbury: Prepared by Resource Futures.

Xeros Technology Group, 2021. *Xeros Technologies website.* Retrieved on 24/03/2021 from www.xerostech.com/technologies

Xu, X., Hou, Q., Xue, Y., Jian, Y., & Wang, L., 2018. Pollution characteristics and fate of microfibers in the wastewater from textile dyeing wastewater treatment plant. *Water Sci. Technol.,* 78, 2046–2054. doi:10.2166/wst.2018.476

Yang, L., Qiao, F., Lei, K., Li, H., Kang, Y., Cui, S., An, L., 2019. Microfiber release from different fabrics during washing. *Environ. Pollut.,* 249, 136–143. doi:10.1016/j.envpol.2019.03.011

Zambrano, M. C., Pawlak, J. J., Daystar, J., Ankeny, M., Cheng, J. J., Venditti, R. A., 2019. Microfibers generated from the laundering of cotton, rayon and polyester based fabrics and their aquatic biodegradation. *Mar. Pollut. Bull.,* 142, 394–407. doi:10.1016/j.marpolbul.2019.02.062

11
POLICIES AND PERSPECTIVES ON REGULATING MICROPLASTIC FIBRE POLLUTION

Esther Kentin and Gaia Battaglia

Introduction

Less than ten years ago most of us would not have thought that a baby blanket made out of fleece could be considered as a threat to human health and the environment. But now we know: there is an abundance of research identifying products and garments made of synthetic materials as a source of plastic pollution that is here to stay. Microplastic fibres (MPFs) are persistent, bioaccumulative and have entered the food chain of marine organisms and humans. Fibres travel by air and currents to remote places, such as the Arctic regions and the deep sea. Rain, snow, air, soil and drinking water have been found to contain microplastic (MP) pollution, with synthetic fibres being the main culprit. The effects on the environment and human health are not yet known, however research on these subjects has intensified throughout the world. At the same time, the production and use of synthetic fibres is growing, as there is worldwide an increasing demand for synthetic textiles, due to their many perks, such as low costs, strength, light weight, colour fastness and water resistance (Muthu, 2017). The search for solutions is not a simple one, but as with plastic pollution in general, it requires a multistakeholder and 'wicked problem' approach (Belontz et al., 2019; Landon-Lane, 2018). The challenges of regulating MPF pollution are acknowledged by the authors, and we proceed with our review of the science and solutions with the understanding that there is not a one-size-fits-all solution. After a short summary of the relevant scientific evidence, we will proceed with an overview of life-cycle assessment methods of textiles to identify the phases and stakeholders involved. We will then turn to the regulation and policy initiatives on textiles and microplastics (MPs) pollution to find that these fields are separate domains. We will then turn to the legal principles on which action can be based and continue with existing and prospective policy options to tackle the issue and to integrate environmental concerns into textiles regulation. It will be

DOI: 10.4324/9781003165385-13

clarified that the preferable options are those which prevent the emission of MPFs, but that upstream solutions must be combined with downstream approaches. With this in mind, the policy options are grouped according to the phase of the textiles' life-cycle they address. The aim of the chapter is not to single out the best or most feasible option in general, but rather to present many options which can be suitable to different situations and degrees of evidence and technological advancement.

Method

We have studied the evidence concerning MPFs and scrutinized studies to find recommendations from the field (Web of science, Science Direct, searches on microplastics, fibres and textiles). We looked into all types of legislation and policies on local, national, regional and international levels, including legislation concerning other types of pollution. We collected suggestions from international organizations, like UNEP, and regional organizations, in particular the EU, and NGOs. For our section on possible policy options, we took an open and non-exclusive approach: anything that could be applicable to prevent pollution by MPFs from textiles was analyzed and considered. We do not intend to be exhaustive, as the research field is moving quickly. Every month dozens of articles on MPs are published and new solutions may be offered. We hope this chapter may inspire those working or intending to work in the textile and fashion industries to contribute to the prevention of MPFs in our environment. Furthermore, the hope is to raise awareness among all stakeholders and policymakers on national and international level who may take inspiration from this review and implement those options that are most suitable to the circumstances of their systems.

Evidence on microplastic fibre release

Since the discovery of MPs in the environment, research has exploded, especially in the last decade (Buchanan, 1971; Carpenter & Smith, 1972; Provencher et al., 2020; Thompson et al., 2004). At first studies were focused on MPs in the marine environment, but today research pertains to various aspects of MP pollution, from effects on lung tissue to the presence in agricultural soil. While knowledge gaps continue to emerge, we hereby focus on what we do know, in particular regarding MPFs. MPs are considered as a persistent pollutant caused by human activities, accumulating in all environmental compartments: marine, freshwater, aerial and terrestrial. Plastic pollution is ubiquitous, as MPs are found everywhere, from remote arctic areas to the deep sea. A relationship between the abundance of MPs and human population density has been reported through research at shorelines, finding 250% more MPs in disposal sites of sewage, while polyester and acrylic fibres were dominating (Browne et al., 2011). In the southern European seas, a large part of MPFs settle on the sea floor in coastal areas, and through the preferential dispersal pathway of sand-sized materials, a vast number of MPFs ultimately end up in the deep sea (Sanchez-Vidal, Thompson, Canals, & De Haan, 2018). In the Arctic Ocean, more than 90% of the MPs found were fibres, and the majority of these consisted of polyester. It was assumed that these were from home laundry through wastewater and atmospheric delivery (Ross et al., 2021). In Parisian freshwater, anthropogenic fibres, both synthetic and non-synthetic, are widespread, while in German rivers, synthetic fibres make up for 40% of the MPs found (Wagner et al., 2014). In the UK, MPFs are the dominant type of MPs found in the Thames basin, while in a study in Italy the share of MPFs varies (Fischer, Paglialonga, Czech, & Tamminga, 2016; Horton, Svendsen, Williams, Spurgeon, & Lahive, 2017). Some Chinese studies indicate that the most frequent shape of MPs detected in freshwater is fibre (Su et al., 2016; Wang, Ndungu, Li, & Wang, 2017). In other studies on MPs in freshwater, MPFs were detected but not always specified or counted separately (Eriksen et al., 2013). While wastewater treatment may prevent MPs from entering aquatic environments, the residue in the form of sewage sludge is identified as a major source of MPs in agricultural soils when it is used as fertilizer (Zubris & Richards, 2005). MPFs are detectable in soils up to 15 years after application. Other sources include the use of mulch film and fertilizers (Weithmann et al., 2018). MPs were also detected and measured beyond agricultural soils. In US conservation parks, up to 70% of found synthetic materials were identified as 'synthetic microfibers', assumingly transported over long distances in the atmosphere (Brahney, Hallerud, Heim, Hahnenberger, & Sukumaran, 2020). The effects on terrestrial ecosystems are largely unknown, though gaining attention (Rillig & Lehmann, 2020). The existence of aerial pathways for MPFs to remote areas means that pollution of MPFs is unavoidable once they are released. A further concern pertains to the air quality itself and possible inhalation of MPs by humans and animals (Dris et al., 2017; Gasperi et al., 2018; Prata, 2018). A study in London reported the highest deposition rates of MPs measured until now, with 92%, being MPFs, and most of these being acrylic and polyester (Wright, Ulke, Font, Chan, & Kelly, 2020). It was suggested that if clothing and other textiles are the main sources, there might be a correlation with densely populated areas, as suggested before in relation to coastal waters. Synthetic fibres make up over 60% of the world fibre consumption, and the production of synthetic fibres is growing at an annual rate of 6.6% (Gasperi et al., 2018; Grand View Research, 2021; Salvador Cesa, Turra, & Baruque-Ramos, 2017). These figures point to an increase of MPFs in the environment if such growth proceeds without control, as degradation rates are assumed to be low (Sait et al., 2021). The effects of MP pollution on human and animal health are uncertain, although there is evidence of negative effects (Foley, Feiner, Malinich, & Höök, 2018; Henry, Laitala, & Klepp, 2019; Prata, 2018). Ingestion has been observed in various organisms, as well as a preference for fibrous shapes, which leads to accumulation and transfer through marine food chains (Wright, Thompson, & Galloway, 2013). Effects on population of planktonic crustaceans were recorded following exposure to MPs in a lab setting and reported as reduction of reproductive capacity (Bosker, Olthof, Vijver, Baas, & Barmentlo, 2019; Jaikumar, Brun, Vijver, & Bosker, 2019). Research on human exposure to MPFs is emerging, building upon studies on occupational exposure in the plastic industry and those on fine particulate matter. Respiratory diseases have been recorded, and other adverse health effects can be expected, in particular in susceptible individuals, which already suffer from fine particulate matter (Akhbarizadeh et al., 2021; Kelly & Fussell, 2015; Prata, 2018). Exposure through food has also been recorded, either as MPs entered in the human food chain or through contamination by packaging and deposition, although effects on human health are yet unknown (Carbery, O'Connor, & Palanisami, 2018; Rist, Carney Almroth, Hartmann, & Karlsson, 2018; Shruti, Pérez-Guevara, Elizalde-Martínez, & Kutralam-Muniasamy, 2020). Most studies regarding the release of MPFs of textiles focus on the use and disposal phase of textiles, and in particular on release during washing (De Falco, Di Pace, Cocca, & Avella, 2019; Napper & Thompson, 2016; Pirc, Vidmar, Mozer, & Kržan, 2016; Özkan & Gündoğdu, 2021). Some studies address the technical aspects of textiles: type of filament, yarns, and fabrics, finishing treatments and the effects of these aspects on shedding (De Falco, Cocca, Avella, & Thompson, 2020; De Falco, Cocca, et al., 2019; Jönsson et al., 2018; Mermaids, 2017). In addition, impacts of the processing of surfaces and cutting-methods are being explored (Cai, Mitrano, Heuberger, Hufenus, & Nowack, 2020). Within the research field of textile engineering, there is little attention to the release of MPs, though focus on this form of pollution may increase due to policy developments concerning sustainable textiles.

Life-cycle assessment of textiles and the release of microplastic fibres

Numerous studies have been published on life-cycle assessment (LCA) of textiles, in particular to compare the environmental impact of different fibres (Muthu, 2015, 2020). Other approaches related to environmental impacts and sustainability are ecological footprint measurement, supply- or value-chain assessment, cradle-to-grave/gate and circular economy analyses. These may relate to a certain aspect of environmental impact, such as carbon footprint, while others may attempt to include all aspects. The question of which approach would be most suitable to measure the environmental impact of MPF release goes beyond the scope of this chapter. Any of the approaches may help to identify possible releases and effects, which may lead to finding of potential solutions and mitigation options.

Indicators frequently included in life-cycle assessments or footprint analyses are (Muthu, 2015):

- land usage and degradation
- water usage and contamination
- energy usage
- depletion of natural resources
- use of pesticides, biocides and fertilizers
- use of chemicals
- packaging
- transport
- emissions of pollutants and CO_2

* waste generation
* human health impacts
* noise, light, odour and heat pollution

The inclusion of MPFs emission as an indicator is not common practice yet in environmental impact studies on textiles. A benchmark study comparing cotton with synthetic textiles conducted in 2014 concluded that acrylic and polyester could be considered as textiles with the least impact on the environment, though the release of MPFs in the manufacturing or use phase was not included in the assessment (Van Der Velden, Patel, & Vogtländer, 2014). Recently, the first steps have been set to validate the inclusion of MPF loss in environmental assessments, and as the evidence on MPF loss is growing, it is expected that soon this will be mainstream (Henry et al., 2019). There are essentially two options for including the release of MPFs as an indicator. Most obvious is to label MPF release as a pollutant, as an emission of a chemical. While research concerning the toxicity of MPs is still ongoing (Manshoven et al., 2019), the European Chemical Agency has labelled MPs as a non-threshold substance for the purpose of risk assessment, due to its persistent and bioaccumulative properties (ECHA, 2019). Also within several other fora, MP pollution is considered as marine litter or chemical pollutant in the aquatic environment, for example by the United Nations Environment Programme. This applies as well for the aerial environment: release of MPFs falls under the definition of fine particulate matter pollution, which affects air quality, both outdoor and indoor. The second option is to bring the release of MPFs under the indicator of waste generation. MPF pollution may be indicated as unrecovered waste, thus a loss within the circular economy approach.

While numerous studies have pointed out the release of MPs during washing of textiles, evidence on emissions of MPFs during other phases of production, use or disposal is scarce. There is evidence that textiles release MPFs into the air and the indoor environment during use, through wearing clothes and sitting on furniture, though there is hardly any data on quantity or sources (De Falco et al., 2020). Studies have, however, suggested that most preferable solutions may be found in the manufacturing and production phase. Using the LCA method for identifying interventions or policy options to prevent MPF release of synthetic textiles throughout the life-cycle, five phases are distinguished:

* Production of fibres, yarns and fabric
* Manufacturing of garment and product
* Distribution
* Use
* End-of-life stage

The raw materials phase, crude oil manufacture and preparation of chips, has been left out in this study as this phase does not deal with MPF pollution specifically. Policy options such as prevention of pellet loss and best management practices on site and during transportation have been developed and implemented, though we have not included these in our analysis as they do not specifically concern MPF pollution. The manufacturing phase has been divided in the production of fibres, yarns and fabric, and the manufacturing of garments and products. There may be some overlap in these phases, as for example both yarns, fabrics and garments can be dyed or treated with coatings. Essential for the LCA of garments are the developments in the fashion industry and its changing dynamics. From two collections a year, to fast-fashion, to ultrafast-fashion, it is expected that the ever-shorter life-cycles of garments will have a negative effect on MPF release. While it may be complex to compare the environmental impact of different garments made of different fibres, there is a consensus that the shorter lifespans of garments come with additional environmental costs (Yang, Song, & Tong, 2017). Reconciling the trend of fast-fashion with sustainability may present the biggest challenge for fashion brands and the production industry. Nevertheless, we see increasingly national and international initiatives of fashion brands and organizations towards sustainability in the broadest scope, such as those by Patagonia, the Milan Green Carpet Fashion Awards and the UN Alliance for Sustainable Fashion. It seems that consumers are ready for these changes (Grazzini, Acuti, & Aiello, 2021).

Regulating microplastic pollution from textiles

Regulation of textiles

International law regarding textiles is largely concentrated on trade in textiles, providing market access and removing trade barriers, such as quotas and tariffs. The past WTO Agreement on Textiles and Clothing (ATC) included an Annex with a list of products that covered more or less any fibre, yarn or textile product, whether natural or man-made, from 'combed wool in fragments', 'boys pyjamas' to 'mattresses' and 'carpets'. While categories of products were mentioned, no further standards or rules were set. The ATC was terminated in 2005, and textiles now fall under the General Agreement on Trade and Tariffs, without further specification. So, presently, despite the textile industry being a true global and major sector in the world economy, there are no binding rules or specifications for textiles on a global level. On a regional and bilateral level, agreements on trade in textiles continue to be negotiated, mostly regulating the access of, restrictions on and treatment of export and import of textile products, including yarns, fabrics and clothing.

Beyond trade agreements, there are basically two regional regulations regarding the labelling of textile products. The European Textile Regulation regulates fibre names, the labelling and marking of fibre composition of textile products for the European market (Regulation (EU) No.1007/2011). This regulation standardizes the names of textile fibres and the indications appearing on labels, on marking and on documents at the various stages of production, processing and distribution. It also lays down methods for official tests to determine fibre composition. Its main goal is to harmonize the names and testing methods of textiles to achieve a proper functioning of the internal market. The regulation is not mandated to protect human health or the environment, and only refers to human health aspects in relating to allergic reactions, providing for a technical file for new textile fibres with scientific information including possible adverse effects on human health. The second regulation is the Mercosur Technical Regulation on Labelling of Textile Products (MERCOSUR/GMC/RES. No. 62/18). This South American regulation goes beyond the EU regulation, by requiring country of origin and mandatory care labelling on the basis of ISO standard 3758. In many other countries, labelling of fibre composition is regulated by national law, such as the Canadian Textile Labelling Act, the Chinese mandatory standards GB 5296.4, the Indian Textile Regulation 1988 and the US Textile Fiber Products Identification Act. Sometimes these national regulations also include care labelling, such as in the United States, though in most countries this is voluntary. In Europe, the ISO standard 3758, developed together with GINETEX, is adopted by 18 countries. Other countries have their own standards, such as the Chinese GB/T 8685 and the US ASTM D5489 (Intertek, 2019). Labelling obligations may constitute a technical barrier to trade and could be potentially a violation of WTO rules, though generally, if the labelling is non-discriminatory and offers benefits for consumers, it is considered consistent with WTO rules.

In 2021, the EU took the first steps to adopt an EU Strategy for Textiles (European Commission, Ares(2021)67453). As part of a broader policy on circularity and climate neutrality, further discussed in the next section, this initiative foresees 'creating conditions and incentives to boost the competitiveness, sustainability and resilience of the EU textiles sector'. Next to promotion of sustainable production processes and sustainable design and collection and recycling of waste textiles, the initiative mentions the tackling of the release of MPs of textiles as a contribution to the European green transition. The strategy is prepared to be adopted at the end of 2021, which may lead to further regulation and policy measures on these issues.

Regulation targeting microplastic pollution in general

From the beginning of the 2000s a number of countries have taken legislative measures to curb plastic pollution, which started with the banning and levying of plastic bags as one of the most visible forms of pollution (UNEP, 2020). The United States was the first country to address MP pollution in its Microbead-Free Water Act in 2015, by banning solid MPs in certain wash-off cosmetic products and more countries followed. Other countries, such as France, Italy, New Zealand, Korea, Taiwan and the UK followed with similar laws. While these measures do not address MPFs of textiles, the adoption of these laws has raised awareness among policymakers on the issue of MP pollution in general.

The European Union has put in place a number of initiatives to address plastic pollution. Next to the plastic bag directive, it adopted the European Strategy for Plastics in a Circular Economy in 2018, presenting wide-ranging although non-binding commitments to action, among which is the development of innovative solutions to prevent MPs from entering the environment (COM(2018)28). MPs are acknowledged as a 'rising problem' on which further research is needed. Measures such as 'better information and minimum requirements' of MPF release from textiles as well as the monitoring of drinking water and extended producer responsibility are envisaged. In line with this strategy, the European Commission requested the European Chemical Agency to prepare a dossier for restricting MPs in certain products under its chemicals' regulation REACH. Although MPFs, not being intentionally added to products, do not fall within the scope of the restriction, the dossier points out that, based on scientific evidence, MPs should be treated as a non-threshold substance for the purpose of risk assessment (ECHA, 2019). Hence, there would be no safe amount which may be released into the environment. In 2019, the European Commission reinforced its commitments through the Green Deal, an ambitious communication outlining a roadmap towards climate neutrality and a clean, circular economy by 2050 (COM(2019)640). Therein, the Commission presents a zero-pollution objective to be achieved by focusing particularly on harmful sources of pollutants such as MPs. The ideas of the Green Deal are further elaborated on in the new Circular Economy Action Plan of 2020 (COM(2020)98). This plan presents several actions relevant to MPFs pollution. Among its key actions is the legislative proposal for a sustainable product policy initiative, based on the widening of the Ecodesign Directive to non-energy-related products such as textiles, which is also mentioned in the EU Strategy for Textiles. Furthermore, the plan suggests the development of labelling, standardization, certification and regulatory measures on unintentionally released MPs, especially from tyres and textiles.

Part of the measures suggested in the new plans will be realized through amendments of existing regulation, such as the Marine Strategy Framework Directive (Directive 2008/56/EC). This directive requires the Member States to carry out monitoring programmes and report on certain enumerated criteria to verify the condition of marine waters. Such criteria were modified in 2017 following a Commission's decision to include an explicit mention of 'micro-litter' as a descriptor. This can prove very valuable to expand the data available and the understanding of MPs concentrations and patterns. Another relevant law is the newly revised Drinking Water Directive (Directive (EU) 2020/2184). The act currently foresees the adoption of a methodology to measure MPs in order to include them on the 'watch list' of substances of concern by the beginning of 2024. Moreover, a deadline is set by 2029 for the submission, on the part of the Commission, of a report regarding the risks for drinking water associated with MPs.

Still undergoing is the revision of the Urban Waste Water Treatment Directive (Council Directive 91/271/EEC). The 2019 Evaluation pinpoints as a shortcoming the lack of inclusion of MPs within the scope of the directive and highlights the issue of MPs captured into wastewater sludge and re-entering the environment through its use in agriculture.

Also on a national and federal level, many countries outside the European Union have set standards regarding the quality of their marine water, freshwater resources and waste water. Explicit measuring of MPs as pollutants is still rare, though California is a promising example (SB-1422 California Safe Drinking Water Act: microplastics). It goes beyond the scope of this chapter to discuss these measures, but it should be stressed that these types of legislation, including legislation regulating air quality, emissions and protection of vulnerable environments, may incorporate measures that lead to the prevention and mitigation of MPF pollution. These measures may be further instigated by international agreements, such as the Ramsar Convention on Wetlands, the World Heritage Convention and the Regional Seas Conventions and Action Plans. There are also many regional and bilateral agreements on rivers, natural parks and other areas that urge states to take measures to prevent pollution.

Regulation targeting microplastic fibre pollution from textiles

At the national level, a limited number of legislative responses have been proposed. In California and Connecticut, bills were submitted to include a warning on release of MPFs on clothing in 2018, but none of them were scheduled for hearing or voting (California's Assembly Bill No. 2379; Connecticut General Assembly No. 341). In 2020, France became the first country in the world to adopt a law preventing MPF pollution from textiles (LOI n° 2020–105, Art 79). As part of its circular economy law, new washing machines must be fitted with a filter for MPFs as of January 2025. The details of this mandatory standard will be specified in a following decree. The European Commission has looked into the possibility of setting requirements on the use of washing machine filters in the context of adoption of ecodesign requirements for washing machines, but it concluded that technical solutions were not mature at that time (European Parliament, E-001371/2020). The Commission announced that by the end of 2025 the possibility of introducing washing machine filters will be considered again.

Voluntary initiatives related to environmental concerns in the textile sector

Relatively recently, environmental and human rights concerns have led to voluntary initiatives by the textiles sector and other organizations. The 2018 Fashion Industry Charter for Climate Action, a Sectoral Engagement activity within the UN Climate Change framework, includes an action plan to move to net-zero Greenhouse gas emissions by 2050. The Charter has been signed by over 120 fashion brands and more than 40 organizations, such as environmental NGOs and fashion organizations, that support the initiative. While the Charter does not deal with MPFs as such, the reduction of GHG emissions may have an effect on the release of MPFs. For example, if renewable and more sustainable materials are developed, MPF release may be reduced or eliminated. Another global initiative is the UN Alliance for Sustainable Fashion, launched in 2019 and composed of UN agencies, to collaborate on the Sustainable Development Goals (SDGs) in the fashion sector. The Alliance aims to encourage the fashion industry, and also governments, to take action according to the SDGs. One of the challenges reviewed is to reduce emissions in the fashion value chain. A document specifically tackling MPs is the Cross Industry Agreement for the prevention of microplastic release into the aquatic environment during the washing of synthetic textiles, an initiative of the European textiles industry, which agreed to develop a harmonized testing method.

Labels are the most visible options for consumers for information about the product and sometimes include additional information regarding care, origin, production method and sustainability. Worldwide, there are more than 100 voluntary ecolabels that may be available for and applicable to textiles. Some internationally operating labels are the Global Organic Textile Standard (GOTS), the Oeko-Tex Standards 100 and the EU Ecolabel (2014/350/EU). No ecolabel includes standards regarding the release of MPFs yet. An initiative set up by GINETEX, a fashion association for textile care, is Clevercare.info. This logo can be added to the washing instructions and it guides consumers to more sustainable care practices, such as washing at lower temperatures and drying textiles naturally instead of in the dryer.

Policy options for preventing and mitigating pollution by microplastic fibres from textiles

General principles on environmental pollution

In action to developing specific environmental laws to control MPF pollution, preventative measures on MPFs may be included in regulatory frameworks that deal with water use, circular economy, health and even consumer protection. General environmental law principles, binding upon states and between states, play a role in the interpretation and application of the law, and these principles are applicable to all activities affecting the environment (Sands, 2018). Among the most relevant principles for the prevention and mitigation of MPF pollution is, firstly, the prevention principle. This principle requires states to prevent environmental pollution as much as possible, placing a due diligence duty on governments to adopt appropriate rules and to enforce these. There is a general consensus that the emission of man-made substances, not occurring in the natural environment, should be prevented. Secondly, the precautionary principle provides guidance where there is scientific uncertainty regarding the effects and consequences of the activity. This principle is often referred to in relation to measures to curb plastic pollution as there are gaps in knowledge regarding the risks for animal and human health, and ecosystems. Despite these gaps, there is ample evidence regarding the presence of MPs in all compartments of the environment, and given the fact that plastic is man-made and persistent, MPs cause disturbance of the natural environment indefinitely. A third principle applicable to the regulation of MPF pollution is the polluter-pays principle. Increasingly we see this principle applied in EU law, in particular in the shape of Extended Producer Responsibility (EPR) (Raubenheimer

& Urho, 2020). The EPR approach requires producers to take responsibility for their products throughout the products' life cycle, including the post-consumer phase (OECD, 2001). The EU Single-Use Plastics Directive of 2019 embraces this approach for ten categories of plastic products (Directive (EU) 2019/904). Next to environmental law principles, policy approaches have been developed in the research and policy context, and those are being progressively incorporated by some states and the EU into governance. The concept of circular economy is such an approach, adopted by the European Commission as one the main blocks of the Green Deal. A circular economy can be defined as 'a regenerative system in which resource input and waste, emission, and energy leakage are minimized by slowing, closing, and narrowing material and energy loops' (Geissdoerfer, Savaget, Bocken, & Hultink, 2017). Among the tools to achieve the circular economy are ecodesign and life-cycle management. Another relevant and related concept is the waste hierarchy. This concept elaborates on sustainability and life-cycle assessment by identifying the most favourable options for waste management at the end-of-life stage of products. At the top of the waste hierarchy is prevention, followed by minimization and reuse.

Principles and policy concepts should guide policy makers to adopt appropriate regulation and rank options according to the waste hierarchy. While science-based decision making is essential to evaluate the efficacy of prevention methods, risk assessment may be perceived differently by scientists and policymakers and, ultimately, law making may lead to compromise that is not wholly satisfactory to environmentalists, regulators or the industry. It should be noted that more systemic options may require serious investments and changes which cannot be realized overnight. In the meantime, so-called 'no-regret' options, measures which are worth implementing without having certainty about the risks, may be – although not the preferable or upstream – a more suitable approach. These are options relatively easy to implement that are also cost-effective and efficient in preventing or mitigating pollution and its effects. Furthermore, as with other complex environmental problems, policy options need to be complementary. As long as synthetic textiles are used, MPFs may be released in every phase. While upstream measures are generally preferred as they may prevent emissions at a later stage, abrasion in the use phase is unavoidable. The life-cycle approach will be helpful to identify complementary policies in each phase. In addition, policies targeted to prevent environmental impacts after release and transfer of MPs between environmental compartments will be discussed. Table 11.1 provides an overview of identified policies in the literature which are further reviewed and assessed later in this chapter.

Policy options along the life cycle phases of textiles

Production of fibres, yarns and fabric

Despite the scarce attention for MPs in the field of textile engineering, there is comprehensive knowledge about abrasion and durability of yarns and fabrics. In

TABLE 11.1 Selection of policy options collected from literature and reports

Phase	Process	Policy options
Production of fibres, yarns, and fabric		
	General	(ISO) Standards on abrasion/durability, microplastic release
		Criterion on durability
		Textile design (fibre, yarn, fabric): avoiding textiles characteristics with high MPF release
		Fee on durability as part of EPR scheme
		Best practices in fibre, yarn and fabric production
		Avoid processed surface, such as fleece, plain brushed and microfiber
		Treatment of textile factory effluent
	Fibre production	Improve melting, fineness, regularity of fibres
	Yarn production	Increase tensile strength and other technical quality measures
		Tightly constructed yarns
		Higher twisting yarns when using recycled polyester, improve quality of recycled yarn
		Yarn size above microfibre range
		Avoid rotor spinning
	Fabric production	Fabrics with compact structure (woven, highly twisted yarns, continuous filaments)
		Knitting techniques to reduce fibre release
		Remove microparticles from fabric at production stage, in-line vacuum system
		Laser-cut textiles instead of scissor-cut
	Wet treatment	Dying of yarn instead of fabric/garment
	Finishing	Pre-washing with filter
		Preventative coating
		Limited use of finishing agent
		Avoid brushing
Manufacturing of garment and product		
	Garment manufacturing	(ISO) standards on abrasion/durability, microplastic release
		Maximum threshold for fibre release, ban for non-conformity
		Ecodesign, garment design: long-lasting product, compatible with end of life recycling
		Ecodesign requirements: resistance to pilling and abrasion
		More use of natural fibre fabrics
		Ultrasound cutting in cut and sew process
	Finishing	Pre-washing with filter
		Preventative (biodegradable) coating, surface coating
		Vacuum exhaustion
	Labelling	Testing and certification abrasion and MPF release of garments

Phase	Process	Policy options
Distribution and retail		
	Labelling	Consumer information on abrasion, preventative measures (washing and drying instructions)
		Ranking textiles fibres with regard of sustainability
	Packaging	Consumer information on abrasion, preventative measures (washing and drying instructions)
	Retail	Tax on products including synthetic polymers
		Visibility of sustainable products
Use		
	Wearing	Extending the life of garments/products
		Wash before wear preventing inhalation
	Washing	Filters on washing machines (EPR for textile producers)
		Performance standards on washing machine and industrial laundries
		Awareness raising (washing instructions, detergents, low temperature)
		Development of test protocols, test for fibre release of textiles
		Detergents development
		Laundry bags
		Avoid long and stressful washing cycles, optimise washing conditions
	Drying	Filters on dryers
Use		Measure microfibre loss during use
End-of-life/disposal		
	Reuse	EPR policy for reuse and recycling stimulating ecodesign
	Recycling	Monitoring of quality
After release in environment		
	Water	Monitoring, development of sampling methods
		Filtering sewage water, ultrafiltering, wastewater treatment
		Standards and methods for filtering
		Quality standards for wastewater
		Reuse of microplastic waste with clay into composite particle
	Soil	Quality standards for sewage sludge
		Preventing sewage sludge with microplastics as fertilizer
		Sludge treatment
	Air	Monitoring

(Continued)

TABLE 11.1 (Continued)

Phase	Process	Policy options
General		
	Research	Develop methods for shedding measurement
		Development of software for fibre identification
		Promotion of innovation by pricing and subsidy incentives
		Collaboration of textile and environmental science
	Testing	Standardization of methods of detecting MPFs
	LCA	Microfibres as indicator
		Research on knowledge gaps
		Product development and process optimalisation through LCA/EIAs
	Consumer/producer behaviour	Reducing production and consumption of fast fashion

Sources: Bauer et al., 2018; Browne et al., 2011; Bukhari, Carrasco-Gallego, & Ponce-Cueto, 2018; Cai et al., 2020; Carney Almroth et al., 2018; Dalla Fontana, Mossotti, & Montarsolo, 2020; De Falco et al., 2020; De Falco, Cocca, et al., 2019; De Falco, Di Pace, et al., 2019; Dris, Gasperi, Rocher, & Tassin, 2018; Eunomia & ICF, 2018; European Commission & Directorate-General for Research and Innovation, 2019; European Commission, Directorate-General for Environment, Hogg, Jones, & Papineschi, 2020; Gasperi et al., 2018; He, Li, & Zhu, 2019; Henry et al., 2018; Henry, Laitala, & Klepp, 2019; International Wool Textile Organisation, 2020; Jönsson et al., 2018; Kentin, 2018; Lant, Hayward, Peththawadu, Sheridan, & Dean, 2020; Mahon et al., 2017; Manshoven et al., 2019; Mermaids, 2017; Napper & Thompson, 2016; Nieminen, Linke, Tobler, & Beke, 2007; O'Brien et al., 2020; OECD, 2020; Palacios-Mateo, Van Der Meer, & Seide, 2021; Palm et al., 2015; RIVM, 2019; Roos, Levenstam Arturin, & Hanning, 2017; SAPEA, 2019; Sun, Dai, Wang, van Loosdrecht, & Ni, 2019; Sundt, Syversen, Skogesal, & Schulze, 2016; The Pew Charitable Trusts & SYSTEMIQ, 2020; Vassilenko, Watkins, Chastain, Posacka, & Ross, 2019; Weis, 2018; Yang et al., 2017; Zhang & Chen, 2020.

particular in the field of technical and high performance textiles, such as for military applications and for protective clothing, abrasion resistance is an important feature. The techniques to produce those textiles are well known and include aspects as fibre use, yarn and thread manufacturing, weaving and knitting technology, and finishing methods (McLoughlin & Sabir, 2018). Abrasion and durability of textiles for upholstery are measured by methods such as the Martindale test, operational since the 1940s. This test measures the number of cycles needed to produce yarn breakage and is mostly used for home textiles (de Castellar, Saurí, Martí, & Manich, 2004). The test is defined in ISO and ASTM standards, next to other test methods, such as the forming of lint (ISO 12945, 12947, ASTM D4966; ASTM D3884, D3885, D3886, D4157, D4158; ISO 9073). While there is awareness of sustainability issues like water and energy use, use of chemicals and CO_2 emission, the attention for MPs in the field of textile engineering is negligible, at least in the literature. Loss of MPs may fit in the broader spectrum of improving durability under the umbrella of sustainability.

In the field of pollution-oriented research on MPFs, there is increasing interest in the production process of textiles. Key is to connect these two now-separated research fields. The use of knowledge of the textile industry to produce less shedding textiles is a fundamental step to tackle MPF release at the source. This process could be complemented with developing testing methods, standard setting and certification. A first step in this direction is made by the European Committee for Standardization and ISO in developing a test method for fibre loss during washing, which could be adopted in voluntary or binding regulation (CEN/TC 248/WG 37 – Microplastics from textiles sources; ISO/TC 38 Textiles, ISO/DIS 4484). Further policies could include incentives for innovation in the textile sector by creating funds and subsidies. Implementing EPR for materials in the form of raising a fee in relation to durability or, more specifically, to fibre loss could steer producers to better options and, at the same time, have them pay for producing polluting materials. These policies may fit in and amend existing textiles regulations on materials, either at the national, regional or international level.

Manufacturing of garment and product

The manufacturing of garments is discussed here as a separate phase since it involves different stakeholders. Fashion brands, designers and retailers take the lead in garment and product development, and they have affinity with consumer choices and preferences. Since consumer awareness on sustainability in general and on MPs more specifically is increasing, a reaction of the branch will follow. Some brands have taken up sustainability as its major selling feature, while others include products that are 'more sustainable'. The choice for natural textiles by some brands has a direct effect on the release of MPs in respect to that specific piece of garment. Nevertheless, the share of synthetic textiles is increasing and, given the limited production capacity of natural fibres due to available agricultural land, synthetic textiles are here to stay (Gasperi et al., 2018; Muthu, 2020). The selection of materials for garment and product is part of the design phase, as well as the choice for finishing treatments, such as pre-washing and coatings. Ecodesign measures may set parameters for garments and products, or even a maximum threshold for fibre release (Eunomia & ICF, 2018). Consumers can be informed by garment and product labelling, alongside the already mandatory information on fibres and care instruction. While these kinds of environmental standards on products may be new for the textile industry, these developments have previously been taken in other sectors, such as the automotive and electronics sector. Furthermore, the policy options in the materials phase mentioned earlier may apply similarly in the production phase, for example EPR for garments and products related to fibre loss as part of a sustainability assessment. Complimentary to the measures directed to prevent MPF loss during use by the consumer, best management practices and preventative measures during production and manufacturing can be taken to prevent release during these phases, both as protecting workers through occupational measures and as preventing emissions into the environment.

Distribution and retail

While stakeholders in this phase may have little influence on MPF loss of products, they are the link between production and use. Retail can play a role in informing consumers on MPF loss of the product and on preventative measures during use. Tools for supplying this information are product and sale websites, tags or labels on products, and packaging. Tax incentives, based on sustainability assessment including fibre loss, could persuade customers to buy more sustainable products.

Use

Since laundering was identified as one of the major sources of MPs in the environment, many studies focused on solutions for this source. Awareness raising among consumers on MPF loss of textiles is often seen as a starting point for policies: by using liquid detergent, a fully loaded machine and at low temperature, some MPF release can be prevented during washing. In addition, considerable attention has been devoted to the filtering of washing effluent either at the washing machine or, as will be discussed next, at wastewater treatment plants. France has taken the first steps to prescribe inbuilt filters in washing machines from 2025, although technical details are not known yet. The EU will consider filters in evaluating the ecodesign requirements on washing machines. Further measures could pertain to the development of washing detergents that could prevent MPF release and the use of fibre-capturing laundry bags for use during washing. Filters capturing MPFs in dryers could be a next preventative step during laundering. The prevention of MPF pollution during use can further be achieved by extending the life of garments as the highest release takes place during the first washing cycles. Washing before wearing may reduce MPF release into the air during the first period of wearing, which can also be achieved by pre-washing in the manufacturing phase.

End-of-life stage

Not much is known about the release of MPFs in the end-of-life stage, at disposal in landfills or incineration. A number of studies have assessed the release of MPFs of recycled materials, such as r-PET, concluding that these materials may lead to higher release (Özkan & Gündoğdu, 2021). Measures leading to innovation and improving quality in the manufacturing process of recycled fabrics, followed up by standard setting, could mitigate this effect.

After release into the environment

As presently few of the policies mentioned earlier are in place, MP release from textiles is a major contributor to MP pollution. Particularly in wastewater, MPs with fibrous shape dominate. Filtering and other methods of treatment have been suggested, but only in a few countries, technologies are applied that substantially remove MPs (Sun et al., 2019). For sewage sludge, technologies for removing MPs are in an initial stage (Zhang & Chen, 2020). Developing methods and technologies and setting standards for wastewater treatment in an international context continues to be essential, as MP pollution is a global phenomenon. In addition, policies regarding sewage sludge should be considered, such as stopping the use of sewage sludge on agricultural land, setting quality standards for the use of sludge, or developing efficient and economical treatments of sludge to prevent and minimize the transfer of MPs to the terrestrial environment. It remains of utmost importance to include MPs, and more specifically MPFs, into monitoring mechanisms of water, marine and air quality regulation. Monitoring is essential to assess the result of policies, and, more importantly, the foundation of our 'state of the environment'.

Evaluation and conclusions

This chapter aimed to assess science, regulation and policies on MPF pollution from textiles and in this section we evaluate our findings. Solutions have been suggested by scientists studying the presence and effects of MPFs, while policymakers begin to consider how to regulate the release of MPFs. The present legislation on textiles is weak on environmental aspects, while there is no environmental regulation that addresses the sources of MPF pollution. The scientific uncertainty regarding the effects of MP pollution on human health and the environment may postpone stricter legislation for the near future, though the legislative initiatives of the EU are hopeful. Although some voluntary initiatives have been taken, the textile industry in general must fully acknowledge the pollution from MPFs by its products. The obligation of producers to prevent said pollution as much as possible and to pay for mitigation measures and clean-ups arises from general legal principles as the products cause an unavoidable spill of MPFs into the environment, much like exhaust from cars or smokestacks that we all acknowledge must be controlled at the source. However, these obligations are not enforceable – although recent climate change litigation may open up possibilities – unless policymakers and regulators implement them through the adoption of binding measures. There is a lot to win, and some bold steps must be taken. Overall, five recommendations can be made:

- Raise awareness on microplastic fibre pollution among all stakeholders.

Awareness on MP pollution among consumers is slowly growing, inter alia through reports in the media. However, MP pollution cannot yet be considered an environmental problem of general knowledge. Solutions that are often mentioned in research are optimal washing conditions, such as low temperature and liquid detergent. But unless consumers are well informed, behaviour will not change (Heidbreder, Bablok, Drews, & Menzel, 2019). Other factors for behavioural change are practicability and convenience, habits and the perceived responsibility for the problem. If measures such as labelling will be taken, consumers should understand the consequences of their behaviour. Labelling alone is not effective unless the public is receptive to the information which it provides. Within the textiles and fashion industry, there is some attention for MP pollution, but current evidence, in particular on toxicity, is considered insufficient to justify taking measures. Individual brands adopt their own strategy, but the share of synthetic materials and low quality fast-fashion is still growing. Whether this is the consequence of ignorance or deliberate neglect, the textile industry should be fully aware of its crucial role in tackling MPF pollution. In addition, policymakers, as drivers of regulation, should gain knowledge of both the evidence and uncertainties related to MPF research. The highlighting of uncertainties, such as on toxicity, may be used as a political argument for avoiding regulation (Avgerinopoulou, 2019), but the evidence that is out, such as ubiquitous presence of MPs in the global environment and its persistent and bioaccumulative characteristics, should suffice as ground for preventative measures or at least no-regret measures.

- Enhance collaboration between science communities for innovation in textiles.

Taking into account the preference for solutions at the source, innovation in textile engineering to prevent MPF release is key. Collaboration in research programmes between textile scientists and scientists working on the detection of MPs is recommended and an open source approach could accelerate innovation. Considerable knowledge on abrasion and durability is already present in literature on textiles (Annis, 2012; McLoughlin & Sabir, 2018; Paul, 2014; Zhang, 2014), though not connected with MPF loss. In addition, there is broad knowledge on LCA and sustainability issues in the textile science and positive initiatives like the Sustainable Apparel Coalition, The Microfibre Consortium, Wear Off Microplastic Alliance and the Microfiber Partnership of Ocean Wise Plastics Lab can be mentioned. There are also some textiles and fashion brands working on microplastic shedding and test methods. But generally, this knowledge is only slowly incorporated by the industry in a fragmentary way.

- Integrate environmental policy on microplastic fibres in textiles regulation.

Regulation of textiles, in particular regarding environmental issues, lags behind other sectors. For instance, the regulation and policies of the automotive and electronic sectors have gone through a development, which brought the inclusion of environmental aspects such as emissions, waste and recycling, and energy use.

For the textile sector, we found no binding environmental standards, no recycling prescriptions and no environmental product requirements. The environmental footprint of the apparel industry is actually growing in step with the increase in production, on the one hand because of the fast-fashion trend, and on the other hand by an increased demand in developing countries (Remy, 2016). As initiatives such as the EU Strategy for Textiles and the UN Alliance for Sustainable Fashion gain momentum, MPs should be tackled therein. LCA might clarify the impact of the textile products, and the stakeholders involved, and, subsequently, identify the measures that lead to more sustainable products, such as prescribing production methods and product standards.

• Take no-regret measures.

As pointed out earlier in the chapter, measures taken at the source are preferable, but it might take some time before these more systemic solutions are in place. In the meantime, solutions that are already available should be taken to prevent MPF pollution as much as possible. Research on wastewater treatment shows that there are effective methods in some countries that could be adopted elsewhere. Installation of filters on washing machines and dryers could also help in places where wastewater treatment is less optimal. Filtering of indoor air – taking advantage of necessary improvements of ventilation due to COVID-19 – could improve both indoor and outdoor air quality. Through the adoption of the EPR approach, costs for these measures could be transferred to textiles producers and the fashion industry, for example by raising taxes on most polluting fabrics and garments.

• Improve monitoring of microplastic fibre pollution.

Finally, MPF pollution should be monitored in all environmental compartments to measure the effects of policies and anticipate deterioration of the environment. In many countries, monitoring is regulated, and MPFs as a sub-category of MPs could be included as indicator. The EU Marine Strategy Framework Directive now includes micro-litter, but this could be further specified into MPs with fibrous shape. Also, in the aerial environment, specification of MPFs as a subcategory of fine particulate matter should be considered when monitoring air quality. Moreover, monitoring is essential to build evidence and reduce uncertainty regarding the sources and fate of MPF pollution.

Acknowledgements

This work was supported by the Leiden University Fund/Kroese-Duijsters Fund. The authors would like to thank the students of the Leiden Advocacy Project on Plastic, in particular Anouk Campagne, for their contribution to the research.

References

Akhbarizadeh, R., Dobaradaran, S., Amouei Torkmahalleh, M., Saeedi, R., Aibaghi, R., & Faraji Ghasemi, F. 2021. Suspended fine particulate matter (PM2.5), microplastics (MPs), and polycyclic aromatic hydrocarbons (PAHs) in air: Their possible relationships and health implications. *Environ Res, 192*, 110339. https://doi.org/10.1016/j.envres.2020.110339

Annis, P. A. 2012. *Understanding and improving the durability of textiles.* Cambridge, UK: Woodhead Publishing.

Avgerinopoulou, D.-T. 2019. *Science-based lawmaking: How to effectively integrate science in international environmental law.* Cham: Springer.

Bauer, B., Watson, D., Gylling, A., Remmen, A., Hauris Lysemose, M., Hohenthal, C., & Jönbrink, A.-K. 2018. Potential ecodesign requirements for textiles and furniture. *Nordic Council of Ministers.* https://norden.diva-portal.org/smash/get/diva2:1221509/FULLTEXT01.pdf

Belontz, S. L., Corcoran, P. L., Davis, H., Hill, K. A., Jazvac, K., Robertson, K., & Wood, K. 2019. Embracing an interdisciplinary approach to plastics pollution awareness and action. *Ambio, 48*(8), 855–866. https://doi.org/10.1007/s13280-018-1126-8

Bosker, T., Olthof, G., Vijver, M. G., Baas, J., & Barmentlo, S. H. 2019. Significant decline of Daphnia magna population biomass due to microplastic exposure. *Environ Pollut, 250*, 669–675. https://doi.org/10.1016/j.envpol.2019.04.067

Brahney, J., Hallerud, M., Heim, E., Hahnenberger, M., & Sukumaran, S. 2020. Plastic rain in protected areas of the United States. *Science (American Association for the Advancement of Science), 368*(6496), 1257–1260. https://doi.org/10.1126/science.aaz5819

Browne, M. A., Crump, P., Niven, S. J., Teuten, E., Tonkin, A., Galloway, T., & Thompson, R. 2011. Accumulation of microplastic on shorelines worldwide: Sources and sinks. *Environ Sci Technol, 45*(21), 9175–9179. https://doi.org/10.1021/es201811s

Buchanan, J. B. 1971. Pollution by synthetic fibres. *Mar Pollut Bull, 2*(2), 23–23. https://doi.org/10.1016/0025–326X(71)90136–6

Bukhari, M. A., Carrasco-Gallego, R., & Ponce-Cueto, E. 2018. Developing a national programme for textiles and clothing recovery. *Waste Manag Res, 36*(4), 321–331. https://doi.org/10.1177/0734242x18759190

Cai, Y., Mitrano, D. M., Heuberger, M., Hufenus, R., & Nowack, B. 2020. The origin of microplastic fiber in polyester textiles: The textile production process matters. *J Clean Prod, 267*, 121970. https://doi.org/10.1016/j.jclepro.2020.121970

Carbery, M., O'Connor, W., & Palanisami, T. 2018. Trophic transfer of microplastics and mixed contaminants in the marine food web and implications for human health. *Environ Int, 115*, 400–409. https://doi.org/10.1016/j.envint.2018.03.007

Carney Almroth, B. M., Åström, L., Roslund, S., Petersson, H., Johansson, M., & Persson, N.-K. 2018. Quantifying shedding of synthetic fibers from textiles; a source of microplastics released into the environment. *Environ Sci Pollut Res, 25*(2), 1191–1199. https://doi.org/10.1007/s11356-017-0528-7

Carpenter, E. J., & Smith, K. L. 1972. Plastics on the Sargasso sea surface. *Science, 175*(4027), 1240. https://doi.org/10.1126/science.175.4027.1240

Dalla Fontana, G., Mossotti, R., & Montarsolo, A. 2020. Assessment of microplastics release from polyester fabrics: The impact of different washing conditions. *Environ Pollut, 264*, 113960–113960.

de Castellar, M. D., Saurí, R. M., Martí, M., & Manich, A. M. 2004. Further progress on the abrasion kinetic modelling of woven fabrics using the martindale abrasion tester. *J Text Inst, 95*(1–6), 369–379. https://doi.org/10.1533/joti.2004.0024

De Falco, F., Cocca, M., Avella, M., & Thompson, R. C. 2020. Microfiber release to water, via laundering, and to air, via everyday use: A comparison between polyester clothing with differing textile parameters. *Environ Sci Technol, 54*(6), 3288–3296. https://doi. org/10.1021/acs.est.9b06892

De Falco, F., Cocca, M., Guarino, V., Gentile, G., Ambrogi, V., Ambrosio, L., & Avella, M. 2019. Novel finishing treatments of polyamide fabrics by electrofluidodynamic process to reduce microplastic release during washings. *Polym degrad stab, 165*, 110–116. https:// doi.org/10.1016/j.polymdegradstab.2019.05.001

De Falco, F., Di Pace, E., Cocca, M., & Avella, M. 2019. The contribution of washing processes of synthetic clothes to microplastic pollution. *Sci Rep, 9*(1). https://doi. org/10.1038/s41598-019-43023-x

Dris, R., Gasperi, J., Mirande, C., Mandin, C., Guerrouache, M., Langlois, V., & Tassin, B. 2017. A first overview of textile fibers, including microplastics, in indoor and outdoor environments. *Environ Pollut, 221*, 453–458. https://doi.org/10.1016/j. envpol.2016.12.013

Dris, R., Gasperi, J., Rocher, V., & Tassin, B. 2018. Synthetic and non-synthetic anthropogenic fibers in a river under the impact of Paris Megacity: Sampling methodological aspects and flux estimations. *Sci Total Environ*, 618, 157–164. https://doi.org/10.1016/j. scitotenv.2017.11.009

ECHA, European Chemical Agency. 2019. *Annex XV restriction report – proposal for restriction – intentionally added microplastics*. Helsinki: ECHA https://echa.europa.eu/ documents/10162/05bd96e3-b969-0a7c-c6d0-441182893720

Eriksen, M., Mason, S., Wilson, S., Box, C., Zellers, A., Edwards, W., . . . Amato, S. 2013. Microplastic pollution in the surface waters of the Laurentian Great Lakes. *Mar Pollut Bull*, 77(1–2), 177–182. https://doi.org/10.1016/j.marpolbul.2013.10.007

Eunomia & ICF. 2018. *Investigating options for reducing releases in the aquatic environment of microplastics emitted by (but not intentionally added in) products. Final Report*. London/Bristol: Eunomia, ICF. https://www.eunomia.co.uk/reports-tools/investigating-options-for-reducing-releases-in-the-aquatic-environment-of-microplastics-emitted-by-products/

European Commission, Directorate-General for Environment, Hogg, D., Jones, P., Papineschi, J. 2020. Study to support preparation of the Commission's guidance for extended producer responsibility scheme: recommendations for guidance. *Publications Office*. https://data.europa.eu/doi/10.2779/301067

European Commission, Directorate-General for Research and Innovation. 2019. Environmental and health risks of microplastic pollution. *Publications Office*. https://data.europa. eu/doi/10.2777/54199

Fischer, E. K., Paglialonga, L., Czech, E., & Tamminga, M. 2016. Microplastic pollution in lakes and lake shoreline sediments: A case study on Lake Bolsena and Lake Chiusi (central Italy). *Environ Pollut, 213*, 648–657. https://doi.org/10.1016/j.envpol.2016.03.012

Foley, C. J., Feiner, Z. S., Malinich, T. D., & Höök, T. O. 2018. A meta-analysis of the effects of exposure to microplastics on fish and aquatic invertebrates. *Sci Total Environ, 631–632*, 550–559. https://doi.org/10.1016/j.scitotenv.2018.03.046

Gasperi, J., Wright, S. L., Dris, R., Collard, F., Mandin, C., Guerrouache, M., . . . Tassin, B. 2018. Microplastics in air: Are we breathing it in? *Curr Opin Environ Sci Health, 1*, 1–5. https://doi.org/10.1016/j.coesh.2017.10.002

Geissdoerfer, M., Savaget, P., Bocken, N. M. P., & Hultink, E. J. 2017. *The circular economy – A new sustainability paradigm?* https://doi.org/10.17863/CAM.7193

Grazzini, L., Acuti, D., & Aiello, G. 2021. Solving the puzzle of sustainable fashion consumption: The role of consumers' implicit attitudes and perceived warmth. *J Clean Prod, 287*. https://doi.org/10.1016/j.jclepro.2020.125579

He, X., Li, H., & Zhu, J. 2019. A value-added insight of reusing microplastic waste: Carrier particle in fluidized bed bioreactor for simultaneous carbon and nitrogen removal from septic wastewater. *Biochem Eng J, 151,* 107300. https://doi.org/10.1016/j.bej.2019.107300

Heidbreder, L. M., Bablok, I., Drews, S., & Menzel, C. 2019. Tackling the plastic problem: A review on perceptions, behaviors, and interventions. *Sci Total Environ, 668,* 1077–1093. https://doi.org/10.1016/j.scitotenv.2019.02.437

Henry, B., Laitala, K., & Klepp, I. G. 2018. *Microplastic pollution from textiles: A literature review.* Oslo: Consumption Research Norway – SIFO. https://oda.oslomet.no/oda-xmlui/bitstream/handle/20.500.12199/5360/OR1%20-%20Microplastic%20pollution%20from%20textiles%20-%20A%20literature%20review.pdf?sequence=1&isAllowed=y

Henry, B., Laitala, K., & Klepp, I. G. 2019. Microfibres from apparel and home textiles: Prospects for including microplastics in environmental sustainability assessment. *Sci Total Environ, 652,* 483–494. https://doi.org/10.1016/j.scitotenv.2018.10.166

Horton, A. A., Svendsen, C., Williams, R. J., Spurgeon, D. J., & Lahive, E. 2017. Large microplastic particles in sediments of tributaries of the River Thames, UK: Abundance, sources and methods for effective quantification. *Mar Pollut Bull, 114*(1), 218–226. https://doi.org/10.1016/j.marpolbul.2016.09.004

International Wool Textile Organisation. 2020. *Wool in aquatic environments.* Brussels: IWTO. https://iwto.org/wp-content/uploads/2020/04/IWTO_Wool-Aquatic.pdf

Intertek. 2019. *Care label recommendations: Weaving quality into your clothing, textiles and footwear.* Intertek https://www.intertek.com/uploadedFiles/Intertek/Divisions/Consumer_Goods/Media/PDFs/Services/Low%20Res%20CompleteCareLabelling.pdf

Jaikumar, G., Brun, N. R., Vijver, M. G., & Bosker, T. 2019. Reproductive toxicity of primary and secondary microplastics to three cladocerans during chronic exposure. *Environ Pollut, 249,* 638–646. https://doi.org/10.1016/j.envpol.2019.03.085

Jönsson, C., Levenstam Arturin, O., Hanning, A.-C., Landin, R., Holmström, E., & Roos, S. 2018. Microplastics Shedding from textiles: Developing analytical method for measurement of shed material representing release during domestic washing. *Sustainability (Basel, Switzerland), 10*(7), 2457. https://doi.org/10.3390/su10072457

Kelly, F. J., & Fussell, J. C. 2015. Air pollution and public health: emerging hazards and improved understanding of risk. *Environ Geochem Health, 37*(4), 631–649. https://doi.org/10.1007/s10653-015-9720-1

Kentin, E. 2018. Restricting microplastics in the European Union: Process and criteria under REACH. *Euro Physical J Plus, 133*(10), 425.

Landon-Lane, M. 2018. Corporate social responsibility in marine plastic debris governance. *Mar Pollut Bull, 127,* 310–319. https://doi.org/10.1016/j.marpolbul.2017.11.054

Lant, N. J., Hayward, A. S., Peththawadu, M. M. D., Sheridan, K. J., & Dean, J. R. 2020. Microfiber release from real soiled consumer laundry and the impact of fabric care products and washing conditions. *PLOS ONE, 15*(6), e0233332. https://doi.org/10.1371/journal.pone.0233332

Mahon, A. M., O'Connell, B., Healy, M. G., O'Connor, I., Officer, R., Nash, R., & Morrison, L. 2017. Microplastics in Sewage Sludge: Effects of Treatment. *Environ Sci Technol, 51*(2), 810–818. https://doi.org/10.1021/acs.est.6b04048

Manshoven, S., Christis, M., Vercalsteren, A., Arnold, M., Nicolau, M., Lafond, E., . . . Coscieme, L. 2019. *Textiles and the environment in a circular economy.* Eionet Report – ETC/WMGE 2019/6. European Topic Centre Waste and Materials in a Green Economy. https://www.eionet.europa.eu/etcs/etc-wmge/products/etc-wmge-reports/textiles-and-the-environment-in-a-circular-economy/@@download/file/ETC-WMGE_report_final%20for%20website_updated%202020.pdf

McLoughlin, J., & Sabir, T. 2018. *High-performance apparel: Materials, development, and applications*. Duxford: Woodhead Publishing

Mermaids. 2017. *Handbook for zero microplastics from textiles and laundry*. Amsterdam: Mermaids Ocean Clean Wash. https://www.oceancleanwash.org/wp-content/uploads/2019/08/Handbook-for-zero-microplastics-from-textiles-and-laundry-developed.pdf

Muthu, S. S. 2015. *Handbook of life cycle assessment (LCA) of textiles and clothing*. Cambridge: Woodhead Publishing.

Muthu, S. S. 2017. *Sustainable fibres and textiles*. Duxford: Woodhead Publishing

Muthu, S. S. 2020. *Assessing the environmental impact of textiles and the clothing supply chain*. Duxford: Woodhead Publishing

Napper, I. E., & Thompson, R. C. 2016. Release of synthetic microplastic plastic fibres from domestic washing machines: Effects of fabric type and washing conditions. *Mar Pollut Bull, 112*(1–2), 39–45. https://doi.org/10.1016/j.marpolbul.2016.09.025

Nieminen, E., Linke, M., Tobler, M., & Beke, B. V. 2007. EU COST Action 628: Life cycle assessment (LCA) of textile products, eco-efficiency and definition of best available technology (BAT) of textile processing. *J Cleaner Product, 15*(13), 1259–1270. https://doi.org/10.1016/j.jclepro.2006.07.011

O'Brien, S., Okoffo, E. D., O'Brien, J. W., Ribeiro, F., Wang, X., Wright, S. L., . . . Thomas, K. V. 2020. Airborne emissions of microplastic fibres from domestic laundry dryers. *Sci Total Environ, 747*, 141175. https://doi.org/10.1016/j.scitotenv.2020.141175

OECD. 2001. *Extended producer responsibility: A guidance manual for governments*. Paris: OECD Publishing.

OECD. 2020. *Summary note. Workshop on Microplastics from Synthetic Textiles: Knowledge, Mitigation, and Policy*. Paris: OECD. https://www.oecd.org/water/Workshop_MP_Textile_Summary_Note_FINAL.pdf

Özkan, İ., & Gündoğdu, S. 2021. Investigation on the microfiber release under controlled washings from the knitted fabrics produced by recycled and virgin polyester yarns. *J Text Inst, 112*(2), 264–272. https://doi.org/10.1080/00405000.2020.1741760

Palacios-Mateo, C., Van Der Meer, Y., & Seide, G. 2021. Analysis of the polyester clothing value chain to identify key intervention points for sustainability. *Environ Sci Europe, 33*(1). https://doi.org/10.1186/s12302-020-00447-x

Palm, D., Elander, M., Watson, D., Kiørboe, N., Rubach, S., Hanssen, O.-J., & Gíslason, S. 2015. The Nordic textile commitment: A proposal of a common quality requirement sys-tem for textile collection, sorting, reuse and recycling. *Nordic Council of Ministers 2014*. http://norden.diva-portal.org/smash/get/diva2:790973/FULLTEXT01.pdf

Paul, R. 2014. *Functional finishes for textiles: Improving comfort, performance and protection*. Cambridge: Woodhead Publishing.

Pirc, U., Vidmar, M., Mozer, A., & Kržan, A. 2016. Emissions of microplastic fibers from microfiber fleece during domestic washing. *Environ Sci Pollut Res Int, 23*(21), 22206–22211. https://doi.org/10.1007/s11356-016-7703-0

Prata, J. C. 2018. Airborne microplastics: Consequences to human health? *Environ Pollut, 234*, 115–126. https://doi.org/10.1016/j.envpol.2017.11.043

Provencher, J. F., Covernton, G. A., Moore, R. C., Horn, D. A., Conkle, J. L., & Lusher, A. L. 2020. Proceed with caution: The need to raise the publication bar for microplastics research. *Sci Total Environ, 748*, 141426–141426. https://doi.org/10.1016/j.scitotenv.2020.141426

Raubenheimer, K., & Urho, N. 2020. Rethinking global governance of plastics: The role of industry. *Mar Pollut, 113*, 103802. https://doi.org/10.1016/j.marpol.2019.103802

Remy, N., Speelman, E., & Swartz, S. 2016. *Style that's sustainable: A new fast-fashion formula*. McKinsey&Company. https://www.mckinsey.com/business-functions/sustainability/our-insights/style-thats-sustainable-a-new-fast-fashion-formula

Grand View Research 2021. *Synthetic fibers market growth analysis report, 2021–2028.*

Rillig, M. C., & Lehmann, A. 2020. Microplastic in terrestrial ecosystems. *Science, 368*(6498), 1430–1431. https://doi.org/10.1126/science.abb5979

Rist, S., Carney Almroth, B., Hartmann, N. B., & Karlsson, T. M. 2018. A critical perspective on early communications concerning human health aspects of microplastics. *Sci Total Environ, 626*, 720–726. https://doi.org/10.1016/j.scitotenv.2018.01.092

RIVM. 2019. *Factsheet microplastics in Nederlandse wateren (Fact sheet microplastics in Dutch waters).* Bilthoven: RIVM. https://www.rivm.nl/sites/default/files/2019-06/Factsheet%20Microplastics%20in%20Nederlandse%20wateren.pdf

Ross, P. S., Chastain, S., Vassilenko, E., Etemadifar, A., Zimmermann, S., Quesnel, S.-A., . . . Williams, B. 2021. Pervasive distribution of polyester fibres in the Arctic Ocean is driven by Atlantic inputs. *Nat Commun, 12*(1). https://doi.org/10.1038/s41467-020-20347-1

Roos, S., Levenstam Arturin, O., & Hanning, A.-C. 2017. *Microplastics shedding from polyester fabrics.* Mistra Future Fashion Report, Swerea. http://mistrafuturefashion.com/new-report-on-microplastics-from-polyester-fabrics/

Sait, S. T. L., Sørensen, L., Kubowicz, S., Vike-Jonas, K., Gonzalez, S. V., Asimakopoulos, A. G., & Booth, A. M. 2021. Microplastic fibres from synthetic textiles: Environmental degradation and additive chemical content. *Environ Pollut, 268*, 115745. https://doi.org/10.1016/j.envpol.2020.115745

Salvador Cesa, F., Turra, A., & Baruque-Ramos, J. 2017. Synthetic fibers as microplastics in the marine environment: A review from textile perspective with a focus on domestic washings. *Sci Total Environ, 598*, 1116–1129. https://doi.org/10.1016/j.scitotenv.2017.04.172

Sanchez-Vidal, A., Thompson, R. C., Canals, M., & De Haan, W. P. 2018. The imprint of microfibres in southern European deep seas. *PLoS ONE, 13*(11), e0207033. https://doi.org/10.1371/journal.pone.0207033

Sands, P. 2018. *Principles of international environmental law* (Fourth edition). Cambridge, UK; New York, NY: Cambridge University Press.

Science Advice for Policy by European Academies (SAPEA). 2019. *A scientific perspective on microplastics in nature and society.* Berlin: SAPEA. https://doi.org/10.26356/microplastics

Shruti, V. C., Pérez-Guevara, F., Elizalde-Martínez, I., & Kutralam-Muniasamy, G. 2020. First study of its kind on the microplastic contamination of soft drinks, cold tea and energy drinks: Future research and environmental considerations. *Sci Total Environ, 726*, 138580. https://doi.org/10.1016/j.scitotenv.2020.138580

Su, L., Xue, Y., Li, L., Yang, D., Kolandhasamy, P., Li, D., & Shi, H. 2016. Microplastics in Taihu Lake, China. *Environ Pollut, 216*, 711–719. https://doi.org/10.1016/j.envpol.2016.06.036

Sun, J., Dai, X., Wang, Q., van Loosdrecht, M. C. M., & Ni, B.-J. 2019. Microplastics in wastewater treatment plants: Detection, occurrence and removal. *Water Res, 152*, 21–37. https://doi.org/10.1016/j.watres.2018.12.050

Sundt, P., Syversen, F., Skogesal, O., & Schulze, P.-E. 2016. *Primary microplastic-pollution: Measures and reduction potentials in Norway.* Norwegian Environment Agency. https://www.miljodirektoratet.no/globalassets/publikasjoner/M545/M545.pdf

The Pew Charitable Trusts & SYSTEMIQ. 2020. *Breaking the plastic wave: A comprehensive assessment of pathways towards stopping ocean plastic pollution.* The Pew Charitable Trusts. https://www.pewtrusts.org/-/media/assets/2020/07/breakingtheplasticwave_report.pdf

Thompson, R. C., Olsen, Y., Mitchell, R. P., Davis, A., Rowland, S. J., John, A. W. G., . . . Russell, A. E. 2004. Lost at sea: Where is all the plastic? *Science, 304*(5672), 838.

UNEP. 2020. *Tackling plastic pollution: Legislative guide for the regulation of single-use plastic products*. Nairobi: UNEP. https://www.unep.org/resources/toolkits-manuals-and-guides/tackling-plastic-pollution-legislative-guide-regulation.

Van Der Velden, N. M., Patel, M. K., & Vogtländer, J. G. 2014. LCA benchmarking study on textiles made of cotton, polyester, nylon, acryl, or elastane. *Int J LCA, 19*(2), 331–356. https://doi.org/10.1007/s11367-013-0626-9

Vassilenko, K., Watkins, M., Chastain, S., Posacka, A., & Ross, P. S. 2019. Me, my clothes and the ocean: The role of textiles in microfiber pollution. *Science Feature*. Vancouver: Ocean Wise Conservation Association. https://assets.ctfassets.net/fsquhe7zbn68/4MQ9y89yx4KeyHv9Svynyq/8434de64585e9d2cfbcd3c46627c7a4a/Research_MicrofibersReport_191004-e.pdf

Wagner, M., Scherer, C., Alvarez-Muñoz, D., Brennholt, N., Bourrain, X., Buchinger, S., . . . Reifferscheid, G. 2014. Microplastics in freshwater ecosystems: what we know and what we need to know. *Environ Sci Eur, 26*(1). https://doi.org/10.1186/s12302-014-0012-7

Wang, W., Ndungu, A. W., Li, Z., & Wang, J. 2017. Microplastics pollution in inland freshwaters of China: A case study in urban surface waters of Wuhan, China. *Sci Total Environ, 575*, 1369–1374. https://doi.org/10.1016/j.scitotenv.2016.09.213

Weis, J. S. 2018. Cooperative work is needed between textile scientists and environmental scientists to tackle the problems of pollution by microfibers. *J Textile Apparel Technol Manag, 10*(3).

Weithmann, N., Möller, J. N., Löder, M. G. J., Piehl, S., Laforsch, C., & Freitag, R., 2018. Organic fertilizer as a vehicle for the entry of microplastic into the environment. *Sci Adv, 4*(4), eaap8060–eaap8060. https://doi.org/10.1126/sciadv.aap8060

Wright, S. L., Thompson, R. C., & Galloway, T. S. 2013. The physical impacts of microplastics on marine organisms: A review. *Environ Pollut, 178*, 483–492. https://doi.org/10.1016/j.envpol.2013.02.031

Wright, S. L., Ulke, J., Font, A., Chan, K. L. A., & Kelly, F. J. 2020. Atmospheric microplastic deposition in an urban environment and an evaluation of transport. *Environ Int, 136*, 105411–105411. https://doi.org/10.1016/j.envint.2019.105411

Yang, S., Song, Y., & Tong, S. 2017. Sustainable retailing in the fashion industry: A systematic literature review. *Sustainability, 9*(7), 1266. https://doi.org/10.3390/su9071266

Zhang, D. 2014. *Advances in filament spinning of polymers and textiles*. Cambridge: Woodhead Publishing.

Zhang, Z., & Chen, Y. 2020. Effects of microplastics on wastewater and sewage sludge treatment and their removal: A review. *Chem Eng J, 382*, 122955. https://doi.org/10.1016/j.cej.2019.122955

Zubris, K. A. V., & Richards, B. K. 2005. Synthetic fibers as an indicator of land application of sludge. *Environ Pollut, 138*(2), 201–211. https://doi.org/10.1016/j.envpol.2005.04.013

12

SUMMARY

Judith S. Weis, Francesca De Falco and Mariacristina Cocca

The first part of this book has discussed the environmental fate and effects of microplastics, especially microfibers from textiles. The chapters have focused on the aquatic environment because that is where most of the studies to date have focused and where microplastics were first found. The major source of these aquatic microfibers is textiles, which shed them in washing machines which cannot trap them, and thus release them in the wastewater (De Falco et al. 2019). While wastewater treatment plants can collect most of them, the quantities released are still overwhelming. In recent years, more attention is being paid to the terrestrial environment, since it has been recently discovered that microfibers are also released from textiles while being dried in dryers (Kapp and Miller 2020) and while being worn (De Falco et al. 2020). Furthermore, the microfibers trapped by sewage treatment plants end up in the sludge, which is often applied to land (Gavigan et al. 2020). Most recently, it has been demonstrated that microfibers are released during the manufacture of threads and textiles. All steps along the textile supply chain from the manufacturer who makes synthetic yarn from plastic pellets, to the factory that stitches together the clothes, are estimated to release 265 million pounds of microfibers per year (The Nature Conservancy 2021). These releases are primarily into the air, and intensive research is underway to learn the fate and effects of these air pollutants.

In Chapter 2, Barrows and Neumann demonstrate that measuring the quantities of microplastics in aquatic environments lacks standardized field and laboratory methodologies, despite concerted streamlining efforts made by the scientific community. Initial microplastic research focused heavily on sampling marine surface environments using a variety of techniques. The most common collecting technique involves pulling nets along the water. This technique greatly undercounts the smaller sized particles and long thin microfibres, which tend to go through the pores of the net. Whole (bulk) water samples, after being filtered, give more accurate

DOI: 10.4324/9781003165385-14

counts of microfibres. Despite these major problems and inaccuracies of using nets, the process remains popular. The field has expanded to sample microplastic from freshwater, air, ice, snow, the water column, the deep sea, sediment, animals, and human food and beverages. Initial sediment collections were along shorelines, but once researchers realized the ubiquity of microplastics, field sampling expanded to include many more environments: freshwater sediments, sand, mud, estuaries, soil, and organisms. Sediment samples are usually collected with cores to sample the upper layers of sediment where microfibers settle; examination of deeper layers can give a historic record of plastic use. To document airborne microplastic abundance, scientists can measure passive deposition by leaving filters, adhesive pads, bottles, or petri dishes out for a specified amount of time to collect microplastics settling out of the air (Zhang et al. 2020). Rain samplers (funnel leading to a collection bottle) measure wet deposition of microplastics while simultaneously measuring rainfall. Standardizing collection procedures from such variable sampling environments has proven difficult. After collection, field samples will have to undergo a laboratory process to prepare for microfiber identification. Laboratory processing and analysis have also been diverse. The preparation technique is often determined by the matrices of the sample. Manipulation of the sample to remove non-plastic materials is often necessary to extract and/or measure microplastic. A range of analytical techniques is used to identify the polymer type in microplastic samples e.g. light microscopy, gas chromatography mass spectrometry (GC/MS), pyrolysis GC/MS (py-GC/MS), micro-Fourier-Transform Infrared spectroscopy (μ-FTIR), and μ-Raman spectroscopy.

Chapter 3, by Provencher et al., provides an overview of the animals known to ingest microplastics, and highlights organism interactions and habitat exposures leading to microplastic uptake. Many animals ingest microplastics, therefore supporting the likelihood that microplastics undergo trophic transfer. In the aquatic environment, microbes can attach to and form a biofilm around MP particles, which can alter vertical transport as well as sorption and release of contaminants by the MPs, which may have ecological consequences. The odor of the biofilm is often what stimulates the animal to consume it. The community of microbes on MPs (the "plastisphere") is the subject of intense study by microbiologists. Organisms that inhabit marine surface waters are likely to encounter microplastics that are less dense than seawater, such as polystyrene (PS), polypropylene (PP), and polyethylene (PE), while benthic organisms are more likely to encounter denser polymers, including polyethylene terephthalate (PET) and polyvinyl chloride (PVC), so exposures are different depending on habitat. It is primarily dense microfibres that have been found in benthic invertebrates, including in the deep sea, reflecting their prevalence in that environment.

Species that breed or congregate in high densities may also act as microplastic concentrators in the environment. Furthermore, migratory animals may influence the fate and transport of microplastics by transporting microplastics across ecosystem boundaries, therefore facilitating exposure to microplastics in relatively remote regions. MPs are small enough that they can be ingested by migratory species, and then deposited at the end of the migration (colony or breeding area) in feces, regurgitations, or mortality. Species that move across different habitats can also play a role as vectors and concentrators of MPs in the environment at the local scale. Seabird defecation and regurgitation may act as a marine-to-terrestrial pathway; thus migratory birds may play a role in introducing plastics back to terrestrial ecosystems. While small organisms may directly ingest MPs as food items, thus allowing MPs to enter food webs, larger organisms likely acquire many MPs through trophic transfer rather than directly ingesting them, or they may create some MPs internally from breaking down consumed macroplastics. Although both abiotic and biotic processes impact the extent to which microplastic exposure and resulting hazard may be characterized, understanding predator-prey relationships and how trophic transfer may result in greater exposure are important to consider as we monitor, and attempt to mitigate effects of, plastic pollution in the environment.

In Chapter 4, Granek et al. note that the diverse fibre types used in textile production suggests that these fibres can have diverse effects on organisms and ecosystems, particularly since comparative studies indicate that fibres may be more toxic to exposed organisms than other microplastic shapes. Even bioplastics, which are designed to reduce waste due to their biodegradability, are often disposed of in a way that does not allow them to biodegrade. Both synthetic and bioplastic fibres can adhere to or be taken up and internalized by organisms, leading to biological effects at the cellular to organismal levels, with potential ecological effects on populations and communities. At the biochemical/cellular level, effects of synthetic fibres include changes in gene expression and enzyme activity, DNA damage, and retention of zinc (El-Gendy et al. 2020). Tissue and organ systems of many species experience negative effects when exposed to synthetic fibres (Bucci et al. 2020; Jacob et al. 2020). Physical organ damage, including inflammation and tissue damage, has been observed in fish and crustaceans (Qiao et al. 2019; Barboza et al. 2020; Welden and Cowie 2016). At the organism level, nylon microfibres (10–100 μm) have been shown to accumulate in the gut of *Mytilus edulis* and reduce their feeding rate on phytoplankton by about 20% (Christoforou et al. 2020). Many of these studies used concentrations far exceeding levels found in the environment. A few studies used environmentally realistic concentrations. Exposure to polypropylene fibres at environmentally relevant concentrations of 3 fibres/L every four days produced adverse effects on Pacific mole crabs (*Emerita analoga*) (Horn et al. 2020). Lifespan decreased and egg incubation time decreased (Horn et al. 2020). In fish, exposure to synthetic fibres and microspheres of length 1–5μm at concentrations of 0.26 and 0.69 mg/L can slow swim speed and alter behaviour (Barboza et al. 2018), making fish more likely to exhibit erratic behaviour and end up farther from the shelter of reefs, which could increase predation on exposed fish.

Effects of microfibre exposure vary by fibre type, environmental degradation, and the organism exposed; however, studies indicate that most species take up fibres and many show negative effects when exposed to synthetic and bio-based plastics. Though organisms may also take up natural fibres, there is very little research on

how these fibres affect organisms in the environment. This chapter broadly cat-
egorizes materials as synthetic and semi-synthetic, bioplastics, and natural fibres,
examines effects on taxonomic groups representing diverse ecosystem types, and
discusses future research needs.

In Chapter 5, Carney Almroth et al. review the toxicology of chemicals associated with microplastics. There has been considerable research on chemicals that are
included in plastic, such as phthalates and bisphenols, and environmental chemicals
that attach to particles, such as PCBs and metals. However, there are many unique
chemicals associated with textile microfibres, such as dyes, surfactants, perfluorinated compounds (PFCs), flame-retardants, antimicrobial agents (e.g. triclosan,
silver nanoparticles), nonylphenol ethoxylate, aromatic amines, and numerous others that can produce stain resistance or water repellance. The textile industry uses
up to 8,000 different chemical compounds and an average textile mill produces an
effluent of 1.6 million liters per day (Carney Almroth et al. 2021). The toxicity of
leachates from textiles is considerable, showing effects on gene expression, cytotox-
icity, embryo development, and behaviour (Carney Almroth et al. 2021).

Numerous factors need to be considered when differentiating between impacts
caused by physical exposure to particles (fibres) versus chemical leachates. Most of
microplastic toxicity studies do not examine effects of fibres, yet Bucci et al. (2020)
suggest that the effects of fibre ingestion may differ from other particle shapes (e.g.,
microbeads or fragments). Further, the gut retention time of fibres can be longer
than other particles (Qiao, Deng et al. 2019; Bour, Hossain et al. 2020). In addition, the chemical composition of microfibres should be considered in toxicity
testing. The chemical composition can be complex, including the type of polymer and the associated chemical additives and sorbed chemicals. More research
involving various natural, semi-synthetic and synthetic polymers is needed to
better understand the role of polymer composition in toxicity. Some of the chemicals intentionally added to textiles and those that are unintentionally sorbed from
the environment are known toxicants that can have damaging effects on exposed
organisms. The chemical mixture associated with fibres is of concern for biota
since microfibres may be vectors for chemical contaminants that accumulate on
fibres, as well as chemicals intentionally applied to textile fibres during manufacturing. Most experimental studies do not attempt to delineate the relative importance
of the physical nature of the fibres versus the chemical contaminants. Numerous
factors can affect responses, including the material composition of the particle, the
size, shape, density, and surface properties of the particle, as well as the chemical
profile of the particle. Chemical exposure routes can be diverse (e.g. direct uptake
from the environment, uptake via food chain), and the role of ingested fibres as
a vector remains to be determined. As of now, there is currently no empirical,
experimental evidence demonstrating release of chemicals from textile fibres in
the environment that would confirm their importance as vectors and/or sources of
chemicals. Evidence suggests that chemical releases from fibres are minimal compared to other emissions (e.g., ventilation, dust removal/disposal), probably due
in part to the low total mass of microfibres discharged during laundering and that

evidence indicates that chemicals are removed from fibres and solubilized into wash water (Saini, Rauert et al. 2016; Kvasnicka, Cohen Huba et al. 2021)

Microplastic research represents a very multidisciplinary field that involves different disciplines from biology and ecotoxicology to textile and material sciences. Without the interconnection and collaboration among these different disciplines, it is difficult to thoroughly comprehend the problem and impact of microplastic pollution, let alone to identify mitigation measures. For this reason, the second part of the book gathers chapters more focused on microfibres from the textile and material science point of view. The aim is to identify the key factors influencing microfibre release, route, and persistence in the environment in order to point out possible mitigation solutions at different levels, from textile production and laundry to wastewater treatment and textile end-of-life. Then, these intervention points that need to be taken into account by a dedicated legislation and regulation framework that address the problem of microfibre pollution.

In Chapter 6, Napper and Thompson analyzed the different methodologies applied to quantify microfibre shedding during laundering. The washing process of synthetic textiles is a key source of microfibre pollution and, therefore, it is of pivotal importance to understand the quantities of microfibres shed during a wash and how and which parameters influence such release. The chapter reviews the main studies in recent years that have developed methodologies to quantify microfibre shedding and have investigated different parameters. First of all, textile factors were discussed like the polymer composition of the fibres, textile construction characteristics like type of yarn, twist, etc. and fabric age. Then, mechanical and chemical factors were assessed and summarized, including washing machine type, temperature, and type of detergent used. The data related to these parameters of influence were obtained using different methodologies. Such methods are all based on the filtration of the effluents coming from the washing tests performed but are all different in other aspects. For example, the load composition used in the washing tests varies, both in terms of weight and material composition of the fabrics tested. Moreover, some test methodologies use real washing machines, whereas others use laboratory equipment that, for instance, simulates the mechanical action of a washing machine by using steel balls. Other differences among the studies involve the filtration system used (i.e., filter pore sizes) and the analysis applied to evaluate the quantity of microfibres released (i.e., weight vs number of microfibres shed). It is clear that there is the strong need to develop uniform and standardized methodologies to quantify microfibre release from textile washing. However, the chapter also shows that even in the absence of a consistent methodology, the data collected up to now already allow us to prioritize some key mitigation actions, as further discussed later in the book.

After microfibres are released during textile washing processes, they enter the sewage systems (where present) and arrive to wastewater treatment plants (WWTPs) which are not specifically designed to remove them. In Chapter 7, Sol et al. discuss the main aspects related to WWTPs as a route for microplastics. This is of particular importance since the European Parliament is considering tackling the presence of microplastics in treated water and sewage sludge (European Parliament 2019). A recent study of 38 WWTPs in 11 countries showed that microplastic abundance in influent was between 0.28 and $6.10 \cdot 10^2$ particles/L when the wastewater was coming from municipal activities, and fibres were the most abundant type of particles (Liu et al. 2021). In general, WWTPs can reach efficiencies higher than 90% in removing microplastics, but this also depends on the technologies applied by the specific plant. Sol et al. provided an overview of the different stages a WWTP may have: pre-treatment, primary, secondary, and tertiary treatment. They also highlighted that when high efficiencies are achieved, microplastics are mostly entrained in sludge, which can be used as agricultural fertilizer which then becomes a source of microplastics in soil. Therefore, new technologies need to be developed and this chapter provides an overview of the major available ones, including bioremediation, electrostatic separators, magnetic nanoparticles, or froth flotation. However, these technologies still need to be optimized for the application at large scale and, currently, there is no cost-effective technology able to remove small microplastics with dimensions between 10 and 300 μm and microfibres. Most promising technologies to remove microfibres could be primary settling and coagulation/flocculation processes to be optimized and combined with other technologies applied in tertiary treatments. In this way it could be possible to achieve an efficiency of 93% in removing microfibres from wastewater.

In Chapter 8, Lott et al. discuss the different aspects of the degradation of microplastics, and specifically of microfibres, in the marine environment. Clarifications are provided on the different mechanisms involved in the environmental fate of plastic materials. The chapter presents an overview of the different mechanisms that lead to microplastic/fibre degradation, discussing the roles of solar radiation, oxygen, water, surface-to-volume ratio, and mechanical impact. Besides these mechanisms, biotic processes are also described in terms of types of microbes involved, biomass formation, and mineralization with consequent biodegradation of the material. The biodegradation of specific polymers, both synthetic and natural, is also reviewed, focusing on the polymers most used to produce fibres for textiles or fishing/aquaculture applications (i.e. polyethylene terephthalate, polyamide, cellulose, etc.). In this respect, biodegradation could be considered a desired material property to tackle the problem of microplastic pollution, especially for some applications like mulch films, slow-release fertilizer capsules and seed coating in agriculture, knitted and non-woven fibers for geotextiles in landscaping, and feeding pipes and mussel nets in aquaculture. In all these cases, biodegradability represents a desired property since such materials could be easily lost and difficult to retrieve.

Chapter 9 by Ipsmiller and Bartl focuses on the textile processing chain and on which solutions can be applied at the end-of-life stage of textiles to prevent pollution and microfibre release. In general, textile manufacturing, from raw materials to fibres, yarn, and fabric production (including dyeing and finishing), consumes massive quantities of energy and other resources, with significant greenhouse gas emissions.

In addition, a huge amount of textile waste is annually produced, waste that can be classified as post-industrial (material generated during textile production) or post-consumer (textiles disposed after use). The chapter discusses the current legislation and application of collection, sorting, re-use, and recycling of textile waste. In particular, the main available recycling technologies are reviewed, including grinder-cutting, polymer, and monomer recycling. An important aspect highlighted is the lack of data and information on the environmental impact of recycling technologies. Moreover, recycling is an approach that deals with the symptoms of the problem, not with the very source of it. Therefore, measures need to be applied to prevent the production of textile waste in the first place.

To better explore the possibilities to reduce microfibre production in other stages of textile life, Chapter 10 by De Falco and Cocca provides an overview of the possible technologies and solutions that can be applied or further developed and implemented to mitigate microfibre pollution from textiles. The chapter analyzes actions that can be applied at two different levels, textile production and laundry. Concerning the first one, data are already available from different research studies that suggest which textile parameters should be taken into account during textile design and production. Moreover, finishing treatments that create a protective thin layer on the surface on the fabric also showed promising results in terms of microfibre release mitigation. Similarly, scientific data are also available on which laundry practices should be preferred to reduce microfibre release (i.e. liquid detergent, low temperature and spin, etc.). Great efforts are also being made by different companies to produce filtration systems for washing machines. The collaboration among relevant industries and stakeholders and research centres and academia will be strategic and fundamental to implement such mitigation actions.

Finally, Chapter 11 by Kentin and Battaglia focuses on government policies that have been adopted or proposed to reduce textile microfibres in the environment. The chapter provides an overview of policy options suitable to different situations and degrees of evidence and technological advancement, with the aim of inspiring the textile industry and policymakers to prevent and address microplastic fibre pollution. Through a study of evidence about microplastic fibres, combined with a review of existing legislation and policies worldwide, (including relevant policies not directly targeting microplastic fibres) and input from international organizations and specialized studies, five main recommendations have emerged. Firstly, raising awareness among consumers, the textile industry, and policymakers is key to the implementation and success of any policies, as they depend on behavioural changes. Secondly, collaboration between textile scientists and scientists working on detection of microplastics is recommended, as new high performing textiles may help prevent microfibre release. Thirdly, environmental policies regarding microplastic fibres should be integrated within textile regulations, given that this sector is the source of the problem. Fourthly, pending the development and implementation of measures at the source, the adoption of measures such as wastewater treatment and washing machine or ventilation filters is to be supported. Such measures should be funded preferably by Extended Producer Responsibility schemes.

Lastly, microplastic fibre pollution should be monitored in all environmental compartments to measure the effects of policies and build evidence as to reduce uncertainty and better anticipate deterioration of the environment.

References

Barboza, L. G. A., Lopes, C., Oliveira, P., Bessa, F., Otero, V., Henriques, B., Raimundo, J., Caetano, M., Vale, C., Guilhermino, L. 2020. Microplastics in wild fish from North East Atlantic Ocean and its potential for causing neurotoxic effects, lipid oxidative damage, and human health risks associated with ingestion exposure. *Sci Total Environ* 717, 134625. https://doi.org/10.1016/j.scitotenv.2019.134625

Barboza, L. G. A., Vieira, L. R., Guilhermino, L. 2018. Single and combined effects of microplastics and mercury on juveniles of the European seabass (*Dicentrarchus labrax*): Changes in behavioural responses and reduction of swimming velocity and resistance time. *Environ Pollut* 236, 1014–1019. https://doi.org/10.1016/j.envpol.2017.12.082

Bour, A., Hossain, S., Taylor, M., Summer, M., Carney Almroth, B. 2020. Synthetic microfiber and microbead exposure and retention time in model aquatic species under different exposure scenarios. *Front. Environ. Sci.*, https://doi.org/10.3389/fenvs.2020.00083

Bucci, K., Tulio, M., Rochman, C. M. 2020. What is known and unknown about the effects of plastic pollution: A meta-analysis and systematic review. *Ecol Appl* 30(2). https://doi.org/10.1002/eap.2044

Carney Almroth, B., Cartine, J., Jonander, C., et al. 2021. Assessing the effects of textile leachates in fish using multiple testing methods: From gene expression to behavior. *Ecotox Environ Saf* 207, 111523. https://doi.org/10.1016/j.ecoenv.2020.111523

Christoforou, E., Dominoni, D. M., Lindström, J., Stilo, G., Spatharis, S. 2020. Effects of long-term exposure to microfibres on ecosystem services provided by coastal mussels. *Environ Pollut* 266, 115184. https://doi.org/10.1016/j.envpol.2020.115184

De Falco, F., Cocca, M., Avella, M., Thompson, R. C. 2020. Microfiber release to water, via laundering, and to air, via everyday use: A comparison between polyester clothing with differing textile parameters. *Environ Sci Technol* 54(6), 3288–3296. https://doi.org/10.1021/acs.est.9b06892

De Falco, F., Di Pace, E., Cocca, M. *et al.* 2019. The contribution of washing processes of synthetic clothes to microplastic pollution. *Sci Rep* 9, 6633. https://doi.org/10.1038/s41598-019-43023-x

El-Gendy, A. H., Augustyniak, M., Toto, N. A., Al Farraj, S., El-Samad, L. M. 2020. Oxidative stress parameters, DNA damage and expression of HSP70 and MT in midgut of *Trachyderma hispida* (Forskål, 1775) (Coleoptera: Tenebrionidae) from a textile industry area. *Environ Pollut* 267, 115661. https://doi.org/10.1016/j.envpol.2020.115661

European Parliament. 2019. *Minimum requirements for water reuse.* Available at: www.europarl.europa.eu/RegData/seance_pleniere/textes_adoptes/provisoire/2019/02-12/0071/P8_TA-PROV(2019)0071_EN.pdf.

Gavigan, J., Kefela, T., Macadam-Somer, I., Suh, S., Geyer, R. 2020. Synthetic microfiber emissions to land rival those to waterbodies and are growing. *PLoS ONE* 15(9), e0237839. https://doi.org/10.1371/journal.pone.0237839

Horn, D. A., Granek, E. F., Steele, C. L. 2020. Effects of environmentally relevant concentrations of microplastic fibres on Pacific mole crab (*Emerita analoga*) mortality and reproduction. *Limnol Oceanogr Lett* 5(1), 74–83. https://doi.org/10.1002/lol2.10137

Jacob, H., Besson, M., Swarzenski, P. W., Lecchini, D., Metian, M. 2020. Effects of virgin micro- and nanoplastics on fish: Trends, meta-analysis, and perspectives. *Environ Sci Technol* 54(8), 4733–4745. https://doi.org/10.1021/acs.est.9b05995

Kapp, K. J., Miller, R. Z. 2020. Electric clothes dryers: An underestimated source of microfiber pollution. *PLoS ONE* 15(10), e0239165. https://doi.org/10.1371/journal.pone.0239165

Kvasnicka, J., Cohen Huba, E., Rodgers, T., Diamond, M. 2021. Textile washing conveys SVOCs from indoors to outdoors: Application and evaluation of a residential multimedia model. *Environ Sci Technol*. in press.

Liu, W., Zhang, J., Liu, H., Guo, X., Zhang, X., Yao, X., Cao, Z., Zhang, T. 2021. A review of the removal of microplastics in global wastewater treatment plants: Characteristics and mechanisms. *Environ Int* 146, 106277. https://doi.org/10.1016/j.envint.2020.106277

The Nature Conservancy. 2021. *Toward eliminating pre-consumer emissions of microplastics from the textile industry*, p. 20.

Qiao, R., Deng, Y., Zhang, S., Wolosker, M. B., Zhu, Q., Ren, H., Zhang, Y. 2019. Accumulation of different shapes of microplastics initiates intestinal injury and gut microbiota dysbiosis in the gut of zebrafish. *Chemosphere* 236, 124334. https://doi.org/10.1016/j.chemosphere.2019.07.065

Saini, A., Rauert, C., Simpson, M. J., Harrad, S., Diamond, M. L. 2016. Characterizing the sorption of polybrominated diphenyl ethers (PBDEs) to cotton and polyester fabrics under controlled conditions. *Sci Total Environ* 563–564, 99–107. https://doi.org/10.1016/j.scitotenv.2016.04.099

Welden, N. A. C., Cowie, P. R. 2016. Long-term microplastic retention causes reduced body condition in the langoustine, Nephrops norvegicus. *Environ Pollut* 218, 895–900. https://doi.org/10.1016/j.envpol.2016.08.020

Zhang, Y., Kang, S., Allen, S., Allen, D., Gao, T., Sillanpää, M. 2020. Atmospheric microplastics: A review on current status and perspectives. *Earth Sci Rev* 203, 103118. https://doi.org/10.1016/j.earscirev.2020.103118

INDEX

Printed in the United States
by Baker & Taylor Publisher Services